Sucheta Mazumdar
Asian American Studies
U C B.

FARM WORKERS, AGRIBUSINESS, AND THE STATE

FARM WORKERS, AGRIBUSINESS, AND THE STATE

LINDA C. MAJKA
THEO J. MAJKA

TEMPLE UNIVERSITY PRESS, PHILADELPHIA

Temple University Press, Philadelphia 19122
© 1982 by Temple University. All rights reserved
Published 1982
Printed in the United States of America

Library of Congress Cataloging in Publication Data

Majka, Linda C.
  Farm workers, agribusiness, and the state.

  Bibliography; p.
  Includes index.
    1. Agricultural laborers—California—History—
20th century. 2. Trade-unions—Agricultural
laborers—California—History—20th century.
3. Agriculture—Economic aspects—California—
History—20th century. 4. Agriculture and state—
California—History—20th century. I. Majka,
Theo J. II. Title.
HD1527.C2M23   1982   331.88-13-09794   82-10652
ISBN 0-87722-256-8

CONTENTS

HD1527
C 2H23
1982
cop. X1

PREFACE

Our approach to farm worker unionization was influenced by living and working in California during the resurgence of the farm labor movement led by the United Farm Workers of America (UFW). The experience offered us the opportunity to observe directly the working conditions of farm labor, the organizing activity of the UFW, the mobilization of resources by the union, the creation of a public attentive to the situation of farm workers, and the emergence and implementation of reforms.

Direct observation and provisional analysis of research issues were facilitated by access to informed observers, including informants in a variety of roles within the UFW, as well as social scientists. We were able to share ideas with and obtain information from UFW staff, including high officials and strategists, the editor of the UFW newspaper, boycott coordinators, field office organizers and officials, rank and file members and strikers, legal and community volunteers, and former UFW members. There were also many opportunities to discuss ideas and observations with others interested in farm labor unionization attempts: attorneys, Democratic club members, clergy, religious and community organization members, trade unionists, Teamster rank and file, community activists, Democratic party officials, and nonunionized farm workers. Particularly helpful were background interviews with journalists who have written extensively on farm labor: Dick Meister, Doug Foster, Mark Day, Harry Bernstein, Sam Kushner, and Ron Taylor.

Dick Flacks, Bill Chambliss, Rich Appelbaum, Craig Jenkins, Pat Donnelly, Steve McNamee, and Morris Friedell provided helpful comments on individual chapters or earlier drafts. Bob Thomas and Dan Clawson gave thorough readings of the entire manuscript and made valuable suggestions for improving the final copy. Many other colleagues, students, and friends, too numerous to list, offered encouragement, made suggestions, raised arguments, gave shelter, and provided a supportive audience.

For assistance in our field research we wish to thank Noelie Rodriguez, Holly Seerley, Armando R. H. Cobos, Jerry Cohen, Jim Drake, Chris Hartmire, Vivian Drake, and Fred Ross, Sr.

We are grateful to student research assistants and typists for their essential contributions: Nita Hertel, Kathy Royer, Marc Ruhi Frank, and Marilyn Loomis. Helping with elements of the final draft were Kathy Royer, Beverly Bostion, Nancy Schiml, and Lou Cooper.

Proofreading and our first (informal) reviews were done by Mark Lehman and Anita Cochran. Thanks are especially due to Anita for preparing the index. Production editor, Candy Hawley, organized the final stages of the publishing process graciously.

Our copyeditor, Jane Barry, deserves special appreciation for the quality of her critical attention to the manuscript. Finally, the advice and support of our editor at Temple University Press brought this research to its completion: our warmest thanks to Michael Ames.

The research is organized chronologically. The following chapters document the struggles as well as the forces which have operated to keep agricultural labor easily exploitable and powerless. Beginning with the Chinese in agriculture in 1870, the study carries the analysis to the present unionization movement over one hundred years later.

INTRODUCTION

This book concerns farm workers, their struggle with the large growers of California, and the ways government at all levels has intervened to regulate political and economic conflict. Our object is not simply to describe past and present farm labor unions. Instead, we wish to understand why the farm labor question has been unable to subside as a social issue, in spite of a century of predictions that it is "solved."

Farm worker unions have acted as both labor movements and organizations of insurgent poor people. We survey how and why for a century farm workers campaigned, protested, marched, picketed, disrupted production, held strikes, called boycotts, and sought contracts to gain their class interests. At the same time growers, acting either as individuals or in associations, fought unionization, urged importation or repatriation of foreign-born workers, and employed vigilantes and strikebreakers, all to insure a plentiful supply of workers at low wages.

The actions of the state in regulating this conflict have contradicted one's reasonable expectations. This is not a history of the progressive enfranchisement of a subordinate group. Rather, as will become clear, state policies contained shifts and reversals; periods of repression and attempts to suppress insurgency were alternated with reforms. During the rise of farm worker unionism, government at all levels used law enforcement, injunctions, troops, braceros, immigration quotas, discriminatory laws, and relief regulations, with infrequent intervals of reforms and labor legislation. We seek to explain why government policy toward farm workers has alternately had the effect of undermining farm labor organizations and, at other times, attempting to guarantee their existence.

Recent accounts of journalists concerned with farm worker struggles have tended primarily to describe events rather than interpret them as a form of worker protest and insurgency.[1] Instead, we have been concerned with establishing long-term patterns in the emergence of militancy and attempting to explain the paradoxes involved in the responses of the state.

We view farm worker organizations both as social movements and as worker organizations shaped by the exigencies of American labor struggles. Histories of labor relations tend to neglect farm labor because analysts have been accustomed to focus on urban workers, industrial unions, and the white labor force. General studies of organized labor remain unlikely to refer in any detail to agricultural workers.[2]

For portions of this history we were able to use secondary sources, since a great deal of work has been done on earlier periods. Also included are data from some primary sources not widely available or previously analyzed. The treatment of the UFW both incorporates the accounts of journalists and scientific studies and reflects our direct knowledge of and involvement in the movement.

In the course of discussing this research with our families, we made a discovery that gave us a sense of continuity with the past: a grandfather and great-uncle had been involved in farm labor protest as young men. Franciszek Majka (age 23) and his brother Michal Majka (age 24) left Poland, traveling by the vessel *H.F. Glade*, and arrived in Honolulu on 6 October 1898. They were in the company of workers destined for Hawaii's sugar plantations. Before departing for San Francisco three years later, they joined in a protest against working conditions on one of the plantations and were arrested and jailed for participating in a sit-down strike.

While working briefly as boycott organizers for the United Farm Workers during the mid-1970s, we first became aware of the particularly rich tradition of farm labor unionism preceding the appearance of Cesar Chavez and the National Farm Workers Association in the national spotlight in 1965. Our book is a product of an encounter with this history as well as a deep interest in the progress of the UFW. Contrary to the prevailing view, farm workers have not historically been docile, let alone reconciled to their circumstances. The better-known strikes are not momentary exceptions, but rather part of a long-term pattern of farm labor activism using mass defiance and whatever political and economic help was offered to improve the conditions of work and life. The UFW is simply the latest and by far the most successful example of a series of agricultural labor unionization efforts throughout this century.

There are several advantages in arranging the research into distinct historical periods as we have done. Similarities and differences in the cases can be easily compared and contrasted. The arrangement allows one to examine the interplay of factors without letting the distinctiveness of each period distract attention from the unfolding of larger processes over time. Concrete historical instances can also be used to reflect upon and modify particular theories. For those readers not concerned with theoretical analysis, however, the book is arranged so that they can easily follow the course of events.

When the manuscript was in its early stages, we contacted Carey McWilliams about the possibility of his writing a foreword for the book. He expressed an interest, but his death prevented us from pursuing this possibility. To readers familiar with McWilliams's *Factories in the Field*, first published in 1939, our debt to his work will be apparent.

During the course of our field research and our work for the UFW, we witnessed an extraordinary occurrence. Accompanying the growth of activism among farm workers was the progressive development of a vast reservoir of ability. Formerly anonymous individuals, oppressed in their jobs and disregarded by the surrounding community, were in the course of their struggles becoming skillful speakers, leaders, organizers, teachers, analysts, and strategists. Direct observation of the changes experienced by so many people reinforced our sense of how much is foreclosed under normal circumstances. Regardless of the level of its material abundance, a society (or organization) whose institutionalized relationships of hierarchy and inequality routinely frustrate the development of such human qualities must be judged impoverished.

The sociologist C. Wright Mills, in *The Power Elite*, saw in postwar America an increasing separation between two modes of human activity: that of making history and that of meeting the requirements of everyday life. The privilege of affecting history was becoming monopolized as a conscious activity of a small group of powerful men.[3] Regardless of the insight of Mills's judgment, this study demonstrates that the rest of us can, under certain circumstances, interrupt the ability of elites to construct and maintain the structures and relationships that reflect and sustain their advantageous positions. Powerless people can affect history through collective action. Farm workers throughout this century, and especially since 1965, have affected agricultural history through their efforts to improve the circumstances of their everyday lives. To these women and men this book is dedicated.

FARM WORKERS, AGRIBUSINESS, AND THE STATE

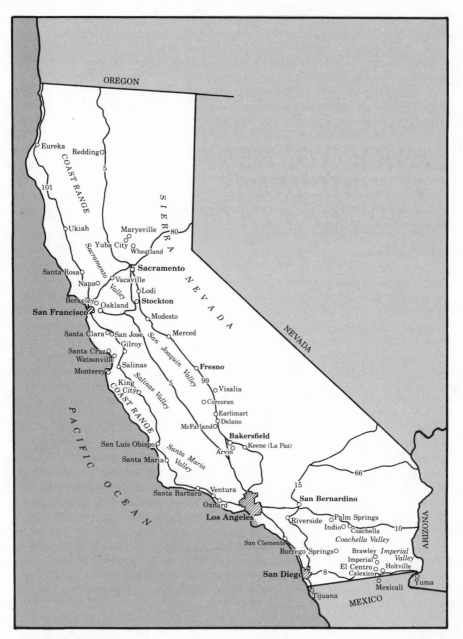

Map of California

CHAPTER 1

FARM WORKER UNIONISM AND STATE INTERVENTION

A social history of agricultural labor in California from 1870 to the present establishes several patterns in the relationship among agricultural workers, the agricultural landowners or growers, and what will be defined as the state. These patterns relate to the repeated attempts by farm workers to organize, the prominence of certain kinds of "control" issues in their demands, the weakness of most organizing efforts as reflected in defeats or merely temporary gains, the intransigence of most growers, and shifts in government policies and actions. These patterns have set the context within which the United Farm Workers, AFL-CIO, under the leadership of Cesar Chavez, has attempted to organize agricultural workers in California during the sixties, seventies, and early eighties.

THE FARM LABOR MARKET

Large-scale production has dominated California agriculture virtually since statehood. Variously described during the past century as the "grower-shipper interests," the "farm factories," and most recently "corporate agriculture" and "agribusiness," these operations have become increasingly concentrated. Concurrently, there has been a decline in the number of farms, especially small farms.[1] Many large growers have had various formal connections with corporations related to agribusiness, such as banks, processors, and shippers. In addition, corporate involvement in agricultural production has increased to the point that by 1970 one-fourth to one-third of cropland production came from corporate farms. Forty-six percent of

California corporate farms have operations in two or more states. Moreover, half of the acreage of corporate farms is held by corporations engaged in businesses other than agricultural production. In the southern San Joaquin Valley, the initial organizational base of the UFW, eleven agricultural corporations alone control over one million acres of land.[2]

Corporations involved in agricultural production are of three types. First there are family corporations engaged in farming. Some of these are quite extensive. Bruce Church, Inc., for example, whose "Red Coach" brand of lettuce has been the target of a recent UFW boycott, is a wholly owned family corporation growing lettuce, celery, cantaloupes, broccoli, spinach, carrots, tomatoes, cotton, alfalfa, and feed grains on 20,000 acres in California and Arizona.[3] Other large agricultural operations are publicly owned corporations primarily engaged in food processing or distribution. Some prominent examples are Del Monte, Libby McNeil and Libby, H. J. Heinz, Coca Cola, Ralston-Purina, Green Giant, DiGiorgio, Great Western Sugar, Heublein, Safeway Stores, and United Brands. Finally there are publicly owned corporations that have substantial investments in agriculture but whose main operations are in nonfood areas. Tenneco, for example, whose operations have extended from petroleum to pipelines, chemicals, shipbuilding, and farm machinery, has farm operations covering 35,000 acres and has become the nation's largest shipper of fresh fruits and vegetables. Other prominent corporations that have invested in agriculture include Dow Chemical, Purex, Standard Oil of California, Gulf and Western, Boeing, Getty Oil, Goodyear Tire and Rubber, Union Carbide, Sterling Precision, Prudential Insurance, Kaiser Aluminum, Penn-Central, and Southern Pacific.[4]

Large agricultural operations have been the employers of an increasing proportion of seasonal farm workers. California, the leader in employment of both migrant and nonmigrant seasonal farm labor, appears to have a fairly constant number of field workers. The average annual employment of seasonal workers in 1975 was 117,000. Of this number, 17,000 were classified as intrastate migrants, 13,000 as interstate migrants and 87,000 as locals, that is, workers who commute from their homes to jobs in the vicinity. These figures exclude farmers and unpaid family members (70,000) and year-round permanent employees (99,000). The average number of seasonal farm workers in California in 1975 actually represented a slight increase from a low of 110,000 in 1972 and was similar to the average from 1966–69.[5]

Large-scale agricultural operations have provided the primary source of employment for farm labor in California. The California food-producing industry has undergone considerable change within the last hundred years in terms of concentration of ownership, size, corporate involvement, technology of production, and crops harvested. Nevertheless, agricultural growers' desire for certain kinds of workers has remained remarkably constant. Growers have sought a labor force that is essentially passive, powerless, tractable, and unorganized, and as a whole they have vehemently resisted the numerous agricultural unionization attempts marking the history of California agriculture. The growth of corporate-owned operations has not appeared to alter this pattern. As a result of their successes, growers have been able to keep labor costs down and in the process render agricultural workers one of the lowest-paid segments of the working class.[6]

We will describe how, in order to secure a labor force with the preferred characteristics, the growers have employed a succession of nonwhite minorities excluded from the predominantly white, urban-based labor union movement. From 1870 to the present, Chinese, Japanese, Mexicans, and Filipinos, to mention only the most numerous groups, have at different times dominated the agricultural labor force. At their first introduction into the fields, they served as a controllable work force. Contrary to their employers' expectations, however, when a homogeneous minority group became the dominant labor supply in certain types of harvest work, it began to organize, demand wage and other concessions, challenge the growers' control of working and employment conditions, and strike if it met grower intransigence. The Chinese alone were excluded from this pattern and remained basically compliant with the terms of their employment, in large part because they were subjected to an exceptional campaign of discrimination and suppression throughout the West. When labor unrest and organization became widespread and the group no longer was the source of low-wage, powerless labor, the large agricultural landowners attempted to undermine its dominant position in the agricultural labor force and hire another group to undercut the organized. Some members of the previous group still remained to compete with the newer workers on terms set by the growers, but with little of their former power. Ethnic diversity has been a further insurance against successful organization, for rivalries and distrust among ethnic factions have hindered collective actions. Gradually obstacles were overcome, organizational efforts

increased, and strikes were called. Then growers would look elsewhere in the chronically oversupplied agricultural labor market for a
source of low-wage, unorganized workers, and the cycle would be
repeated.

The California farm workers' struggle to organize throughout this
century is a remarkable passage in working class history. The struggles varied in intensity, organization, tactics, duration, specific
grievances, leadership, and extent of mass involvement. The survival
and growth of the United Farm Workers Union under the leadership
of Cesar Chavez during the past twenty years are extraordinary,
considering that the vast majority of past farm labor associations had
only a brief existence. The poverty of their constituents and the
overwhelming strength of their opponents made the organizations
extremely vulnerable. Exposed to many of the barriers confronting
previous unions, the UFW has nevertheless been able to endure and
act effectively in the interests of farm workers.

FARM WORKER PROTEST

We have selected several major focal points around which to organize
our presentation of historical evidence and analysis of its most significant patterns. Three are critical. First, contrary to what might be
expected, a significant number of organizational attempts and
strikes went beyond seeking wage concessions and raised demands
for changes in hiring practices and greater control by labor over
employment and conditions of work. We will examine these demands.
Second, until the UFW's most recent drives, agricultural workers
have been unable to implement permanent improvements in these
conditions. This weakness has remained for each group of workers,
despite the variety of strategies, organizational structures, and leadership styles that we will analyze here. Finally, patterns of responses
by the state will be closely examined for each period.

Many of the more prolonged periods of insurgency involved demands for unionization and concurrent alterations in the method of
labor recruitment and hiring. Farm workers have consistently
sought guarantees of stable employment and changes in existing
work practices as well as increased wages. These control objectives
have the potential to transform the established methods of agricultural labor recruitment and hiring to the advantage of labor. The
practice of hiring directly or through labor contractors has functioned
to place control over the labor force with the employers. Workers
have been exposed to severe forms of exploitation with little countervailing power except the ability to disrupt production.

The prevalence of hiring demands and other control issues contradicts most expectations concerning low-wage, low-skilled workers.
Control issues challenge the prevailing patterns of the utilization of
labor and the conditions of work. They are aimed at adapting the
production process to worker needs, narrowing the area of management's arbitrary power, and incorporating worker representatives
into decision-making processes within the company.[7] Most authorities on control issues have identified them primarily as the concern
of workers in advanced sectors of production.[8] Low-wage and low-
skilled workers in nonunionized sectors of production with a low
organic composition of capital are believed to be almost exclusively
concerned with wage issues out of the need to defend their existing
standard of living. Besides the recruitment issue, however, agricultural workers have repeatedly fought for union recognition, improvements in health and safety conditions in the fields, the creation
of tolerable living conditions in labor camps, the limitation of working hours, the elimination of excessive charges for meals in the camps
and at the work site, and the rehiring of strikers without discrimination. Before the UFW these control issues were not as well developed,
since no union or worker organization had sufficiently established
itself to be able to pursue the implementation of these demands.
Nevertheless, their prevalence over time indicates a realization of
the need to challenge the growers' unilateral control over conditions
of employment and work as well as alter the prevailing norms for
exploitation before long-term qualitative improvement in the circumstances of farm workers could take place.

During the UFW era control issues have been elaborated to an
unprecedented extent. Along with seeking wage gains, the UFW has
specifically attempted to eliminate the labor contractor system and
establish a union hiring hall, gain union recognition and contracts,
institute a seniority system through the hiring hall, end illegal child
labor, control pesticide use, establish ranch committees of workers to
handle problems with employers, and regulate the mechanization of
agriculture to prevent a massive displacement of workers. The significance of control issues in agriculture labor insurgency is under-
lined by the poverty of most farm workers throughout this century.

In order to evaluate the successes and failures of farm worker
struggles of various periods, it is necessary to examine the factors
that contribute to the strength of collective action and social movements. Sociologists and social historians who analyze social movements have tended to explain their rise and fate in terms of such
factors as social strains and dislocations, rising expectations, rapid

social change, relative and absolute deprivation, and class antagonism. But there is another approach that is more relevant to the
practical understanding of what facilitates or inhibits such movements. This is called the "resource mobilization" approach. Varied in
content and emphasis, this approach focuses on the same kinds of
questions that have concerned social movement leaders and practical
theorists. The relevant issues are how people can organize, pool their
resources, and wield power effectively. In particular, this approach
examines the variety of resources that must be mobilized in order to
achieve success. Resources may come from the constituents of the
movement or from sympathetic supporters external to it.[9] The mobilization of resources creates a source of power for those who seek to
influence or change the policies of a political system.[10] Viewed in this
way, social movements are best analyzed as extensions of normal
political channels.

Questions relevant to mobilization involve two distinct kinds of
resources. The first involve the collectivity upon which the movement
is based: how a constituency can be mobilized; what issues or events
might activate it; what are the best targets or goals; what the most
effective structure, leadership, and division of labor are; and what
strategies can best achieve gains and minimize the adverse effects of
social control. Resources within the collectivity include the time
people have available to spend on movement activities, the presence
of a common culture and heritage, the similarity of people's understanding of their common situation, the availability of money, and
the proclivity to engage in cooperative, collective endeavors. These
will be referred to as "internal resources."

Other resources can be mobilized that are in the strict sense external to the collectivity. The important questions here concern how
outside individuals, organizations, and structures can be mobilized to
contribute to the success of the movement. How might a political
alliance with other groups and organizations be initiated and sustained? How might a large, diffuse sympathetic public be created? In
what ways can the media be used to the movement's advantage? How
can political leaders and elites be persuaded to support it? The kinds
of assistance that sources outside the collectivity can provide a social
movement will be called "external resources."

Our research on agricultural labor unionization attempts in California has led us to make several generalizations concerning variables critical to the success of these efforts. First, the predominance of
failures and short-term gains is not due to the unwillingness of farm
workers to engage in struggles. The internal resources of agricul-

tural workers have been repeatedly mobilized, as indicated by the numerous instances of strike activity and unionization attempts. Farm labor organizations have been quite diverse in their kinds of leadership, size and structure, ideologies, strategies, tactics, and specific goals. Ethnic homogeneity and shared cultural traditions have often created unusually high levels of worker solidarity. Farm workers have shared the recognition of collective oppression and selected common targets to oppose. They have displayed a willingness to endure repression from authorities and sacrifice their meager resources in the hope of improved future conditions. Concessions have, however, been temporary. Typically they are withdrawn after the threat of strikes and disruption of the harvest has passed. The institutional power of farm labor by itself is weak—a factor shared with other segments of the poor. Under ordinary circumstances farm workers lack the institutional leverage necessary for the long-term survival of their organizations and of the concessions ceded during periods of labor defiance.[11]

What has been critically lacking during most strikes and unionization attempts is the mobilization of external resources, simply because few have been available. The success of a movement is related to the ability of its leaders to gain external support, promote alliances with other movements and organizations, legitimate the movement through the media, enlist elites in the cause, and obtain concrete gains through political channels. The possibility of assembling this kind of support simply did not exist for farm labor for most of its history.

There are two related reasons for this failure to mobilize external resources: the pervasiveness of racism and the division between agricultural and urban labor. Since agricultural labor has been predominantly nonwhite, historically its demands for better conditions have not been sympathetically received, and the support of sympathizers has been overshadowed by the power of the interests that benefited from the existing pattern of labor exploitation. Political leaders and the media tended either to ignore the labor conditions prevailing in agriculture or to be hostile to suggestions for change. During earlier periods urban-based labor unions, logically farm labor's most suitable allies, offered little support to the several attempts to establish agricultural labor unions under the American Federation of Labor. There is ample evidence that earlier in this century organized labor in general took little interest in the unionization of nonwhites. Segregationist beliefs dominated labor ideology, especially at the national level. For a significant portion of its history, organized labor promoted policies of racial exclusion. In California white-dominated unions, which held considerable political power during the late 1800s, were primary proponents of discriminatory legislation aimed at nonwhites and often excluded them from union membership.

In fact, before the late 1950s, when unions agreed to support the antibracero movement, urban-based labor unions offered significant support for agricultural labor demands only when the farm workers involved were predominantly white: during the 1913–17 insurgency, led by the Industrial Workers of the World, of mostly white hop- and wheat-field workers, and during the attempts to organize whites from the Dust Bowl region who had migrated to the California fields in the latter part of the Depression. Support for other organizing attempts, if forthcoming at all, was brief, meager, noncommital, and inconsequential.

As a result, racism in general and the racism of white labor in particular strengthened the already established divisions between agricultural and urban labor. Historically there has been little mobility between the agricultural sector and skilled urban occupations. Agriculture was simply outside the occupational areas that labor unions were concerned with organizing. The segmentation of occupations produced what several researchers have termed a "dual labor market." Markets for nonwhites have been disproportionately centered in agriculture and low-skilled, low-wage urban jobs, while markets for whites include the higher-skilled, better-paying industrial, manufacturing, and craft occupations. These two labor markets drew from different sources of labor, had their own mechanisms for recruitment and training, and produced barriers to block mobility for the less privileged. This separation, enhanced by racial divisions, prompted the more privileged, predominantly white labor force to view advancements by nonwhites as threats to their living standards and occupational security. The option of incorporating nonwhite agricultural workers into existing labor federations like the AFL did not prevail until relatively recently.

Urban union organizers regarded agricultural workers as unorganizable. This attitude was based in part on unsupported assumptions regarding various nonwhite ethnic groups and their cultures. But the belief also prevailed among union organizers that the migratory patterns associated with much agricultural work did not provide a stable base for unionization. This opinion became self-fulfilling. Social historians have noted that successful protest movements among agricultural workers and other rural peoples throughout the world typically have received urban-based support for mobilization, and this support has been a critical factor in achieving gains.[12] Until fairly recently, however, this kind of support was not widely available for nonwhite farm workers until changes in race relations, largely initiated by the civil rights movement, made it possible for the NFWA-UFW to forge alliances with urban groups and mobilize resources external to the farm worker population.

FARM WORKERS AND STATE CONTROL

The most critical result of the lack of external resources has been the inability of farm worker movements and organizations to channel or influence government reactions and policies. With several exceptions, most notably in the present period, agricultural labor has simply lacked the leverage on government agencies and officials necessary for the institutionalization of the changes it has sought. Consequently the effects of government actions and policies throughout this history have been overwhelmingly in direct support of the interests of the large growers.

It will be shown how the growers, either as individuals or through their organizations, have been unable by themselves to regulate the agricultural labor supply completely to their own advantage. They have often been successful in recruiting groups they considered desirable both inside and outside the United States. But many of the forces that channeled groups into the agricultural labor market, such as changes in immigration laws and their enforcement, economic depressions, discrimination, migration patterns, and conditions prevailing in other countries, were largely outside the growers' control. The state, therefore, has periodically intervened to regulate and manipulate the agricultural labor supply. Its shifting policies and practices were a crucial determinant of the kinds of capital-labor relationships that have been characteristic of agriculture.

Agricultural workers have been particularly vulnerable to state power. They have in the past lacked sufficient countervailing power to offset grower pressure on the state, and as nonwhites they have often been subjected to racial discrimination, which prevented them from exercising electoral power commensurate with their numbers or building a political power base. Subsequent chapters will show that, during most periods, state intervention has served the immediate interests of the large growers by helping maintain their control over the work force. Changes in immigration laws and their enforcement, the repression of farm worker unionization efforts, discriminatory legislation directed against nonwhites, and the government-directed bracero programs are the most outstanding examples of state regulation of the agricultural labor supply. In agricultural areas themselves, law enforcement officials and local courts routinely have taken the side of growers in labor disputes and cooperated with attempts to recruit strikebreakers and limit strike activity. Many state actions have had the effect of either eliminating unionization efforts altogether or undermining the dominant position within the labor supply of an organized and militant group. By this process the labor source of California agriculture has periodically undergone shifts in composition.

State intervention secured for growers a labor focce that was in each case initially powerless, controllable, inexpensive, and unorganized. Yet it has not prevented attempts at organization by nearly every group engaged in agriculture for any considerable length of time. Confronted with an increasingly organized and militant agricultural work force, the state response typically has been to help promote the migration or immigration of a replacement labor supply, setting the stage for the following period of labor insurgency.

More complex, and perhaps ultimately more significant, are interventions aimed at mediating agricultural conflicts by attempting to provide certain guarantees to labor. Mediation efforts are exceptions to the predominant pattern of governmental response and have been undertaken largely over the opposition of the growers. During two relatively brief periods—the late 1930s and the era beginning in 1975 and continuing until at least the early 1980s—the state has acted to provide support for efforts aimed at unionizing California's agricultural labor force. This intervention has led not only to vital wage gains for farm workers, but, as we shall show, to alterations of the balance of power between agricultural capital and labor. One of the primary concerns of this study is to analyze the conditions and circumstances giving rise to state mediation as an exception to the long tradition of state support for the growers' immediate interests. Also important are the implications of state mediation: the limitations it imposes upon insurgent organizations, its power to channel militancy in certain directions, and its effects on future labor insurgency, unionization, and alliances with sympathetic individuals and organizations.

We will argue that state mediation has the potential to alter drastically the relationship between farm labor and capital. Control over hiring procedures, job seniority, the terms of employment, and the work process itself may be shifted toward labor. Thus, government efforts providing the basis for unionization are treated as historically significant events rather than ameliorative reform measures that leave class relationships unchanged.

To interpret the state response to farm labor insurgency, we have utilized elements from several recent attempts to develop an analysis of state policies and functions that differs from both pluralist political theory and classical Marxism. The former analyzes reforms undertaken by the state as complex responses to conflicting social demands. Claims upon the state are manifested by election preferences, political pressure, and organized interests, all generated from outside the state itself. With its variety of corrective and adaptive mechanisms, the state is viewed as a neutral agency, given legitimacy through some combination of normative consensus and majority preference. As a result, the state is believed to be a neutral mediator that does not consistently give advantage to any one segment of the population. In positing that reforms stem from the kind of representative process to which most groups have access, pluralist analysis tends to ignore the ways in which the institutional context of reforms can limit their potential impact: for example, the constraints imposed within Western societies by the necessity of maintaining markets, profits, and capital accumulation in the private sector.

The second approach is the one most often associated with the Leninist tradition within Marxism. State actions are interpreted as simply functioning to insure the domination of a capitalist class. A corollary of this view is the idea that reforms under capitalism are something of a sham, designed primarily to preempt growing discontent and curb radicalization. Certainly any attempt to apply a Marxian analysis to the study of political crises and state actions has to focus on the state's bias in favor of capital. But an approach is needed that differentiates among the various state responses to the conflicts and crises generated by insurgency. Underlying conflicts and contradictions must be located on the level of the state, and the balance of forces making demands upon the state in any given situation should be assessed.

The need for another approach has led to a renewed interest in formulating "theories of the capitalist state." This has arisen largely within the context of a far broader intellectual project to revitalize Marxian theory by freeing it from the constraints imposed in the past by textual ritualism and canonical dogma. While taking seriously the fundamental questions posed by classical Marxism, much of this analysis is deeply rooted in sociological tradition; in fact, a substantial proportion of those involved are also pursuing academic careers in sociology, anthropology, history, and political science. In some countries, such as France, recent developments in Marxian theory are at least loosely associated with national political developments, while in others, like the United States, the connection is less evident.

Instead of viewing the state solely as an instrument of class domination, it is more useful to examine "contradictions" within state policies and government interventions. The generality of such an approach has naturally produced a diversity of analysis, each analyst differing on what constitutes a contradiction. However, all share the recognition that the state performs a number of functions related to insuring the continued viability of a social system containing specific relations of dominance and subordination, including work relations. The growing importance of the state in regulating economic activity increases the number and variety of state activities, some of which may conflict with others under certain conditions. Thus, both economic and social stability may be difficult to obtain simply because the fulfillment of one is detrimental to the achievement of the other.

As a representative of this approach, James O'Connor analyzes the capitalist state in terms of its function of creating and maintaining the conditions for profitable capital accumulation while preserving social harmony through winning mass acceptance for its programs and policies. Besides providing infrastructural support, the state must legitimize its specific relationship to the accumulation process by appearing to pursue the interests of society as a whole. The dual functions of accumulation and legitimation are conceived of as contradictory. For example, the state's use of coercive powers to maintain private accumulation may deprive it of legitimation and support for its policies.[13] These related but potentially contradictory processes, both critical to the functioning of the capitalist state, place state intervention within a particular historical context and demonstrate the limits imposed on its possible actions. Given particular circumstances of intense class struggle, the ability of the state to rationalize capital accumulation is limited if further immediate disruptions are to be avoided. On a general level the state is treated as an equal partner with the competitive and monopoly sectors of the economy in furthering the accumulation process, thus divesting the state of much of its superstructural character. The centrality of the state forces its decision-makers to weigh political strategies. The possibility exists that political conflict within as well as outside the state may increase and state responses show a contradictory character.

Contradictory state responses lead to consideration of government policies that are at odds with the immediate interests of capital and state functions that go beyond those only involving accumulation. It is reasonable to ask what kinds of limits prevent government from undertaking profoundly anticapitalist solutions, especially in times of crisis. One method of confronting these issues is provided by what has been called "structuralist" Marxist theory, an approach that has been a major catalyst of debate. According to structuralists, the functions the state undertakes are determined by the structure and contradictions of society as a whole. The problem is not to interpret state actions as stemming from the power of specific individuals inside or outside government or from the influence over the state exercised by a ruling class. Rather, structuralists analyze what operations the state must perform to reproduce capitalist society as a whole.

The works of Nicos Poulantzas contain perhaps the most developed example of a structuralist approach to the capitalist state.[14] His analysis treats the state as the agent that must mediate various conflicts, especially those between social classes. Structural contradictions are especially pronounced at the level of the state and define it as the place where social transformations occur.[15] The fundamental issue is how the state reproduces class relations in ways that enhance the interests of the dominant classes.

Poulantzas argues that the state represents the political interests of the dominant classes as a whole rather than the specific economic interests of particular segments of capital. This is so even though the state is not composed of or controlled by representatives of the dominant classes. The capitalist class is too segmented and concerned with divergent, parochial interests to represent adequately its general political interests. Thus, the state must be able to free itself from direction or manipulation by segments of capital if it is to represent the long-term political interests of the capitalist class as a whole: a position defined as "relative autonomy." This transcendence of specific capitalist interests allows the state to serve as an integrative mechanism and enhances its ability to insure the long-term dominance of capital.

Correspondingly the state is capable of guaranteeing the economic interests of subordinate classes even when to do so is contrary to the short-term interests of the capitalist class in profit maximization and control over the labor force. The state is often forced to make concessions by the political and economic struggles of subordinate classes.

However, such concessions do not necessarily threaten the more general political interests of the dominant classes or the conditions for capital accumulation.

Moreover, even while guaranteeing reforms beneficial to subordinate classes, the state also attempts to undermine their political strength and potential to win further concessions. This is accomplished by depoliticizing their struggles and absorbing class conflicts into state structures that appear to represent the interests of society as a whole. The possibility that subordinate classes will organize politically is also undermined by reinforcing their divisions and their economic isolation from each other.[16] Instead of providing the insurgents with the groundwork or structural basis for better defending their interests and launching future challenges, reforms act as mechanisms of ideological indoctrination, since basic capitalist structures are left intact. The emphasis, then, of structural Marxists, and especially Poulantzas, is on the ways that mediation by the state maintains the long term viability of a capitalist mode of production with its accompanying class relationships through repressing potential threats, or more significantly, keeping oppositional forces isolated, legally restricted, and lacking in political power—even when they are able to translate their insurgency into concrete concessions.

A number of writers have responded critically to structuralist Marxism. All stress that the structural analysis of the state concerns itself only with how the state reproduces capitalist social relations and ignores the possibility that the state might promote solutions that erode the political and economic dominance of capital. In its extreme form, the structuralist position sets up a determinism whereby a system called capitalism absorbs all challenges to its hegemony short of revolutionary transformation.

Two critical arguments emerge. First, although structuralists regard the state as a condensation of class relations, they emphasize the processes by which the state reproduces capitalist class domination, even in the face of substantial working-class pressures. They slight the possibility that the state might be unable under certain circumstances to reproduce class relations. Several critics argue that class struggles shape the state as much as the state limits class struggles.[17] However useful it may be to specify the general functions of the capitalist state, it is also possible that the state might not realize these functions under all circumstances. Thus, the state may be analyzed as a constantly shifting entity whose position at any moment depends on the strengths of the particular forces brought to bear upon it. In this way particular actors within the state, such as elected officials, become important elements within the political class struggle and cannot be dismissed as mere instruments channeling insurgency by subordinate classes in directions that minimize its effect. In fact, like the actions of elected officials, the internal structure of the state may be determined in part by the struggles of subordinate classes.

Second, implicit within structural Marxism is the idea that the state has a crisis-management function, but the full implications of this have not been developed. In particular, crisis-management might give the state itself an interest in resolving intense conflicts in ways that insure stability, independent in theory from the entire class structure or mode of production. Instead, there are compelling reasons why state managers ordinarily pursue procapitalist policies, such as the dependence of the state apparatus (as well as political careers) on economic growth, facilitated by profitable investment in the private sector. However, the structuralist approach does not elaborate on the possibility that the state's fundamental interest in maintaining order may lead it during crisis periods to enforce concessions that shift power toward subordinate classes.[18]

The analytical framework we have used can now be summarized. The capitalist state is involved in the dual functions of stimulating capital accumulation in the private sector and legitimating its policies by appearing to pursue the general interest of the entire society. These potentially contradictory functions contain an opportunity for subordinate groups to force government concessions. Short-term gains, however, are not synonymous with alterations in the balance of power between oppositional forces. While mediating conflicts, the state also attempts to circumscribe them in order to keep class relations intact. During periods of crisis, this may mean forcing reforms over the opposition of powerful segments of capital. By absorbing class conflicts into government agencies and regulating them through bureaucratic procedures, the state can best preserve the general political interests of the dominant class.

The state's ability to accomplish such objectives is qualified by the strength of protest and the interest of government officials in managing crises successfully. Because they are not fully accountable to capital, politicians and state officials do not necessarily know how to mediate conflicts in ways that reproduce class relationships and insure the long-term interests of capital. Instead, class struggles may dominate the development of state structures and win the kind of concessions that shift power toward subordinate classes, best described by the phrase "nonreformist reforms."

It might seem ironic to readers of the next chapters that we emphasize state mediation and reforms when they have been largely absent
during this history. Instead, what has been impressively evident is
the consistency of state intervention on behalf of immediate economic
concerns of growers. Given the dominant position of agriculture in
California's economic history, the prevalence of straightforward government attempts to insure the immediate profits of agribusiness is
not surprising. However, whenever grower tactics and government
intervention were not immediately able to restore stability and pre-
dictability to production, the economic centrality of agriculture gave
insurgents leverage. In order to gain permanent concessions, farm
labor needed and still needs to break the bonds that united the state
and agribusiness. State support for agricultural unionization is crucial if any substantial, enduring changes benefiting the workers are
to take place. For example, the UFW could not have survived indefinitely without the support of elements of the state, not because of
any lack of support among farm workers or assistance by a sympathetic public but rather because of the power of the growers and their
allies.

Federal, state, and local governments obviously differ in their
ability to influence the agricultural labor situation. Local government agencies, especially the courts and police, have overwhelmingly acted in the immediate interests of growers; their ability to act,
however, is limited to such immediate situations as intervening in a
strike or helping recruit local sources of labor. The California and
federal governments possess the wider scope of influence necessary to
create or maintain particular forms of capital-labor relationships and
mediate agricultural labor conflicts. For this reason they will receive
primary emphasis here. "State," as we use the word, includes significantly more than is ordinarily associated with the word "government." It involves, for example, law enforcement agencies, courts,
prisons, government-funded agricultural research projects, government commissions and associations concerned with policy formation.

The struggle over the unionization of farm labor takes place within
the logic of the capitalist organization of agriculture. Control over the
work force and labor process is thought to be the prerogative of
management. Also, inexpensive labor costs are one way of reducing
the total costs of production and thereby increasing profits, but the
substandard wages prevailing throughout much of California's history do not appear to be essential for the financial solvency of agribusiness. Wages have periodically risen in response to farm worker
threats or actual disruption of production, only to be reduced after the

insurgency subsided. The concentrated ownership of agricultural production in California has created the possibility of realizing many of labor's demands without undermining the financial viability of large-scale agricultural production. However—and this fact is often ignored—the same concentration has given agricultural capital substantial resources for combating labor demands and unionization efforts. Nevertheless, changes are now occurring in the relationship between agricultural labor and capital, and they should continue in the near future. These gains have been and will be won by labor rather than conceded in advance by capital. In this sense people do make their own history, but they are constrained by the institutional contexts within which their struggles take place.

CHAPTER 2

CHINESE IMMIGRATION AND THE SEPARATION OF RURAL AND URBAN LABOR

The first group of workers to be utilized in California's agricultural expansion were Chinese immigrants who contributed the bulk of farm labor from 1870 until 1893, a period that saw an intense campaign against their immigration. White workers in mining regions, skilled trades in urban areas, and labor unions bitterly opposed their presence. Anti-Chinese sentiment within the working class led to Chinese isolation and, consequently, their situation as an acutely exploitable labor force. Even before they were introduced into the fields in large numbers, they were exposed to intense exploitation. Also, confinement of Chinese immigrants to undesirable urban jobs and to agricultural work strengthened the separation between white and nonwhite segments of the working class. Employment of Chinese in agriculture was concentrated in labor-intensive crops, initiating another dominant pattern in California's agricultural history. While they were the fields, growers were unconstrained in setting conditions of employment.

The context of the development of the above patterns derived from the hostility Chinese immigrants encountered in mining regions and, especially, urban areas. As a result, it is necessary to concentrate on the situation in cities, particularly San Francisco, in order to understand the magnitude of opposition which forced Chinese workers to seek employment in agriculture on terms largely dictated by their employers. While opposition to the Chinese was widespread, the anti-Chinese sentiments and actions of the white working class were particularly important. Not only did organized labor's hostility toward the Chinese initiate a strict separation of urban and agricultural employment sectors in which nonwhites would be concentrated in the latter, but it also made any semblance of working class unity a virtual impossibility. Nonwhite farm workers were prevented from forming strategic alliances with organized labor and denied any substantial external resources which might be used to create and sustain protest and institute agricultural labor reforms.

CHINESE LABOR AND URBAN UNIONS

The use of Chinese immigrant labor was a critical factor supporting economic development in California. Initially most of the Chinese population in California worked in mines and on railroad construction, including that of the transcontinental railroad.[1] Beginning in the 1860s they were also employed in California's newly developing agricultural lands, together with a small proportion of Native Americans and whites. In addition, Chinese immigrants were hired by land companies to provide the labor necessary to reclaim nearly five million acres of fertile swamp lands in the San Francisco Bay region and the Sacramento–San Joaquin River delta. An official of a land reclamation company estimated to a Congressional commission that through various forms of unskilled labor, the Chinese produced $60 to $90 million in wealth annually, an amount exceeding the output of California's mines.[2]

Organized labor played a major role in forming working class consciousness on the Chinese question and shaping legislation affecting Chinese workers. At first labor unions were indifferent to Chinese workers. Unions developed in a relatively privileged situation simultaneously with the growth of the state's population following the gold rush. Since California remained primarily unindustrialized until after 1900, unions were concentrated in the skilled trades and centered in urban areas, particularly San Francisco. The conditions of labor in the early years hastened union recognition and advancement. Labor was initially in demand to manufacture the pipes, cables, pumps, hoisting engines, and milling machinery supplied to the mining camps. When the Civil War drastically limited imports from the eastern United States, unions were organized to counter the effects of rising prices. In a geographically isolated area with a general shortage of workers like nineteenth-century California, strikes were exceedingly effective during times of economic expansion. Without a surplus of unemployed, it was difficult to recruit strikebreakers. Distance served as a protective shield for the early unions.[3]

Certain short-run economic interests of skilled labor were served by segregationist attitudes toward the Chinese. Restriction of Chinese laborers to the more undesirable jobs meant that a substantial segment of labor could not readily be used to displace striking skilled workers. Early Chinese immigrants were evicted from the mines by the imposition in 1850 of a foreign miners tax, which many could not pay. White miners agitated against them in fear of the possible effects of their competition.[4] Forced into the cities, Chinese workers initially engaged in unskilled occupations and were employed as domestics and cooks. As such their presence was not opposed by white labor. As continued immigration swelled the number of urban Chinese residents, they gradually moved into skilled trades, which began to bring them into increasing competition with white workers.[5]

During economic downturns white working-class resentment against the giving of increasingly scarce jobs to Chinese workers deprived both groups of a potential source of mutual support and exposed the Chinese population to harsh working and living conditions. As a distinct segment of the working class, they were vulnerable to exploitation as cheap labor. Culturally, socially, and linguistically separated from potential allies, they became a despised minority, a scapegoat for problems arising from the fluctuations of the economy. They were subject to discriminatory restrictions that deprived them of legal protection and institutionalized methods of redressing injury. Regarded as inferior and shunned by the labor movement, the Chinese were essentially powerless to remedy the situation in which they found themselves. As events unfolded, they withdrew from contact with the rest of society and, with certain notable exceptions in urban areas, became passive and tractable.

THE EXCLUSION CAMPAIGN

Organized opposition to Chinese immigration in the cities began in 1859 with the establishment of the People's Protective Union. The union emerged as the culmination of a boycott campaign against employers who hired Chinese workers in the cigar-making trade. Later it called a wider boycott against the products of all employers of Chinese, but this was largely unsuccessful.[6] Labor had scarcely become organized when it began promoting anti-Chinese agitation. A march of 2,000 workers up Market Street in San Francisco in June 1867 in support of an eight-hour work day ended with a warning, delivered by a leader of the Stonecutters' Union, that capital planned to block the eight-hour-day law by importing "the lowest caste of the human race in China." The *San Francisco Daily* said that the demonstration showed "the determination that prevails among a large and intelligent body of workingmen to adopt eight hours as a day's work, and also, in a measure to protest against Chinese labor being introduced so as to interfere with the rights of white workingmen."[7]

Because Chinese workers were regarded as an economic threat rather than a political resource, legal protections for Chinese were interpreted as an attack on white workers. Reports of concessions made by the U.S. government to China in exchange for investment opportunities overseas served as a catalyst for racist sentiment. Anti-Chinese actions escalated in reaction to the ratification of the Burlingame Treaty with China in 1868. This treaty was bitterly opposed by much of California's population. The most objectionable provision was one granting Chinese in the United States "the same privileges, immunities, and exemptions in respect to travel or residence as may be . . . enjoyed by the citizens of the most favored nations."[8] While stopping short of allowing naturalization, it did prohibit a number of options in the mistreatment of Chinese and precluded limitation of Chinese immigration in the future.[9]

For the federal government the rationale of the treaty was clear. The actions of federal officials were oriented toward insuring the long-term interests of entrepreneurs with domestic and international operations. Throughout the late nineteenth century, the executive branch of the federal government acted as the regulator and coordinator of entry into the markets of the Far East by American business. This delicate position required care not to offend the Asian governments, which might easily shut the door to American investment. The Burlingame Treaty of 1868 extended privileges of trade and commerce granted by previous treaties of 1844 and 1856. In earlier decades the government had allowed Chinese immigration as a way of promoting a supply of cheap labor for the West Coast. The same pattern of involvement by the federal government was largely repeated with respect to the Japanese nearly four decades later.

During the next several years anti-Chinese activity by white labor grew substantially. Associations formed to lobby for abrogation of the Burlingame Treaty successfully petitioned both the Democratic and Republican parties in California to adopt anti-Chinese provisions in their platforms. Labor organizations were not alone in their ideology and their aggressive agitation against the Chinese. Prominent intellectuals joined the attack by expanding the ideology and giving it an aura of legitimacy by blaming the Chinese for their own victimization. Henry George was a notable example. Early in his career as a politician and intellectual, George contributed a rationale for labor's anti-Chinese stance. Before 1869 his writings emphasized that monopolies were responsible for curtailing the income of workers and producing unemployment and economic stagnation. In 1869, however, in a letter to the *New York Tribune*, George argued that continued Chinese immigration would permit the Chinese to take over one occupation after another, reducing white wages and setting up a depressive economic spiral. The exploitation of Chinese would transfer wealth from the producers to the property owners: the capitalists and the landlords. The problem would attain national proportions, George argued, as Chinese labor was utilized in the Midwest and East. Chinese labor accentuated the trend toward monopoly. The result would make "the rich richer and the poor poorer."[10] The two components of this prediction were a rational economic argument and an emotional hostility to the Chinese. As John Stuart Mill pointed out, George's argument took for granted that the Chinese could never be assimilated.[11]

What ultimately gave organized labor the leverage it needed on the Chinese question was participation by business owners and manufacturers in the anti-Chinese campaign. By 1873 business interests had begun to feel threatened by Chinese immigration and gradually joined labor in demanding exclusion. As long as the Chinese worked for wages and under conditions set by their white employers, they were enthusiastically welcomed. As soon as the Chinese learned to use the strike as a means of improving wages and working conditions and began establishing their own shops, hiring their own countrymen, reducing the Chinese labor available to white employers, and undercutting their white business and manufacturing competition, certain businessmen allied themselves with organized labor.[12] In view of the generally radical stance of labor at the time, this agreement of capital and labor was incongruous. But from this point on, considerable progress was made in restricting Chinese immigration.

The strategy of the ironic alliance had two fronts. It successfully pressured the California legislature to pass anti-Chinese laws and later moved Congress to cancel the Burlingame Treaty. The California legislation was primarily aimed at placing financial burdens on the Chinese and preventing them from earning a livelihood. For example, one law imposed a $1,000 fine on anyone who brought an Asian into California without first presenting evidence of his good character. Asians were forbidden to work on the construction of certain irrigation and reclamation projects. Stiff taxes were imposed on Chinese operating laundry businesses. A law aimed at breaking up Chinatown areas in cities by forbidding the renting of rooms in which there was less than five hundred cubic feet of air per person was passed first by San Francisco and later by the California legislature. Lodgers and landlords were subject to heavy fines and imprisonment.[13] The laws were used as harassment devices until ruled unconstitutional several years after their passage. On a number of occasions during the 1870s, delegations representing the state of California were sent to Washington, D.C., to pressure the federal government for Chinese exclusion. In 1876 both national political parties inserted anti-Chinese planks in their platforms. In 1877 a commission appointed by Congress the previous year to investigate the California situation recommended immediate action to restrict Chinese immigration. In 1879 both houses of Congress passed a law limiting the number of Chinese immigrants to fifteen per vessel. President Hayes's veto of the measure prompted a California referendum on Chinese exclusion in the fall of that year in which 154,638 voted for exclusion and only 833 against.[14]

These, then, were the general features of the opposition to the employment of Chinese and its effect on civil liberties. Specific historical experiences determined the extent and form of anti-Chinese prejudice. Events during the depression of the mid-1870s illustrated the process by which the Chinese became objects of racial hostility and were forced into a position in which they had little choice but to accept farm labor under exploitative circumstances.

ECONOMIC DECLINE AND IMMIGRANT LABOR

It would be misleading to conclude that exclusionary attitudes toward the Chinese were simply a product of prejudice, an assumption prevalent in race relations research. Instead, patterns in the expression of racism often reflect the conditions of class conflict. Racial prejudices can be reinforced, manipulated to deflect social protest, and utilized against the interests of the subordinate class during capital-labor struggles. With respect to the Chinese, heightened attitudes of racial hostility generated a climate of political support for discriminatory legislation which had the effect of promoting wider segmentation of the labor market. Racism directed against Asians lent a rationale for state regulation of the labor supply in the interests of capital.

It is no accident that the height of the Chinese exclusion campaign coincided with the depression of the mid-1870s, a time of severe dislocation for workers in the West. In 1876, the year of the worst financial and economic conditions for California, 23,000 Chinese entered the state while thousands of white workers were unemployed.[15] In addition, California was at this time experiencing a serious drought. The California historian Hubert Howe Bancroft estimated 15,000 unemployed in San Francisco alone in the spring of 1877, accounting for 20 to 25 percent of the labor force.[16] Increasingly, local and state politicians took up anti-Chinese positions and actively sought the support of anticoolie clubs. Political figures lent a certain legitimacy to the more militant anti-Chinese actions largely undertaken by workers' organizations.

Political organizations of the working class gave expression to the severe disruptions and discontent workers were experiencing in the depression of the 1870s. At the time the only body in California capable of speaking for white workers and unemployed people as a whole was the newly formed Workingmen's party of the United States. It had absorbed many of the members of the International Workingmen's Association after the latter disbanded. Through this group large numbers of white workers became organized. Several chapters of the party were formed in San Francisco and one in Sacramento. Contemporary observers believed that labor was headed for a confrontation with capital. One notable study concluded from interviews with spectators and participants in party and union activities as well as analysis of local newspapers "the masses seemed ready, and only awaiting an excuse, to let loose their discontent and pillage the city [San Francisco]."[17] But the slogan eventually adopted by the Workingmen's party to channel their discontent was "The Chinese must go!"[18]

When labor activism and disturbances became widespread in 1877, little attention was initially given to the Chinese question. Emphasis was placed instead on confronting the Central Pacific Railroad, which had recently lowered wages and was being struck in the East. Organized labor also actively opposed the granting of governmental subsidies, including land, to private parties. In numerous statements it vigorously denounced the encroachment of capital on the rights and privileges of the general population. Soon, however, a group of leaders emerged who directed the party's attention to the Chinese question.

On 23 July anti-Chinese elements gained influence over a segment of a crowd gathered adjacent to San Francisco's City Hall. The crowd had assembled to hear speeches demanding an eight-hour day and nationalization of the railroads, the two primary points of a widely discussed socialist program. Even though the Chinese were not mentioned in any of the speeches, bands of men influenced by anti-coolie agitators in the crowd broke off from the main gathering to hunt for victims. Twenty to thirty Chinese wash houses were broken into that night. For the next several nights, disturbances took the form of attacks on businesses targeted in part because of their alleged support of Chinese presence in California. The disorder also included battles with police, physical assaults on the Chinese community, and the murders of several Chinese.[19]

The manner of containment of the protest was not arbitrary. A pattern in law enforcement emerged: violence was successfully displaced from the property of major economic institutions and directed instead against Chinese people and businesses. The United States Mint, the Mission Woolen Mills, the Pacific Mail Steamship Company, and other denounced establishments were well protected by the police, the militia, and a volunteer group of "law and order" citizens called the "pick handle brigade" after the weapons furnished them. When crowds found that they could not assail these companies, they shifted to attacking Chinese establishments. Although police made attempts at dispersal, the crowds were successful in destroying a Chinese Methodist Church, numerous Chinese laundries, and other businesses not afforded police protection. The stage had been set before the mass onslaught against the Chinese community: over the last few years, small bands of white workers had repeatedly attacked individual Chinese with impunity.[20]

Aggression against Chinese had been tested and found sufficient as a mobilizing objective for working-class protesters. Shortly after the mass actions dissipated, a new labor party arose and concentrated more intensively on the issue of Chinese exclusion. The new Workingmen's party of California was formed in October 1877, with Dennis Kearney as president. Kearney, a self-educated Irish ex-seaman who owned a draying business in the city, was particularly vehement on the Chinese issue. Although bitter denunciations of capital were distributed throughout his speeches, he successfully focused working-class mass activism on the movement for Chinese exclusion. Under his leadership over 7,000 marchers participated in the Workingmen's Thanksgiving Day parade of 1877, which the *San Francisco Examiner* described as "a great demonstration against coolie labor."[21]

Opportunities to reorient the white workers' movement or even to debate the mobilization around anti-Chinese goals were never actually realized. During 1878 competition arose between two party factions, differentiated in part by their stands on the Chinese question. Kearney's rival, Frank Roney, thought the party's position on the Chinese was "brutal," but he went along with it for pragmatic reasons. Kearney appears to have had more workers on his side, as evidenced by his popularity as a sandlot speaker.[22]

The opposition to the Chinese contrasted ironically with the Workingmen's party's otherwise consistent concern for the interests of the poor and its condemnation of the abuses of established wealth and power. Its platform consisted of a series of proposals designed, according to the party, to wrest state power from the rich and give it to the people, destroy land monopoly, and institute a system of progressive taxation to eliminate the accumulation of large amounts of wealth in private hands. The party also pledged to elect only workingmen to office and provide for the poor and disabled. These proposals were interspersed with condemnation of those employing Chinese and threats against the Chinese themselves. The new party soon superseded the Workingmen's party of the United States, which eventually merged with it. Not surprisingly, it was on the Chinese question that the Workingmen's party of California was able to weld seemingly improbable alliances and gain electoral victories that increased pressure on the federal government to alter its position on Chinese immigration.

Although by 1878 the Workingmen's party had become a major political force in California, it failed to implement any of its anticapitalist proposals. In fact, its effectiveness was limited to marshaling support for anti-Chinese legislation. Chinese exclusion and discriminatory legislation were goals neither the Republicans nor the Democrats opposed, and the party's primary legacy was its role in escalating anti-Chinese sentiment and agitation. It was a purpose not at odds with the interests of most other classes in California at the time.

Just as the expression of protest by white workers was deflected into racial hostility, the success of the legislative program of the Workingmen's party was limited to its racial agenda. The party's role in drafting the 1879 revision of the California constitution illustrated how its political goals were largely thwarted. After electoral victories by the party in a number of locations around the state, the California legislature devised a plan for the selection of delegates to the constitutional convention that included 32 delegates-at-large chosen by a statewide vote to supplement the 120 delegates elected by senatorial districts. These delegates-at-large were added as protection against control of the convention by Workingmen's party delegates and formed the nucleus of the convention's conservative, business-oriented bloc. Nevertheless, the Workingmen candidates won all 30 delegate positions from San Francisco and added 21 more positions from other areas. Thus, Workingmen made up an impressive one-third of all delegates at the 1978 convention.[23]

The votes of a third of the delegates to the constitutional convention were not going to be enough to pass laws designed to dismantle corporate power in the state. The best the Workingmen could do was to align with agrarian delegates in order to pass what might be described as a Granger platform. The alliance sought regulatory powers and modest reforms to curb the power of corporations, especially the railroad companies. Included were reforms of taxation and limits on land ownership. Many corporations, however, were able in subsequent years to defy state authority and circumvent these laws, and the regulatory agencies eventually came to serve the very interests they were supposed to superintend.[24] The Workingmen failed to write into the constitution the mandatory eight-hour day, one of their primary objectives. Even a proposal to establish a bureau of labor statistics was voted down.[25]

In contrast Workingmen delegates did take the lead in establishing a set of anti-Chinese clauses to which there was little opposition. The constitution subjected Chinese to measures aimed at cutting off their means of livelihood as well as depriving them of any possible political influence.[26] Article XIX stated that no Chinese could be employed on any state, county, municipal, or other public works project. In addition, Chinese could not be employed by corporations operating under California laws. Chinese were also forbidden to vote (along with any "idiot, insane person, or person convicted of any infamous crime").[27] Incorporated cities and towns were authorized to remove Chinese from their boundries or designate areas within which they must live. These anti-Chinese clauses were invalidated by the federal courts in March 1880. They did, however, serve to reinforce widespread opposition to Chinese presence and promote anti-Chinese actions.

The new constitution met opposition, but not on humanitarian grounds. Primarily because of the modest anticapital reforms contained in it, its adoption was opposed by business, merchant, landowner, and other propertied interests as well as the leading newspapers, with the exception of the San Francisco Chronicle. In May 1879 the constitution was adopted in a special referendum by a vote of 77,959 to 67,134.[28] However, 99 percent (150,000 to 900 votes) favored exclusion of Chinese immigrants on the accompanying referendum as a reaction to President Hayes's veto of anti-Chinese legislation.[29]

Singling out a minority for discriminatory legislation had the effect of sanctioning assaults on minority members themselves. With the passage of the constitution, unemployed white workers in cities suffering from four years of economic depression attempted to enforce its anti-Chinese provisions and attacked companies that employed

Chinese. In San Francisco, a number of companies discharged Chinese workers and hired white workers in their place. It was in connection with these outbreaks that Dennis Kearney, now president of the Workingmen's party and a popular spokesman for the unemployed, was arrested and prosecuted, although appeals later reversed his conviction.

Also in 1880, President Hayes had vetoed a bill prohibiting any sea-going vessel from carrying more than fifteen "Mongolian" passengers on any voyage to the United States. The veto was interpreted as a way of stalling for time in order to make the necessary adjustments leading to Chinese exclusion. In general, after giving approval by noninvolvement for over two decades of escalating anti-Chinese animosity, federal officials chose to continue to acquiesce to discrimination. They were at this point confronted with the possibility of widespread insurrections by white workers in California and were being pressured by other anti-Chinese forces in East Coast labor organizations. As a response, during the summer of 1879 the federal government sent a delegation to China to renegotiate the Burlingame Treaty. Renegotiation was completed in 1880. New provisions granted the United States the option to "regulate, limit or suspend" but not "entirely prohibit" the immigration of Chinese laborers.[30] The new treaty gave the United States the authority to restrict Chinese immigration.

Federal intervention in the form of further legislation continued to reflect anti-Chinese sentiment. The Chinese Exclusion Act was passed in 1882, suspending Chinese immigration for ten years. President Arthur signed the act on 6 May. Besides suspending the immigration of Chinese laborers, it prohibited federal and state courts from naturalizing Chinese. Restrictions were renewed in 1892 and again in 1902. In 1904 they were extended without time limit. As a result, the Chinese population of California decreased from 75,000 in 1880 to 72,000 in 1890 and then went into a long decline.

Once legitimated by public authority, attacks on the livelihood and personal security of the Chinese would not readily subside, even with Chinese exclusion. Attention in San Francisco turned to organizing boycotts to pressure employers to discharge Chinese and hire whites in their place in enterprises where Chinese labor was concentrated, particularly the boot- and shoe-making, cigar-making, and laundry trades. Most of the pressure was organized by the Representative Assembly of Trades and Labor Unions (the Trades Assembly), which grew out of a caucus of unionists who opposed Kearney's leadership in the Workingmen's party. By 1882 the decline in unemployment had reduced Kearney's main constituency, and the Workingmen's party quickly vanished. The Trades Assembly became the principal organization of the white working class in San Francisco.

It would be a mistake to assume that opposition to Chinese employment stemmed from a general competition for jobs. Direct competition between unionists and Chinese was limited by a dual labor market. Competition between whites and Chinese concentrated in the manufacturing of consumer goods, which employed mostly unskilled labor. The unskilled, or secondary, labor market was almost entirely nonunionized. The more unionized sectors of metal trades, construction, and maritime industries experienced very little Chinese entry.[31] Nor was the problem the backwardness of the Chinese labor force. If the basis for trade unionist opposition to Chinese workers had been their presumed lack of class consciousness and resistance to organization, there was less reason in the 1880s to hold these assumptions than there had been in any previous decade. Chinese workers became increasingly organized in urban areas during the 1880s. Strikes among Chinese employed in cigar making successfully raised wages to the point that by 1885 the wages of white and Chinese cigar makers had begun to overlap.[32] This growth in Chinese militancy was hard to reconcile with the trade union argument that Chinese were unorganizable, unassimilable, and acquiescent to low wages and poor working conditions. Still, the response of the San Francisco local of the Cigar Makers' International Union was to attempt to place white men in cigar factories that had exclusively employed Chinese as part of a long-term plan for driving Chinese from the cigar-making trade, and especially from the more skilled and better-paying positions that Chinese were increasingly occupying.[33] Only a few trade union leaders raised the ideals of working-class solidarity and internationalism and posed the alternative of integrating Chinese into white unions.

Through its active participation and leadership in the exclusion campaign, organized labor in effect curbed its drive for the more egalitarian goals that were also at stake in the 1870s and 1880s. The unions failed to pursue such goals as the limitation of land ownership, the redistribution of wealth through progressive taxation, and stringent public control over private enterprise. Even more importantly, trade union involvement in the general movement against the Chinese gave Chinese workers little choice but to seek agricultural jobs. Excluded from skilled jobs in the primary sector, pressured out of unskilled manufacturing jobs by trade union boycotts, they became an isolated and exploitable labor force. Through the campaign to prohibit Chinese immigration urban labor unions initially became involved in the supply of labor to large growers.

LOW-WAGE FARM LABOR

The availability of a work force with few options but to accept agricultural labor under exploitative conditions gave an enormous subsidy to large growers. Chinese labor was in large part responsible for the progress of California's fruit production and the emergence of a wealthy class of landowners between 1870 and 1895. By the 1870s the profitability of wheat farming had deteriorated in California as a result of the development of wheat production in the Mississippi Valley. The transition to a more profitable crop was facilitated by the completion of the transcontinental railroad in 1869, the creation of the refrigeration car, the appropriate climate and soil conditions obtaining in California, and irrigation.[34] But what finally permitted the shift to citrus and deciduous fruit growing was the labor provided by Chinese: the work of clearing, diking, ditching, draining, irrigating, and harvesting the new crops.[35] Authorities disagree about the extent to which Chinese labor was utilized during these decades, but it is clear that by 1880 they dominated the agricultural labor supply, occupying from 75 to 90 percent of the positions in the fields. In 1886 the California Bureau of Labor estimated that the Chinese supplied about seven-eighths of all agricultural labor.[36] That Chinese workers were concentrated in agriculture is evident: Chinese composed only 7.5 percent of the California population in 1880.[37]

The Chinese employed by the growers were compliant. Organized strikes by Chinese workers in urban trades did not carry over to the Chinese in rural areas. Appearing for hire at harvest season, they worked hard and long for little pay, made few complaints, and disappeared as soon as the harvest season was over into urban areas or the small Chinatowns that had sprung up in many rural towns. Large agricultural landowners found them an ideal supply of farm labor and have tried to duplicate the pattern of Chinese employment during successive decades. For half a century, growers publicly expressed a desire for a return of labor conditions prevailing during the time of Chinese employment.

The supply of Chinese field labor continually increased as disturbances of the mid-1870s were followed by a migration of Chinese to rural areas. While most sections of California experienced a relative decline in Chinese population, in agricultural regions the proportion of Chinese continued to increase during the 1880s.[38] Smaller orchardists who had to compete with the large growers did not profit to the same degree from this supply of inexpensive labor because they employed, at most, a half-dozen white farm hands. Chinese employment gave the large growers a distinct advantage over other farmers and sent their small competitors into the ranks of the anti-Chinese movement. (For similar reasons many small urban manufacturers opposed Chinese immigration, whereas large manufacturers turned against it only when the Chinese began to organize among themselves in the trades where they were concentrated.) Wheat farmers and cattle ranchers, still a substantial proportion of the large landowners, were indifferent to the issue, since their much smaller labor needs were adequately filled by white laborers. Large fruit producers thus came to be isolated in their support of continued immigration.

With the passage of the Chinese Exclusion Act, much of the focus of anti-Chinese actions shifted to rural areas. By 1885 thousands of new immigrants from the eastern part of the United States had poured into California and were unable to find employment. Anti-Chinese riots spread to rural areas throughout the West. Thirty Chinese were killed by white miners in Rock Springs, Wyoming, in 1885. Chinese residents were driven out of Seattle and Tacoma, Washington, and Eureka, Marysville, Truckee, Nicolaus, and other California cities in the spring of 1886.[39] In many of these incidents there appeared to be substantial participation by white workingmen, especially in the mining and lumber regions, and leadership was often provided by local assemblies of the Knights of Labor.[40] In 1888 Congress passed the Scott Act, which closed the door on 20,000 Chinese who had left the United States but had intended to return.

In the last decade of the nineteenth century, depressed economic conditions again caused distress for the working class as a whole and especially the Chinese minority. The desperation accompanying the economic decline was again partly channeled into hostility against the Chinese. The depression beginning in 1893 swelled California's unemployed population. Jobless workers from the Midwest and Rocky Mountain regions flooded into the state. The *Coast Seaman's Journal* reported that San Francisco had not witnessed such destitution, suffering, and poverty in twenty-five years. Throughout the valleys of California unemployed white workers erupted against the Chinese. In Fresno, when it was learned that a thousand unemployed men were en route from Denver, the local chief of police, fearing a riot, begged the growers in the area to discharge the Chinese they employed in order to make room for the newest immigrants.[41]

Both the California and Federal governments appeared to invite reactions against Chinese presence in the United States by singling them out for restrictive legislation. For example, an immediate impetus for anti-Chinese riots was the passage of the Geary Act by Congress in 1892. Named for California Democratic Congressman Thomas Geary of Sonoma County, the legislation not only continued Chinese exclusion for another ten years, but provided for the deportation of all Chinese illegally present in the United States. In addition, it placed the burden of proof of legal residence on the Chinese themselves.[42] All Chinese laborers were required to register under the act within one year. American lawyers advised Chinese not to comply, since they assumed that the act was unconstitutional, but the Supreme Court upheld it. It has been estimated that up to 95 percent of the Chinese failed to register and were legally subject to deportation. These circumstances allowed white workers in the rural districts to claim they were enforcing the law when they proceeded to drive the Chinese out of the fields.

Disturbances quickly spread throughout California from the Napa Valley and as far north as Ukiah to the citrus districts in the south. The *Los Angeles Times* reported in August and September of 1893 at least one anti-Chinese demonstration in each of thirteen towns in agricultural areas. Fresno, Bakersfield, Redlands, and San Bernardino experienced severe or prolonged disturbances.[43] Chinese were literally taken from the fields and camps and loaded onto the first trains out of town. Their camps and rural Chinatowns were razed; the inhabitants were threatened and killed. The Chinese fled for shelter to the cities from which many had been driven eighteen years before. By 1895 white workers were replacing Chinese in the fields in large numbers.

Growers, smaller farmers, and local townspeople generally did not participate in the anti-Chinese demonstrations in agricultural areas. The owners of large citrus groves, orchards, and vineyards, who were dependent on Chinese harvest labor, urged moderation. They gave up their opposition to Chinese exclusion only under duress. In fact, the displacement of the Chinese did not expose the growers to an economic loss. Unemployment had made available a generally sufficient quantity of white workers to replace the Chinese they had driven out. In 1902 Congress responded by extending Chinese exclusion indefinitely, prohibiting the immigration of Chinese laborers from island territories of the United States to the mainland, and continuing to deny the Chinese naturalization.[44] This action completed the first major transition in the California agricultural labor force.

CHINESE EXCLUSION AND ORGANIZED LABOR

The stance of California labor organizations and the white working class was mirrored nationally. Similar anti-Chinese positions emerged within the labor movement in several other Pacific Coast and Rocky Mountain states, and these were often accompanied by outbreaks more violent than those in California. On the East Coast, after fewer than one hundred Chinese laborers were used as strikebreakers at a North Adams, Massachusetts, shoe factory in 1870, national labor organizations moved into the forefront of the anti-Chinese movement, fearful of an imagined army of Asian workers that would undermine white labor's standard of living. Both Terence Powderly of the Knights of Labor and Samuel Gompers of the American Federation of Labor were vehement opponents of Asian immigration. Their position initiated a tendency within the American labor movement to disregard nonwhite segments of the working class and leave the largely nonwhite agricultural work force unorganized, easily exploited, and without hope of organized labor's support.

Labor's decision to campaign for the exclusion of the Chinese set the pattern for the relationship between the predominantly white, urban-based labor unions and the nonwhite groups that dominated agricultural labor. Implicit in the decision was a denial of the possibility of enlisting the Chinese and integrating them into existing labor organizations. Labor analysts cited cultural differences, social and linguistic barriers, residential segregation, lower wage levels, and Chinese conservatism, loyalty to the employer, and lack of class consciousness. These assumptions were questionable at best. For example, during 1913–18 the Industrial Workers of the World (IWW) were successfully able to organize agricultural labor in the West, including remnants of the earlier Chinese farm workers. Nevertheless, trade unions did not consider alliances with Chinese workers viable. The intense oppression of the Chinese population denied them political and economic leverage and precluded successful self-organization. They remained essentially powerless throughout the period.

The denial by the unions of the possibility of participation by the Chinese re-emerged and was directed against other nonwhite groups on many occasions during the next half century. Organized labor resisted Japanese, Filipino, and finally Mexican immigration. Even when the nonwhite workers who continuously dominated California's agricultural labor were able to organize themselves, established unions generally remained aloof, and agricultural workers had to overcome the barriers to unionization by themselves. When they temporarily succeeded, they were deprived of their logical allies. Without support, concessions granted by growers had a short life, and agricultural workers were unable to consolidate their gains. External resources were grievously lacking.

As a result, little was done during the first sixty years of the twentieth century to prevent the segregation of the white and minority segments of the working class. Nonwhite workers dominated field labor, while white workers were concentrated in urban-based industries, manufacturing, and trades. The agricultural group remained unorganized and endured conditions of persistent economic deprivation. During the late nineteenth century, prejudice within the working class led organized labor to pressure government to translate the anti-Chinese sentiment into law. Organized labor's support for discriminatory legislation gave the state a political basis for regulation of the agricultural labor supply in the long term interests of capital.

State action during this period may appear to be an anomaly when compared to later patterns. Government restriction of Chinese immigration cut off an ideal source of labor for the large agricultural landowners and pressure exerted by organized labor, both nationally and in California, was a primary stimulus of exclusion. However, by the time of the renegotiation of the Burlingame Treaty, growers who utilized Chinese workers were virtually isolated in favoring continued unrestricted immigration. Other segments of capital no longer profited from Chinese immigration and the issue had become an explosive one. Further, Chinese exclusion represented a "safe" concession to organized labor. The Workingmen's party's socialist program had become deflected toward racist ends which it did, in fact, achieve. The results were discriminatory ordinances and federal intervention setting a precedent for later regulation of the supply of labor to large growers. Also, state policies had the effect of maintaining dual labor market conditions and promoting wider differences between the two groups of workers. In these important respects the experience of the Chinese was not unique. They were the first workers in the succession of available and readily exploited immigrant groups passing through the fields in a pattern of labor supply and utilization that has yet to be fully transcended.

CHAPTER 3

JAPANESE FARM LABOR AND LAND TENURE

The immigration of Japanese workers was a pattern-setting solution to the labor problem of large growers in California. It marked the first instance in which growers succeeded in using the federal government to manipulate the supply of agricultural workers in their direct interest. Japanese immigration and employment in agriculture took place under disadvantageous conditions imposed from the outset. Japanese workers faced the dual labor market dividing rural and urban workers, policies of racial exclusion on the part of organized labor, and the growers' interest in maintaining a large controllable seasonal labor force at low wages. The growers could not accomplish the maintenance of exploitative conditions by themselves. In this chapter we will show how the federal government came to their aid. The circumstances of agricultural labor for future farm workers were also conditioned by another pattern initiated during the time Japanese workers were the major source of labor: the decline in alternative ways of work in California agriculture, particularly the opportunity for field workers to become working farmers on small acreages. State laws regulating land ownership by racial minorities were at the time an important means of limiting alternatives to the system of seasonal labor at low wages.

For Japanese farm workers the need to organize was obvious. They were the first group of foreign-born farm workers to demonstrate what became the persistent response of immigrant workers to the conditions of California agriculture. At first immigrant groups were tractable under low wages and harsh working conditions. Then,

when a single ethnic group came to supply the bulk of harvest labor
for a particular crop, they organized and held strikes to improve
working and living conditions. It is significant that beginning with
the Japanese, farm worker agitation has tended to center on control
over work as much as on the attempt to improve wages.

JAPANESE WORKERS AND LABOR ASSOCIATIONS

At first Japanese workers provided an ideal solution to the problem of
finding a low-cost source of labor. The Chinese movement back to the
cities had created a crisis for California agriculture. Many of the jobs
vacated by the Chinese were filled by white workers forced out of
their jobs by the depression of the 1890s. These workers sought to
maintain the high level of wages typical of urban jobs, and they built
the first movement in California to organize agricultural laborers.
Large growers had few options but to meet their wage demands. In
the late 1890s, however, there was a sharp increase in the immigration of Japanese. To the growers' satisfaction, they moved immediately into agricultural jobs at wages actually lower than those
paid to the remaining Chinese. The Japanese successfully replaced
white workers, and because of this displacement, organized labor
regarded them with distrust and antagonism. The improvement in
the conditions of field work had lasted less than a decade.

Japanese entry into the fields occurred in stages. Immigration
began around 1885, mainly to the developing plantations in Hawaii.
Previously emigration from Japan had been illegal. Like the
Chinese, the Japanese were ineligible for naturalization. After several years in Hawaii, Japanese began coming to the West Coast, but
substantial immigration to the United States did not begin until over
a decade later. Until 1898 the number of Japanese entering was less
than 2,000 a year. This number climbed to 12,000 by 1900 and
averaged approximately 6,600 annually over the next decade.[1]

At this stage Japanese immigrants were concentrated in California, largely in agricultural areas. A conservative estimate by the
California commissioner of labor in 1913 reported that 65 percent of
the Japanese in California were involved in agriculture as laborers or
farmers.[2] Japanese farm workers tended to concentrate in areas
where labor-intensive crops were produced. By 1913 the percentage
of labor represented by the Japanese on white-owned or -operated
farms was 87 percent for berries, 66 percent for sugar beets, 52
percent for grapes, 46 percent for vegetables, and 37 percent for citrus
and deciduous fruits, but only 7 percent for hops, hay, and grains.[3]

Other appraisals place their share of the labor market at a considerably higher percentage, with one estimating they represented from 65 to 85 percent of various vegetable labor, nearly 100 percent for sugar beets, 90 percent for berries and 70 percent for deciduous fruit.[4] The Japanese were thus concentrated in the areas of produce that growers turned to during the agricultural crisis of the 1890s. They therefore dominated the labor supply of the intensive specialized sector that accounted for approximately half of the agricultural produce in California.[5]

At first the Japanese were not a threat to the low labor costs of agriculture. On the contrary, as mentioned earlier, their influx into field jobs around 1900 successfully stemmed the movement of white farm workers to organize for higher pay. The first attempt at organizing agricultural labor took place around this time, but with the increased employment of Japanese laborers at wages far below those demanded by white workers, organizational attempts quickly failed, and whites moved out of agricultural employment.[6] In the Imperial Valley in the extreme southern part of the state, Mexican as well as Japanese labor was utilized to force whites out of jobs.[7] Generally speaking, early Japanese farm laborers underbid every other group engaged in agricultural production. As a result, they represented a superexploitable source of farm labor, as had the Chinese before them. Growers came to rely increasingly on their employment and encouraged further immigration.[8]

Ironically, California growers were able to obtain the passage of a protective tariff by arguing that such legislation was essential to maintain high wage standards for American labor. As early as 1898, however, a report by the Industrial Commission on Immigration documented that most of the labor in sugar beet fields was performed by Japanese workers.[9] Sugar beets were a labor-intensive cash crop producing quick profits and needing little capitalization. In spite of demands from labor and small growers to break up the land conglomerates, Congress passed the Dingley Tariff Act of 1897. The tariff created a highly profitable market for the new sugar beet growers by imposing a heavy duty on imported sugar. The main beneficiary was what was then called the Sugar Trust, formed by the merger in 1902 of the Spreckles sugar beet growing empire in California and the eastern American Sugar Refining Company. The duty imposed on imported sugar was the equivalent of an annual subsidy of $140 million to California sugar beet growers.[10]

Organizing trade unions was not an option for Japanese farm workers. A noteworthy incident during the early years of Japanese employment illustrates the continued policy of organized labor toward nonwhite workers. A strike of approximately one thousand Japanese and Mexican sugar beet workers in Oxnard in 1903 resulted in several concessions by growers. This prompted the California State Federation of Labor to pass a resolution to place an organizer in the fields. One official of the federation stated that the resolution "virtually breaks the ice on the question of forming the Orientals into unions and so keeping them from scabbing on white people, in place of not recognizing Asiatics as at present."[11] When the resolution was forwarded to the executive council of the AFL, it was virtually ignored. The Oxnard workers created the Sugar Beet and Farm Laborers' Union of Oxnard and applied to the AFL for a charter. In reply, Samuel Gompers asked for assurances that the union would "under no circumstances accept membership of any Chinese or Japanese."[12] Subsequently the charter was denied.

As Japanese workers began to dominate an increasing segment of agricultural production, their position changed. Japanese field workers organized labor associations and designated secretaries who were put in charge of locating and coordinating jobs for their members. This process of organizing and dealing with employers through a spokesperson not only rationalized to some extent the employment of agricultural labor but later came to be used in collective bargaining and strike actions. Unlike the labor contractors of more recent decades, who have acted as middlemen between growers and farm workers, Japanese labor association secretaries essentially identified with the interests of the laborers. Often they were simply field workers whom the work group selected as spokespersons. Sometimes they were "camp bosses," who maintained lodging for workers even during the off season. Living with the work crews, they had greater contact and identification with workers than did the labor contractors who appeared in later decades.[13]

It is significant that the issues on which Japanese farm workers focused their militancy extended beyond wages. Field workers and their labor association leaders aimed to gain control over hiring, to the extent of enforcing a closed shop when possible. Work crews and representatives developed agreements over territory and in some cases even created exclusive job areas.[14] The leaders also formed associations to reduce price cutting and competition among work crews.[15]

Strikes generally took place when the employer was at a strategic disadvantage—at the harvest. Growers at the time complained that the Japanese were "merciless" in their strikes and would strike without provocation. Their power was greater than mere numbers, since their predominance in certain crops made harvest-time strikes especially effective. In fact, the increasing reliance on harvest strikes as a tactic to force a rise in wages was a vital factor in turning large growers toward agitation for Japanese exclusion. Work slowdowns were an alternative to harvest strikes. The slowdowns succeeded in converting payment in many areas from an hourly rate to a piece rate high enough to allow laborers to combine their harvest-season income to purchase or lease land for themselves.[16] For through their strategic position in the labor force, the Japanese could inflict severe financial losses by withholding labor from growers who refused to lease or sell land to Japanese. They were thus able to buy or rent land in some of the most fertile sections of the state.[17]

Militant tactics had been impossible before the early 1900s because of racial and ethnic divisions. The proceedings of the 1907 convention of the California Fruit Growers expressed a growing resentment against the current labor force and recalled the advantages of using Chinese labor. According to the proceedings, the Chinese "were patient, plodding, and uncomplaining in the performance of the most menial service. They submitted to anything, never violating a contract," while the Japanese were "a tricky and cunning lot, who break contracts and become quite independent. They are not organized into unions, but their clannishness seems to operate as a union would."[18]

Japanese workers started the first major phase of rural labor militancy, using strikes, job actions, slowdowns, boycotts, and other militant tactics in a pattern to be repeated during each successive wave of farm worker unionism. The initial stage of organizing illustrates farm workers' concern from the outset with control issues as a prerequisite to basic improvement in the situation of harvest labor. But certain enduring limitations of farm worker movements were also apparent in the beginning phase of insurgency. Japanese labor unrest was localized. Although strikes and work slowdowns were widespread, no statewide organization emerged that could act in the interests of all the Japanese employed in the fields. They failed to build a political power base from which the government could be confronted when discriminatory actions were directed against them. Real advances for agricultural workers depended upon wider organization and alliances than the Japanese were able to achieve.

JAPANESE LAND TENURE

Racial hiring policies were not the only means used by growers to maintain an exploitable seasonal labor force. The subordination of farm workers also depended upon a restriction of their access to land ownership. The artificial scarcity of land perpetuated farm worker subordination and prevented mobility for their ethnic group.

Growers had two powerful reasons for opposing Japanese immigration by 1910. Because of organizing by their ethnic associations, Japanese were no longer a source of inexpensive, efficient, and docile labor, and, and, perhaps more importantly, they were moving swiftly into landowner and tenant status. Unlike Chinese immigrants, the Japanese had their origins largely in a rural class of small landowners and had higher aspirations than unskilled coolie labor. While many had relatively poor origins, their class placed special importance on owning land, and the immigrants attempted to duplicate their former conditions in the United States. The rapidity with which Japanese moved into land ownership and tenancy was largely due to their willingness to pay competitively high prices for land and to offer a higher bid than others for the leasing of land or sharecropping arrangements. Once in position as owners or lessees of agricultural land, they employed their own countrymen almost exclusively. Approximately 96 percent of the laborers employed on Japanese-managed agricultural lands were Japanese. This had the effect of depriving white landowners of labor and increasing the effectiveness of Japanese workers' strikers and slowdowns. By 1907 Japanese laborers were the highest-paid farm labor group in the state.[19]

It is a common misconception that it was the amount and extent of Japanese land ownership that spurred large growers to join the anti-Japanese movement. It was not, in fact, the acreage actually owned by Japanese that threatened the large growers.[20] The amount of agricultural land leased, under share, and under contract put the acreage under Japanese control at a figure many times that for mere ownership. In 1905 Japanese owned only about 2,500 acres, but they managed 62,000 acres. By 1910, when Japanese ownership had risen to 17,000 acres, land under their management amounted to 195,000 acres.[21] Nevertheless, the Japanese share did not represent a great proportion of the state's improved agricultural land. Although estimates vary widely, it is safe to assume that by 1910 the Japanese controlled, through ownership, lease, share, or contract arrangements, much less than 5 percent of the state's agricultural land and perhaps as little as 1 percent.

However, the degree of influence Japanese tenants and landowners had in California is understated by these modest acreage statistics for several reasons. Japanese holdings were concentrated in comparatively few localities, thus giving them control over a large proportion of agricultural production in specific areas. In the Vaca Valley they leased or owned approximately half the land under cultivation for fruit and grapes. Around Florin, just south of Sacramento, they owned or leased about one-third of the land. Other areas of comparable concentration were along the American River near Sacramento, the lower Sacramento River area, Livingston, the lower San Joaquin River area, and the Newcastle district. Thus, some 70 percent of the agricultural land controlled by Japanese was in twelve of the state's fifty-eight counties.[22] Moreover, the Japanese growers specialized in the production of certain crops in which their countrymen were employed as farm laborers. In a 1910 Census Bureau report, Japanese-managed lands accounted for about half of all acreage for strawberries, one-third of acreage producing all berries combined, about one-seventh of potato acreage, and one-tenth of land producing various vegetables.[23] By 1919 the market value of crops produced on lands owned, leased, or under share arrangement by Japanese was $67 million, just over 10 percent of the total value of California agricultural crops.[24] They made a crucial contribution to establishing and expanding the production of berries and vegetables in the state. These are labor-intensive crops and require a substantially greater amount of labor per acre than, for example, hops and grains. The value of crop yield per acre was nearly twice the state's average.

Paralleling the rising share of land under Japanese control was another subtle threat, with implications potentially more damaging to the growing conglomerates. In California, monopolization of land had been the rule from the outset, producing a pattern of land use very different from that obtaining in the rest of the country at the time. Japanese farms successfully competed with large-scale agriculture despite the fact that their operations were relatively small. Fifty-six percent of Japanese farms had less than 30 acres and 83 percent less than 75 acres, while the average California farm had 317 acres in 1910.[25] One reason for the difference was the Japanese concentration on crops requiring intensive cultivation. The pattern of small land holdings reversed a trend toward increasingly large units of production in every crop area, and such holdings competed with the larger units by yielding higher productivity at lower cost. This Japanese success clearly represented a challenge to large landowners, since it demonstrated that land conglomerates were not a more rational system for agricultural production and were, in fact, considerably less efficient in many cases. This fact is consistent with worldwide observations of the competitive advantages of small farms in cash crop production. As one authority noted, "In most export crops the small holding is the most efficient form of agricultural organization."[26] In the production of vegetables and fruits, the optimum acreage was quite small. Radical and socialist parties cited this fact when arguing that land conglomerates should be broken up and farm land disposed of in small tracts to a greater number of people. The Workingmen's party had included this position in its platform, and at the time when Japanese control over agricultural land was at its height, the IWW advocated similar measures.

In a relatively brief period, large agricultural growers moved from a position of enthusiastic support for Japanese immigration and employment in the fields to opposition to their entry and control over farm land. Growers, beginning to look elsewhere for a source of efficient low-wage labor, turned to the state and joined forces with other anti-Japanese elements, particularly organized labor. As with the Chinese, the authority of the California government proved insufficient to accomplish a change in the labor source. It was the federal government that successfully reversed Japanese influence in the fields.

At first agitation for the curtailment of Japanese immigration came from organized labor and was concentrated in San Francisco. Anti-Japanese agitation began there in earnest in 1900 with mass meetings and a quarantine of the city's Japanese and Chinese quarters. By 1904 national labor organizations had become involved, and the AFL passed a resolution at its national convention asking Congress to exclude further Japanese immigration. A series of sensational articles in the *San Francisco Chronicle* in February 1905 initiated a more intense campaign against the Japanese. The articles linked Japanese immigrants to crime and poverty and charged that they were "an evil in the public schools" and "a menace to American women." In that year both houses of the California legislature passed without opposition a resolution urging Congress to suspend Japanese immigration.[27] By this time growers no longer represented a barrier to anti-Japanese legislation at the state level. In fact, both major California farm organizations supported Japanese exclusion, whereas a few years earlier they had enthusiastically welcomed Japanese immigrants.

The Roosevelt administration viewed the events in California with increasing concern, though not because of any pro-Japanese feelings. As evidenced from private communications, Roosevelt's personal views on the Japanese question were basically similar to those of the proponents of exclusion.[28] However, Japan's recent devastation of two Russian fleets and the severe damage it inflicted on the Russian army dictated that continued political and economic access to the Far East by the United States could be insured only through friendly relations between the two governments. When the San Francisco school board acted in late 1906 to segregate whites and Asians in city schools, and when in early 1907 the California legislature seemed likely to pass anti-Japanese legislation, the Roosevelt administration quickly moved to stifle explicit anti-Japanese acts. At the same time it entered into negotiations with the Japanese government that accomplished the ultimate objective of the exclusionists: the suspension of Japanese immigration.[29]

The Gentlemen's Agreement between the Roosevelt administration and the government of Japan was concluded in late 1907 and early 1908. It was not a formal declaration or treaty but an understanding. The Japanese government agreed not to issue passports for the continental United States to skilled or unskilled laborers. These categories included most Japanese immigrants at the time. Exceptions were made for laborers who had previously been to the United States and for the wives and children of Japanese laborers already there. Indications are that the Gentlemen's Agreement was successful in curtailing the immigration of Japanese workers. From 1909 to 1913 approximately 21,500 Japanese were admitted to the United States while 27,000 departed. Arrivals were primarily under the categories allowed by the agreement, most being women and children.[30] By concluding the Gentlemen's Agreement with Japan, the Roosevelt administration had achieved the goal of restricting the immigration of Japanese labor and at the same time prevented the rupture of the stable relationship between the United States and the government of Japan by avoiding the racist overtones that had characterized the efforts of the California legislature.

Although the predominance of Japanese farm laborers in certain segments of California agriculture began to decline, complete erosion was postponed until the large-scale influx of Mexican workers for jobs in the fields during World War I. In the meantime, the growing number of Japanese families continued to disturb the patriotic groups, including the American Legion and the Native Sons of the Golden West, who had been among the leading anti-Japanese elements. The decline in Japanese immigration did, however, reduce the interest of organized labor. Trade unionists maintained an anti-Japanese stance for some time, but they no longer took such an active part in the controversy.

As was noted above, the Japanese provided the initial example of an emerging pattern of state manipulation of the agricultural labor supply. At the point when growers no longer found a certain source of agricultural labor desirable, government institutions came to their aid by excluding the group and providing another that, at least in the beginning, supplied growers with low-wage, compliant workers. State involvement was crucial, since large growers could never have engineered such relatively smooth transitions from one labor force to another by independent action. As regulator of the labor supply, the state insured an uninterrupted source of inexpensive labor and thus undermined conditions for effective, permanent labor organization. The added ingredient of racial prejudice deprived the minority groups furnishing the labor supply of support from other segments of the population, notably organized labor.

STATE INTERVENTION AND THE HEGEMONY OF LARGE-SCALE FARMING

As was true of manipulating the labor supply, regulating access to land could not be accomplished by economic means alone. It was in the short-run interests of certain growers to sell or lease land to Japanese farmers, since they were willing to pay above-market prices. However, Japanese family farms competed very successfully with large-scale enterprises in certain cash crops. Instead of economic mechanisms growers would have to use their special access to political channels to gain state intervention in the service of their long-run interest in the hegemony of large-scale farming. Especially through their power and influence over legislators from agricultural regions and within the two national political parties, large growers were able to secure the political and legal means to maintain land tenure privileges. The principal method used in California to limit economic competition from small farms was legislation limiting the right to pursue a profit in agriculture according to the ethnicity of the farmer.

White agricultural landowners became alarmed that even after the Gentlemen's Agreement of 1907 had for the most part eliminated new immigration, there was no leveling off of the amount of land under Japanese control. Although the proportion of Japanese among agricultural workers had begun to decline, the amount of farm land owned and leased by Japanese expanded rapidly. To white agricultural landowners, the increasing number of Japanese families on these lands represented competition and even a possible eroding of the viability of large-scale land ownership. Not surprisingly, an increasing segment began to look to the government as an instrument to protect the dominance of large-scale agricultural production.

A number of anti-Japanese bills, including several dealing with land ownership, were introduced in the California legislature after

1907. Most were sponsored by legislators from agricultural districts.[31] One of the most important of these was the Webb-Henry Bill of the Alien Lands Act, introduced in January 1913. At the time a Progressive Republican, Hiram Johnson, was governor, while the national administration was Democratic. Unlike the state Democratic Party, the Progressive Republican Party had not incorporated anti-Japanese proposals into its platform, but only indicated support for the prohibition of Japanese land ownership and Japanese exclusion. Although the national Democratic platform did not contain anti-Japanese provisions either, nationally the Democratic Party was more closely identified with anti-Asian positions. During his presidential campaign in 1914, Woodrow Wilson published an anti-Asian statement to achieve greater consistency between the national and the California state Democratic platforms.[32]

A concise statement of the rationale for discriminatory legislation had been given as early as 1910 by the California labor commissioner, John MacKenzie. He concluded: "Japanese ambition is to progess beyond mere servility. . . . The moment that this ambition was exercised, that moment the Japanese ceases to be an ideal laborer."[33] Japanese ambitions to own or lease small tracts of farm land were incompatible with a system of agricultural land monopolization and the maintenance of a large pool of low-wage labor. The president of the Los Angeles County Farm Bureau Federation summarized its position when he stated during hearings by the Congressional Committee on Japanese Immigration, reported in 1921, that his organization opposed "Japanese being permitted to lease, rent or own agricultural land."[34]

The national government continued to seek to satisfy the demands of anti-Japanese forces led by large growers without giving offense to the Japanese government. The conditions were similar to those generating the Gentlemen's Agreement six years earlier, although different political parties were in power. When it became clear that the California legislature was about to pass legislation prohibiting Japanese ownership of agricultural lands, President Wilson sent Secretary of State William Jennings Bryan to Sacramento to confer with the governor and legislators on the bill. Although it seems Bryan had little of importance to say to state officials, his visit did insure that the legislation was technically compatible with the provisions of the 1911 treaty between the United States and Japan and was phrased so as to give the minimum of offense to the Japanese government.[35] It was generally acknowledged, however, that any restriction on Japanese property ownership would provoke objections from the government of Japan. Bryan arrived in Sacramento on 28 April, and on 2 May an amended version of the Webb-Henry Bill passed the state senate by a vote of 35 to 2 and passed the assembly the following day 72 to 3. At President Wilson's request, Governor Johnson waited until May 19 to sign the bill in order to allow the president time to explain its provisions to the Japanese government.[36]

Under the Alien Lands Act, aliens who were ineligible for citizenship could no longer purchase and own real property, nor could they sell or bequeath land to other aliens ineligible for citizenship. Since the federal government discriminated against East Asians by prohibiting them from becoming citizens through naturalization, this act also applied to Hindus, Filipinos, and Chinese, but it was clearly directed against the Japanese. Such aliens were allowed to lease agricultural land for a period not exceeding three years, with the possibility of renewal. The law did not prohibit Japanese who had previously bought land from keeping it, nor did it place restrictions upon those of Japanese descent born in the United States, a category almost entirely composed of small children at the time of the bill's passage. Two contradictory features of the legislation prevented it from being effective. The major goal was to discourage further Japanese control over the state's agricultural production. However, the bill was written in such a way that it did not hinder large landowners from profiting from business dealings with Japanese. As noted earlier, Japanese on the whole paid significantly higher prices than others when buying or leasing land. While there existed nearly unanimous agreement among the growers that it was desirable to inhibit Japanese expansion into the fields, few were willing individually to deny themselves the capital resulting from selling and leasing agricultural land to Japanese. There was a contradiction between the broader class interest of the large growers in insuring continuous hegemony over agricultural production and the more narrow and immediate interests of many individual growers.

Leasing land to Japanese posed few problems under the Alien Lands Act. Although it forbade the sale of farm land to Japanese nationals or corporations in which Japanese held a controlling interest, the law was circumvented by selling land to Japanese children born in the United States, who were of course citizens, and appointing their parents as guardians of the land. Likewise, several corporations in which Japanese had legally only a minority interest were formed to invest in agricultural land. As a result, farm land controlled by Japanese increased from 282,000 acres in 1913 to 458,000 acres in 1920, with the acreage owned nearly tripling during this period (from 27,000 acres to 75,000 acres).[37]

By 1919 it was obvious that the Alien Lands Act was not serving the development of large-scale agricultural production. Consequently, large grower organizations backed a movement to strengthen the act by closing the loopholes. In effecting a more severe measure, the California government acted to preserve the interests of large agriculture while limiting the short-run advantages of certain large landowner interests. That large growers could not check a threat to their hegemony and were even profiting from it is testimony to the competitive aspects of capitalist agriculture and the absence of long-term planning to insure class hegemony over agricultural production. State intervention was essential to keep short-term individual interests from interfering with the development of corporate agriculture.

The 1920 Alien Lands Act was put on the ballot and passed as an initiative measure by 668,000 to 222,000 votes in round figures. The most significant feature of the new law was that it forbade the leasing of agricultural lands or acquisition of stock in land corporations by Japanese. It also prohibited Japanese parents from acting as guardians for their children. (This section was later ruled unconstitutional under the Fourteenth Amendment.) In 1923 the law was amended to prohibit even cropping contracts. Thus, Japanese who had not previously owned land were limited to working as hired labor in the fields.[38] This law became a model for similar legislation adopted in Washington, Oregon, Arizona, Colorado, Delaware, Nebraska, Texas, Idaho, and New Mexico.[39] The Alien Lands Act in California stayed on the books until 1956, when a ballot initiative invalidated it, although by the 1930s, with the disappearance of the Japanese threat to corporate agriculture, the law was virtually inactive in many communities.[40]

Since local authorities were vested with its enforcement, the statute could be circumvented whenever it served the interest of local officials, as several authorities have documented.[41] However, Japanese control of agricultural land rapidly declined after 1920. By 1925 the amount of land owned and leased by Japanese was roughly equivalent to the 1914 total.[42] A trend that would have seriously challenged the hegemony of corporate agriculture had been reversed.

Japanese began to move from rural to urban areas after being excluded from farm ownership. Many who stayed in agriculture were concentrated in the cultivation of the small, scattered units adjacent to urban areas known as truck farms. Others became managers of large farms as Mexican and Filipino workers began to make up the bulk of agricultural labor. Further Japanese immigration was officially prohibited by the federal Immigration Act of 1924.

Stigmatized, powerless, and isolated, Japanese people were effectively blocked in their attempt to secure more advantageous positions as agricultural workers or as agricultural landowners and tenants. They lacked the means to defy upper-class control over political power in the way they had for a time challenged upper-class control over land. When large growers escalated economic competition into political conflict, Japanese farmers were without the civil means to defend their interests. Denied full citizenship status, Japanese faced formidable limits to their participation in politics and access to the legal system. Racist attitudes within the larger society blocked the alliances needed to create a movement to protect their organizations and small businesses.

The mass evacuation of Japanese during World War II gave large agricultural landowners control of the remaining Japanese farms. All of the white grower organizations supported evacuation, and the Western Growers Protective Association, the Associated Farmers, and the California Farm Bureau were especially vocal. Although Japanese regained much of their property after the war, they failed to recover their special province in California agriculture, which had centered on truck farms and specialty crops. Estimates of the property losses of Japanese range from $350 to $500 million, and the proportion of Japanese wage and salary workers employed by non-Japanese jumped from 20 percent before the war to 70 percent after.[43]

With the exclusion of the Japanese and the subsequent preemption of their right to own and lease land, an important era of California agricultural labor ended. Large growers had successfully turned to the state to guarantee their hegemony in California agriculture. By the time of massive Mexican immigration and employment in the fields during World War I, basic patterns had been established that have kept farm labor a separate and disadvantaged segment of the working class.

CHAPTER 4

FARM WORKER INSURGENCY AND THE REGULATION OF IMMIGRATION

Since farm labor conflict is essentially a struggle between competing class interests rather than a form of racial disturbance, it should come as no surprise that rural strife continued even when the group supplying harvest labor was predominantly white. The second major wave of farm worker protest occurred in the years just before World War I in crop areas where white workers made up the bulk of the harvest labor force. Turmoil centered around attempts by the Industrial Workers of the World (IWW or Wobblies) to direct agricultural labor protest. Racial differences were not as significant a factor as they had been when they added to the complexity of rural unrest involving the Japanese and Chinese. Instead, from the first significant clash in the hop fields, it is clear that there was a conflict based on class interests. Farm workers struggled to gain improvement in wages, working conditions, and living arrangements, while large agricultural landowners fought them with coordinated and severe opposition.

To see that insurgency was necessary from the point of view of the farm workers, we need only review the functions of mass defiance as they appeared in this second stage in the long-term pattern of farm worker militancy. Mass protest was crucial in gaining whatever concessions were won from growers, who normally opposed any involvement in the conditions of farm labor as a violation of their short-run interests. They continued, in fact, to oppose amelioration even when some government officials intervened to attempt reforms alleviating some of the worse conditions prevailing in the fields.

This period of IWW organizing and its aftermath provides an excellent example of what appears as paradoxical government actions. In response to insurgency, the state pursued two contrasting policies simultaneously: reform and repression. Government agencies and officials initiated reforms to redress the worst grievances of farm workers. However, other agencies reacted with repression to quell the conditions of discontent and revolt. When insurgency subsided, concessions were eroded, and farm workers were again left powerless. The apparent paradox disappears when the contradictory nature of state policies and interventions is considered. During times of intense unrest, government agencies respond to several conflicting demands placed upon them. Government officials themselves have a profound interest in successfully managing crises, and while insurgency remains significant, this usually means placation through concessions in order to preserve legitimacy of state actions. However, if these concessions do not become institutionalized, either because the opposition is too strong or the insurgents too weak, then the stage is set for a rapid reversal. Without significant oppositional force either from insurgency or from more institutionalized means, there is little that would prevent the state in acting exclusively as an instrument promoting capital accumulation. Before and after IWW-led protests this was mostly the case. But even during this brief period of modest reforms, the structural weakness of farm workers and the failure of the IWW to effectively solicit and direct external resources enhanced the ability of the state to eliminate this threat to unconstrained grower control over the labor force. With the removal of the IWW and the onset of U.S. involvement in World War I, reforms were quickly eroded.

THE IWW AND FARM WORKER INSURGENCY

Before the IWW, attempts at organizing agricultural labor were sporadic and amounted to little more than isolated strikes, although several gained temporary concessions. The lack of strong and consistent support by the AFL for union activities in the rural sector resulted in very limited and brief organizing efforts, some lasting less than a single harvest season. Animosity to Asian labor also inhibited unionization attempts. In contrast, the IWW stood from the outset against discrimination based on race, color, or nationality. At its third convention—held in 1907, during the height of the controversy surrounding Japanese immigration—an IWW delegate from California remarked that "the whole fight against the Japanese is the fight of the middle class of California, in which they employ the labor faker to back it up." He added, however, that it would be "practically useless" for the IWW to attempt to organize Japanese workers at that time.[1] Although the IWW included workers of diverse national origins, it was mainly active in areas where whites dominated the labor force: the wheat and hop fields, where migratory white "blindlestiffs" were employed, rather than the orchards and vegetable farms where Asian labor was utilized.

A series of "free speech" fights in several California cities from 1910 to 1912 won the IWW the right to maintain headquarters, distribute literature, and hold public meetings. By 1913 the IWW had begun to recruit members among migratory workers. Intermittent strikes and labor disruptions occurred in the fields in 1913 and throughout the war years. One of the first strikes, now referred to as the "Wheatland riot" or the "Wheatland strike," was the largest agricultural labor disturbance in California to that time.

Detailed accounts of the Wheatland riot are available elsewhere.[2] Following the common practice, the E. B. Durst hop ranch near Wheatland had advertised throughout California, Nevada, and southern Oregon that 3,000 pickers were needed for the 1913 harvest, although only 1,500 would actually be employed. By early August, 2,800 workers speaking twenty-seven languages had assembled to discover that only half of them could obtain work, and then at depressed wages due to the oversupply. Despite the diversity in nationality, the majority of the workers were white. A committee of hop-pickers, most of them familiar with the IWW's militant syndicalism, submitted a list of ten demands to the ranch owner, including such improvements in working and living conditions as the provision of drinking water in the fields twice a day, better sanitary conditions in the camps, and a flat rate of $1.25 per hundredweight of hops picked. The committee had the overwhelming support of the assembled workers, who organized a mass meeting in order to call a strike if these demands were not met. During the meeting a deputy sheriff fired a shot in the air, and other deputies threatened to shoot the assembled workers. A riot ensued that left the district attorney, a deputy sheriff, and two hop-pickers dead. The district attorney and deputy sheriff were killed by a Puerto Rican worker who had disarmed one of the lawmen. He, in turn, was killed by another deputy. Most workers immediately fled the area. The state militia dispatched to the scene the next morning arrested some of those remaining.

During the following months, sheriffs, aided by over a hundred deputized detectives from the Burns Agency, engaged in a manhunt of extraordinary proportions, arresting hundreds of hop-pickers and

Wobblies throughout the West. Many had not been present at the Durst Ranch at the time of the disturbance. Some were severely beaten, tortured, threatened, or bribed to gain confessions that would help the authorities arrest prominent California IWW leaders. Many of those arrested were held incommunicado for weeks.[3] Wobbly Herman Suhr, who was present at Wheatland, was seized in Arizona by private detectives and shipped without legal formalities to California in a boxcar. The authorities were evidently more interested in punishing the IWW than in determining responsibility for the killings. Writing over twenty years later, Carey McWilliams described the period of the arrests as "one of the most amazing reigns of terror that California has ever witnessed."[4]

Four of the arrested finally came to trial on murder charges, including Suhr and IWW organizer, Richard "Blackie" Ford, a former Wobbly, who had addressed the crowd. It was soon obvious that the government's case was weak. Many California trade unions rallied to the Wobblies' defense and passed resolutions condemning the trial. Despite their antipathy toward the IWW, AFL unions were the largest contributors to the Wheatland defense fund. Support within the working class was widespread, and over 100,000 workers were involved in protest activities.[5]

The trial began in January 1914 in Marysville, near Wheatland. The local press had vehemently attacked both the IWW and individual defendants for months before the trial, and yet a defense motion for a change of venue was denied. The trial judge had been a long-time friend of the slain district attorney, and the special state-appointed prosecutor was the attorney for the California Hop Growers Association.[6] After two weeks a jury of fourteen, including eight farmers and the part-time gardener of the slain district attorney's widow, convicted Ford and Suhr of second-degree murder, on grounds that they were guilty of conspiracy to murder as leaders of the strike that resulted in the shootings. They were both sentenced to life imprisonment in Folsom penitentiary, and bail was denied pending appeal.

In response the IWW called a strike by all hop-pickers, starting in the spring of 1914, on ranches not meeting a set of demands for improved wages and working conditions. It was hoped that the strike and the resulting economic pressure would bring about the release of Ford and Suhr. The strike was endorsed by AFL councils in Sacramento, San Diego, and Fresno. Japanese hop-pickers did not participate in the campaign, fearing that their presence would cause the AFL to withhold approval, but they placed advertisements supporting it in Japanese-language papers.[7] Most California hop growers conceded the increased wages and improved working conditions the IWW demanded well in advance of the strike deadline.[8] With Ford and Suhr still behind bars, however, the IWW initiated a month-long hop-pickers' strike in August. According to a recent study of the Wheatland riot and its aftermath, the strike "had succeeded in both scaring and punishing many hop farmers in California for their alleged complicity in the 'railroading' of Ford and Suhr." A prominent Wheatland hop grower and one of the trial's original prosecutors even testified in support of a pardon for Ford and Suhr.[9]

In the 1915 season, the IWW turned to a general boycott of all hop fields, processors, and their products. Reports of fires in the hop and wheat fields filled California newspapers throughout the summer. Although concrete evidence was never produced, most newspapers, growers, and California officials were convinced that nearly all were set by Wobblies. Most analysts now believe that some fires may have been set by individual IWW supporters, but there was no systematic or coordinated IWW plan to burn fields. Before the IWW campaign, field fires had simply been attributed to natural causes attending a dry, hot harvest season.

In September 1915 Governor Hiram Johnson denied Ford and Suhr's appeal for a pardon:

> By a forced construction of the law of conspiracy of an industrial revolt, those who had committed no wrong themselves were convicted of a heinous offense. . . . a survey of the entire case, while not authorizing a pardon, would justify a mitigation of the sentence imposed. . . . But so long as in behalf of these men the threats of injury and sabotage continue, so long as the preachment exists in their behalf in the state of California, so long as incendiarism is attempted, I will neither listen to appeals for clemency on behalf of Ford and Suhr, nor in any fashion consider the shortening of their terms of imprisonment.[10]

Ford was eventually paroled in 1925 but was immediately rearrested and charged with the death of the deputy sheriff during the Wheatland riot. Again he was tried in Marysville, but this time he was acquitted on the basis of the same evidence on which he had been found guilty of the murder of the district attorney eleven years before. Suhr was paroled without incident in 1926.

Despite these setbacks the IWW continued its agitation in the fields. By the end of 1915, Durst and his associates were complaining that they could not effectively manage their business because of IWW activity, even after their creation of a private police force of armed guards, gunmen, and detectives.[11] By 1917 the IWW estimated that the Ford and Suhr convictions had cost the growers $10 million annually; the growers admitted to a total loss of $15 to $20 million.[12] With the prospect of continuing losses, various California agencies moved toward improving some of the worst conditions of agricultural labor while recommending increased repression and elimination of the IWW as a force in California agriculture. Foremost in reform efforts was the state Commission on Immigration and Housing, chaired by Simon J. Lubin. The essence of its approach was contained in a 1914 letter to Governor Johnson from Professor Carleton Parker, then the executive secretary of the commission. Parker proposed that improved labor conditions would reduce the appeal of the Wobblies. The Immigration Commission had the means, he wrote, "to clean up this abuse [unsanitary labor camps] this summer, insure a decent standard of comfort to the seasonal worker and take away the argument and talking weapon of the agitator." He added, "I am convinced . . . our service will be as imperative and essential to the farmer and employer as to the laborer."[13]

The commission began making annual reports to the governor in 1914. Its work was the first systematic attempt to investigate and report conditions in the fields and use the findings as a basis for reform recommendations. It revealed conditions that had existed for decades: the lack of decent housing, sanitation facilities, and safeguards against injury; low wages; poor diet; and insecurity of employment. Legislation was passed over grower opposition to improve the conditions of migratory laborers, while the commission did as much as its jurisdiction allowed toward the same end. For the first time in their history, many fields had fresh water available free of charge, and landowners could be forced to clean up their camps for migratory workers. Improvements were so impressive that even the IWW noted that while many other conditions needed to be changed, if the improvements made since the Wheatland riot "were the sum total of our several years' work, the organization would still justify its existence."[14]

Despite these reforms, the state continued to insure a supply of controllable labor. The reforms to some extent legitimated farm worker grievances, but they stopped short of changing the predominantly migratory pattern of agricultural labor and the arbitrary power of the employer or contractor over hiring and firing. Some of the reform measures no doubt had the effect of undercutting the wider public's sympathy for the insurgents. For its part, the IWW showed little inclination toward developing a formal organization.

The collection of dues was irregular. The union treasury amounted simply to accumulated strike funds. The many headquarters were "not places for executive direction of the union as much as gregarious centers where the lodging house inhabitant or the hobo with his blanket [could] find light, a stove, and companionship."[15] Behind its revolutionary rhetoric, the IWW pursued many of the goals of industrial unionism. Agitation included wage issues but went considerably beyond them. IWW demands covered all the conditions of life for the harvest laborer. An unsanitary camp was enough to generate a walkout. Organizing agricultural workers in the Midwest, the IWW demanded a ten-hour day, 50 cents an hour overtime, a daily wage of $3.00, clean sleeping places, tolerable board, and no discrimination against union members.[16] Like succeeding unions of field workers, the IWW relied upon mass participation and direct action tactics: picketing, peaceful strikes, production slowdowns, sabotage, and the crop-wide strikes. The IWW's basic strategy was to escalate mass defiance to take advantage of the relatively rare times when protest can compel concessions from elites.

Unlike later farm worker unions, the IWW refused to sign contracts with employers, regarding them as an agreement to cooperate with the exploiters of the workers. For the Wobblies only constant agitation could yield a qualitative improvement in the field worker's situation.[17] Accordingly, IWW organizing was decentralized. As one observer commented, "every one of the 5000 laborers in California who have been at some time connected with the I.W.W. considers himself a "camp delegate" with walking papers to organize a camp local."[18] IWW activists were thus in a good position to recognize and make effective use of the great potential for disruption that is the ultimate source of the power of agricultural workers. A relatively homogeneous mass of workers, poorly paid but crucial to production, could recognize the advantages of collective action. By escalating the momentum of protest, the IWW was able to force a break in the usual pattern of government accommodation of elites. As the threat of disruption intensified, the state was compelled to offer concessions in the hope of dissipating collective anger and unrest.

STATE OPPOSITION TO THE IWW

Concessions were also part of a broader strategy to channel the political behavior of protesters away from disruption. Thus, it is not surprising that at the same time reforms were instituted, the state directed repression against the insurgents. Attacks begun against the IWW in California were part of a more general repression of the

Wobblies in areas where they had gained considerable influence, such as the lumber regions of the Pacific Northwest, agricultural areas in the Midwest and Rocky Mountain regions, and several industrial areas. Late in 1915 a grower organization issued an appeal to President Wilson to eradicate the IWW through federal prosecution. The appeal was immediately endorsed by the governors of California, Oregon, Washington, and Utah. President Wilson authorized an inquiry by the Department of Justice to amass evidence to prosecute IWW leaders on interstate conspiracy charges. The Justice Department turned to the Commission on Immigration and Housing for information on violations of federal law by IWW leaders. The commission was, however, unable to expose any definite violations of federal law, a finding corroborated through investigation by agents of the Department of Justice. Simon Lubin, the head of the commission, recommended that the law be modified to permit federal prosecution of IWW readers. The suggestion was adopted a short time later through the passage of Espionage and Selective Service acts.[19]

The year 1917 saw the last but the most active period of IWW-led labor unrest in the California fields. A strike early in the year in the vineyards around Fresno spread quickly to neighboring counties. It was settled when growers agreed to an eight-hour day and a daily wage of $2.50. Japanese workers had joined the strike and benefited from the concessions granted. In April picker strikes closed packing houses in Riverside and Redlands. Later, in June, a farm labor strike near Turlock caused a loss of 1,000 carloads of cantaloupe. Throughout the summer, newspapers carried frequent stories of sabotage in the fields.

Labor unrest, and with it the trend toward better wages and working conditions, ended abruptly in September 1917, as the federal government launched a campaign to suppress the IWW. Over a thousand IWW members were arrested nationwide that month; later, 160 were convicted of criminal syndicalism under the Espionage Act passed that June. Almost a hundred Wobblies were given sentences of from one to twenty years and fines of over $3 million.[20] Part of a general suppression of radical groups, the attacks eliminated opposition to the U.S. entrance into World War I. Sacramento was one of the sites of major IWW trials. All 46 defendants in the California IWW conspiracy cases were found guilty of conspiring to violate the U.S. Constitution and the Espionage Act and obstructing the war activities of the government.[21] The number of Socialist party locals nationwide was reduced from 5,000 to 3,500 during the War while virtually the entire IWW leadership was imprisoned.[22] In Fresno, on 6 September 1917, the IWW headquarters was raided and nineteen Wobblies arrested. Later raids were carried out by federal agents in Stockton and Hanford, where, as in Fresno, IWW organizers had been urging workers to strike. The Department of Justice went so far as to open an office in Fresno and ask all growers with labor trouble to make reports to it.[23] Several labor historians have attributed the IWW's national decline to the federal roundup of its leaders.[24]

After the elimination of IWW influence in the California fields, wartime profits for agricultural landowners soared. In a further effort to hinder field unions, additional workers were recruited for harvest labor, some with the cooperation of the government, ostensibly to help the war effort. Boy Scouts and YMCA members were employed with the assistance of public agencies. California schools for boys signed contracts to supply labor. Schools in Napa were closed early in 1918 so that children could work on the harvest, a practice that later became common in agricultural regions. The Woman's Land Army of America, California Division, supervised the placement of hundreds of women in the fields. Even deaf mutes in Berkeley were taken from their school and sent into agricultural regions. That year the $2 million prune and grape harvest in the area was accomplished at a labor cost of $20,000, or 1 percent of the value of the crops. Decent wages and working conditions were apparently incompatible with winning a war. A bulletin of the Twelfth Federal Reserve Bank in San Francisco, issued just five days before the initiation of federal prosecution of the Wobblies, the Socialist Party, and other antiwar radicals, declared that the rising cost of farm labor "hampers the effectiveness of this country's efforts."[25]

Reforms achieved during the period of IWW insurgency were never permanently implemented. The raids against the IWW preceded a drastic lowering of farm labor wages. As the threat of disruption passed, political leaders had little incentive to respond to grievances. The continued unresponsiveness of the California government to the need for agricultural reform during and after the war spurred Simon Lubin to resign in disgust from the Commission on Immigration and Housing. Ironically, the withdrawal of concessions was partly an outcome of the role of Lubin and the commission in the suppression of the IWW. The erosion of the position of farm labor set the stage for the tremendous labor upheaval in the California fields during the Depression years.

The correspondence between IWW agitation and agricultural reform is often overlooked by those who condemn the IWW either for its radicalism or for its failure to establish itself as a permanent orga-

nization in the California fields. It is true that for all their expressed
commitment to organizing migratory workers, the Wobblies actually
did very little toward building union membership. The Wheatland
riot was a spontaneous eruption. Later, the IWW's primary goal was
to gain the release of Ford and Suhr rather than to initiate an
organization of migratory workers. It is sometimes argued that it
"squandered an opportunity created by the surge of support for the
IWW among migratory workers after the Wheatland troubles to
begin building a strong, permanent labor movement in far western
agriculture."[26] In fact the IWW did attempt a more conventional
organization-building strategy in 1916, chartering a California chapter of the IWW-affiliated Agricultural Workers Organization, which
was then active in the Midwest. It disappeared after a few months,
the victim of factional infighting and sectarianism.[27] The external
support offered to the IWW campaign, while impressive, was not
readily transformed into resources which could be utilized to institutionalize concessions.

The IWW successfully used the Ford and Suhr issue to attract
sympathetic attention, escalate defiance, and win concessions that
for a time altered the deplorable conditions of migratory labor. Given
the relative isolation of the IWW from the labor movement, its
repression by government agencies, the onset of World War I, the
abundant supply of agricultural workers, and finally its own ideological orientation, which viewed labor contracts as acts of "class col-
laboration," it is likely that the IWW accomplished all that was
realistically possible. The results of its agitation compared favorably
with a concurrent unionization campaign conducted in California by
the AFL: Although the AFL had several locals, employed a staff of
organizers, and maintained a "mild and conciliatory attitude," its
campaign brought few results and was of little consequence.[28]

Because concessions to farm workers were undertaken without
guaranteeing labor's right to organize, government-sponsored reforms had the potential, in conjunction with repression of worker
organizations, to prevent future insurgency. As a result, government
policies were crucial in undermining insurgency and maintaining
the character of capital-labor relations in the fields. The California
and federal governments both participated in limiting the influence
of the IWW. Repression of the IWW and its virtual elimination from
California combined with reforms aimed at improving working conditions in the fields. By using a strategy of simultaneous reform and
repression, the state sought to reduce the likelihood of future disruption of the capital accumulation process in agriculture. Thus, the

state acted in the long term political interests of the growers, even though the growers themselves opposed reforms.

However, the contradictory aspects of these actions prevented any long term solution. Preserving stable future capital accumulation by eliminating IWW pressure did not rest comfortably with attempting some of the more modest reforms the IWW had sought. IWW-promoted insurgency had been the stimulus for government sponsored reforms. Without that force, government policies became exclusively oriented toward promoting capital accumulation, again through managing the labor supply in ways which supplied growers with controllable and inexpensive labor.

After insurgency subsided and the IWW was virtually eliminated through federal prosecution, migratory workers were almost powerless to prevent effacement of newly-won improvements in wages and working and living conditions. Although the IWW in theory recognized strikes and industrial union issues as a means of challenging the unilateral control of work by the capitalist class, their farm labor struggles left the system of labor exploitation intact. In refusing to sign contracts the union protected itself from compromises with employers but did little to alter their basic independence. Although the strikes challenged the growers' unilateral control over wage rates, union activity never reached the roots of exploitation in the labor contractor system.

The pattern of temporary concessions, especially over wages, made in response to insurgency and then taken back when labor peace prevails has recurred throughout California's agricultural history. The temporary nature of improvements indicates a profound weakness in agricultural unionization campaigns that do not attempt—or that fail—to institutionalize structural changes in capital-labor relationships.

MEXICAN AND FILIPINO IMMIGRATION

After the threat of labor militancy subsided, growers were again free to dictate the terms of agricultural employment. Using whatever means were available to keep the labor force quiescent and unorganized, they aimed to hold labor costs to a minimum and maintain control over the work force. Such a strategy was not without its contradictions. Growers' opposition to reforms and the lack of improvement in the conditions of agricultural labor led whites, Mexicans, and Filipinos to participate in strikes, labor boycotts, and other strategies aimed at organizing the agricultural labor force.

The U.S. entry into World War I provided the rationale for the federal government to encourage large-scale immigration of Mexicans for seasonal work. There had been Mexican labor in the fields for years, especially in border areas, but never on the scale it reached during the war. Mexican workers had been recruited and used extensively by railroad and mining companies in the Southwest since early in the century. The railroads joined large growers in exerting pressure on Congress to continue permitting relatively open Mexican immigration throughout the 1920s. Before World War I Mexicans were just one of a number of ethnic groups represented in the farm labor force. Because of their small numbers, they were not in a position to negotiate with their employers. By 1920, however, they had become the largest single element in California's agricultural labor supply, making up over 50 percent of migratory workers. Their predominance continued throughout the decade and made successful unionization and strikes possible during the late 1920s.

Before 1917 Mexican workers entered the United States with little difficulty. The Immigration Act of February 1917, however, instituted requirements of literacy and the payment of an $8.00 head tax for aliens over sixteen. This created difficulties for potential immigrants from countries like Mexico where poverty and illiteracy were widespread. In fact, Department of Labor statistics show that 7,500 Mexicans were denied entry into the United States in the first full year of the law's operation as a result of these requirements.[29]

The beginning of U.S. involvement in World War I effectively curtailed the enforcement of the Immigration Act in limiting Mexican immigration. Immediately upon the passage of the law, Southwestern growers besieged the Department of Labor with accounts of severe labor shortages. In response Secretary of Labor William B. Wilson issued in May 1917 an order waiving the literacy test, head tax, and a prohibition against the entry of contract labor in the temporary admission of Mexican agricultural workers.[30] The Southwestern growers, however, wanted all restrictions on Mexican immigration eliminated. Food Administrator Herbert Hoover, one of the primary supporters of the large growers in Washington, lobbied for the removal of the head tax for all Mexican workers and the elimination of the six-month limit placed on Mexican residence in the United States.[31] Joining the growers in these demands were railroad and mining interests, who had utilized inexpensive Mexican labor for years. By June 1918 many of the restrictions had been eliminated. Mexican workers were entitled to stay in the United States for the duration of the war and were permitted to work in mining, railroad, and construction projects in addition to agriculture.[32] After the war the temporary admission program was continually extended, first to 1919, then 1920, and finally to 1921. Upon its expiration the enforcement of the Immigration Act became so lax that grower access to Mexican labor was virtually unhampered.

The temporary admission program was of immense financial benefit to the growers. The widespread availability of Mexican workers made possible the introduction of cotton farming to the Southwest, which became one of the area's most prominent and profitable agricultural industries. But the program only supplemented the regular immigration of those meeting the requirements of law. Further encouragement of Mexican immigration for menial work came with the passage of the comprehensive Immigration Act of 1924. For the first time the immigration of certain nationalities was limited by quotas.

Immigration from Mexico, however, was not restricted by a quota. Additionally, all Mexicans were classified as "white" in order to circumvent a clause in the Immigration Act which prohibited entry to anyone having "more than 50 percent Indian blood," a provision which would have normally applied to a large portion of Mexican workers. Combined with massive illegal immigration, these measures insured a vast supply of Mexican workers to be used by agricultural landowners to keep labor costs at a low level and guarantee an adequate harvest labor force. Furthermore, border officials themselves admitted that illegal entries equaled or exceeded legal ones.[33] During the 1920s estimates of the proportion of Mexican farm laborers in the California agricultural work force of 200,000 ranged from 50 to 75 percent.

Like earlier Japanese immigrants, the Mexicans were welcomed into the fields by the growers. They quickly replaced Japanese, Hindus, and whites. Besides cultural and language barriers and the AFL's opposition to their presence, other characteristics of Mexican farm workers made them an easily exploitable labor source. A substantial number, if not the majority, were only in the United States for the harvest season and would return to Mexico upon its conclusion. They generally earned more money during the harvest season in the Southwestern United States than they could in Mexico, and growers frequently used this fact to justify the low wages prevailing in agriculture. Moreover, because of illegal entry and numerous unintended technical violations of immigration laws, up to 80 percent of Mexican workers in the United States were legally subject to deportation, a threat growers used repeatedly to discourage organization efforts among them.[34] The 1927 convention of the Fruit Growers of California debated whether to encourage Puerto Rican migration to California or continue Mexican immigration. An official, expressing the consensus, stated that since Puerto Rico was a United States possession, "We cannot handle them [Puerto Ricans] like Mexicans. A Porto [sic] Rican has as much right to stay as we have. He cannot be exported as can a Mexican who becomes indigent."[35]

The only threats to this arrangement were two pieces of legislation considered by Congress in 1925 and 1926. The Box Bill and the Harris Bill would have placed Mexican immigration on a quota basis, with an allotment of only 1,575 per year. Sponsored by Representative John Box of East Texas and Senator William Harris of Georgia, the bills were strongly supported by the AFL and small farmers, who claimed that they could not compete with large growers utilizing low-wage Mexican labor. Both Box and Harris despised Mexicans on racial grounds and, more importantly, represented cotton-growing constituencies competing with the Southwestern cotton growers. Restricting the availability of labor would give the cotton growers in the South a competitive advantage.[36] Organized labor wanted Mexican immigration restricted on both racial and economic grounds: AFL President William Green argued that Mexican restriction was necessary to protect American workers from adverse competition; other union representatives claimed that Mexicans were genetically inferior and thus unassimilable.[37] The arguments echoed similar ones used by white labor against the previous immigration of Japanese and Chinese and reflected the racial divisions within the working population.

The testimony of agriculture lobbyists demonstrated that economic self-interest was at the core of their antirestriction position. One lobbyist, S. Parker Frisselle, the owner of 5,000 acres of California agricultural land and a member of the Fresno Chamber of Commerce, the California Federated Farm Bureau, and the California Development Association, told a Congressional committee considering the bills that "we in California would greatly prefer some setup in which our peak labor demands might be met and upon completion of our harvest these laborers would be returned to their home country."[38] He indicated that the Mexicans filled this requirement and added that they did not become landowners. He told the committee, "The Mexican is not aggressive. He is amenable to suggestions and does his work. He does not take the Chinese or Japanese attitudes." Frisselle characterized the Mexican as "a man who gives us no trouble. He takes his orders and follows them."[39] In a speech before the Commonwealth Club of California, it was stated that "the Mexican peon is at present the backbone of our menial labor supply. . . .

some of our largest agricultural crops are so dependent upon Mexican labor that many farmers feel that it is indispensable."[40] At the same meeting an official of the Southern Pacific Railroad, which had profited from low-wage Mexican labor, remarked that the immigration quota should not be applied to the Mexican worker because "he is not radical in the slightest respect" and "is easily controlled by those in authority."[41]

The agricultural interests of the border and mountain states acted as one to oppose the bills, as did many railroad, cattle, and mining interests. Within the executive branch only the Department of Labor favored the bills; the departments of Agriculture, Interior, and State opposed them.[42] Pressured by conflicting interests during hearings on the Box Bill, the House Immigration and Naturalization Committee decided to do nothing. Ultimately neither piece of restrictionist legislation was voted on by Congress. This inaction satisfied the large growers and stimulated increasingly heated controversy over Mexican workers in the Southwest. Another Box-Harris bill restricting Mexican immigration was introduced in 1928. Although as unsuccessful as the previous efforts, it served as a warning.

Agricultural landowners, realizing that legislation might drastically limit their supply of Mexican labor, began to recruit Filipino laborers in large numbers as possible replacements. At first the bulk of Filipino immigration came from the Hawaiian Islands, where Filipinos had been employed on sugar cane plantations. The Filipino population in the United States rose from 5,600 in 1920, most of them students, to 56,000 in 1930, largely concentrated on the Pacific Coast and engaged in farm production.[43] Filipino immigrants were unique in several respects. Ninety percent were males; nearly all were single. Approximately 85 percent were under the age of thirty.[44] Since the Philippine Islands were then a possession of the United States, Filipinos were not subjected to immigration laws and thus could not be legally restricted. However, they were not eligible for citizenship unless they had served in the U.S. armed forces. Although never as numerous as Mexican laborers, they did undercut other field workers in some area, notably those where Japanese and whites were employed.[45] In fact, when first recruited, Filipino field workers were paid the lowest wage of all minority groups and tended to be employed as stoop laborers. Their lack of visible family ties gave them the mobility growers found desirable, though in later years it may have increased the militancy of their strikes.

While not actually needed to replace Mexican field laborers since the feared restrictions never occurred, Filipino immigration served grower interests in two ways. First, it created an excess labor supply as an added insurance against organization efforts and the need for wage raises to attract sufficient workers. Many who argued at the time that Filipino and Mexican agricultural workers were not in direct competition with whites admitted that few whites would work for such wages. Second, the animosity that quickly developed between Mexicans and Filipinos served to divide the farm labor force and inhibit organization. A report of the California Department of Industrial Relations in 1930 stated that growers preferred to "employ a mixture of laborers of various races, speaking diverse languages, and not accustomed to mingling with each other. The practice is intended to avoid labor trouble which might result from having a homogeneous group of laborers."[46]

With labor costs kept at a minimum and the agricultural proletariat fragmented, California farm land became more concentrated. Larger and larger tracts were owned by fewer individuals or corporations. The La Follette Committee reported that by 1930 more than one-third of all large-scale farms in the United States (defined as those having a gross annual output of more than $30,000) were located in California. Within California they composed only 2 percent of the total number of farms but produced 29 percent of all agricultural output, while the largest 10 percent of California farms controlled 80 percent of the state's farm land and produced more than 50 percent of its agricultural products.[47] Sixty percent of the large-scale truck farms and fruit farms in the nation were in California.

Correspondingly, a trend toward "rationalization" or coordination of agricultural production arose. Organizations were formed to standardize marketing procedures for various crops. Several are still in existence. The most prominent were the San Joaquin Labor Bureau (cotton, raisins, and fruit), Western Growers Protective Association, (vegetable and melon producers), the Grower-Shipper Vegetable Association (lettuce), and the California Fruit Growers Exchange (citrus fruit). These grower organizations eventually came to coordinate labor employment, meeting to estimate labor requirements for the next harvest, fix a uniform wage to be paid by member growers, and coordinate plans for recruiting workers. The result of continuous labor recruitment was, according to the U.S. Department of Agriculture, a chronic oversupply of farm labor in California throughout the 1920s.[48]

The success of large-scale agricultural production stood in stark contrast to the situation of the 200,000 farm workers employed in the state during the 1920s. Mexican labor made possible an immense expansion of labor-intensive crops. Truck farm crops increased by 50 percent, fruit and nuts by 30 percent, and cotton by 400 percent.[49] The concentration of land ownership and the labor-intensive nature of the highly valuable crops produced had increasingly created what labor economists called "the industrialization of labor relations,"[50] a process virtually completed during the 1920s. In 1929 slightly more than 25 percent of the people employed in agriculture in the United States were wage laborers. In California the proportion of wage laborers was 60 percent, the highest of any state in the nation.[51] The wage workers were overwhelmingly nonwhites and were disproportionately utilized by large growers rather than small farmers. A 1928 survey of 1,200 farms made by the University of California College of Agriculture found that 90 percent of farms exceeding 640 acres used Mexican labor, while only 38 percent under 20 acres did so.[52]

The large growers had gained an extraordinary degree of control over agricultural labor. The labor surplus kept labor costs to a minimum. In 1928, a peak year in agriculture, Mexican farm workers earned an average of 35 cents an hour. Oversupply and low wages also reinforced the migratory nature of agricultural work. Most Mexican farm workers followed the crops, either alone or with families. As much as one-third of the harvest season might be spent looking for employment. School attendance for children was minimal. Constant movement allowed no opportunity to put down roots. Mexicans were accustomed to poverty but not to the lack of a stable community of residence and the accompanying isolation. Often they traveled with a labor contractor who arranged employment with a grower for a fee in addition to taking a percentage of the wages if he also served as a field supervisor. The contractor system was preferred by growers, since it exempted them from the legal responsibility for setting wages and providing workers' compensation. After the harvest, workers who did not return to Mexico migrated to Mexican barrios in nearby cities to search for temporary employment.

The immediate effect of easing immigration restrictions was to make it possible to employ massive numbers of Mexican workers in the fields. The indirect effect of state immigration policy was to reinforce the labor contractor system and enhance grower control of the work force. The contractor became thoroughly entrenched, answerable as an employment agent to the grower but serving as an intermediary, an interpreter, and a field-crew leader for the workers. Growers retained control over such matters as the timing of work, the amount of production, and general overseeing and surveillance. The contractor, however, was the visible source of authority. In the event of worker grievances, the contractor could claim that they concerned matters out of his or her control, since growers had set working conditions by a prior (usually oral) agreement. Contractors typically identified with the employer, were entrepreneurs themselves, and had no use for union organizers. This is the system many analysts regard as the primary barrier to unionization and self-determination by farm workers.

MANIPULATING IMMIGRATION AND REPATRIATION

Mexican and Filipino farm workers began in time to rebel against their low wages and conditions of employment. They met formidable obstacles, imposed by their weak bargaining position and the continued refusal by the AFL to back unionization efforts in the fields.

Late in 1927 a number of local Mexican unions combined to form the Confederacion de Uniones Obreras Mexicanas (Confederation of Mexican Labor Unions). Their constitution shared the analysis of some American leftist organizations endorsing "class struggle" and "integration into a single union of all labor in the world to combat international finance."[53] For farm labor, it called for better wages, an end to exploitation by labor contractors, and the elimination of employment agencies and commissaries, which functioned to keep farm workers dependent on their employers and restrict their control over working conditions and wages. The Confederation actually accomplished little, but it was a sign of the radicalization of the agricultural labor force, which was to turn the California fields into a battleground for most of the 1930s.

Mexican workers focused their militancy on wages and control issues, especially the elimination of the labor contractor system. A strike of Mexican cantaloupe workers near El Centro and Brawley in 1928 was soon broken by the arrest of many strikers, but it resulted in small wage gains and the temporary elimination of some widespread abuses in the contractor system. Two years later, in January 1930, another large strike occurred in the same valley. Five thousand Mexican, Japanese, and Filipino workers participated. The Communist party's Trade Union Unity League (TUUL) became involved and recruited a number of new members during the disturbance. This strike was broken by large-scale violence on the part of growers and local authorities. Having worked with Japanese and Mexican organizations for several years, the Communist party was in a position to provide leadership to the fledgling farm labor movement. After a second strike less than a month later in the same area, mainly by white packing-shed workers, the TUUL's affiliate, the Agricultural

Workers Industrial League (AWIL), called for a mass meeting in April to plan strategy for the elimination of the labor contractor system and job speedups and a means of dealing with unemployment. The meeting never took place. One week before it was scheduled to be held, the local sheriff led a group of deputies, policemen, and privately hired thugs into an AWIL meeting and removed all 108 persons found there to the El Centro County Jail.[54] Eight union leaders were convicted under California's criminal syndicalist law. Of the eight, two were Mexican, one Filipino, and one Japanese. In a preview of tactics carried out by local authorities and vigilante groups throughout the 1930s, the commander of the local American Legion post remarked that "the way to kill the Red plague is to dynamite it out. That's what we did in Imperial County. The judge who tried the Communists was a Legionnaire, 50 percent of the jurors were veterans. What chance did the Communists have?"[55]

Strikes by Mexican and Filipino agricultural workers continued, many of them under the leadership of the Communist party's Cannery and Agricultural Workers Industrial Union (CAWIU), which had grown out of AWIL. They culminated in the 1933 San Joaquin Valley cotton strike which involved 18,000 workers, 75 percent of them Mexicans. Filipino farm workers often formed their own labor organizations, the Filipino Labor Union formed during the summer of 1934 being the most important. It grew to ten branches and several thousand members by 1936, and closely cooperated with several independent Mexican unions. Centered in Santa Maria Valley, its members were involved in several successful strikes noteworthy for cooperation among Filipino, Mexican, and white workers. Filipinos in general refused to undercut other labor and held especially militant and disruptive strikes.[56]

In the early Depression years it became clear that Mexican and Filipino participation in militant strikes had abruptly ended grower preference for them as a source of farm labor. Expanding the labor supply from Mexico and the Philippines was not as effective in countering radicalization and unionization as it had been in the past, since militancy among the immigrant workers was rapidly increasing. By 1930 rising unemployment forced white workers into the fields, where they were utilized by growers to decrease their dependency on other sources of labor.[57] For the next few years, agencies within the California and federal governments took measures to stem the flow of Mexican and Filipino immigrants and to return a portion of those in the United States to Mexico and the Philippine Islands. These repatriation efforts cannot be understood outside the context of the Depression's mass unemployment and budgetary strains. Actions were undertaken to reduce the surplus labor supply and thus reduce government welfare expenditures. That these actions often were not solely or even primarily intended to manipulate the labor supply for the agricultural sector did not in any sense reduce their overall benefits for the growers. In this instance, government management of Depression-created crises coincided with the more specific interests of large-scale agriculture and grower-shipper interests in reducing the number of foreign born.

At first growers continued their opposition to attempts to restrict the immigration of agricultural labor. But as rising unemployment was sending out-of-state white workers and local labor into the fields and reducing the growers' need for Mexican and Filipino labor, crop production was declining sharply. As a result, labor requirements were drastically reduced just as the agricultural labor supply was threatening to swell to unprecedented proportions. The growers grumbled at first about the administrative restrictions on Mexican immigration that began in 1929 and 1930, but they soon ceased their complaints.[58] Although it was not apparent in 1930, the reduction in the number of Mexicans and Filipinos available for agricultural labor cut into the population that in a few years would be the most militant segment of the labor force.

The U.S. State Department achieved a reduction in Mexican immigration simply by enforcing statutes of the 1917 Immigration Act that had been consistently waived throughout the 1920s to allow temporary Mexican immigration: the literacy test and the head tax. Consular officers began to refuse to grant visas on grounds that, if strictly applied, could have all but stopped immigration from Mexico. From July 1929 through February 1930, the number of visas issued to Mexicans declined seventy-five percent compared with the average number issued during the preceding five years.[59] After March 1930 no visas were granted to Mexicans who were common laborers and had not previously resided in the United States. In 1929 Congress passed legislation for the first time setting penalties for illegal entry. Those caught for the first violation were subject to one year in prison or a $1,000 fine. Penalties for recidivists were considerably harsher. The Border Patrol was strengthened. Established in 1925, it was initially understaffed and underfunded and mostly concerned with enforcing customs and alcoholic prohibition laws, but by the early Depression years it had developed into an efficient organization. By all accounts the Border Patrol and the enforcement of laws penalizing illegal entry were extremely effective in reducing illegal Mexican immigration. At the same time, the new visa requirements and their strict enforcement substantially curtailed legal immigration. The number of legal Mexican immigrants dropped from an annual average of 62,000 between 1923 and 1929 to 11,800 during 1930 and 2,500 during 1931.[60]

Under Depression conditions members of Congress became more disposed to legislate restrictions against Mexican immigration. A bill introduced by Senator William Harris of Georgia passed the Senate in May 1930, but the Hoover administration successfully prevented the House version from coming to a vote. Officials of the State Department argued that the bill would enrage officials in Mexico, and perhaps most Latin American countries, and would be detrimental to American interests in Latin America.[61] Other measures undertaken by the government, however, were accomplishing the same purpose as the Harris bill. Perhaps the most significant were a series of drives for the deportation and repatriation of Mexicans living in the United States.

Most of the repatriation was formally voluntary; it stemmed from discouragement over the lack of employment opportunities and the punitive treatment of the Mexican population in the United States. Repatriation began almost as soon as the Depression set in, but it increased after a series of deportation raids by the U.S. Bureau of Immigration in 1931. Enthusiastically implemented by Secretary of Labor William Doak, a recent Hoover appointee, searches by bureau officials were conducted throughout the nation. Southern California was an area of intensive focus; there the searches were more like raids on Mexican communities.[62] People found to be subject to deportation were given the opportunity to depart voluntarily and were driven to the border. Others were formally deported. According to bureau statistics, between June 1930 and June 1931 the agency deported or promoted the voluntary departure from the United States of 30,000 people, the majority of whom were Mexicans.[63] Thousands of Mexicans were deported from Los Angeles alone, while the *New York Times* reported that 75,000 Mexicans and Mexican Americans had left Southern California in 1931.[64]

After the federal raids subsided, Los Angeles County sponsored a series of repatriation trains to Mexico to lessen the county's relief burden by reducing the number of Mexicans on relief. Passage was free for any Mexican or Mexican American. By the end of 1933, fifteen repatriation trains had removed approximately 12,700 people from Los Angeles, for an estimated financial saving to the county of $435,000.[65] After 1933 repatriation pressures tapered off, with the last train leaving in March 1934.

Although most of the federal raids and all of the repatriation drives in Southern California were in urban areas, chiefly Los Angeles, they had a strong effect on the agricultural labor force. A large proportion of those repatriated from the cities during the winter were actually part of the farm labor supply; they had simply moved to urban areas during the off season to search for work. Moreover, the raids and repatriation drives produced a climate of fear and uncertainty, which combined with the lack of employment opportunities to create a massive, unsupervised, individual repatriation movement. In fact, government-supervised repatriation accounted for only a small percentage of the Mexicans returning south during this period. According to the Office of Social Statistics in Mexico City, the number of Mexican repatriates for the years 1930 through 1933 was 312,000. Other estimates range as high as 400,000. In 1931—the year of the deportation raids—alone, 125,000 returned.[66] Many of the deportations had political overtones. Articles in the *Nation* and *New Republic* during the period accused the Bureau of Immigration of harassing ethnic radicals with threats of deportation, and during a berry-pickers' strike in Southern California, the local Chamber of Commerce and the growers attempted to remove large numbers of strikers through county repatriation.[67]

Filipino workers were likewise subjected to discriminatory government policies aimed at influencing the racial composition (and political behavior) of the agricultural labor supply. Representative Richard Webb of California introduced legislation in 1928 aimed at their exclusion which was strongly endorsed by the state AFL organization.[68] It was soon determined, however, that since the Philippine Islands were still a U.S. possession, Filipino immigration could not be legally restricted.

Filipino immigration was placed on a quota basis with the passage of the Philippine Islands Independence Act of 1934, and this amounted to Filipino exclusion. Representative Webb sponsored further legislation—H.R. 6464, signed by President Roosevelt in July 1935—which provided free transportation to the Philippine Islands for Filipinos residing in the United States. Advertisements designed to persuade as many Filipinos as possible to take up the offer made little mention of the section of the bill that read: "No Filipino who receives the benefits of this act shall be entitled to return to the continental United States."[69] The program had little success, coming as it did well into the Depression. Filipinos reportedly regarded it with suspicion.

The experience of Mexican and Filipino workers provides a classic example of governmental manipulation of the agricultural labor supply. Through changes in immigration policies and practices, loosening immigration restrictions made possible massive employment of Mexican workers in Southwestern agribusiness. But when Depression conditions as well as initial indications of growing worker militancy undermined their utility to growers, immigration of Mexican and Filipino workers was drastically curtailed and deportation and repatriation efforts were initiated.

While a similar strategy was successful against Japanese farm workers, this time it failed to halt unionization efforts. Although unemployed whites had begun to replace Mexican and Filipino agricultural workers even before the Dust Bowl migration of the later Depression years, labor strife continued to increase in California's fields. The 1930s witnessed the most extensive series of farm labor strikes in U.S. history, rivaled only by the strikes of the 1960s and 1970s. The threat of continued disruption of agricultural production motivated government officials and agencies by the end of the decade to seek an accommodation with labor and attempt to stabilize the farm labor force, in part through providing the means for reducing its predominantly migratory pattern. This agricultural counterpart of the industrial strife and governmental response occurring during the Depression has been largely ignored by labor historians.

CHAPTER 5

THE GREAT DEPRESSION AND THE RISE OF FARM LABOR UNIONISM

The Depression era of the thirties initiated the third major stage of agricultural labor militancy. This period of farm worker protest paralleled the first fifteen years of the UFW era in its high level of strike activity and in the number of workers involved in labor disputes. Both periods were characterized by coordinated and vehement opposition by growers to unionization. And in both periods the state participated in attempts to quell expressions of discontent. Only when insurgency could not be dissipated was it moved to mediate the conflict.

Unlike previous episodes of farm worker militancy, unionization efforts during the early years of the Depression took place at a time of profound economic dislocation and political crisis. The era as a whole was characterized by heightened class consciousness. In rural areas of California a number of spontaneous labor disturbances erupted. The union assuming leadership in many of the strikes was the Cannery and Agricultural Workers Industrial Union (CAWIU). It sent organizers to strike areas to escalate protests, coordinate the disruption of agricultural production, and gain concessions through mass defiance. In this chapter we will consider the strengths and limitations of CAWIU, the vigilante terror that confronted it, the repression of the organization, and the tendency, which we have noted before, for grower concessions to be eroded with the waning of protest.

CAWIU was significantly limited during its brief existence by its inability to mobilize external resources. Outside support was slight in comparison with the forces seeking to repress farm worker insurgency. CAWIU was fairly successful in turning workers' willingness to strike into temporary gains, but it was less successful in establishing union organizations that could prolong these concessions. Nevertheless, the early Depression years witnessed the emergence of a public sympathetic to agricultural labor unionization. This public was to expand during the remaining Depression years and in the late thirties help create the possibility of more permanent reforms and the unionization of California's agricultural work force.

THE GROWTH OF CAWIU

During the thirties California witnessed the largest series of strikes thus far in U.S. agricultural history. CAWIU, the union that led most of the strikes in the years from 1930 through 1934, was affiliated with the Communist party. It worked closely with other organizations and unions, notably Mexican and Filipino ones; similar to the IWW, CAWIU rejected the AFL's bias against nonwhites. Its rise created the possibility of organizing farm labor across ethnic lines.

The onset of the Depression brought steadily declining wages for agricultural as well as industrial workers. According to a 1936 report of the California State Emergency Relief Administration, wages for Mexican migrants fell from an average of thirty-five cents an hour in 1928 to fourteen cents an hour in 1933.[1] Housing and living conditions had also worsened since the California Immigration and Housing Commission declined into an ineffective organization. Rural strikes and organizational activities occurring in response to Depression conditions have frequently been overlooked by labor historians, who tend to concentrate on the industrial strife of the period. Nevertheless, rural strikes took no subordinate place in California at the time, and many observers described them as class warfare in the fields. The years 1930–32 witnessed ten major strikes in California agriculture, with three involving more than a thousand workers. CAWIU participated in all the larger strikes. Most were spontaneous disturbances in which CAWIU provided leadership only after the strike had commenced. Few gains were won during the series, but they helped CAWIU organizers develop organizing techniques and strike strategy that were successfully utilized in later struggles.

Control issues had a prominent part in field worker strikes involving CAWIU, and such nonwage demands were more varied and better defined than they had been in the two previous stages of farm worker insurgency. Strike issues did, of course, include wage gains; frequently the demand was for a basic wage of $2.50 for an eight-hour day, with time and a half for overtime. But CAWIU also demanded

union recognition, preferential hiring through the union as intermediary, election of rank and file worker committees to negotiate
with employers, and hiring without discrimination on grounds of
race, color, union affiliation, or strike participation. If successful,
CAWIU demands would essentially have eliminated the labor contractor system.[2] CAWIU also raised a number of secondary control
issues reflecting the local situation of strikers: improved housing, an
end to evictions from grower-maintained labor camps, and abolition
of charges for living quarters, for example. Disputes sometimes involved sanitary conditions and the provision of clean drinking water
at the work site, free transporation, work implements, and medical
services. Farm workers themselves determined the specific strike
demands by consensus during intensive strike meetings.[3]

Also developed during the early Depression years were cooperative
ties between the growers, law enforcement agencies, and local vigilante groups partly composed of prominent citizens. The intensity
and effectiveness of their coordinated opposition to farm worker
strikes is illustrated by the first of a continuous series of labor
disputes to spread throughout California in the early thirties. In
November 1932 a strike of orchard-pruners involving about four
hundred Mexican, Filipino, and white workers took place on the
ranch of Congressman Frank Buck in Vacaville. Specially deputized
recruits were used to break up strike meetings. Six strike leaders
were taken out of Vacaville jail and driven twenty miles from town,
where forty masked men "flogged them with tug straps, clipped their
heads with sheep clippers, and poured red enamel over them."[4] The
strike was lost and finally called off in late January 1933, but more
disturbances followed during 1933 and part of 1934.

For our purposes it will not be necessary to describe in detail all the
major strikes of the period. Instead, we will summarize briefly in
order to illustrate the demands and tactics of strikers, the response of
growers, law enforcement agencies, vigilante groups, and government, and finally the outcome of the insurgency. The strikes included
a series of general crop-wide walkouts, mostly under CAWIU leadership. Strikes began in 1933 during the pea harvest in the Santa
Clara Valley and the berry harvest in El Monte, just east of Los
Angeles, continued throughout the summer, and reached a climax in
the San Joaquin Valley cotton strike in October of that year. The El
Monte strike began when the predominantly Mexican workers
walked out of the Los Angeles County berry fields, 80 percent of
which were leased or owned by Japanese in violation of the California
Alien Lands Act. Pay was as low as nine cents an hour; the union was

demanding twenty-five cents. As agricultural landowners, the Japanese reacted as their white counterparts did: they recruited strikebreakers to replace the workers who had walked out. Under CAWIU leadership, and with the cooperation of the Mexican workers' union, the Confederacion de Uniones de Campesinos y Obreros Mexicanos (CUCOM), the strike spread to encompass some 7,000 workers in celery and onions as well as berries. The Mexican consul and U.S. Department of Labor officials intervened and brought wages up to twenty cents an hour for the strikers, but only by arranging an agreement between growers and the less radical CUCOM that was intended to erode workers' support for CAWIU. Farm workers who remained loyal to CAWIU by staying out on strike witnessed their jobs being filled by Japanese laborers and schoolchildren who had been enlisted as strikebreakers.

A general crop strike of peach-pickers that summer involved an estimated 6,000 workers. Substantial organizing took place among workers before the strike, and mass picketing was effective and coordinated. The peach dispute spread to seven counties in the upper San Joaquin and the lower Sacramento valleys. Starting in Tulare, the strike spread to Merced, Modesto, Stockton, and even the Marysville-Chico district, nearly 300 miles from Tulare. In every struck field, the workers registered substantial wage gains. By August CAWIU membership had increased to over 8,000, compared with 3,000 the month before.[5] A grape strike involving 500 pickers around Lodi and Fresno failed to win significant gains and is remembered chiefly for the way it was suppressed. Seventy members of a local vigilante group were sworn in as special deputies. With the local police, they followed roving pickets and arrested them on charges of disturbing the peace whenever the pickets attempted to interfere with the crop harvest.[6]

The cotton strike of 1933 climaxed the harvest season. It began in early October in the southern San Joaquin Valley, centering in Kern, King, and Tulare counties, where more than half California's cotton was grown. Rapidly spreading to encompass the entire valley, it involved some 18,000 workers, well over half, and perhaps as many as 90 percent, of the cotton harvest workers needed. Approximately 75 percent of these were Mexicans or of Mexican descent.

Cotton production in the valley had rapidly developed during the 1920s and replaced less profitable crops. California cotton was a superior form; the weight produced per acre was over three times the national average. Although only 1,500 acres were devoted to producing cotton in 1921, there were approximately 300,000 cotton acres in

1935 and nearly 600,000 in 1937.[7] The late fall and winter harvesting season for cotton helped bridge the gap between October and January, when little field labor was traditionally needed. The development of cotton production occurred after large-scale cash-crop agriculture had been firmly established in California. It brought with it a system of coordination and control among large cotton growers, enabling them to exert the pressure needed to keep small growers in line. The Anderson Clayton Company alone ginned 35 percent of the cotton in California and Arizona. Large growers and processors with ties to financial institutions operated through the Agricultural Labor Bureau of San Joaquin Valley to standardize wage rates for chopping and picking throughout the cotton-growing area. Pressure from banks and processing companies, whose services were essential for continued production, kept wages and working conditions nearly uniform throughout the area.

The coordination of cotton production did not, however, benefit those who actually worked in the fields. In fact, it left little room for laborers to negotiate with individual employers. The wage for cotton chopping fell from $1.46 an acre in 1930 to 66 cents in 1932. The wages for cotton picking also declined from over $1.00 a hundredweight in the late 1920s to 40 cents in 1932. The growers customarily met in Fresno in the fall, under the auspices of the San Joaquin Valley Agricultural Labor Bureau, to determine wages for the whole industry. The 1933 rates were set at 72 cents an acre for cotton chopping and 60 cents a hundredweight for cotton picking, only slight advances over the 1932 rate.[8] Thus, the stage was set for the October strike.

At the height of the strike, roving picket bands covered a 114-mile stretch of the San Joaquin Valley from Bakersfield to Merced. CAWIU demanded a picking rate of $1.00 per hundredweight, the abolition of labor contractors, union hiring without discrimination, and union recognition. Worker loyalty toward CAWIU increased during the strike, and thousands of new workers were recruited into the union. CAWIU locals were established throughout the valley, with headquarters in Tulare. Relief for strikers came from sympathetic persons and organizations, much of it gathered by the Workers International Relief, affiliated with the Communist party. The State Emergency Relief Administration, which was under federal direction, provided aid for some of the strikers. The federal relief foreshadowed more extensive efforts by the federal government later in the decade to stabilize the agricultural labor force. Interestingly, a number of small cotton growers who had suffered from the domination of the large cotton interests also supported the strike.

Growers evicted strikers from the company-owned housing provided for the pickers, but the evictions actually helped the strike, since a number of emergency tent colonies were formed and served as centers for strike activities. Local police, supplemented at times by the state highway patrol, conducted massive arrests of pickets and strikers. In one incident, a vigilante group opened fire without warning on unarmed workers leaving a union meeting in Pixley, killing two and wounding several. Eleven ranchers were subsequently arrested and charged with murder, but despite positive identification by witnesses, all were acquitted.

The Roosevelt administration at first remained passive while strikers were murdered by armed growers and illegal wholesale arrests of pickets took place. The California government cut off relief payments, and Federal Employment Agencies attempted to recruit strikebreakers, but the influence of CAWIU expanded nonetheless. As the strike threatened to spread to California's entire crop of ripening cotton, government officials and institutions moved toward promoting reconciliation between the conflicting parties. The Roosevelt administration made several unsuccessful attempts to settle the dispute. National Recovery Administration official George Creel, a journalist active in reform movements during the Progressive Era and chairman of the Committee on Public Information created by President Wilson to mobilize public support for the war, was sent to the tent camp at Corcoran. There he was refused admittance by the strikers and was booed when he pleaded with them over a loudspeaker to return to the fields. The conciliator of the U.S. Department of Labor made some progress but was unable to bring about an end to the strike. The Mexican consul, Enrique Bravo, unsuccessfully appealed to the workers to abandon the strike in the name of continued peaceful relations between the United States and Mexico.

Resolution finally was achieved through a fact-finding committee appointed by Governor James Rolph and headed by the University of California labor historian Ira B. Cross. The committee condemned the conduct of the growers and the massive violation of the civil liberties of farm workers and recommended a compromise rate of 75 cents a hundredweight for cotton picking. Under pressure from the Federal Intermediate Credit Bank, the Agricultural Labor Bureau of the San Joaquin Valley voted to accept the wage scale "in the interest of good American citizenship, law and order, and in order to forestall the spread of communism and radicalism and to protect the harvesting of other crops."[9] CAWIU was under pressure at the time because of the suspension of food relief by the State Emergency Relief Administration and the dispatching to the main strike areas of highway patrol officers who threatened further arrests of strike leaders if the strike continued. While the settlement was a compromise, it enhanced the prestige of CAWIU among agricultural laborers. Their leaders claimed that it represented a major victory, and many growers signed contracts with the Union. Membership in CAWIU rose to well over 20,000 by the end of the 1933 harvest season. The cotton strike, the largest of its kind in U.S. agricultural history thus far, had lasted twenty-four days.

The strikes led by CAWIU in 1933 and early 1934 also stimulated labor activity in fields where the union was not actually present, and several nonunion strikes succeeded in winning gains. During 1933 a total of thirty-seven strikes involving fourteen crops, 48,000 agricultural workers, and a loss of 670,000 work days was reported. CAWIU led twenty-four of the strikes, or 65 percent of the total. These twenty-four strikes brought out 38,000 workers, approximately 79 percent of those participating in agricultural labor disputes that year. Twenty-one of them resulted in gains for the workers, while slightly over half of the other strikes—led by AFL affiliates or independent unions or spontaneous eruptions—were completely lost.[10] Thus, CAWIU established itself as an effective force.

CAWIU's initial success illustrated the functions of mass defiance. Grievances had continued for decades with no redress until the outbreak of protest and the threat to disrupt production compelled elites to search for ways to manage labor's discontent. The conciliation secured by CAWIU was a direct result of the union's effectiveness in coordinating and amplifying mass protest. Ultimately, though, its comparative lack of external resources made the gains it achieved short-lived.

THE CAWIU PROGRAM AND ITS LIMITATIONS

Control issues occupied a large place in CAWIU's program and in strikers' demands. In interviews tape recorded for the University of California, a former CAWIU district organizer, Caroline Decker Gladstein, recalled that even the earliest strikes demanded the abolition of the labor contractor and union recognition.[11] According to Dorothy Ray Healey, a CAWIU organizer who later became vice president of the United Cannery, Agricultural, Packing and Allied Workers of America (UCAPAWA), a union affiliated with the Committee for Industrial Organizations, it was CAWIU policy to do away with the labor contractor so that workers could see themselves as able to affect their own situation. The immediate need, of course, was to end the contractors' practice of embezzling workers' funds. The rank and file workers' strike committees, she observed, needed very little debate to arrive at consensus on other nonwage grievances like the lack of fresh drinking water, camp sanitation, and decent housing. The strike meeting would typically result in a list of eight or ten of the most important demands rather than a long catalogue of everything that was needed.[12]

Is it possible that such demands were merely a reflection of the rhetoric of CAWIU organizers rather than the experience of farm workers? The evidence of CAWIU tactics and organizers' statements suggest that strike issues reflected farm workers' reaction to conditions in the fields. Healey pointed out that CAWIU emphasized the importance of worker committees in developing rank and file leadership and organizing for picketing and negotiations, and she recalled the daily three- or four-hour meetings attended by strikers to mobilize workers, discuss grievances and strike demands, and acquire the knowledge to go beyond wage demands.[13]

According to most analysts, CAWIU failed to sustain its organizations because of its shortcomings as a labor union. Apparently CAWIU never resolved the basic problem faced by most organizations with the goal of transforming social institutions: balancing ultimate ends with the necessity of achieving immediate concessions and victories based on negotiation and conciliation. Pressure from the Communist party to inject more anticapitalist ideology into dealings with grower-shipper interests interfered with the winning of concrete gains for the workers to demonstrate CAWIU's capability as an effective bargaining agent. Especially in the early period of its existence, CAWIU would sometimes enter a dispute in progress— either a spontaneous walkout or a strike called by another union— and attempt to provide leadership. Sometimes the intrusion was resented; more often than not it was welcomed. Since the union was essentially an outside force, however, it could not systematically plan and coordinate the strikes in which it became involved, and they were often chaotic. On the other hand, worker support for the union was greatly increased by such actions as the cotton and peach strikes of 1933, which were not only well planned and executed, but also generally successful in winning gains for the workers.

CAWIU as an organization did not emerge from farm worker experience; rather, it was formed by people who did not intimately understand the social situation of the many segments of agricultural labor. This lack of background created the union's most substantial problem. The two most prominent CAWIU organizers in the California fields were Pat Chambers, a thirty-one-year-old construction worker, and Caroline Decker, a twenty-year-old Party member who had already been involved in a Kentucky coal strike. Nearly all of the initial CAWIU volunteer organizers, including Chambers and Decker, were unfamiliar with agriculture. Moreover, since the main organizational focus of the union was on strikes, membership would drastically decline after a particular harvest. Of the more than 20,000 in CAWIU at the end of the 1933 harvest season, only about 1,000 were committed to the ideology and goals of the union and formed the cadre of the communist movement among agricultural workers. According to one leftist critic of the union, even some of these were siphoned out of the fields and into Communist party organizations, thus depriving the union of its most class-conscious and militant members.[14] Since the rest largely dispersed after a harvest, little consolidation of gains could be made.

Another substantial barrier to the development of a stable organization was the isolation of CAWIU in the fields. Donald Henderson, who was to become the first president of the CIO's UCAPAWA, noted that CAWIU had no formal ties to the trade union movement in California and encountered considerable hostility from officials of AFL unions, who viewed attempts to organize agricultural workers as doomed to failure. As a result, CAWIU was effectively denied one valuable external resource. Although its goals included the organization of cannery and related workers, it concentrated on migratory field labor. This emphasis deprived the union of the stable group of regular, year-round employees that a base among canners would provide and confined it to small cities and rural areas, where it was difficult to stop the terrorist activities of vigilantes.[15]

Liberal critics pointed to the revolutionary aims of the union as the source of its difficulty in reaching an accommodation with the grower-shipper interests: growers were likely to view a CAWIU strike as a "rule or ruin" struggle, and they could easily enlist the help of local vigilante groups and law enforcement officials to "get the reds out." While it was undoubtedly true that the union's ideology helped mobilize reactionary elements, large agricultural growers have historically utilized their power and alliances to defeat all organizational efforts by their field labor, ideologically radical or otherwise. Such critics also complained that CAWIU's radicalism prevented potential supporters from offering their assistance.[16] In fact, the strikes and the growers' reactions succeeded in focusing widespread attention on the conditions of agricultural labor for the first time since the IWW-led insurgency twenty years before. The sympathetic public attracted by CAWIU efforts would become an important element in reform attempts by government agencies later during the Depression.

The same analysts pointed to the disparity between the radical orientation of CAWIU and the more modest objectives of higher wages and better working conditions sought by most workers, suggesting that there was a difference in goals between the leadership and the mass membership. Despite the evidence of massive participation in insurgency, they contend, "relatively few workers supported the CAWIU."[17] But the notion that "outside ideologies" dictated CAWIU's orientation has been exaggerated. Tactics, strategies, goals, organizational forms, and analyses were developed in response to particular situations. CAWIU organizers may have talked about the necessity of class struggle and the overthrow of capitalism, but they helped lead, coordinate, and support direct actions to improve wages and working and living conditions. The disruption of agricultural production led by CAWIU resulted in significant, if short-lived, gains and, in pursuing grower concessions, the union received widespread worker support. It was, moreover, the only labor organization of any consequence concerned with farm labor at the time. Perhaps a more accurate assessment is that CAWIU accomplished what was possible given the brevity of its existence, the comparative lack of resources, and the antipathy of urban trade unions.

The communist issue was exploited by growers to win sympathy for their antilabor stance and justify violent tactics against farm workers. Referring to the Imperial Valley strikes of 1934, General Pelham D. Glassford, an Arizona farmer serving as the special conciliator of the U.S. Department of Labor, wrote in a report to the Valley's board of supervisors:

> After more than 2 months of observation and investigation in Imperial Valley, it is my conviction that a group of growers have exploited a "communist" hysteria for the advancement of their own interests; that they have welcomed labor agitation, which they could brand as "Red," as a means of sustaining supremacy by mob rule, thereby preserving what is so essential to their profits, cheap labor; that they have succeeded in drawing into their conspiracy certain county officials who have become the principal tool of their machines.[18]

The resistance generated by the agricultural interests was not in fact significantly different from that offered to other farm labor unions, both before and after the period. However, a new tactic was introduced to undermine worker support for the militant CAWIU. Before the January 1934 lettuce strike, growers, hoping to prevent a CAWIU organization drive, agreed to negotiate with the recently revived Imperial Valley Workers' Union, which had been dormant since 1929. Union officials later accused the growers of failing to uphold the agreement, and the Mexican union turned to CAWIU for aid. While the strike was in progress, growers established a company union to rival CAWIU and refused to hire anyone who was not a member. This "union" received little worker support, but after the strike was crushed, workers gradually joined it in order to work.[19] The grower strategy of cooperating with a rival union or forming a company union in order to undermine an effective organization was to be applied again in the future.

CAWIU's organizational difficulties might not have been insurmountable, given sufficient time for the union to grow. Its efforts in the fields only began in earnest in the fall of 1932, and a mere year later it led the largest strike of farm workers in U.S. history. There are indications that just before it was destroyed by vigilantes and the government, CAWIU was moving toward correcting some of its more serious deficiencies. In its second annual convention in early 1934, the union criticized itself for having a leadership largely made up of people unfamiliar with the situation of agricultural workers. A resolution was passed to bring rank and file workers into leadership capacities and involve them in decisions affecting the direction of strikes. Strike committees were to be democratically elected. Also, the assumption of the leadership of spontaneous strikes was analyzed and blamed for the union's defeats. Instead solid organization and adequate preliminary planning were to be given particular emphasis. The union also directed some of its organizers to concentrate on cannery workers, who would provide a stable source of membership and crucial support for agricultural strikes.[20] Thus, CAWIU was taking steps toward making itself a more effective organization.

Whether CAWIU would have been able to establish a solid organization is open to question. It remained a loose conglomeration of organizers throughout its brief existence. Caroline Decker has admitted that the union was incapable of serving as a bargaining agent for the workers on a continuing basis.[21] Most of the workers did not accept the union's communist orientation, as is evidenced by the lack of grass-roots effort to reconstruct CAWIU after the union's leadership was imprisoned. But CAWIU was effective in escalating defiance and providing tactical expertise and leadership, and it was extraordinarily successful in winning grower concessions. Over 85 percent of the 1933 strikes in which the union participated won gains, compared to gains achieved by less than 50 percent of other strikes involving only spontaneous action or led by small AFL-affiliated unions. CAWIU strikes or the threat of strikes were primarily responsible for raising the average pay of California farm workers by a third.[22] Still, it must be admitted that the gains won were mostly temporary. The elimination of CAWIU brought with it a drastic decline in strike activity and a rapid effacement of many of the gains insurgent workers had achieved.

THE DEMISE OF CAWIU

Independent of any of CAWIU's shortcomings, a wave of repression against the union began in 1934. After the cotton strike was resolved, the center of activity once again moved south to the winter harvests of lettuce and peas in the Imperial Valley. Early in January lettuce workers voted to strike, and in February about 4,000 pea-pickers walked out. Few gains resulted from these and related strikes in the area. The suppression of the strikes was violent even by California standards. Strike leaders were arrested, union meetings tear-gassed, union-sponsored parades and rallies broken up, and Mexican colonies and labor camps raided; and a lawyer for the American Civil Liberties Union was kidnapped and dumped in the desert.[23] During this period, an organization called the Associated Farmers was formed as a loose configuration of vigilante groups in agricultural regions. It institutionalized and gave a certain legitimacy to the antilabor terrorist activity that had frequently occurred during the previous five years. This unofficial repression contributed to the instability of the farm labor problem by generating combat whenever farm workers shed their passivity.

Strikes continued under CAWIU leadship until mid-1934. Of the fifteen strikes reported in 1934, ten were under CAWIU leadership or influence. A June strike of 1,000 apricot-pickers against three of the larger grower-shipper interests in Contra Costa County witnessed wholesale arrests under an antipicketing order. Aided by seventy-five specially deputized men, the local authorities placed 150 pickets in a corral and later escorted them to the county line. Thirteen leaders were arrested. The *Oakland Tribune* called the action a "round-up and deportation of undesirable agitators," while the San Francisco Labor Council labeled the arrests "outrages by mobs of farmers aided and abetted by State highway police."[24]

The wave of repression against CAWIU during the summer of 1934 was part of a more general antiunion campaign in response to the growth of labor discontent throughout the United States. On the

West Coast, the Pacific Coast Maritime Strike was in progress. A general strike was called in San Francisco on July 19 that lasted for three days. The strike was led largely by the International Longshoreman's Union (ILU) and was supported by CAWIU. Harry Bridges, president of the ILU, was able to persuade some rank and file members of AFL unions to break with their more conservative leaders for the duration of the strike. The National Guard eventually moved onto the San Francisco waterfront to suppress it. Before that, however, on July 20, the second day of the strike, police aided by a group of vigilantes raided the CAWIU headquarters, library, and school in Sacramento, arresting eighteen of the leaders—including Caroline Decker and Pat Chambers—on criminal syndicalism charges. They were accused specifically of committing "crime, sabotage, violence, or unlawful methods of terrorism with intent to approve, advocate, or further the doctrine of criminal syndicalism," as the law stated. For the next two months, a campaign against both urban and rural labor raged. Worker meeting places were raided and shut down; individual workers were beaten up, kidnapped, and arrested. The *Nation* of 29 August 1934 carried a two-and-a-half-page list of acts of violence by police and gangs of vigilantes against workers throughout California. Nearly every agricultural center was the scene of attacks, as were waterfront areas.[25] The reaction to the general strike and other labor disturbances was most strongly felt in the fields—not surprisingly, given the central position of agriculture in the California economy and the numerous ties between financial institutions and large grower-shipper interests. By the fall the bulk of the CAWIU leadership was in jail.

The November trial of sixteen defendants, fifteen of whom had been arrested during the Sacramento raid in July, marked the second time that California had invoked an antisyndicalism law to smash a militant farm labor organization. The prosecution's case hinged largely on tapping the political prejudices of the middle-class jury. For three weeks in the Sacramento courtroom, the prosecution read excerpts from communist literature seized in the raid, emphasizing passages expected to particularly upset the politically unsophisticated jurors. The Associated Farmers invested much time and money in aiding the prosecution. One member of the group's executive committee lent his secretary to the Sacramento County district attorney. They persuaded the district attorney of Imperial County four hundred miles to the south to assist the prosecution and paid his expenses, and they hired an official of the Los Angeles Police Intelligence unit to assist in the case. In all, the Associated Farmers spent nearly $14,000 to help secure the conviction of CAWIU leaders.[26]

On 1 April 1935 eight of the defendants, including Decker and Chambers, were convicted and sent to jail. Later their convictions were reversed on appeal, but the union-smashing job was by then complete. On 17 March 1935 the union's parent organization, the TUUL, and all affiliated organizations, including CAWIU itself, were dissolved by the Communist party. Organizers were encouraged to merge with independent and AFL unions as part of the Communist party's newly initiated "popular front" strategy.

The elimination of CAWIU brought about a drastic decline in field strike activity. Not only was there now no union or organization to coordinate crop-wide strikes but the localized strikes that occurred spontaneously or under the leadership of small independent unions were ruthlessly handled by local law enforcement agencies and the Associated Farmers. Few gains were made by agricultural workers in the years immediately after the arrest of the CAWIU leadership, for labor had neither the power nor the organization to contend with private groups acting in cooperation with local police forces to suppress labor organizations.

Although loosely coordinated statewide by the Associated Farmers, most antiunion activity, including vigilantism, originated at the local level. The California and federal governments were conspicuously slow to stem antiunion activities, including mob attacks and violations of civil liberties. In fact, the California government had been responsible for the single most significant blow to unionism in the period when it arrested virtually the entire California leadership of CAWIU. Violent opposition to agricultural unionization was thus permitted to continue throughout most of the Depression.

The repression of CAWIU and the non-intervention by the California and federal governments during periods of intense, violent antiunion action in the fields, in effect placed the state in the position of promoting agricultural capital accumulation through keeping labor costs to a minimum. However, this time suppression of farm labor activism was only temporary, and since state policies were not oriented toward securing acceptance by agricultural labor, unionization efforts continued throughout the decade.

Despite the repression, organizational efforts again commenced, led initially by small local unions. Eventually the persistence of field labor militancy and unionization efforts, and the violent opposition they aroused, prompted both the California government and the

Roosevelt administration to attempt to improve some of the worst conditions of migratory field labor and stabilize the farm labor situation by managing labor disputes and supporting unionization attempts.

THE ASSOCIATED FARMERS

The Associated Farmers were implicated in nearly every instance of the repression of agricultural strikes during this period. Formed in February 1934, just after the San Joaquin cotton strike, by a prominent American Legion official, the group's purpose was to coordinate grower efforts to help each other harvest their crops in the event of emergencies, especially strikes. It also agreed to offer its services to local law enforcement agencies during periods of disorder caused by "picketing and sabotage."[27] On many occasions during the 1930s, local members of the Associated Farmers were deputized so that they could help the police confront labor militancy. At other times the Associated Farmers simply pre-empted the repressive functions of the local sheriff, policed strikes themselves, and made mass arrests. Chapters of the organization were largely composed of local growers, members of such patriotic organizations as the American Legion, businessmen, government officials, and members of the sheriff's department. Within one year, twenty-six counties had active chapters.

The original impetus for establishing such a group came from the Agricultural Labor Subcommittee of the state Chamber of Commerce, meeting in Los Angeles on 6 November 1933, just after the violent and costly cotton strike. The subcommittee drew up two resolutions, later approved by the Chamber's board of directors, calling for enforcement of the state Criminal Syndicalism Act to end agricultural labor agitation and for the enlargement of the Chamber's Farm Labor Committee into a broader Citizen's Committee.[28] The task of organizing this Citizen's Committee was given to S. Parker Frisselle, now a prominent member of the state Chamber of Commerce. He had been owner and manager of a 5,000-acre ranch near Fresno, an active leader in the Agricultural Labor Bureau of the San Joaquin Valley, and a director of the Kern Sunset Oil Company.[29]

An organizing meeting was held on 28 November 1933 in San Francisco. Twenty-four persons attended, including representatives of the Pacific Gas and Electric Company, the Southern Pacific Railroad, the California Packing Corporation (Calpak), and the Bank of America.[30] Further meetings were held in areas where agricultural labor disturbances were anticipated. These meetings generally included representatives from local utility companies and banks as well as the sheriff, the district attorney, the chief of police, and the chairman of the county board of supervisors.[31] The immediate goals of the Associated Farmers were to promote the adoption of local anti-picketing ordinances, begin a publicity program designed to alert the public to the dangers of communism, and secure public support for attacks on agricultural labor unions with radical leadership.

Growers paid only nominal membership dues. According to a report of the first convention, held in May 1934, the president of the group stated that funds would come from banks and utility companies: farmers would staff the organization but leave ultimate control to banks and utilities.[32] Representatives of the State Farm Bureau and the Chamber of Commerce promoted the organization to local farm bureaus, businessmen, and law enforcement officials. The Headquarters were appropriately established in San Francisco. High-level officials in the Canners' League of California, the Southern Pacific Railroad, Standard Oil of California, the American-Hawaiian Steamship Company, and the Bank of America were appointed to solicit funds in their respective fields.[33]

Funds came from some of the largest industrial and financial institutions in the state. Much of the capital was raised by officials of the Pacific Gas and Electric Company and Calpak. Initially most of the money came from northern California interests, the Industrial Association of San Francisco and Calpak being the major contributors. After an upsurge of unionism and strikes in 1936, however, industrial and financial interests in the southern part of the state began to contribute large amounts. Chief among these were the Crown-Willamette Paper Company and the Southern California Edison Company. From its founding to the La Follette Committee hearings in 1939, the group's ten largest contributors—less than 1 percent of all contributors—provided 44.3 percent of its funds. In order of size of their reported donations, the ten were: the Industrial Association of San Francisco, the Dried Fruit Association of California, the Canners' League, the Southern Pacific Railroad, the Southern Californians (a Los Angeles employers' association), the Atcheson, Topeka, and Santa Fe Railroad, the Pacific Gas and Electric Company, the San Joaquin Cotton Oil Company, the Holly Sugar Corporation, and the Spreckles Investment Company.[34]

Most of the industrial supporters of the Associated Farmers were invested in agricultural production or were in allied industrial groups: that is, industries providing goods and services to agriculture (banks, utilities, paper and wood product companies) or industries handling agricultural produce (railroads, trucking companies, shipping companies). Representatives of these corporations often served as directors of local units. On the board of directors of the Kings County unit, for example, were representatives of the First National Bank of Corcoran, the Boston Land Company, and the J. G. Boswell Company, a major cotton-ginning corporation. On the board in Kern County were representatives of the Kern County Land Company, the Bank of America, the Cotton Oil Company, the Farm Implement and Engine Company, the Earl Fruit Company, the First National Bank of Delano, and the San Joaquin Cotton Oil Company.[35] Carey McWilliams, a contemporary observer, described the relationship between the large agricultural landowners and the allied corporate interests as one in which "the large-scale farming interests and the heavy industrial contributors (sometimes the same interests) really run the show," although they are not the ones who "organize mobs to browbeat and coerce agricultural workers." In McWilliams's judgment "the real headquarters of vigilantism in California are to be found on Montgomery Street in San Francisco and not in the green valleys of the state."[36] Similarly, John Steinbeck charged that the Associated Farmers were backed by speculative landowners like Alfred J. Chandler, the publisher of the *Los Angeles Times*, Herbert Hoover, William Randolph Hearst, and the Bank of America.[37]

Some observers at the time interpreted the Associated Farmers as a leading element within an embryonic fascist movement. The documentation of the group's activities lends credibility to this perspective. It successfully campaigned throughout California for antipicketing and "emergency disaster" ordinances. Antipicketing ordinances soon went into effect in every rural county in California and emergency disaster ordinances were enacted in nearly every county and in most cities and towns. These provided for extralegal government machinery with sweeping powers to come into existence whenever a community executive officer declared that an emergency existed. With the exception of a southern California earthquake in 1933, the only emergencies in recent years had been labor agitation and strikes. The Associated Farmers were also active in sponsoring anti-Semitic movies and promoting speakers sympathetic to Nazism throughout California. The group's leaders formed a paramilitary organization called the California Cavaliers, whose expressed purpose was to "stamp out all un-American activities among farm labor." Its chief organizer declared, "We aren't going to stand for any more of these organizers from now on; anyone who peeps about higher wages will wish he hadn't."[38] However it was expressed, opposition to agricultural unionism was the heart of the Associated Farmers' program.

In an interview with a nationwide farm journal in 1937, the group'ǝ
president, Colonel Walter Garrison, argued that the closed shop
would prevent farmers from cooperating in harvesting their crops
and keep college students from being employed and that the hiring
hall would detract from the tradition of treating farm workers like
members of the family.[39] The organization was identified as a major
factor in the smashing of the CAWIU in testimony given before the
La Follette Committee.

The most significant strike of 1935 occurred during August in
Sonoma County, where 2,000 apple-pickers spontaneously struck for
higher wages in the orchards around Santa Rosa and Sebastopol.
They were joined by 2,000 packing-shed workers. Two hundred and
fifty vigilantes raided and disrupted a meeting of pickers and packers, where two Communist party officials were speaking. Three
weeks later these same two officials were tarred and feathered,
beaten, paraded through Santa Rosa, and driven out of the county.
The home of one of the strike organizers was shot up and tear-gassed.
The leaders of the mob were a local banker, the mayor, the local head
of the Federal Re-Employment Bureau, several policemen, a member
of the California legislature, numerous members of the American
Legion, and the president of the local Chamber of Commerce.[40] The
intimidation was so thorough that workers were afraid to come into
the area after the strike was broken, and wages had to be raised just
to attract an adequate harvest labor force. Even wage increases were
not enough: the director of the State Emergency Relief Administration in San Francisco had to take 5,000 men off relief to force them to
supply the needed labor.

San Francisco newspapers reflected a growing polarization of opinion concerning rural vigilantism. Hearst's *San Francisco Examiner*,
always outspoken against farm labor organization and previously
vocally anti-Asian, characteristically glorified the repression, saying
that "the tar and feather party was hailed in Sonoma County as a
direct American answer to the red strike fomentors."[41] The *News* and
the *Chronicle*, on the other hand, called on the California attorney
general to take action against the vigilantes. The *News* called them a
"pack of lawless bullies masquerading as patriots."[42] In response, the
recently elected governor, Frank Merriam, who was hardly more
sympathetic toward farm labor unionization than his predecessor
had been, set up an investigating fund. Twenty-three business and
professional people were arrested on charges of kidnapping and
assault with deadly weapons, but they were quickly acquitted.

Agricultural strikes became more frequent during 1936. Increasingly under the control of the newly formed Federation of Agricultural Workers Union of America (FAWUA) and several AFL affiliates, they began to win limited wage raises. FAWUA was formed through a merger of several independent Mexican, Filipino, and Japanese farm labor unions. It led most of the agricultural strikes of 1936, and although it lacked the radical connections and ideology of CAWIU, its strikes were subjected to a similar degree of repression.

Two of the major strikes in 1936 occurred in the vicinity of Los Angeles. A strike by Mexican and Filipino celery workers in April and May in surrounding communities, including El Monte, Torrance, Norwalk, Bellflower, Palos Verdes, and Dominguez, was met by an armed force of 1,500 "citizens," deputy sheriffs, special guards, and Los Angeles city police, who broke up strikers' parades, meetings, and caravans, fired volleys over the heads of strikers near the fields, and arrested at least a third of those on strike. A number of individual growers wanted to end the conflict by signing agreements with the union but were constrained from doing so by the large grower-shipper interests.[43] Another strike of 2,500 to 3,000 citrus-pickers in Orange County in mid-June was greeted by police and armed guards displaying assorted weapons, ranging from shotguns to submachine guns. Guards were given "shoot to kill" orders by the sheriff. Meetings were broken up by armed men using tear gas. The Associated Farmers organized protection for strikebreakers. Many of the arrested strikers received vagrancy sentences from local judges, timed to run until the approximate end of the harvest season. Even the vice president of the State Federation of Labor and the secretary of the Los Angeles Central Labor Council were arrested while investigating the strike. The celery strike settlement mediated by the U.S. Department of Labor resulted in significant worker gains, while the orange-picker strike was largely defeated.[44]

The violent repression of organizational efforts in agriculture was not restricted to the fields. White lettuce-packers in the Salinas area had organized the Vegetable Packers Union and affiliated with the AFL. The industry-wide contract the union signed with the Grower-Shipper Vegetable Association in 1934 came up for renewal in September 1936. When contract talks stalled, a strike ensued, and the Associated Farmers launched an elaborately planned and executed program for the repression of the strike and the extermination of the union. They hired a reactionary publisher and army reserve officer, Colonel Henry Sanborn, to supervise law enforcement operations in Salinas for the duration of the strike. Although lacking an official position, Colonel Sanborn directed the efforts of the police and sheriffs, organized raids, and ordered arrests. Meanwhile the sheriff called for a general mobilization of all male Salinas residents between the ages of eighteen and forty-five. Twenty-five hundred men were armed, deputized, and used to arrest and intimidate strikers. In addition, Governor Frank Merriam sent in 150 state highway patrolmen, who used tear gas, nausea gas, and clubs against peaceful pickets. This action evoked a threat by the State Federation of Labor to institute recall proceedings against the governor.[45] The report of the National Labor Relations Board concerning the strike stated that "the impression of these events . . . is one of inexcusable police brutality, in many instances bordering on sadism."[46] The strike terminated after six weeks and marked the end of the Vegetable Packers Union.

THE FOUNDING OF UCAPAWA

In the meantime a split had developed within the California State Federation of Labor that had profound implications for agricultural workers. A number of agricultural union locals were given federal charters under AFL jurisdiction and affiliated to nearby central labor councils. Since the disadvantage of having different uncoordinated farm worker unions in each agricultural community was readily apparent, a movement began within the federation to set up a statewide organization that would include cannery and packing shed as well as field workers, organized on an industrial basis rather than along craft lines. This movement was supported by the Maritime Federation of the Pacific, of which the International Longshoremen and Warehousemen's Union (ILWU) was part, and the left wing of the State Federation of Labor. However, a proposal to charter such a union was denied in March 1937 by the Federation's executive committee. More traditional, craft-oriented trade unionists were in control of most of the federation's executive offices and were supported by the Teamsters Union and AFL President William Green. The secretary of the federation, Edward Vandeleur, had long been unenthusiastic about the unionization of agricultural labor. Moreover, a union encompassing the agricultural sector and organized along industrial lines had a potential membership of 250,000, which could be expected to align itself with the left wing of the federation. The executive committee instead held to the craft tradition and decided that processing and field workers should not be in the same union, and, in addition, that the federation should have direct control over any statewide agricultural union.[47]

Repulsed by the Federation's conservativism, supporters of cannery and field worker unionization decided to establish a union

separate from the AFL and affiliate with the newly independent
Committee for Industrial Organizations (CIO). A number of Pacific
Coast maritime unions were then voting to do the same thing, including the Maritime Federation and, with it, the ILWU. The United
Cannery, Agricultural, Packing and Allied Workers of America
(UCAPAWA) was formed in Denver in July 1937 and chartered by
the CIO. The new union was supported by the left wing of the State
Federation of Labor, most of the federally chartered AFL farm labor
unions, the officials of many of the largest Filipino and Mexican farm
worker unions in California, and a number of agricultural unions
based outside California, including the Southern Tenant Farmers
Union. Agricultural unions from Alabama, Florida, New Jersey,
Arizona, Colorado, Michigan, Ohio, Tennessee, and Texas were represented at UCAPAWA's founding convention, reflecting the intended national scope of the new union. As one observer noted, the
convention delegates were "the men who chop cotton, pick fruit, work
in the beet and onion fields . . . oyster shuckers, fish canners."[48]
Blacks, Filipinos, Japanese, Mexicans, and other Latin Americans,
historically slighted by the AFL, were also represented. Among the
matters discussed were a strategy to combat a contemporaneous
campaign to drive a wedge between organized labor and small farm
owners, especially those in the Midwest, and a plan to unite independent small farm owners, tenant farmers, agricultural workers, and
farm cooperatives under a central organization.[49]

   UCAPAWA faced a significantly different context for its unionization drives than any previous union had. In the wake of Depression-
related strikes and protests by industrial workers, the political climate had shifted and produced a federal endorsement of the right of
labor to organize. Before, workers' right to organize had fallen outside the law, and employers had utilized numerous legal and illegal
strategies and devices to fight unionization. Section 7a of the 1933
National Industrial Recovery Act began to undermine employers'
options. Then in July 1935, two years before the founding of
UCAPAWA, the National Labor Relations Act was passed by Congress. The NLRA (or Wagner Act, after its sponsor Democratic Senator Robert F. Wagner of New York) effectively neutralized employer
opposition. The NLRA guarantees employees the right to join labor
organizations and unions and engage in collective bargaining with
employers through their representatives. It also restrains employers
from interfering with unionization efforts, showing favoritism toward one union over another, forming company unions, and discrimi-

nating against union members. The law is administered through the National Labor Relations Board, which conducts elections among employees to determine union preference, if any, and investigates violations of the law on the part of both employers and unions.

The NLRA and other government activity which promoted union recognition by employers was simultaneously cooptive and liberating for the workers. Government intervention created new possibilities for confining capital/labor conflicts within boundaries which did not threaten private control over the economy and capitalism's basic market and profit mechanisms. As Senator Wagner put it, "A free and self-disciplined labor movement . . . is essential to [the] democratic purpose of maintaining our system of free enterprise."[50] Also, in time, the law provided avenues for dampening rank and file militancy and restricting the political power of the newly created unions.

At the time, though, the NLRA was overwhelmingly pro-labor, and government sharply curtailed its repressive response toward strikes. This dramatic shift in state policy further stimulated worker insurgency and led to the establishment of most of the large industrial unions.

Agricultural workers, however, were specifically excluded from coverage under the NLRA. The importance of this exclusion would only be understood later, since it provided the context within which the continued efforts toward unionization of agricultural labor have occurred from the late Depression years to the present. In lieu of coverage under comparable labor legislation, farm workers could only use their power of insurgency to gain concessions and union recognition.

During the 1930s, the political climate supportive of unionization added to labor's strength to gain union recognition and contracts through collective defiance. In fact, in the industrial sector the initial contract breakthroughs at General Motors and U.S. Steel early in 1937 occurred outside the procedures specified by the NLRA. For several years after its passage, the Wagner Act's legitimation of labor's right to organize was perhaps more important for its stimulation of heightened worker militancy resulting in union contracts than for its provisions for government-supervised union recognition elections.[51]

Founders of UCAPAWA put their hopes in the possibility of agricultural workers being able to take advantage of these circumstances. The emergence of the CIO in agricultural labor unionization created the potential for an organizationally stable, national union allied to the industrial unionization movement and benefiting from that movement's resources. Coupled with the growth of nationwide farm labor support groups, the establishment of UCAPAWA helped stimulate a shift in the response of the California and federal governments to the agricultural labor problem.

CHAPTER 6

STATE INTERVENTION AND THE MIGRANCY PROBLEM

Two events shaped the context of unionization attempts and state efforts to mediate capital-labor relations in the agricultural sector in the late 1930s: the Dust Bowl migration and the Farm Security Administration's migratory camp program. As a result of the migration, the majority of field workers in the late 1930s were white; through the camp program, the federal government attempted to stabilize and settle a portion of the migratory agricultural population. It was widely thought at the time that both conditions would be favorable to unionization. Racial divisions within the labor supply appeared to be less critical, as grower organizations and their allies could no longer employ racism to justify their opposition to unionization, and the camps provided a measure of stability that could be used as an organizational resource by UCAPAWA leaders.

The influx of migrants from the Dust Bowl region was the culmination of an accelerated nationwide decline of the class of small farmers and expansion of the rural wage-worker class. This time the growers themselves had less to do with stimulating the transition in the agricultural labor supply than had been true in the past. The effects of the Dust Bowl migration, however, still operated to their advantage.

THE RURAL LABOR SURPLUS

Throughout the United States the Depression years meant a slowing of the half-century trend to movement away from rural areas to cities. Migration from rural to urban areas during the thirties measured only about half the net flow of the twenties.[1] Cities were no longer able to absorb surplus labor from the countryside, which had depended upon urban jobs to draw away part of each generation as it faced shrinking opportunities on the land. During the thirties younger members of rural families stayed with the farms, especially in the areas with the dimmest agricultural prospects. Thus, the poorest areas became "shock absorbers for depression."[2] Agricultural towns grew for the first half of the decade as farmland bordering cities drew urban people into subsistence homesteading. It was estimated at the time that over 3.5 million more people were living on farms than would have been there if the Depression had not occurred and if the demographic patterns of the twenties had prevailed.[3]

The rural labor surplus appeared at a time when agriculture, already staggered by the long decline of the twenties, was sinking further under the force of renewed depression. Countries experiencing the Depression tended to cease imports of farm products. The drastic contraction of export demand created huge surpluses of such commodities as wheat, cotton, and rice. The prices of all farm products reflected a disparity in exchange value for industrial goods. By February 1933 farm products could be exchanged for only half as much in industrial goods as had been possible before World War I. Gross agricultural income in 1932 was less than half that of 1929, although fixed charges, including interest and taxes, did not become proportionately lower. Capital used in agriculture had in January 1933 a value of only $38 billion, compared with $58 billion in 1929 and $79 billion in 1919, but farm debt remained practically unchanged. Credit was restricted as thousands of country banks closed.[4]

Market deterioration meant that the burdens of taxes and mortgage debts rapidly became oppressive. Involuntary sales of farm property due to bank debts or tax delinquency rose. It has been estimated that there were nearly 1.75 million farm business failures among mortgaged owners between 1930 and 1940. Forced transfers of farm real estate took place through tax sales, foreclosures, bankruptcies, loss of title by default of contract, sales to third parties to avoid foreclosure, and surrender of title to the creditor, and other transfers to avoid foreclosure. Data are not available for failures of tenant farmers, but the Bureau of Agricultural Economics estimated that tenants and mortgaged owners together accounted for over 2 million failures in the thirties.[5]

The number of people who owned land declined among those who cultivated and harvested crops for a living. The Depression, which began in agriculture in the twenties, accelerated a half-century trend in loss of farm ownership. From 1880 to 1940, for every census division and for the United States as a whole, there was a fall in the number of owners for each thousand males employed in agriculture. In 1880 there were 547 owners per thousand. Rapid rises in the price of farm land for the next thirty years put farm purchases out of reach for wage workers. The number of owners fell to 451 per thousand by 1920, and to 414 by 1940.[6] In the same period the number of tenants and landless laborers increased. When first counted in the census of 1880, tenants were found to operate 25.6 percent of the farms. By 1925, the census reported, 38.6 percent of American farms were operated by tenants, and in 1930 more than half the farm land and 42.4 percent of farms were operated by tenants. Thereafter, partly as a result of agricultural stabilization measures by the federal government, the number of tenants and sharecroppers began to decline and landless wage labor increased.[7]

As the tillers of the land lost their control of it, their situation proved to be one of bitter insecurity. Tenants had less stability of residence than owners; sharecroppers had less stability than tenants. A report of the Bureau of the Census in 1920 noted that 44.8 percent of white tenants had been on their farms less than two years. Only one in four had been on the same farm five years or more. A study by the Bureau of Agricultural Economics reported widespread instability and insecurity among tenant farmers. In a survey of tenants who had lived less than two years on the farms they were occupying on 1 January 1935, it was found that migrant tenants amounted to 40 to 60 percent of tenant farmers in more than half the counties in America.[8]

The cost to tenant families in terms of the disruption of their lives and social relationships was all the more severe since their migrations frequently took place in destitution. The persistent turnover of farm population was wasteful of productive resources as well as labor, according to the report of the Tolan Commission:

> The farmer who is continually on the move cannot systematically care for fruit trees, shrubbery, and other long-lived vegetation. If he expects to move again soon, he does not find it to his advantage . . . to turn under cover crops to conserve and build up the soil. It is difficult for the mobile farmer to provide and care for livestock. Further it seems that mobility begets more mobility. Because of his apparent instability it becomes increasingly difficult for a mobile farmer to obtain credit facilities to carry out his business operations. Social relations are also continually disrupted as farm families move from community to community.[9]

FARM LABOR MIGRANCY

Even without the Depression there would have been a surplus of field laborers for the existing jobs. Because of the economic crisis, displaced owners, tenants, and even urban unemployed surged into the harvest labor market. In January 1933 the oversupply of farm workers reached a peak. For the United States as a whole, the supply stood at 263 laborers for every 100 jobs. On the basis of census figures, the number of workers required for seasonal agricultural labor has been estimated at between 1 and 2 million for the entire country. A conservative estimate of the number of family dependents and farm laborers themselves was about 6.6 million.[10]

Technological change in agriculture aggravated the insecurity and joblessness of rural workers. There was an increase of over 40 percent in the U.S. population from 1909 to 1939, and there might have been a proportionate increase in agricultural employment if it had not been for technological improvements. Had labor requirements risen in proportion to the population, the number of farm workers needed in 1939 would have been 6.5 million more than were actually employed. The most rapid technological advance in American agriculture took place beginning in the early thirties, displacing thousands of rural workers at a time when cities were incapable of providing employment for their own millions.[11] Mechanization, an important aspect of the new technology, brought the purchase of mechanical cultivators, harvesters, tractors, trucks, and cars into the calculation of the capital required for the production of food. Policies adopted by the New Deal recovery program encouraged the rapid adoption of energy-intensive farming methods. As will be shown later, the way improvements were introduced favored agribusiness, the creation of factory farms, destroyed the jobs of farm workers and tenants, increased poverty and insecurity, and uprooted thousands of families, turning them into migrants.

One migratory worker, a child when his family lost its small farm in Arizona, memorably described why his family had to "follow the crops" in California. Cesar Chavez recalled:

My dad was being turned out of his small plot of land. He had inherited this from his father, who had homesteaded it. I saw my two, three other uncles also moving out. And for the same reason. The bank had foreclosed on the loan.

If the local bank approved, the Government would guarantee the loan and small farmers like my father would continue in business. It so happened the president of the bank was the guy who most wanted

our land. We were surrounded by him: he owned all the land around
us. Of course, he wouldn't pass the loan.

One morning a giant tractor came in, like we had never seen before.
My daddy used to do all his work with horses. So this huge tractor
came in and began to knock down this corral, this small corral where
my father kept his horses. We didn't understand why. In the matter of
a week, the whole face of the land was changed.[12]

Of all the reasons for the migrancy of destitute rural people during
the Depression, perhaps the most famous were the droughts and dust
storms of the mid-thirties. Undoubtedly these accelerated the uproot-
ing of families from the Great Plains: one migration survey of California revealed that about a quarter of the agricultural families
enumerated were from Oklahoma alone, and more than half were
from Missouri, Arkansas, Oklahoma, and Texas.[13] Nevertheless,
wind erosion of the soil succeeded in prying families away from their
homes mainly because it interacted with political and economic circumstances: Depression-related foreclosures and the loss of foreign
markets, rapid innovations in energy-intensive or power farming,
and the concentration of land holdings. As Paul Taylor described the
situation in 1938:

it is not only the parching of the plains and the blowing of the topsoil
which expels these people. If that were all, the return of rain to the
Dust Bowl would end the exodus. But the causes are more deep-seated
and more enduring than the hostile fluctuations of weather. At the
close of the war, prices of cotton and of wheat collapsed, and with
them, many thousands of rural families were shaken from their positions on the agricultural ladder. Farm owners lost the equities in their
farms and became tenants; tenants were reduced to laborers, and farm
laborers did what they could. This process, begun in the depression of
the early twenties, was accelerated by the depression of the early thirties. Then came drought and grasshoppers, and whole sections of the
rural population already loosened by the accumulating forces of successive depressions were finally dislodged by a catastrophe of Nature.
Those not anchored by the farm program and the relief policies of the
Government are seeking refuge by flight.[14]

Although the migrations of the twenties were in fact greater in
volume than those of the thirties, what gave Depression migrations
their desperate character were the years of general dislocation,
poverty, and misery that were their context. After migration many
displaced farmers fell into the ranks of agricultural laborers. Given

the vast oversupply of workers for jobs at the lowest ranks in the rural market, farm laborers arriving in the West frequently met low wages, irregular employment, and the need to migrate from job to job to piece together a living. The conditions behind the "disorganization" of farm labor markets insured that the mobility of farm workers would be exploitative and excessive. Migrancy was waste. While the large seasonal demand for labor by large-scale growers guaranteed that all laborers would get some work some of the time, the oversupply lowered wages to the point that families could barely afford the trip to the next job site. The work of small children was required for survival. The incidence of disease and the lack of medical care testified to the wretched social conditions surrounding the job of harvesting food for large-scale growers.

For their part, growers preferred to hire out-of-state labor brought in by a labor contractor because it gave "a greater degree of control of the labor situation to the employer."[15] Methods used by labor contractors to recruit workers often actually had the effect of lowering wage rates and intensifying the disorganization of the labor market. The contract system invited irresponsibility on the part of the labor brokers, who were often migratory themselves and whose real identities were often unknown to employers. They frequently colluded with the growers: they were as effective as employers in enforcing blacklisting to prevent the organization of workers, and their monopoly over employment functioned like its illegal counterpart in industry, the company union.[16] A report by the President's Commission on Migratory Labor described the abuses of the labor contractor system:

> To the extent that a crew leader or labor contractor recruits labor, he is an employment agent. In this activity are to be found the well-known malpractices of private employment agencies, such as misrepresentation of work opportunities, the charging of excessive fees, and sending workers to places where there are no jobs.[17]

FEDERAL PROGRAMS AND CORPORATE AGRICULTURE

Federal government intervention to relieve the distress of rural families saved many workers from starvation, but it also enriched the largest agribusiness enterprises, reinforced trends toward the concentration of land ownership, and promoted energy-intensive farming. Federal programs ultimately helped to dislodge tenant farmers from their last shred of control over agricultural production. At the time, criticism of federal policy focused specifically on the effects of the Agricultural Adjustment Program. Under the Agricultural Adjustment Act, or "Triple A," the program aimed at soil conservation and improvement in the market price for farm products through restricted production of certain commodities and benefit payments to growers based on their limitation of acreage planted and harvested. Critics charged that the program encouraged large growers and corporations to acquire even more acreage. Absentee owners given incentives to operate large units with a maximum of energy-intensive technology and a minimum of labor displaced thousands of tenants and sharecroppers at a time when the cities were incapable of absorbing them.[18] Defenders of the Triple A pointed out that the program merely stimulated already existing trends toward the enlargement and consolidation of farm land, and in the meantime it raised the level of farm prices and farm income, prevented some foreclosures, and saved some farm operators from ruin.[19]

The criticism, however, was well founded. It was certainly true in the South that tenants were displaced so that landlords could gain the share of the Triple A payments that would otherwise have gone to the tenants. The provisions of the law designed to safeguard tenant interests offered ample loopholes for a landowner willing to profit at the expense of a tenant. It was undeniable that most of the benefits of the program went to growers with a stake in commercial farming. Cash payments to limit acreage and higher prices for farm products on the market did little for the farmer with small acreage and a minimal commercial production.[20] Annual reports of the Triple A showed that participation in programs was higher among large agricultural units than small ones. In certain southern states one-third of the total benefit payments under the 1938 program went to 5 percent of the persons receiving payments.[21] In California in the same year, 43.6 percent of the total benefit payments went to 2 percent of the farms and individuals.[22]

There were contradictions among the agrarian policies pursued by government agencies during the Depression. One set of agencies—represented by the Farm Security Administration, the Resettlement Administration, and economists in the Department of Agriculture—worked toward promoting subsistence farming, diversity, rural cooperatives, and resident ownership. Another set of program administrations—including departments of the Triple A and the Farm Credit Administration, the Soil Conservation Service, and the Federal Surplus Commodities Corporation—acted to benefit large commercial growers, accelerate mechanization, and support the production of food for profit. Only one-tenth of the appropriations made to programs of the U.S. Department of Agriculture in the later Depression years reached the Farm Security Administration, the politically embattled agency specifically concerned with the problems of destitute farmers, Southern sharecroppers and tenants, and farm workers.[23] While large-scale commercial production received incentives under the Triple A program, no minimum standards were set to protect hired labor. Income for agricultural production was increased, while the number of jobs was reduced and competition for agricultural employment drove wages to the lowest levels. Agricultural capital's share of farm income was increased; agricultural labor's was reduced.[24]

A variety of measures demonstrate the trend toward concentration in agricultural capital. In the period from 1910 to 1934, there was an increase of 62 percent in the number of large-scale farms of 1,000 acres and over. The proportion of land in large-scale farms showed an even more striking change. The percentage of land in farms of 500 acres or more in 1910 was 28.5 percent; by 1935 it was 40.2 percent. By 1935 fewer than 3 percent of all the farms in the United States hired more than 40 percent of all the agricultural workers.[25] In California the movement to large-scale farming was well advanced by the thirties. The census of 1930 showed that California contained over 50 percent of the large-scale farms in the United States in poultry, truck crops, and fruit production.[26] If the 1923 index of output is set at 100, the index of output per worker had risen to 125 by 1936. During the same years the index of farm wages per day (without board) fell from 103 to 73.[27] The share of the consumer's dollar reaching the agricultural wage laborer also declined. Wages were made to adjust to the Depression: in some important growing areas wage levels that were at 35 to 50 cents an hour in 1929 had declined to 15 or 16 cents by the spring of 1933. An index of farm wages treating the average 1930 wage as 100 showed a fall to 53 by 1933.[28]

Large-scale growers were in a qualitatively better position than small farmers to survive an economic collapse. The large grower or corporation undoubtedly had better credit and capital connections with banks and other lending institutions. Although dependent on wage labor for harvest operations, large producers, in cooperation with other growers and related agribusiness corporations, were in a position to set wages for a labor market kept in disorganization by the labor contractor system. While the wage bill could represent a source of weakness for large-scale operations, it has traditionally been treated as a "controllable" cost because of the superior economic strength, political power, and social position of agribusiness compared to the destitute, migrant, underemployed masses of wage laborers seeking temporary employment in the fields. In contrast, agricultural employers have long been in the habit of regarding other costs as rigid and unalterable: transportation to markets up to 3,000 miles away, rent, power, water, fertilizer, machinery, and like charges. Paul S. Taylor described this view to the La Follette Commission, which investigated violations of free speech and the rights of labor in the late thirties:

> This acceptance of the view that these [nonwage] costs are what agricultural employers call "uncontrollable elements" may occur sometimes because the employers are allied with or controlled by one or another of the economic interests which fix these costs. Whether for this reason or not, evidently it seems easier for large agricultural employers to organize to control wages than to organize to revise other costs to meet fluctuating economic conditions.[29]

One can only speculate about what dissension would be created within grower associations if they had to consider organizing against, say, power rates or interest charges while including within their ranks board members of the institutions that set these costs. No such discussions need take place so long as wages can be made to react to changes in the growers' economic circumstances.

The prevailing patterns of California agriculture had appeared elsewhere in the nation in the thirties and earlier. In Arizona 7.6 percent of the truck farms spent 45 percent of all the cash used to employ truck farm labor. In small valleys in New Mexico, Utah, and Arizona, the Yakima valley of Washington, the Snake River Valley of Idaho, and the Willamette and Hood River valleys of Oregon, intensive crops depended on migratory families during the harvest season. Migratory labor was used in the Lower Rio Grande Valley and Winter Garden districts of South Texas. New Jersey truck farms, Florida citrus groves, and the onion fields of Hardin County, Ohio, conformed to the same pattern: concentrated land ownership and the use of migratory labor.[30] For the United States as a whole, the index of agricultural wages based on 100 for 1927 fell to 46 in 1933 and rose only to 65 in 1939.[31]

THE DUST BOWL MIGRATION

Displaced and destitute families fleeing the drought arrived in California from the Plains during the mid-thirties. Over half a million people left the south central states of Oklahoma, Arkansas, Texas, and Missouri during the Depression years, and over 300,000 of them came to California.[32] Compared with adjacent decades, migration to California during the 1930s was comparatively small. Slightly over a million people arrived, resulting in a migration-induced rise of 18 percent in the population of the state. This is to be compared with a total migration of 1.9 million during the previous decade (causing a 33 percent rise in the population), and 2.7 million during the following one (for a 40 percent rise).[33] The difference, of course, was that California could better absorb its growth in the other decades. Moreover, Depression-era migrants concentrated in rural areas, resulting in a dramatic growth of the population of rural counties. Between 1935 and 1940 the rural counties of Kern, Yuba, Madera, Tulare, and San Joaquin experienced population increases of 64, 50, 36, 38, and 30 percent respectively. The urban counties of Los Angeles, Alameda, and San Francisco, on the other hand, registered respective population increases of 26, 8, and 1 percent.[34]

California growers and grower organizations contributed to the flow of Dust Bowl refugees into California. Advertisements were placed in newspapers in the Midwest offering agricultural work in California at attractive wages. John Steinbeck, like many other observers, interpreted the Dust Bowl recruitment as an effort to sustain an already oversupplied field labor market so that wages could be kept low and unionization discouraged.[35] Even without grower encouragement, however, the majority of Dust Bowl migrants would most likely have ended up in California anyway.

The massive Dust Bowl Migration to rural California marked still another transition in the agricultural labor supply, although this transition had begun even before most of the migrants reached California. White workers were rapidly replacing Mexican workers in the fields. Due to industrial unemployment and Mexican repatriation, nonwhites represented only 50 percent of the labor camp population as early as the end of 1934, according to estimates of the California Commission on Immigration and Housing.[36] The peak of migration from the Dust Bowl to Arizona and California occurred during the years 1935–37. By 1937 it was apparent that the majority of migratory workers were white.

The Dust Bowl migrants undercut and replaced the more militant and organized Mexican and, to a lesser extent, Filipino workers, but grower representatives expressed ambivalence over the possible long-term effects of using white American workers to supply the bulk of agricultural labor. Since the new migrants were unorganized, most growers preferred them to Mexicans and Filipinos who had already demonstrated their militancy.[37] However, organizations like the Associated Farmers reasoned that "American" workers would be less amenable than foreign-born ones to the prevailing low wages and poor working and living conditions. Dr. George Clements of the Los Angeles Chamber of Commerce, a long-time supporter of the growers, expressed their reservations in 1936:

> This year 90 percent of the labor consisted of migratory labor from the south, mid-south, and south-east. This labor, mostly white, is supposed to supplant the former Mexican laborers. . . . Can we expect these new white transient citizens to fill their place? The white transients are not tractable labor. Being so-called American citizens, they are going to demand the so-called American standard of living. In our own estimation they are going to be the finest pabulum for unionization for either group—the AFL or the subversive elements. They are not going to be satisfied with 160 working days.[38]

John Steinbeck, writing from a different perspective, described the white refugees in a similar way:

> One has only to go into the squatter's camps where the families live on the ground and have no homes, no beds, and no equipment; and one has only to look at the strong purposeful faces often filled with pain and more often, when they see the corporation-held idle lands, filled with anger, to know that this new race is here to stay and that heed must be taken of it.
> It should be understood that with this race the old methods of repression, of starvation wages, of jailing, beating and intimidation are not going to work; these are American people.[39]

Despite these expectations, the initial effect of the Dust Bowl migration was to undermine the potential for change in agricultural employment.[40] At the start of the influx there were several trends signaling improvement for workers. In mid-1933 there were an estimated 186 workers for every 100 jobs in agriculture, but CAWIU still achieved its most notable gains that year. By 1934 there were 142 workers per 100 jobs. It was also reported that a substantial proportion of workers were choosing to stay on relief rather than work at the wages being offered. Even the state Chamber of Commerce admitted to the probability of a substantial wage gain for agricultural workers.

While California's agriculture suffered severely during the initial stages of the Depression and later recovered, the pattern was different for the agricultural work force. The Dust Bowl influx created an oversupply of labor that kept agricultural wages low. Using the average agricultural income for growers in the years 1924–29 as a base index of 100, the index for 1932 was 60. This rose to 112 for 1933 and, despite the effects of the 1937 recession, was 94 for 1939. Using the same base index for agricultural wages, the index was 65 for 1937 and declined to 59 for 1939.[41]

What this meant for migratory workers was destitution. Temporary camps known as ditchbank settlements were commonplace along river banks in the California agricultural valleys. Other rural housing for migrants, such as that in the "Little Oklahomas" that arose on the outskirts of agricultural communities, was poor at best and degrading at worst. Health care, especially that for the children, was substandard. Malnutrition became a problem. Educational programs for children and sanitation facilities were extremely inadequate. Gradually public attention focused on these conditions. At the height of the controversy over Steinbeck's *Grapes of Wrath*, Eleanor Roosevelt toured the state for five days, visiting the ditchbank settlements and talking with migrants. She reported to Congress that Steinbeck had not exaggerated the living conditions of the migrants.[42] Her statement helped stimulate the creation of the House Committee on the Interstate Migration of Destitute Citizens, headed by Representative John Tolan of California. A series of floods in 1938 that washed out many of the ditchbank settlements also propelled the displaced into newspaper headlines and attracted public sympathy.

Despite the increase in public concern, agricultural workers had virtually no protection under such New Deal legislation as the National Labor Relations Act, the Wages and Hours Bill (which set minimum wages and maximum work hours), and the Social Security Act.[43] Their exclusion from such legislation stemmed from Roosevelt's fear that the powerful agricultural bloc in Congress, headed by Southern senators, would prevent the passage of the NLRA and the Social Security Act altogether unless agricultural workers were exempted from their provisions.

THE FSA CAMP PROGRAM

Until late in the Depression the federal government did little to alleviate the specific problems of migratory agricultural workers in California. This would have to wait until the La Follette Committee came to California in 1939. From 1933 to 1938 federal policies and agencies were directed primarily at national conditions and offered help to the migrants only within this context. The most important programs for migratory workers were the Federal Transient Service and the Resettlement Administration, which later became the Farm Security Administration (FSA).

The Federal Transient Service, established in May 1933, was primarily concerned with helping interstate migrants and focused its efforts on unattached men traveling between states. It had little to offer migratory agricultural workers, since migrants traveling within a state did not qualify for most forms of aid. The service also made a rigid distinction between transients and seasonal agricultural workers; some families received aid only as long as they were interstate migrants. The program was terminated in September 1935, having provided limited aid to the first group of Dust Bowl refugees.[44]

During the same years the Federal Emergency Relief Administration provided unemployment relief. The guidelines of its director, Henry Hopkins, established that relief was to be granted solely on the basis of need, thus allowing the allocation of relief funds to workers on strike. This policy made possible the length and success of the 1933 cotton strike. Naturally it was bitterly opposed by the agricultural landowners and the Merriam administration in California. By December 1935 this federal program had been abolished, and responsibility for relief was transferred to the individual states. California established the State Emergency Relief Administration, and Governor Merriam appointed Harold Pomeroy as its director. When Culbert Olson became governor in January 1939, Pomeroy resigned to become executive secretary of the Associated Farmers.[45] As one might expect, Pomeroy instituted much more stringent requirements for relief eligibility than the federal program had.

The most significant and lasting program undertaken by the federal government during this period was the construction of migratory labor camps, initiated by the Resettlement Administration and later transferred to the Farm Security Administration. The camps provided more than just shelter for their residents. They were a resource for union activists because they were outside the control of employers and under the protection of the federal government. The camps were structured as democratic communities and provided health care for their residents. Restraints on the activities of members were minimal. Many analysts looked to the camps as models for a new kind of rural community, which would supply a base for the stabilization and rationalization of the agricultural labor force, including its possible unionization.

The program was created in late 1935 by the Resettlement Administration under the direction of Rexford Tugwell, a member of

Roosevelt's Brain Trust. The idea of migratory labor camps was promoted by the director of Rural Rehabilitation in California, Henry Drobisch, who had observed that one of the primary demands in most of the strikes in 1933 and 1934 was for decent housing. He planned to construct camp housing in California for all of the state's 150,000 to 200,000 migrant workers and spent much of 1935 in Washington lobbying for this project. Shortly after its birth the Resettlement Administration was faced with deciding whether to give priority to a plan similar to that of Drobisch or to relocate Dust Bowl refugees in cooperative community and farming projects. Although several large-scale cooperative farms had been established—more in Arizona than in California—the camp proposal received more attention and won out for pragmatic reasons. The unplanned migration already occurring was relocating people in far greater numbers than any coordinated government effort could. Cooperative farms would take much longer to realize on a large scale and would provoke considerably more opposition from Congress and state governments. The RA-FSA had already aroused severe Congressional criticism because of what was perceived as its collectivist approach. Something had to be accomplished in a short time, and the migratory camp program was more conducive to immediate visible results than collective farm experiments. Although Tugwell ideologically favored the collective farms, he approved plans for the extension of the labor camp program, possibly motivated by his visit to the existing California facilities in October 1935.[46] Although it was perceived as the moderate option at the time, the migratory camp program would have had greater historical significance if it had resulted in the unionization of the agricultural labor force.

By 1940 fifty-six camps, including sixteen mobile camps, were in operation. Eighteen of these were in California, providing for 20,000 to 30,000 migrants. The camps were situated in places where substantial numbers of agricultural workers were employed. Several were in strategic locations along migratory routes. The Arvin camp, for example, was near the southern entrance to the San Joaquin Valley; the Brawley camp was located in the Imperial Valley.[47]

The camp constitution created a legislative council, whose members were to be democratically elected. The council chose the officers of the community court. On paper it was an admirable experiment in democracy, designed to expose the Dust Bowl refugees to managed, cooperative self-government. Unfortunately the setup was at odds with the previous experience of the refugees. As has often been noted, their culture emphasized personal independence, a "beholden to no one" attitude, far removed from the procedural concerns of collective efforts and organizations. Their "rugged individualism" worked against the success of the camp government as well as the unionization efforts of UCAPAWA.[48]

Differences between camp managers and inhabitants generated misunderstandings and frustrations. The FSA decided against hiring social workers and instead selected "sympathetic but vigorous young people with no history of case work technique."[49] Many were graduate students from the University of California. Some were socialists; most were liberals. Nearly all were dedicated to making the experiment in cooperative democracy work, but few could overcome the distance between their orientation and values and the migrants'.

Despite its problems, the camp program had important possibilities. Carey McWilliams, who became the head of the state Division of Immigration and Housing under Culbert Olson, interpreted them as follows:

> The solution of the farm-labor problem can only be achieved through the organization of farm workers. The chief significance of the migratory camps is that they provide an agency through which organization can be achieved. Quite apart from this consideration, however, they are social agencies of great practical importance and they demonstrate that the stabilization of migratory labor can be accomplished. . . . California agriculture would lend itself admirably to collective control and operation, and the long-range significance of the migratory camps consists in the fact that they represent an initial step toward a collective agricultural economy.[50]

This foreshadowing of collective control of the agricultural economy was not lost on agricultural landowners. Although the camps actually saved them money by supplying inexpensive housing for their workers, they forced growers to relinquish some of their control over the work force.[51] Only a few growers opposed the camps because they thought migratory workers were undeserving; in fact, for several years before the program began, grower organizations had publicized the need for better housing.[52] They objected to them because labor organizers in camps did not face all the external barriers to recruiting that their counterparts in private camps, ditchbank settlements, and rural shacktowns did. FSA camp inhabitants were permitted—in fact, usually encouraged—to engage in union activities. Many UCAPAWA local chapters held their meetings on camp grounds. In several instances, UCAPAWA had its strike headquarters in the camps. Moreover, since workers were not living in grower-supplied housing, they could no longer be evicted for striking or becoming union members. In short, the camps became a resource for UCAPAWA.

When the Resettlement Administration first announced the camp program, a group of California growers held a conference to formulate their position. They proposed that the camps be limited to 300 persons each, be located on private property, have meager facilities to emphasize their transient nature, be under the control of a local committee of growers, and be strictly regulated to prevent the spread of "subversive ideas."[53] When these conditions were not met, agricultural landowners and their organizations first opposed the establishment of the camps and later continually sought their removal. Some camps were even boycotted by growers.[54] The camps, however, continued to provide shelter for migrants until World War II reduced the agricultural labor surplus and made them obsolete.

Ironically, it was Mexican and Filipino farm workers who had largely stimulated government aid through their participation in strikes earlier in the decade, but by the time the federal government responded, the majority of field workers were white. Recipients of benefits were mostly white migrants, while nonwhite migrants existing under similar circumstances tended to be left unaided.

CHAPTER 7

STATE INTERVENTION AND THE REVIVAL OF UNIONISM

During the later Depression years, government policy made a definite and significant shift in the direction of support for agricultural labor. Both the federal government and the state of California took actions that in effect supported unionization efforts, undermined antiunion tactics and organizations of agribusiness, and publicized labor conditions and the need for reforms. These attempts represented a reversal of the previous pattern of government intervention; they were exceptions to the prevailing relationship between political elites and dominant agricultural landowners. As long as the alliance between public and private power with respect to agriculture was intact, few, if any, permanent changes in capital-labor relations could be achieved by farm workers. What was necessary was a crisis profound enough to unravel some of the ties between government agencies and officials and the dominant growers and their organizations.

Although the societal crisis posed by the Depression created a general context for reform, specific circumstances in the California fields precipitated the government actions on behalf of farm labor. The first of these was a decade of farm labor unrest affecting diverse crops and distributed over a substantial number of California's agricultural regions. This prolonged labor militancy was accompanied by continuous unionization efforts, some statewide and others more localized. Attempts to deter the momentum toward agricultural unionization had failed; direct repression did no more than temporarily enforce worker compliance. As a result, agricultural production was unstable, constantly facing disruption or the threat of disruption, with no relief in sight.

Farm worker insurgency created the agricultural crisis that was a prerequisite to state mediation. However, a wedge had to be driven between state managers and agribusiness before government efforts could take place over the unified opposition of the large growers and against their immediate economic interests. Agricultural labor accomplished this separation of interests by mobilizing its external resources, which in turn put pressure on government to accommodate labor's demands. UCAPAWA had, theoretically at least, the resources of the CIO behind it and alliances with the broader industrial labor movement. Private citizens' organizations began to publicize the conditions in the fields to a wider audience and lobby for government reforms. Finally, the explicitly reform-oriented administration that came to power in Sacramento in the late thirties was more independent from grower interests than its predecessors had been.

Under these circumstances, elements of the state attempted to overcome the crisis in agriculture by providing certain concessions to labor. The most promising of these was the government's tacit support for unionization efforts. For a time the climate of opinion supported government action to reform agricultural labor conditions and the extension to agricultural labor of the NLRA provisions. There was no preconceived plan or design for state mediation; a series of rather uncoordinated government efforts evolved, a searching and experimenting to find effective policies and actions.

THE OLSON ADMINISTRATION

The election of the Democratic candidate, Culbert Olson, as governor in November 1938 proved to be the immediate pivotal event that shifted the stance of the California government in capital-labor relations. The previous administration, led by Frank Merriam, a Republican, was characterized by an almost single-minded attention to the interests of growers and indifference at best to those of seasonal farm workers. Olson's election culminated the New Deal electoral realignment in California begun during the previous gubernatorial campaign. Before 1934 Democratic Party officials in California had little sympathy with New Deal politics. The shift toward advocacy of New Deal policies was largely stimulated by the EPIC campaign ("End Poverty in California") associated with the writer Upton Sinclair. Sinclair, a long-time Socialist, decided in September 1933 to seek the Democratic nomination for governor and so changed his party registration to Democratic. His campaigns for the Democratic nomination, which he won handily, and later for the governorship advanced the themes of the EPIC campaign.

Sinclair's program was intended to go beyond New Deal policies. It called for a cooperative "production for use" system, in which the state would buy or lease agricultural lands to be cultivated by the unemployed. Factories were to be constructed for the manufacturing of clothes and furniture and the processing of foods. The workers, drawn from the unemployment rolls, were to have access to the items they manufactured and receive scrip money, expendable for goods produced within the production-for-use system.[1] While representing a variation on the work relief programs, it went beyond them to the extent that it proposed, in essence, to set up an alternative productive apparatus with the potential to compete with private enterprise. The program aroused a great deal of enthusiasm. EPIC clubs sprang up throughout the state, although they were heavily concentrated in southern California. By the fall of 1934, their number had increased to 2,000 from 300 the previous January. Carey McWilliams described the EPIC campaign as "without a doubt the first example of a truly grass-roots campaign in the state's political history; a movement formed outside the Democratic Party with the objective of taking it over."[2]

The 1934 gubernatorial campaign was the most bitter in the state's history. It took place in an already polarized atmosphere, stimulated in part by the resurgence of both urban and rural labor movements. It was the year after the most intense series of strikes in the history of U.S. agriculture, most led by the CAWIU, and the year of the waterfront strikes, the repression of worker organizations especially in port areas, the roundup of CAWIU leaders, and the rise of the Associated Farmers. Sinclair's candidacy met with solid newspaper opposition. Even the Roosevelt administration failed to endorse him.[3] He was defeated by the incumbent, Frank Merriam. Sinclair received approximately 38 percent of the votes cast, compared with 49 percent for Merriam and 13 percent for Raymond Haight, the nominee of the Commonwealth and Progressive parties, who campaigned as a "middle of the roader" and largely drew votes away from Sinclair.[4] Sinclair returned to private life, but a number of EPIC-supported candidates were successful in the 1934 election. Twenty-four EPIC-endorsed candidates won seats in the State Assembly and three in the State Senate. Culbert Olson, for example, a staunch supporter of Sinclair's candidacy, was elected the state senator from Los Angeles. The 1934 election marked the emergence of a New Deal Democratic Party with a formidable left-liberal wing.[5]

Olson soon emerged as the leader of the EPIC-liberal bloc in the California legislature. Somewhat more moderate than Sinclair, he was soon recognized as the candidate with the most potential for uniting the various factions of the party, and in August 1938 he easily won the Democratic gubernatorial primary. Ellis Patterson, the party's nominee for lieutenant governor, and Sheridan Downey, the nominee for U.S. senator, also represented the left wing of the party. Downey had been Sinclair's running mate in 1934 and won the nomination in 1938 by badly defeating the Roosevelt-endorsed incumbent, William Gills McAdoo, who represented the moderate wing of the party.[6] At its 1938 national convention, the Communist party's California chairperson identified Olson as the leading progressive candidate and part of the progressive bloc gaining momentum in California politics.[7]

Olson decisively defeated Merriam, winning 52.5 percent of the vote to Merriam's 44.2 percent. His victory was mirrored in Downey's defeat of the Republican nominee for the U.S. Senate, Philip Bancroft. Bancroft had been on the executive committee of the Associated Farmers for the previous four years and had been one of their vice presidents twice during that period. He was also head of the Deciduous Fruit Department of the California Farm Bureau Federation. He campaigned on an antirelief, antilabor, and anti-Communist platform, which bore a close resemblance to the position of the Associated Farmers. Ellis Patterson also won the lieutenant governorship, making it a sweep for the liberal Democrats.

Olson adopted a moderate version of Sinclair's "production for use" program. While he still used the slogans, Olson's ideas were within the New Deal tradition. His approach to California's agriculture and harvest labor was reformist. In his policy reports and later in his testimony to the La Follette and Tolan committees, he did not question the desirability of large-scale agriculture but rather condemned agricultural landowners for their disregard for the welfare of their workers. This position did not threaten the private and corporate ownership of large-scale tracts of agricultural land; it merely sought to reduce conflict. Not all of those in his administration shared his orientation, however. His appointee to head the Division of Immigration and Housing, Carey McWilliams, attacked what he called "industrial agriculture," the production of food for private profit, and appeared to favor a collective system.

Olson did support the inclusion of agricultural workers under the provisions of the NLRA and the extension of existing social welfare benefits to them. He also tacitly endorsed the organization of

farm labor unions. The most promising achievement of his administration in this area was the elimination of several barriers to unionization created by the policies of his predecessor. There was a
significant reversal of policy in the area of relief. In December 1935
the State Relief Administration (SRA) took over the task of providing
relief. In the summer of 1936 Governor Merriam appointed Harold
Pomeroy, who later became executive secretary of the Associated
Farmers, to head the agency. The policy of the SRA was that recipients must fulfill a one-year residency requirement for relief. Those
defined as nonresidents were granted relief only upon the condition
that they leave the state.[8] Relief was denied to anyone who failed to
accept work at the prevailing wages, no matter how low they might
be. Pomeroy summarized the policy as follows: "If business, agriculture, or industry can only pay a certain wage, then we can't give relief
to those who refuse to work at that figure."[9] In effect, the SRA was
upholding the minimal wages prevailing in agriculture. In addition,
people were cut off relief during the harvest season to insure an
oversupply of labor, which in turn reinforced low wages and grower
control over the labor force. This policy was in complete harmony
with the views of the Associated Farmers.[10]

Even while the federal relief program was still in operation, people
had been cut off the relief rolls to provide a harvest-time labor force.
Thousands were suspended during the spring and summer of 1935
and told to work in the fields; in May alone, approximately 2,400
persons were turned over to San Joaquin Valley growers by relief
agencies. The suspensions were repeated during the peak of the
harvest season that fall. Carey McWilliams attended a conference in
November where a Los Angeles relief administrator related that he
had removed 600 families from the relief rolls and ordered them to
work in the Imperial Valley 250 miles away. He also sent a thousand
Filipinos there to insure the docility of the white workers.[11]

With the emergence of the SRA in 1936, this practice became even
more pervasive and coordinated. The policy of channeling relief recipients into the already swollen agricultural labor supply helped
frustrate organizational activities and keep agricultural wages at a
minimum. During the height of the Dust Bowl migration, projects of
the federal Works Progress Administration (WPA) could only help a
small fraction of the new migrants, and FSA camps could provide
inexpensive housing for even fewer. Agricultural workers were
almost completely at the mercy of growers, who nevertheless constantly complained of a labor shortage, demanded that even more
persons be cut off relief, and strenuously opposed new WPA projects.

In 1937 Sonoma County orchard owners demanded that Los Angeles County provide them with 20,000 workers from the relief rolls. The *Los Angeles Evening News* sent a reporter to investigate the situation. He reported that more than enough labor would be available if a higher wage was paid; hundreds of migratory families were destitute; the California unemployment agency was helping arrest union officials; and growers were opposing the efforts of the Resettlement Administration to build a migratory labor camp, fearing that a semi-permanent labor force would be easier to organize.[12]

Dewey Anderson, Olson's appointee as head of the SRA, reversed many of Pomeroy's policies. He announced that the SRA would be completely reorganized under the principle of production for use. The program would include the manufacture of clothes, the production and canning of food, and the distribution of these commodities to the unemployed. He denied that it would have any harmful effect on the private sector of the economy and maintained that it was unrelated to the Sinclair proposal.[13] In the end he was unable even to attempt to put the plan into practice.

With respect to agricultural labor, Anderson announced that the "prevailing wage" policy of the Merriam administration would be replaced by a "fair wage" policy: the SRA would determine what was an adequate agricultural wage, and no person would be removed from relief to work at a lower one. The SRA could not force agricultural landowners to honor this wage, but it could protect people on relief from being forced to accept whatever wage growers offered. In 1939 the Olson administration twice attempted to set this fair wage. In May of that year, Carey McWilliams, acting as Division of Immigration and Housing chief, announced after a public hearing in Madera that the fair wage for cotton-choppers (i.e., weeders and thinners) would be 27½ cents per hour, as opposed to the cotton growers' offer of 20 cents. This was the first time that an administrator had used his right under the Unemployment Relief Act to certify that a job might be declined and the client still remain on relief.[14] The 27½-cent hourly wage or $1.25 per hundredweight was determined to be the fair wage for cotton picking in the fall, while 20 cents per hour or 80 cents per hundredweight had been offered.[15] In both instances, labor strikes had motivated the Division to determine a fair wage in a particular area.

The Olson administration quickly modified its stance, however. Because of vehement opposition to the fair wage policy, Olson called a conference in June of representatives of grower organizations and present and former government officials, including Pomeroy, now with the Associated Farmers, McWilliams, and Anderson. They agreed on a policy by which farm workers and their families would be released from the relief rolls when earnings from agricultural employment for all the employable members of the family would be equal to or in excess of the family's relief budget. They also decided that no government agency should determine wages that agricultural employers would be required to pay.[16] Although not a complete reversal, this change represented a concession to the organized agricultural landowners and a reduction of the reform initiative of the Olson administration. Throughout the Olson era, grower organizations continually sought to achieve even more restrictive relief polices by returning relief to individual counties, and their efforts produced several crucial legislative battles. Although Olson was able to resist such pressures, they put his administration continually on the defensive.

The appointment of Carey McWilliams to head the Division of Immigration and Housing infuriated the Associated Farmers, who referred to him as "Agricultural Pest No. One, outranking pear blight and boll weevil."[17] McWilliams attempted to revitalize the Division, which had been inactive for nearly twenty years. He announced that his inspectors would check carefully for violations of California housing codes in the migrant housing provided by agricultural employers. During his first year in office, the number of inspections of labor camps tripled. Although the division was understaffed and underfunded, it was successful in publicizing the worst conditions in the camps. McWilliams made numerous public appearances throughout California to call attention to the need to improve conditions in the fields. He organized guided tours of the camps for social workers, church leaders, teachers, and homemakers. He even went on the radio to urge people to report the locations of hidden labor camps and violations of the housing code. He later estimated that in 1939 growers spent over one million dollars in improving their labor camps.[18] This appeared to be as much as McWilliams could hope to achieve, since the division employed only four inspectors to look after 4,500 or 5,000 labor camps with a peak-season population of over 150,000 people.

Shortly after his inauguration, Olson called a conference of all California and federal agencies whose concern related to migratory labor. Its purpose was to set up a permanent committee to coordinate various social services of the state and federal governments and correct some of the worst abuses. Also, a Commission on Reemployment was created to study the relief situation. It recommended that 6,000 units of family housing be constructed for approximately 23,000 persons, with an adjacent farming area. To promote production for use, farming operations would be structured on a cooperative basis under the supervision of the FSA and would produce milk, eggs, and vegetables solely for consumption by the occupants of the projects.[19]

Included in Olson's legislative programs were proposals to construct thirty labor camps to augment the FSA program, regulate labor contractors, create a fair wage standard board for agricultural labor, require the registration of private labor camps, and tighten the rules under which private camps were operated.[20] With the exception of the bill to regulate labor contractors, all went down to defeat. A coalition of Republicans and conservative Democrats still controlled the legislature, and the urban areas that provided Olson with the bulk of his political support were badly underrepresented there. Los Angeles County, which contained over half of California's population and whose electorate supported liberal politicians at that time, had only one senator.[21] The conservative coalition was supported by agricultural organizations, including the Farm Bureau and Associated Farmers, and by most of California's other major corporations. The most Olson could do was veto several bills that would have returned the function of relief giving to the individual counties. The Unemployment Relief Appropriation Act of 1940, passed over his veto, raised the residency requirement for relief eligibility to three years, and to five years for any migrant entering the state after 1 June 1940.[22]

The Olson administration next confronted a direct attack on the legitimacy of the SRA. The Democratic assemblyman from Los Angeles, Samuel Yorty, obtained approval to set up a committee to investigate the SRA. Yorty had previously been politically to the left of Olson, but he had recently become a convert to anti-communism. In February 1940 the Yorty committee issued a report charging that for the past two years communists had successfully infiltrated the agency.[23] The report and the publicity it produced made Olson's fight to save the SRA and get adequate appropriations even more difficult.

Olson also had to face difficulties within his own administration. Dewey Anderson resigned from the SRA in August 1939, charging Olson with using the agency to build up a political machine by giving his political supporters appointments within it. There was some substance to the charge, for the SRA was one of the few agencies not under civil service regulations, and Olson's transfer of its offices from San Francisco to Los Angeles was widely interpreted as a move to secure control over the Los Angeles Democratic machine.[24] Olson also broke with Lieutenant Governor Patterson over the 1940 Democratic presidential nomination: Olson favored drafting Roosevelt for a third term, but Patterson hoped to head a left-wing ticket himself and was supported by McWilliams. The Roosevelt-Olson ticket scored a landslide victory in the Democratic presidential primary on 7 May 1940, while the Patterson slate finished last among the four tickets.[25] McWilliams offered to resign his position, but in the end he held on to it for the rest of Olson's tenure as governor.

Olson was defeated in his bid for re-election in 1942 by Earl Warren, who received 57 percent of the vote to Olson's 42 percent. What ultimately undermined Olson's reform program, making it unable to withstand the formidable power of the "economy bloc" in the legislature, was that it came too late in the decade. By the end of 1940, Roosevelt's war-preparedness programs were quickly removing the basis of the agricultural labor problem. California had received more defense contracts than any other state, and emerging defense industries were attracting the labor surplus out of the fields. Olson's administration had little time to overcome legislative barriers before priorities changed.

For a brief period there was, however, a popular belief that changes could be accomplished in the relationship between agricultural capital and labor. Even more important than the administration's limited gains in eliminating barriers to farm labor unionization was the public perception that the administration was behind unionization efforts. This, combined with the action of the federal government and the emergence of private organizations with similar objectives, gave UCAPAWA an opportunity to gain a foothold.

THE LA FOLLETTE AND TOLAN COMMITTEES

The federal government took little notice of the agricultural labor situation in California throughout most of the Depression years. It began to respond only in 1939, when a liberal Democratic administration with an interest in the migrant problem was installed in Sacramento. John Steinbeck's *Grapes of Wrath* was published in March, and McWilliams's *Factories in the Field* was published in May. Darrell Zanuck's film of the Steinbeck novel became popular early in 1940. At this point Congress and the Roosevelt administration began to consider the necessity of national action.

The California Congressional delegation formed a caucus to generate a specific program. Alfred Elliot, a conservative Democratic congressman from rural Tulare County, was selected as its leader. Splits within the caucus developed almost immediately. On one side were the conservatives, like Elliot, who thought the migrants were degenerates and wanted to get them off relief and out of California. Elliot disapproved of increased federal aid and the expansion of the FSA program and instead wanted action aimed at repatriating the migrants.[26] Liberals, on the other hand, represented by Democratic Congressman Jerry Voorhis from southern California and John Tolan from Oakland, viewed the migrants as part of a national problem and wished to relieve the conditions under which they lived. Voorhis proposed federal aid to the states containing the greatest proportion of migrants and to the depressed areas where the migrants originated, a nationwide employment service for agricultural migrants, and uniform residency requirements in all states for relief eligibility.[27] Tolan introduced a House resolution for a Congressional committee to investigate the migrant problem. The resolution at first failed to gain acceptance, but a year later it was reintroduced and passed. The resulting Tolan Committee investigation represented one of the most significant steps taken by the federal government during this period.

Despite the diverse viewpoints of the California Democrats, they submitted a report to Roosevelt in February 1939. The Voorhis-Elliot brief suggested various measures the federal government could undertake to relieve the migrant problem, including the organization of a national farm employment service, the expansion of the FSA camp system into other states to attract migrants away from California, and financing for housing and public education of migrants to lessen California's expenditures.[28] Roosevelt formed his own committee, composed of representatives of the New Deal agencies involved with the migrant situation and headed by WPA administrator F. C. Harrington. Its report, issued on 15 March, concluded that there was little the federal government could do under the existing Congressional mandate. Special legislation was needed to provide for nationwide planning to deal with the problem. The report then suggested several possible courses of action, including the resettlement of migrants in states where suitable employment opportunities existed and granting assistance to migrants willing to repatriate. Although these suggestions did not specifically address the factors that made the situation of the migrants intolerable—the lack of adequate food and housing, the grower-shipper interests, control of the conditions of employment, the hostility of local residents—they did address the need to reduce the surplus labor supply. The effect of the Harrington report, however, was to return the initiative to Congress, and especially to the disunited California delegation.

The Congressional sessions of 1939 and 1940 were extremely frustrating to those wanting a quick federal response to the migrant problem. The California delegation and Congress as a whole could agree on only one point: the migrant problem needed more study. Thus, the resolution Tolan first introduced over a year before was passed on 22 April 1940. It authorized the formation of the House Committee on the Interstate Migration of Destitute Citizens, which became known as the Tolan Committee. The committee did not limit itself to the migratory labor situation in California but gathered information in the migrants' states of origin as well. Perhaps its major contribution was the documentation of the causes of migration, such as the increased use of mechanization in the farms of the South and Midwest, the demise of sharecropping and tenant farming systems, and the rise of the wage system for agricultural workers. Testifying before the committee, Secretary of Labor Frances Perkins criticized the exemption of agricultural labor from federal labor laws.[29] The committee's report remains one of the most comprehensive bodies of information on the sources and nature of migrant problems in the United States.

The Tolan Committee's report came too late to be of practical use, however. The committee itself did not arrive in California until late 1940. By that time the defense industries were already drawing off the surplus agricultural labor supply. Those who testified that migrants had no industrial skills or experience, were only suitable for farm labor, and could not be utilized in the war effort proved to be wrong.[30] While the committee conducted its investigation, the problem was already vanishing. When the report was finally issued, few people in Congress or in the Roosevelt administration were still interested.

While the House was fighting over the appropriate action to take, the Senate did virtually nothing. It had made its major contribution a year earlier when the Senate Subcommittee to Investigate Violations of Free Speech and Assembly and Interference with the Right of Labor to Organize and Bargain Collectively (the La Follette Committee) went to California to investigate the antilabor practices of organized growers. Formed in 1936, the committee was headed by Senator Robert M. La Follette, Jr., of Wisconsin. Its main function was to document employer violations of the NLRA. Since agricultural labor was not covered under the NLRA, the committee had not planned to investigate the situation in the fields of California. However, the election of Olson and increased federal concern with migrant problems in the late 1930s persuaded it to broaden the scope of its investigation. Carey McWilliams claimed that the popularity of his and Steinbeck's books prodded a lukewarm Senator La Follette.[31] The committee reasoned that violations of civil liberties through the antilabor practices of organized growers and local officials gave it sufficient justification to come to California. The Committee's investigation was part of the government's rather haphazard probing into ways to ameliorate the worst circumstances of the migratory labor force.

Several committee staff members had in fact begun a preliminary investigation into California conditions late in 1938, but they abruptly halted in January 1939, when the committee ran out of funds. La Follette himself was coming up for re-election in 1940 in a heavily agricultural state, and he did not want to appear to be engaged in a vendetta against farm organizations. During the course of the California hearings, he was also apparently disturbed by the sympathy of some of his staff for the more left-wing members of California's rural unions.[32] Nevertheless, the growth of national interest in the problems of California agriculture in the spring and summer of 1939 gave the committee ample justification for extending its investigation. In August 1939 the Senate allocated $50,000 to begin the California hearings. McWilliams helped to brief the committee staff and line up witnesses.[33]

The committee held twenty-eight days of public hearings in December 1939 and January 1940 in San Francisco and Los Angeles, calling about four hundred witnesses. Governor Olson was its first witness, presenting a statement prepared by McWilliams. Later McWilliams testified himself and issued a lengthy report on farm labor conditions. The committee collected data in five interrelated areas: the structure and history of California agriculture; the activities of employers' associations; the involvement of these associations with agricultural labor; the impact of their labor policies upon specific organizing drives and strikes; and the cooperation of agricultural and industrial associations to frustrate organization and collective bargaining in both agricultural and nonagricultural areas. Although also concerned with strikebreaking and unionbusting tactics in California industry, the committee concentrated on the fields. The testimony it heard is contained in twenty-seven volumes issued 19 October 1942.[34] It documents the blacklists, the antipicketing ordinances, the vigilante activities, the antilabor police tactics, and the cooperation between agricultural and industrial interests. The Associated Farmers were portrayed as a pivotal organization. Their files were subpoenaed and revealed the extent of their activities.

The report concluded that since California agriculture was at least as concentrated, coordinated, and capitalized as the industrial sector, its workers should be included under federal labor legislation. The committee recommended that control over labor relations in corporate agriculture be placed in the hands of the government rather than grower organizations. Toward this end, they advised that agricultural workers be included under the NLRA, the Social Security Act, the Fair Labor Standards Act, and individual state labor legislation. They also looked favorably on collective action by the workers themselves.[35] The hearings came several months too late to help a large cotton-pickers strike in which UCAPAWA was involved, but several representatives of the committee witnessed it, and one received minor injuries when the Madera police broke up a strike meeting.[36] The hearings gathered greater urgency since they were not only investigating events of two, three, and four years before, but also a pattern threatening to continue.

In retrospect it is clear that the revelations of the La Follette Committee signaled the end of the effectiveness of the Associated Farmers.[37] Attempts to spread the organization to other West Coast states and parts of the Midwest were undermined by the hearings. The Associated Farmers remained a phenomenon solely of California agribusiness, and even in California its effectiveness as a coordinating agency for antilabor forces was reduced. By 1940 unions attempting to organize farm workers were no longer confronted by the intense and violent opposition of the recent past. McWilliams recently wrote that the hearings in effect "put the Associated Farmers out of business."[38] Moreover, the international situation generated antipathy toward organizations with fascist overtones. Antiunion activities continued, but after 1939 they were no longer undertaken or coordinated by the Associated Farmers. The group remained a force influencing the California legislature well into 1941 and continued in existence throughout the forties. But the initiative had by then shifted to agricultural unions and the workers themselves, who realized that their organizing would be supported by elements of the government.

During the middle and late 1930s several private liberal organizations emerged with the intention of publicizing the conditions of migrant laborers and supporting unionization efforts. The Simon J. Lubin Society, named after the first head of the Division of Immigration and Housing, was the most important of these. Founded in 1936, the organization coordinated charitable relief, published numerous pamphlets directed against the Associated Farmers, provided pro-labor speakers, and, most importantly, served as a coordinating agency for agricultural unions, a research service, and a clearinghouse for information about union activities. It also helped persuade the La Follette Committee to extend its investigations into California.[39]

The John Steinbeck Committee to Aid Agricultural Organization was formed in late 1938 with similar goals. Chaired by McWilliams and later by Helen Gahagan Douglas, the organization was more paternalistic and was primarily concerned with the specific problems of the Dust Bowl refugees. It did, however, supply financial support for UCAPAWA, and it strongly endorsed unionization efforts in general.[40]

UCAPAWA AND THE FAILURE TO ORGANIZE

The CIO-affiliated United Cannery, Agricultural, Packing and Allied Workers of America was the primary organization attempting to unite agricultural workers in California during the late 1930s. National in scope, it achieved notable successes in other areas of the country, claiming at one point 40,000 dues-paying members, most of them in Colorado, Wyoming, Florida, and Arizona, and among the fish cannery and seafood workers in the Pacific Northwest and South Atlantic regions.

UCAPAWA had certain advantages that previous California unions had lacked. Its initial unionization efforts were aimed at packing-shed and cannery workers as well as field workers, thereby encompassing nearly the entire process of agricultural production. The strategic strength of such a union would be comparable to that enjoyed in the most advantageous situations in industry. It would have enabled UCAPAWA to avoid the kind of situation that had occurred several times in the past when employers reached an accommodation with cannery and packing-shed workers while using every instrument at their disposal to repress field workers and keep the two segments of the work force divided. Strikes by workers in any segment of the food production process could be supported by the other segments, making the chronic labor surplus from which strikebreakers could be recruited less of a handicap. The more permanent and better-paid cannery and packing workers could provide a stable financial base for the union, and its ties to industrial unions in the CIO could bring monetary assistance, political alliances, publicity, and other external resources. Such support had been noticeably lacking in previous organizational efforts. Within the work force itself, the vertical integration of different types of workers held the promise of breaking down ethnic animosity. Other potential contributors to unionization success were prounion elements within government and sympathetic private organizations. The Olson administration, FSA camps, the Lubin Society, and the Steinbeck Committee were among the external resources capable of mobilization. Yet given its potential, the results of UCAPAWA's efforts were disappointing. Its failure in California was due to a number of factors: the nature of the organization itself, the repression it faced, the unreceptiveness of the people it was trying to organize, and, ultimately, the onset of World War II.

An initial setback was the union's failure to make significant inroads into the processing industries of California. The AFL maintained control over the nonfield workers, and the dispute between the CIO and the state Federation of Labor, which included the Teamsters' Union, prevented cooperation between the two union organizations. Consequently, UCAPAWA's potential remained undeveloped in California.

Its membership included a number of leftists, many with previous experience from the Communist party's dual unionism period, when it organized its own locals in competition with established AFL unions. One of these was Dorothy Ray Healy, who had been active in CAWIU and who became one of UCAPAWA's vice presidents.[41] Many other leftists participated in the Workers Alliance, a national pressure group formed in 1935 to protect unemployment relief from budget cuts. Led by radicals and composed of unemployed workers, the Workers Alliance cooperated with UCAPAWA to prevent its members from serving as strikebreakers. Its membership was transferred to UCAPAWA during the harvest season.[42] As was noted above, however, UCAPAWA conducted its most serious recruiting efforts in the FSA camps. Organizing campaigns took place in at least eight camps, and at least five—Visalia, Arvin, Shafter, Marysville, and Gridley—had active locals of the Workers Alliance or UCAPAWA or both.[43]

UCAPAWA entered the fields on an organized basis for the first time in 1938. The union itself initiated few strikes but felt compelled to direct numerous unorganized and spontaneous strikes when the strikers appealed to it for support.[44] UCAPAWA officials feared that these strikes were draining the union of energy and resources that should have gone toward building a stable organization as a prelude to strike and contract negotiations, and late in the decade they became more selective about the strikes to which they would commit resources and personnel. When the union joined a strike already in progress, the development of strike demands was limited to a few central issues. However, control as well as wage issues were raised under UCAPAWA direction. In various strikes the union sought job stewards in each field, closed shop agreements, drinking water at the job site, the testing of growers' weighing machines, an end to lock-outs, and the hiring of union members and the rehiring of strikers without discrimination. UCAPAWA assumed the leadership of one strike directed specifically against "chiseling" by labor contractors.[45]

UCAPAWA was called in to lead several strikes during its initial year. Twelve strikes involving about 5,500 field workers were reported for 1938. Most were small, localized, and spontaneous. UCAPAWA organizers became involved in most of them, including the three largest: the Sacramento pea-pickers strike (2,000 workers), the Kern County cotton-pickers strike (3,000 workers), and the Santa Ana (Orange County) vegetable strike (750 workers). The pea-pickers' and vegetable workers' walkouts resulted in union victories, but the largest, the cotton-pickers' strike, was defeated. It was called in protest of the growers' offer of 75 cents per hundredweight; the rate the previous year was 90 cents. Union officials, taken by surprise by the strike, rushed organizers to the area. Tactics were reminiscent of those used in the 1933 cotton strike. Caravans of strikers drove from field to field to extend the walkout. The Associated Farmers initiated a blacklist of those involved, refused to negotiate with strike representatives, and ignored mediation offers from the U.S. Department of Labor. Numerous arrests were made by the Kern County sheriff's department under antipicketing ordinances. Harold Pomeroy, then head of the SRA, denied relief to those who refused to work as strikebreakers for the prevailing wage.[46]

The union claimed that many independent growers were ready to agree to the strikers' demands but had been warned by the Associated Farmers that if they gave in they would be unable to obtain loans from banks and cotton-ginning companies to finance next year's crops. Under the unified opposition of the growers and local officials, the strike collapsed, but it had served as a rehearsal for the much larger cotton strike of the following year.[47]

The 1939 harvest season produced strikes fewer in number but larger in scope than there had been for several years. Aware of its organizational weakness, UCAPAWA organizers discouraged strikes unless widespread support could be demonstrated. In fact, the union tried to prevent the 1939 cotton strike in the San Joaquin

Valley, which proved to be the largest in many years, nearing the scale of the 1933 cotton strike.[48] Wages for cotton-pickers were lower in 1939 than they had been in 1934. It was noted earlier that Carey McWilliams as the head of the Division of Immigration and Housing had set 27½ cents per hour or $1.25 per hundredweight as a fair wage, and that no one who refused to work for less would be released from relief rolls. Meanwhile the growers had announced through the Agricultural Labor Bureau of the San Joaquin Valley that the wage would be 20 cents per hour or 80 cents per hundredweight. In the last two years the amount of cotton cultivated had been cut nearly in half under the restrictive program of the AAA: from 670,000 acres in 1937 to 340,000 acres in 1939. This meant, of course, that fewer workers would be employed.

The strike started in the Madera area and quickly spread to involve several thousand workers over a wide area. Even representatives of the Associated Farmers testified to the La Follette Committee that the strike was 75 to 90 percent effective.[49] The Workers Alliance kept its members from working at less than the fair wage set by McWilliams. Strikers again drove in caravans from ranch to ranch to spread the strike, and UCAPAWA used several FSA camps as strike headquarters.

The strike met with the usual opposition. Hundreds of strikers were arrested for violations of the antipicketing ordinances. Growers organized auto convoys of their own to intercept strikers.[50] Striking workers were evicted from private labor camps, and growers did not hesitate to use clubs and display guns when confronting pickets.

The most violent confrontation occurred at a Madera strike rally on 21 October. While the sheriff stood by, 300 growers and vigilantes attacked people at the rally with clubs, fan belts, tire chains, and pick handles. No arrests were made. Governor Olson called in the Highway Patrol, which ended the battle with tear gas.[51] The strike grew to include a number of spontaneous work stoppages in the upper valley. UCAPAWA gained unexpected support from a number of smaller growers who claimed that they had received inequitable treatment under the AAA and resented having no control over the wages set by ginning companies and large growers.[52]

The strike brought mixed results. In most areas strike activity subsided after several weeks. Many growers broke away from the wage standard and accepted a union compromise offer of $1.00 per hundredweight. In other areas the strike continued for several months, usually with no results. When the year ended, UCAPAWA had made little progress in establishing itself as a permanent agricultural union. Nor did 1940 bring great advances, despite the favorable political climate which was further enhanced by the La Follette Committee hearings of December 1939 and January 1940. The union's failure to organize packing-shed workers was obviously undermining its chances of success. Despite the public announcement in 1940 of an ambitious campaign to organize California's agricultural workers, little was accomplished. The national organization had drastically reduced its organizing budget and forced the union locals nationwide to restrict their activities to processing industries accessible to union headquarters in urban areas.[53] The AFL re-entered the fields in 1940, and the little headway it made was at the expense of UCAPAWA. At its 1940 convention, UCAPAWA decided to concentrate on cannery and processing workers, who were covered under the provisions of the NLRA and thus protected from the most effective tactics of the growers.[54]

The major blow of 1940 was the decision of the Filipino Agricultural Labor Association (FALA) to affiliate with the AFL. FALA was organized in 1939 and represented a temporary revival of the tradition of independent, ethnic agricultural unions. It led the only farm worker strike of any importance in the United States in 1940, involving several thousand Filipino celery workers in the Delta area. Most FALA members were more sympathetic to the CIO than the AFL, which had consistently opposed Filipino immigration and tried to exclude Filipinos from organized trades. In the face of UCAPAWA's declining strength, though, FALA voted to affiliate with the AFL, hoping to enlist support from AFL unions in the transportation and canning industries.[55]

UCAPAWA quietly left the California fields early in 1941. By that time the initiative had been lost. In 1944 the union changed its name to the Food, Tobacco, and Allied Workers of America (FTA). In 1951 it was expelled from the CIO for alleged Communist domination.

WHY UCAPAWA FAILED

Part of the reason for UCAPAWA's failure in California can be found within the organization itself. As part of a national union, it was subject to policies dictated at higher levels. The national organization believed that the most advantageous strategy would be to bring large numbers of people into the union as quickly as possible to provide a stable financial base. The California fields were not the place to look for a readily organizable constituency. Moreover, the structure and much of the staff of union locals were not drawn from the agricultural workers themselves, and so there was a cultural barrier between union organizers and workers. Considerably more radical than the Dust Bowl migrants, UCAPAWA organizers issued pamphlets calling for collective action by a united working class to confront a growing pattern of fascist political organization within the United States. The terms and analysis used were ideologically alien, and probably scarcely comprehensible, to those for whom they were intended.[56] The union's urban, class-conscious activists, many with college educations, did not mix well with former small farmers trying to duplicate their previous situation. While the Filipino and Mexican officials and organizers of UCAPAWA were cited by the union as testimony to its international character, there was virtually no mention of Dust Bowl migrants in comparable positions. Thus, it is not surprising that organizing drives failed and that UCAPAWA initiated few successful strikes. Its limited accomplishments came instead from assuming leadership in spontaneous strikes.

The union itself and its supporters blamed its failures on repression by large agricultural landowners, their organizations, the local police, and vigilante groups. Senator La Follette expressed this position in a report on the 1939 cotton strike:

> betrayals of duty by the constituted authorities of Madera are not, it seems clear, to be charged to them alone. Behind and above these officials stand those organizations which, in intimate coordination, loosed and directed forces to beget official and private lawlessness in Madera. The Agricultural Labor Bureau of the San Joaquin Valley and its strong right arm, the Associated Farmers, together fixed and enforced the wage rate which the strikers protested. In the course of their enforcement campaign, the Associated Farmers carried with them, through sheer domination of the local scene, the officials who ought to have administered constitutional laws with equal justice. In short, the Madera strike of 1939 shows that labor relations in that county were lawlessly controlled by a private group strong enough to command the suspension of those laws which they violated and the perversion of other laws to obtain their ends.[57]

That local repression was a major factor is undoubtedly true, but similar activity initiated by growers and local governments did not destroy the IWW and CAWIU, nor has it been ultimately successful against the UFW. If local, coordinated repression was fatal, this was in part the result of the orientation of those the union identified as its primary constituency and their disinclination at that time to support the union.

Most of the Dust Bowl refugees upon whom UCAPAWA concentrated its efforts were former small farm operators who had little

experience with labor unions or collective action. Initially despondent and poverty-stricken, most were not inclined to jeopardize their
brief periods of employment by initiating or supporting strikes
and organizing. Observers of the Dust Bowl refugees have described
the individualism that made them resist unionization and the demoralization, hopelessness, and despondency that made them an
especially pliable source of labor. Like many groups before them,
they were an inexpensive and controllable labor force upon their
introduction into the fields, undermining the hegemony over the
labor supply of a more militant organized group. But unlike most of
the earlier nonwhite groups, the Dust Bowl migrants did not move
gradually toward a less compliant stance, at least not while they
constituted the dominant supply of farm labor. Culturally and ideologically, the white migrants were at this time less organizable than
most of the previous groups in the fields. Their orientation was
manifested in the reluctance of many to accept relief and skepticism,
or even outright hostility, where UCAPAWA was concerned. Many
accepted the equation of the CIO with communism. Researchers who
recorded their attitudes generally reported beliefs consistent with
the position of the Associated Farmers: many Dust Bowl migrants
distrusted the National Labor Relations Board, despised "agitators,"
and believed strikes were fomented to overthrow the government.[58]

The nativism and racism of many of the white migrants also made
them less conducive to organization. Many resented UCAPAWA's
nondiscriminatory policy. Their antiblack prejudices were easily
transferred to Filipinos, Mexicans, and other "foreigners," and made
their inclusion in a union of diverse ethnicity and nationality all the
more difficult. Growers did what they could to exacerbate this antagonism, using the traditional mechanisms of wage determination by
race (usually with the white migrants being paid less), assignment of
different national groups to separate work gangs, and hiring members of one group to break strikes waged by another.[59]

If their position as the dominant agricultural labor force had continued, it is conceivable that the white migrants would have joined a
union or constructed their own. In fact, a large proportion of the
participants in the 1947 DiGiorgio strike, perhaps the most significant strike in the period between 1939 and 1965, were remnants of
the Dust Bowl migration. Five of the six executive board members of
Arvin Local 218 of the National Farm Labor Union (NFLU), which
initiated the DiGiorgio strike, were from Oklahoma, Arkansas, or
Missouri. Ethnic differences this time did not interfere with solidarity; white strikers united with Mexican Americans and Filipinos.[60]

But this occurred a decade later, under different historical circumstances.

Ironically, the "Americanism" of the white migrants, which observers including Steinbeck and McWilliams had believed would make them less tolerant of exploitation, helped them only after they found nonagricultural jobs, in the defense industries and elsewhere, where the fact that they were white made assimilation easier.

Given this constituency, UCAPAWA's emphasis on building a formal, mass-membership, permanent agricultural workers' union thus appears to have been a strategic error. The internal resources needed to build an organization were lacking. Worker insurgency in the form of strikes, slowdowns, picketing, and spontaneous work stoppages was the mechanism that elicited concessions from growers. Agricultural unions had been most effective when they promoted mass defiance, coordinated and strategically advised militant tactics, pressured government agencies to initiate reforms and investigate and correct unfair and illegal grower practices, channeled external support to the workers, and acted as worker representatives in negotiations with growers. These efforts were responsible for whatever concessions the IWW and CAWIU had won. UCAPAWA organizers, in contrast, attempted to enroll a large membership in a formal organization. The union initiated few strikes on its own and instead tried to coordinate and support spontaneous strikes whose participants appealed for help. Committing resources to scattered strikes was perceived as draining the union without returning proportional gains. The district executive board eventually had to rule that no spontaneous strikes would receive support until a district representative had conducted a thorough investigation.

Early in 1940 the union decided to place even greater emphasis on membership building by establishing eight locals in various agricultural districts. An experienced leadership was to direct the locals and maintain union activity in spite of shifts in the migratory work force. The result was a series of defeats. At the national level UCAPAWA concentrated on the processing industries and allocated fewer resources to California field organizing. By early 1941 the union abandoned the effort to organize migratory workers in California.

FAILURE OF STATE MEDIATION

The final chapter in Carey McWilliams's *Factories in the Field*, published just months after McWilliams became one of Governor Olson's most controversial appointees, was entitled "The End of a Cycle."

Written before Olson's election and the emergence of a national
concern with the plight of migratory agricultural workers, the chapter expressed the opinion of many observers of agricultural labor.
"The jig . . . is about up," wrote McWilliams.[61] The emergence of
UCAPAWA, the arrival of the Dust Bowl migrants, and the initial
efforts of the federal government to stabilize the labor force seemed to
mark the end of a pattern of labor exploitation that had utilized a
succession of nonwhite groups cut off from the white urban-based
labor movement. McWilliams documented this system, beginning
with the introduction of Chinese into the fields in 1870, and he felt
that he was writing the system's obituary.

What promised to be the end of an era turned out to be merely
another chapter. Despite favorable circumstances, few lasting
changes were made. The Olson administration could not surmount
the formidable conservative "economy bloc" of Republicans and rural
Democrats in the California legislature. The Associated Farmers
were still active in promoting vigilante repression of strikes with the
cooperation of local officials. Some of the developments thought to be
favorable for unionization turned out to be disappointing.
UCAPAWA shared some of the limitations of earlier organizing
efforts, and it had little perseverence. Dust Bowl migrants as a group
were not at that time a good foundation for a permanent, mass-based
agricultural union.

The resistance of the Dust Bowl migrants to commit their time,
energies, and resources to the long-term objectives of UCAPAWA
made the union's goal of establishing a permanent organization seem
highly improbable. Still, when confronted with the immediacy of
their destitution, a substantial number of the white migrants would
at times overcome demoralization and withhold their labor. The
union failed to escalate the tendencies toward protest among its
membership. UCAPAWA was the largest union to organize field
workers at that time. It offered the potential of alliances with canneries and processing industries, as well as the support of the CIO. It was
possibly the most disappointing failure.

In addition, UCAPAWA's efforts should be analyzed within the
context of the industrial labor movement of the same period. Most of
the gains by industrial workers during the Depression were achieved
before mid-1937 or the point at which UCAPAWA was created. The
May 1935 passage of the NLRA had stimulated a massive upsurge of
worker protest, including picketing, strikes, company union take-
overs, and factory occupations. Nearly half a million men were involved in sit-down strikes during 1936 and early 1937 alone. Unions

became established in mass production industries: in steel, auto-
mobiles, rubber, coal and mining, meat packing, and other basic
industries. Then rank-and-file militancy rapidly fell off during the
sharp recession of 1937–38. Industrialists hardened their stance, and
the Roosevelt administration became less supportive of industrial
unionism for the duration of the Depression. As a result, few additional gains were made by industrial workers between 1937–40.[62] By
the time UCAPAWA began its unionization drive in the fields the
national political situation had shifted against labor, possibly fore-
closing the possibility of establishing a permanent farm labor union.

What ultimately counterbalanced government intervention to stabilize and rationalize the agricultural labor supply was the U.S.
entry into World War II. The contrast with the experiences of industrial unions during the War is significant. The return to prosperity
created renewed militancy among industrial workers. Initial union
contracts were reached with a number of corporations that had resisted during the Depression, and older contracts with other firms
were renegotiated. More importantly, expansion of the federal government's role in labor-management relations for the duration of the
War (through the National War Labor Board) eliminated the remaining vestiges of antiunionism among industrialists and completed the
establishment of unions within American industry.[63]

In the agricultural sector, however, wartime conditions undermined government labor reforms. By mid-1940, preparations for war
were attracting large numbers of migrants to cities, where there were
jobs available that paid well. During 1942 there was an actual shortage of labor in the California fields for the first time. The crisis in
agriculture had passed, and the Olson administration and the federal
government turned their attention from crisis management and reform to insuring growers an adequate supply of labor. This set the
stage for the importation of Mexican braceros, a dominant source of
field labor until the end of 1964, the year before the initial Delano-
area grape strikes. Segments of the state would not again undertake
a policy of facilitating the unionization of agricultural workers for
more than thirty-five years and then it would take another decade of
agricultural labor unrest to stimulate such support. In the meantime
California agribusiness, with the cooperation of the federal government, was presented with a nearly ideal labor situation.

CHAPTER 8

THE STATE AS LABOR CONTRACTOR: THE BRACERO ERA

Beginning in 1942 and extending until the end of 1964, a continuous sequence of bracero programs dominated the relationship between agricultural labor and capital. These constituted a system through which Mexican nationals were recruited for agricultural work for the length of a harvest season. The programs weighed the scales even further in favor of agribusiness, legitimizing its control over the agricultural work force with international agreements. These years appropriately came to be referred to as "the bracero era." Braceros had few of the characteristics of a free agricultural proletariat. Their status, work contracts, and the limitations on their mobility were fixed by law, leading Lee G. Williams, a U.S. Department of Labor official involved in supervising bracero employment from 1959 to 1964, to refer to the programs as "legalized slavery."[1] The influx of braceros represented another transition in the agricultural labor supply, one which brought tremendous economic benefits for agribusiness.

The single most important reason for the long survival of the bracero programs was the support given to large-scale growers by government agencies and officials. Government agents in charge of the programs repeatedly accepted without question grower claims of impending labor shortages and the consequent necessity of importing braceros. Agribusiness, in effect, predetermined the "prevailing wage" and other contract provisions. Complaints filed by domestic and bracero workers were ignored; braceros were allowed, and sometimes ordered, to continue field work during strikes; and union officials were refused access to documents giving the particulars of the bracero programs. The bracero era witnessed the most complete coincidence between government intervention and the interests of agribusiness to date.

Not surprisingly, the bracero programs had negative consequences for nonbracero farm workers. The option of employing braceros was used by growers to undercut the negotiating position of domestic workers. Wages remained exceedingly low, and living and working conditions showed little tendency to improve. Unionization was effectively blocked. Perhaps even more significant was the occupational and residential displacement of domestic workers by the expansion of bracero employment. Domestic farm workers had been gradually settling into many of California's rural towns, establishing permanent residences and obtaining most of their employment within commuting distance of their homes. The migratory patterns so predominant during the 1930s were slowly disappearing. Both Mexican workers and the remnants of the Dust Bowl migration were remaining in one location for increasingly long periods. They were being stabilized, becoming what Mexicans referred to as "locales." The growth of bracero employment reversed this trend. Beginning in the agricultural regions close to the Mexican border, growers hired fewer domestic workers. With less work to sustain them, many families pulled up roots and moved farther north, again attempting to establish permanent residences. But the braceros followed. After Public Law 78 gave the bracero program the sanction of federal law in 1951, bracero employment spread to nearly every agricultural region in California. Bracero labor dominated a few crops, composed a significant proportion of the work force for many others, and supplemented the domestic labor force for most of the rest. As a result, fewer domestic workers could survive on farm labor jobs, and many left the agricultural regions altogether. Combined with agricultural mechanization, most notably of cotton, the rapid growth in the number of bracero workers provided one of the major stimuli for the rapid urbanization of the Mexican and Mexican American population within the United States.

BRACERO AGREEMENTS, 1942–1951

The history of the bracero programs can be divided into two periods. The first period, from 1942 to 1951, was characterized by a series of temporary agreements that left growers essentially free to determine their labor needs while the federal government provided financial support and administrative facilities. This initial decade of the system's existence witnessed several shifting, erratic experiments with government and grower management that served to underline the unstable nature of the programs themselves.

The initial agreement that provided Mexican nationals for Southwestern farms was formalized after a period of negotiations by an exchange of diplomatic notes between the governments of Mexico and the United States on 4 August 1942.[2] Growers had complained in the past of labor shortages, but they began to insist that the problem was urgent when preparations for war began in 1940.[3] Early in 1942 Secretary of Agriculture Claude Wickard directed the Department of Agriculture to prepare several tentative proposals for the importation of foreign workers. Concurrently, Governor Olson of California sent a telegram to the secretaries of State, Labor, and Agriculture imploring them to allow Mexican nationals into the fields. The telegram read in part: "Without a substantial number of Mexicans the situation is certain to be disasterous to the entire victory program, despite our united efforts in the mobilization of youth and city dwellers for emergency farm work."[4]

There did in fact appear to be a need for a supplementary source of rural labor. Even those active at the time in farm labor organizing admitted that field labor was in short supply during the war. But had harvest work been made more attractive and employment stabilized and coordinated, perhaps through implementation of the reforms proposed during the late 1930s, the wartime labor shortage in the fields might have been reduced, and might have made the bracero programs unnecessary.

While the federal government provided the channels to supply growers with bracero labor, it had to contend with objections from other interested parties. Labor unions opposed the programs virtually from the start, charging that the labor shortage had been manufactured by growers to prevent improvements in the living conditions of field workers. The AFL also feared competition from Mexican workers in the skilled trades if the programs were extended to urban occupations or if adequate safeguards preventing braceros from deserting the fields for urban jobs were not instituted and enforced. As a result, occupations for Mexican workers under the bracero programs were strictly limited.

The primary obstacle to instituting the bracero programs was the Mexican government. Mexico had expressed ambivalence toward the initial proposals. Relations between the United States and Mexico had been strained by the treatment Mexican citizens and Mexican Americans had received in the United States in the past. The Mexican government did not want to sanction a recreation of the type of exploitation experienced by Mexican field workers during World War I, and the harassment, discrimination, and repatriation drives directed against Mexicans and Mexican Americans during the early Depression years were only a decade in the past. On the other hand, Mexico realized the substantial benefits in the form of the additional revenue that the program would provide, and these considerations won out.

The bracero agreement, signed on 23 July and formalized twelve days later, contained more comprehensive provisions for the protection of the workers than any subsequent agreement. Since there was a pressing need for bracero labor at that time, Mexican officials could negotiate from a position of strength, and most of the protective provisions were included at their insistence. A year later, the safeguards of the program began to be eroded, and bracero programs instituted after the war were still less adequate in protecting either domestic workers or braceros. The 1942 agreement established four guidelines that remained throughout the twenty-two-year history of the programs. Mexican contract workers would be exempt from U.S. military service. They would not be subject to discriminatory acts of any kind. They would be guaranteed transportation, living expenses, and repatriation. Finally, and most importantly, they were not to be used to replace domestic workers or to depress farm wages.[5]

Other clauses of the agreement set out wage and employment conditions. Wages were to be at the prevailing rate for the area, and in no case would they be less than 30 cents an hour. Piece rates were to be comparable. Braceros were guaranteed work for 75 percent of the contract period, and if this requirement could not be met, they were to receive the equivalent of $3.00 a day for subsistence in food, money, or a combination of the two. For all days they were unemployed, braceros were to receive meals, housing, and medical care "on the same basis as American workers." Ten percent of the braceros' earnings were deducted and placed in a savings fund that was transferred to Mexico's Agricultural Credit Bank and payable to the individual bracero upon his return to Mexico. Later, in 1948, this provision was abandoned: although the money reached the Mexican bank, it often did not subsequently reach the braceros.[6]

Another clause designated the U.S. government as the "employer" in bracero contracts. This provision proved to be a pivotal one. It meant that the federal government took responsibility for supplying braceros to individual growers or their associations; in effect, it placed the government in the position of a huge labor contractor. The government paid for the braceros' transportation and living expenses while they were en route from Mexico to the American employers and back again. Only in the first year of the program's operation was the government reimbursed for these expenses by growers employing braceros. The federal government's role in implementing the bracero programs represented a tremendous subsidy for those utilizing bracero labor. Still, many growers were critical of some of the contract provisions, and their organizations tried to eliminate such features as housing and transportation standards, prevailing wage provisions, and guaranteed subsistence and unemployment payments. Many growers also disliked the selection of the Farm Security Administration as the administrative agency for the program because of the FSA's support for agricultural labor reforms during the 1930s. Unsure of the advantages and durability of the programs, growers supplemented domestic and bracero labor with large numbers of undocumented Mexican nationals until a more permanent and advantageous bracero program was instituted in the 1950s. These undocumented workers were paid even less than braceros. However, although they sometimes composed a large part of the harvest labor force—an official of the Wage Stabilization Board estimated that illegal workers made up 60 percent of the work force employed in the 1951 tomato harvest—there was always the danger of arrest or voluntary departure. More importantly, no method existed to insure the presence of an adequate number of undocumented workers for harvest operations year after year.

Several studies have documented how a contract labor system of this sort lends itself to exploitation and abuse of both foreign and domestic workers.[7] It is not difficult to see how exploitation of braceros could occur within the terms of the 1942 agreement, even without the frequent and systematic abuses and violations that were to become the norm. The requirement that braceros receive the same housing, medical attention, and board as domestic workers was virtually meaningless. The greater part of domestic workers had no medical coverage themselves, for example. The prohibition against discrimination was all but impossible to enforce, but Texas was forbidden to use braceros for five years because of past treatment of Mexicans and Mexican Americans in the state.

Similarly, it was hard to argue convincingly that braceros did not adversely affect domestic employment and wages. The influx of braceros helped recreate the oversupply of agricultural labor that in the past had been critical in preventing farm labor stabilization and in keeping wages low and workers unorganized. It also created yet another group that could be used to divide the agricultural labor force. Few braceros would protest against the conditions under which they lived and worked. If they did, they could be and often were deported.

Rises in farm labor wages were inversely related to the percentage of braceros employed in a particular region. California's agricultural sector was the primary user of bracero labor. Wages for cotton picking there increased 136 percent between 1940 and 1945, compared with an average nationwide wage increase of 211 percent. In Texas, which was not permitted to import braceros during these years, wages for cotton-pickers increased 236 percent. The situation was reversed between 1947 and 1950, when bracero employment in Texas cotton-picking operations skyrocketed and the number of braceros employed in cotton picking in California actually declined. During this period cotton-picking wages stayed constant nationally, rose in California by 15 percent, and declined in Texas by 11 percent. These and similar data led the President's Commission on Migratory Labor to conclude that "the agencies of Government responsible for importing and contracting foreign labor have not been successful in protecting domestic farm labor from detrimental effects of imported contract alien labor. We find alien labor has depressed farm wages and, therefore, has been detrimental to domestic labor."[8]

The depressive effect of bracero employment on farm labor wages was felt not only in cotton production but throughout the agricultural sector. The massive introduction of braceros into California effectively froze wages in some crop areas and actually brought them down in others. As a result, farm wages in the United States declined as a proportion of manufacturing wages. This decline was especially severe in California. In 1948, when the number of braceros was still comparatively small, U.S. farm wages stood at 55 percent of manufacturing wages nationally, and California farm wages were somewhat higher at 64.7 percent of national manufacturing wages. By 1959, at the height of the bracero programs, farm wages nationally had dropped 13 percentage points, to 42 percent of manufacturing wages. In California the drop was even more precipitous: a decline of 18.1 percentage points to 46.6 percent. After the termination of the bracero programs in 1964, farm wages began a slow ascent, reaching 46 percent of manufacturing wages nationally and 49.8 percent in California by 1967.[9]

The specific mechanism for creating labor shortages to justify importing braceros has been described in detail by Ernesto Galarza. Grower associations submitted estimates of the number of braceros needed for the next harvest period. These figures were prepared by the growers themselves to reflect what they considered the optimal number of braceros. Grower associations determined prevailing wages much as they had during the 1930s. Individual employers went through the motions of advertising for domestic workers at a low wage level, knowing that few would accept field work at such rates. In this manner a manipulated and artificial labor shortage was created. Even when there were a sufficient number of domestic workers willing to accept the low wages advertised, braceros were often illegally hired instead: they were less likely to strike or disrupt harvest operations. In fact, there is no record of even a single bracero-initiated strike for the life of the programs. Instead, braceros were frequently used to replace striking domestic workers. The few times braceros refused to work in fields that were the sites of labor disputes were exceptions to a general pattern.[10]

The limited guarantees against certain kinds of exploitation and abuses were eroded less than a year after the first program began. The FSA acted in strict accordance with the provisions of the initial braceros agreement during its first months of operation.[11] A personal representative of California governor Earl Warren therefore told a Senate committee that the FSA was the wrong agency to administer the program and that the agency was making it difficult for growers to get along with their bracero workers.[12] As a result, on 1 July 1943 administrative control of the bracero programs was transferred from the FSA to the War Manpower Commission, a change that Carey McWilliams described as "tantamount to turning the whole program over to the farm associations."[13]

The initial bracero agreement was originally intended to terminate at the close of World War II. Many observers predicted that its end would stimulate well-organized and potentially successful unionization drives. Workers returning to the fields had experienced the benefits of collective bargaining in industry and were likely to be dissatisfied with conditions in agriculture.[14] Moreover, in 1945 and 1946 the International Longshoremen and Warehousemen's Union (ILWU) set a precedent for farm labor unionization by organizing Hawaiian sugar and pineapple workers, including a substantial number of field workers. With the anticipated exit of braceros, the oversupply of agricultural workers would temporarily be removed, and domestic workers would be in a favorable negotiating position.

Growers had similar expectations. Major grower organizations predictably claimed that a field labor shortage was imminent should the bracero agreement be ended, and with it would come serious instability in food production with consequent detrimental effects on national economic growth. To buttress support for an extension of the agreement, figures were published demonstrating a steady increase in the number of undocumented Mexicans entering the United States, the implication being that the Southwest would be flooded with illegal immigrants if bracero importation were abruptly ended. The irony was that Southwestern growers themselves were increasing their employment of undocumented workers while using their presence to argue in favor of continued bracero certification. Acquiescing to the interests of agribusiness and ignoring the protests of organized labor, Congress extended the bracero programs several times, beginning in December 1945. This concession probably prevented a return to farm labor insurgency and the movement for labor reform begun during the previous decade.

Beginning in 1948, several significant changes occurred in the bracero agreements. The programs were transferred from the War Manpower Commission to the Bureau of Employment Security, an agency of the Department of Labor. The bureau in turn utilized the services of the California Farm Placement Bureau, an agency with a history of close cooperation with growers and virtually complete inattention to complaints by farm workers.[15]

Most of the other changes were equally favorable to agribusiness. Unlike the initial bracero contracts, the new agreements did not stipulate a minimum wage or piece-rate guarantee. No formal mechanism was established to insure compliance with the contract, and the former unemployment pay of $3.00 a day was dropped. Texas was now participating in the programs and would soon rival California in the number of braceros used.[16]

The most significant change in the program was that the federal government was no longer the recruiter and contractor of bracero labor. That task was taken over by individual growers and their representatives. The grower-employer now had to pay round-trip transportation costs from Mexico and post a $25.00 bond guaranteeing transportation home. Naturally this requirement met with disapproval. Many growers claimed that too many braceros "skipped"—that is, illegally left the job to seek more attractive positions in industry or elsewhere in agriculture, causing forfeiture of the bond.

Despite this objection, many observers thought that agribusiness had achieved an ideal situation. Direct grower recruitment had been established, and many of the previous protections and restrictions had been removed. Moreover, enforcement of the contracts was likely to be loose; only the U.S. Employment Service was given undefined

duties in this area. In practice this meant that the federal government no longer guaranteed fulfillment of bracero contracts.[17] As a
result, agribusiness was virtually in charge of every phase of the
bracero programs.

Still, direct recruitment had some critical drawbacks. It had been
easier and less expensive to let a government agency handle the
recruitment, allocation, and transportation of braceros, especially
with some of the protections for braceros eliminated. The new contracts represented a step toward a loose contract, although many
growers considered the minimum four-month contract unnecessarily
long. The programs were also still designated as temporary. Growers
could not be guaranteed that bracero labor would be available in the
future. In retrospect, however, it can be seen that direct grower
recruitment served to keep the machinery of the programs in operation until a more permanent basis for the agreements was established with the passage of Public Law 78 in 1951.

Agribusiness has never adequately regulated its labor supply
when left to its own devices. The history of agricultural labor is
replete with examples of government intervention to regulate and
manage transitions in the work force. Corporate agriculture has been
unable either to establish a systematic, rational, and regulated mode
of labor recruitment or to prevent abuse of the labor force. Continued
uncertainty about the ability of the farm labor market to supply labor
for the next harvest or the next decade has historically stimulated
growers to create a surplus labor supply for field work. Because of this
tradition of ineffectiveness, direct grower recruitment of braceros
and the reduction of involvement by the federal government worked
against the long-term interests of agribusiness. Even large grower
associations had no systematic conduits for recruitment and distribution of workers through which braceros could be channeled. As a
result, under direct grower recruitment the number of braceros used
in California actually declined. The program was also less stable
than under pre-1948 agreements and could be terminated
quickly. In fact, abuses of braceros and regular violations of contracts
under the direct recruitment system soon resulted in a threat by
Mexico to cut off the programs entirely. What was needed to preserve
the viability of bracero labor was government intervention to coordinate the entire process again and provide a minimal guarantee of
contract enforcement. The passage of Public Law 78 in 1951 accomplished this on terms very favorable to agribusiness and also institutionalized the programs on a more permanent basis, making them
less vulnerable to sudden termination. After this, grower demand for

undocumented workers virtually disappeared. Shortly thereafter the federal government undertook a successful campaign to close the border to illegal immigration.

From the end of the war to the closing of the border in 1954, braceros and undocumented Mexican nationals dominated the labor force in many crop areas in California and throughout the Southwest. Between 1942 and 1950, over 430,000 Mexicans passed through bracero contract centers. The programs began cautiously; only 4,200 Mexican workers participated during the first year. This figure rose to 53,000 in 1943, and later it fluctuated between a low of 19,600 in 1947 and a high of 107,000 in 1949. The latter figure reflected the impact of the initial use of braceros in Texas. The actual number of braceros working in the United States was much greater than these figures indicate because of contract extensions and renewals. California used over half of the braceros contracted.[18] In 1948–50, when the use of braceros in California was at a low point because of the inefficiency of direct grower recruitment, braceros were concentrated in the southern counties of the state and in Riverside, Ventura, and Monterey counties, where growers were well organized.[19] After the federal government became involved in bracero recruitment again in 1951, the number of braceros skyrocketed, and their labor was utilized in nearly every agricultural region in the state.

The proportion of undocumented Mexican nationals at work in the California fields during this period is impossible to ascertain. Growers employing workers supplied by labor contractors were perhaps unsure of the proportion themselves. The best systematic evidence of trends in illegal traffic is the number of deportations by the Border Patrol, but this figure can be misleading, as enforcement changed drastically over a short time. Moreover, only a small proportion of those apprehended were actually working in the fields. When a check was made of farm laborers, the number removed from any particular field generally was small and usually represented only a fraction of the undocumented workers employed at the time. Nevertheless, statistics of the Immigration and Naturalization Service can provide a rough picture of the rise of illegal immigration.

From 1940 to 1943, the number of undocumented Mexicans deported from the United States ranged from 5,100 to 8,900. This rose to 29,000 in 1944; to 69,000 in 1945; and to 101,000 in 1946. It continued to rise steadily, reaching a peak of 920,000 in 1954, before declining sharply when the border was closed.[20] In 1948, for example, estimates placed the number of undocumented workers in California between 35,000 and 60,000, with 4,000 to 6,000 situated in the Imperial

Valley alone.[21] The pattern of deportations confirms the comments of many observers that the use of undocumented agricultural workers rose sharply after World War II as added insurance against labor organization and a rise in labor costs.

THE DIGIORGIO STRIKE

The only significant agricultural labor activity for most of the bracero era was undertaken by the National Farm Labor Union (NFLU), chartered by the AFL in 1946. Its president was H. L. Mitchell, former president of the Southern Tenant Farmers Union, a union active during the 1930s in Arkansas, Louisiana, Texas, and Oklahoma and at one time affiliated with UCAPAWA. Its director of organizations, Henry Hasiwar, was a veteran of several industrial union drives during the previous decade. Ernesto Galarza, who became responsible for union publicity and who would later write extensively on both the union and the bracero programs, had been a political liaison for several Latin American unions and had a Ph.D. in economics from Columbia University. Although the NFLU was national in scope, its largest strike took place in Kern County, California, against the DiGiorgio Fruit Corporation and involved workers from the small southern San Joaquin Valley towns of Arvin, Lamont, and Weedpatch.

The DiGiorgio Fruit Corporation, with its extensive financial empire and corporate ties, was a prime example of agribusiness. The corporation owned farms, orchards, packing sheds, and brokerage facilities. Concentrated in California, its holdings stretched from Borrego Valley in northeastern San Diego County 600 miles north to Marysville. The site of the strike, DiGiorgio Farms, encompassed 11,000 acres of grapes, fruit orchards, and vegetables within a 19-mile perimeter. DiGiorgio Farms was among the first to introduce bracero labor into the San Joaquin Valley. In Florida the corporation operated several thousand acres of citrus orchards. It also managed a chain of produce auctions in Baltimore, Chicago, Pittsburgh, New York, and Cincinnati at which it sold its products as well as those of other growers on a commission basis. Appropriately, the corporation's headquarters were located not in an agricultural region but on Montgomery Street in San Francisco.[22]

The corporation was closely controlled by the DiGiorgio family. The founder, Joseph, had numerous ties in corporate and financial circles. His nephew, Robert, served on the boards of the Bank of America, the Union Oil Company, and other enterprises collateral to agribusiness. The corporation had helped organize the Associated Farmers during the 1930s and solicited contributions in the corporate world for its operations. The corporation was extensive enough to be indicted by a federal grand jury in 1942, with some of its associates in the produce trade, "for wrongful and unlawful combination to fix, control, peg and stabilize prices . . . by controlling and restricting the channels and methods of distribution."[23] The corporation bargained collectively with teamsters, cannery workers, and longshoremen, but not with its farm workers.

DiGiorgio Farms drew much of its manpower from surrounding towns like Arvin and Lamont, the homes of many former Mexican and Dust Bowl migrants who had stabilized their residence and reduced their dependency on seasonal jobs. These workers formed the core of Local 218 of the NFLU. Other DiGiorgio workers—Mexicans, Filipinos, and whites—were housed on ethnically segregated company property. Wages typically were low: 80 to 85 cents an hour with no extra pay added to the base rate for overtime or night work. Crews could be called to work at any time, including Sundays. Seniority was nonexistent in the fields and packing sheds, and workers could be fired on the spot with no chance of appeal.[24] By September 1947 the NFLU had signed up and received union dues from 858 of the 1,345 employees on DiGiorgio's payroll. A list of demands was issued calling for a raise of ten cents an hour, seniority rights, and union recognition. Joseph and Robert DiGiorgio refused to reply.

The strike began on 1 October, immediately reducing DiGiorgio's labor force by two-thirds. The union claimed that a majority of shed and field workers, irrigators, and tractor drivers participated in the strike, and all of the 130 braceros employed by DiGiorgio at the time initially joined it. This prompted the corporation to call in the Kern County sheriff and a field representative from the U.S. Department of Agriculture. What they said to the striking braceros is not known, since the only other witnesses to the conversation were senior DiGiorgio officers, but the braceros resumed work immediately.[25] Braceros were particularly vulnerable to grower reprisals. Failure to work meant deportation and little chance of being recontracted in the future. Although bracero employment during a strike violated the bracero agreement, braceros remained at work in DiGiorgio's fields until 10 November, when pressure by the NFLU stimulated the Department of Agriculture to cancel their contracts. During the six-week interim, they were escorted by government officials through NFLU picket lines.[26] Supplemented by undocumented workers who faced arrest and deportation if they supported the strike, braceros formed the core of DiGiorgio's labor force until a crew of strikebreakers were recruited, some traveling from as far away as Texas.

The union maintained picket lines around the DiGiorgio property for nine months. They ceased only when prohibited by a National Labor Relations Board examiner on the grounds that the union was engaging in a boycott, forbidden by the recently passed Taft-Hartley Amendment to the NLRA. Although agricultural workers were not subject to the provisions of the act, it took seventeen additional months for the injunction to be overturned by the NLRB. By that time the strike had long been lost.[27]

Despite its failure, the DiGiorgio strike could have been a harbinger of future insurgency had the expansion of the bracero programs not undercut this potential. The core of Local 218 was composed of former migrants who had established residential stability and represented a solid foundation for establishing and sustaining a farm worker union. A growing proportion of the farm labor force was becoming localized, creating year-round communities in towns that dotted agricultural regions: Arvin and Lamont in the southern San Joaquin Valley; Delano, Pixley, Earlimart, and McFarland further to the north; Yuba City, Marysville, and Gridley in Sacramento Valley's Peach Bowl. Even in the Imperial Valley towns of Calexico, El Centro, Brawley, Westmoreland, Holtville, Huber, Calipatria, and Imperial, where agricultural jobs were most seriously threatened by braceros and undocumented workers, the beginnings of stable farm worker communities could be discerned.

Moreover, long-standing ethnic animosities were being overcome. Although workers themselves often referred to Local 218 as an "Okie Union," in itself something of significance given the antiunion disposition of many Dust Bowl migrants ten years before, the union refused to draw lines among members of different ethnicities. Instead, the critical divisions were between workers of different citizenship and employment status: domestics, braceros, and undocumented Mexican nationals.

Despite the growing residential stability of domestic workers, the growers' ability to displace them in favor of braceros and undocumented workers, especially during strikes, prevented the NFLU from establishing a series of stable farm worker locals throughout the state. The union continued to organize and coordinate strike activity with varying degrees of success, but concessions by growers were temporary, typically lasting only for the duration of a specific harvest.

In a September 1949 strike, one of the largest led by the NFLU, several thousand cottonpickers in four San Joaquin Valley counties won their modest demand that a wage cut be rescinded and that the rate remain the same as the previous year's—$3.00 per hundred pounds. One of the people on the mobile picket line was Cesar Chavez, who was then twenty-one years old and participating in his first strike.[28] Smaller-scale NFLU-led strikes continued over the next several years: potatopickers around Wasco, Schafter, and McFarland in 1950; tomato harvesters near Tracy in 1950; Imperial Valley melonpickers in 1951 and 1952. By 1952 the union had organized nine strikes, but none had resulted in union recognition, and only the 1952 Los Banos melon strike in northwest Fresno County was resolved through negotiation. Many of the strikes were stimulated by the substantial wage cuts that accompanied the growing concentration of braceros in particular crops. At best the strikes could only rescind wage reductions. Braceros continued to displace domestic workers over a wider geographical area and in a growing number of crops.

Unless the bracero programs were eliminated or curtailed and grower access to undocumented workers was limited, Ernesto Galarza, the NFLU director of research and education, concluded that efforts to organize the farm labor force were "doomed in advance." The union's primary goal in the decade after the DiGiorgio strike became the exposure of the deleterious effects of the bracero programs on domestic farm workers' employment and wages and systematic violation of the terms of the bracero agreements.[29] This goal the union single-mindedly pursued over an eight-year period beginning in 1952, keeping the bracero issue surrounded in controversy. Its long-term goals were the repeal of Public Law 78 and the disclosure of the extent of undocumented worker traffic. Given the unfavorable environment for organizing, the conservative disposition of the California and federal administrations during this period, and the customary lack of support from industrial and urban unions, this appears to have been a realistic appraisal of what was possible. The NFLU achieved only limited success in the fields, but its exposés of the practical, day-to-day operations of the bracero programs represented a major contribution toward terminating Public Law 78 and thus establishing the preconditions for the rise of the United Farm Workers.

The struggle between the NFLU and DiGiorgio did not end with the union's withdrawal of its picket line. In November 1949 a subcommittee of the House Committee on Education and Labor held two days of hearings in Bakersfield on the DiGiorgio strike. This action was in part prompted by a libel suit the corporation had filed against the NFLU for showing a prounion film, "Poverty in the Valley of Plenty." The film was sponsored by a number of trade unions, including the Hollywood Film Council, AFL, which produced and distributed it. Among those considered to narrate the film was the president of the Screen Actors Guild, Ronald Reagan, then a Democrat, but Harry Flannery was finally selected.[30]

Representative Cleveland Baily from West Virginia, the author of a resolution to repeal the Taft-Hartley Act, was chairman of the subcommittee. Also on the subcommittee was Representative Thomas Werdel, whose congressional district encompassed Kern County and DiGiorgio Farms and who belonged to the same law firm as a member of the DiGiorgio family.[31] Werdel was in fact instrumental in arranging the hearings. Other subcommittee members were Richard Nixon of California, Tom Steed of Oklahoma, Thruston B. Morton of Kentucky, and Leonard Irving of Missouri. Nixon was serving his second term in Congress, and his political career was midway between the Alger Hiss case and the Senate race against Helen Gahagan Douglas. The hearings were attended by a proagribusiness group calling itself the Special Citizens of Kern County. Among them were some of the strongest and most influential backers of a campaign to support Nixon for senator. They were in Bakersfield to watch him perform, and they were not disappointed.

The hearings themselves, although slanted in favor of the DiGiorgio Corporation, did not arouse much publicity. Congressman Nixon questioned witnesses in such a way as to create the impression that outside agitators were the source of the disturbance and that DiGiorgio's workers had not wanted to strike.[32] The main controversy began nearly four months after the hearings closed, when Werdel inserted into the Appendix of the *Congressional Record* an extension of his remarks that, he said, included a majority report filed by the subcommittee.[33] The alleged subcommittee report severely criticized the NFLU, accused the union of libel, and claimed that no strike had existed. It concluded "that this committee has been induced to spend its time and the taxpayer's money to publicize the leadership of a labor organization which has no contracts, no grievances, no strike, no pickets, and only a handful of members."[34] The report appeared over the signatures of Nixon, Morton, and Steed in the appendix of the *Congressional Record* for 9 March 1950.

Following its release, the "report" was extensively quoted in the national press, as was the DiGiorgio Corporation's claim that it had been vindicated. More importantly, the report was used during the next decade by DiGiorgio's lawyers as evidence in several lawsuits, including one brought in 1960 against the newly formed Agricultural Workers Organizing Committee for its showing of "Poverty in the Valley of Plenty." It was powerful propaganda against agricultural unionization and indirectly helped blunt criticism of the bracero system.

On closer scrutiny, it appears that the report was not the subcommittee's official majority report at all. It never had the authorization of the subcommittee, and it did not pass through its official channels.[35] It was probably written by Werdel and his staff or someone associated with them. Over fifteen years after it was published, neither Steed, Morton, nor Nixon would take credit for writing the report.[36] But the document had served its purpose. With the assumed prestige and authority of a Congressional report, it was used as evidence in lawsuits as well as propaganda for the DiGiorgio Corporation and agribusiness in general. It also indirectly promoted continuation of the bracero agreements by condemning the labor organization that was the system's severest critic. And it helped to lay the foundation for the passage of Public Law 78, which placed the bracero programs on a more permanent basis.

THE INSTITUTIONALIZATION OF THE BRACERO PROGRAMS

It was noted above that in some respects the system of direct recruitment worked against the long-term interests of corporate agriculture. The difficulties of direct recruitment were strikingly illustrated in the spring of 1951, when Mexico announced that it would terminate the bracero agreement unless direct recruitment was eliminated. Mexico had never been pleased with this arrangement and was sensitive to the lack of enforcement of bracero contracts and the systematic abuses of bracero and undocumented Mexican labor. Braceros' dissatisfaction with their treatment had manifested itself in work stoppages, desertions, a flood of mail addressed to Mexican consuls, and appeals for advice to farm worker organizations. Most of their distress went unnoticed and unrecorded.[37]

Mexico's ultimatum prompted agribusiness to turn to the federal government for a solution. Previous bracero programs had been concluded under provisions of immigration laws or wartime emergency measures. To stabilize the bracero agreements, a legislative foundation not yet in existence was needed. Public Law 78 provided the basis for the institutionalization of the programs. It was first introduced in the U.S. Senate by Senator Allen J. Ellender of Louisiana on 27 February 1951 and was sponsored in the House by Representative W. R. Poage of Texas. The only opposition to the legislation among farm organizations came from the Farmers Union, which claimed that it would prove detrimental to the interests of small farmers. Public Law 78 passed both branches of Congress by a comfortable margin. Rejecting the advice of the Department of Labor, President Truman signed it into law on 13 July.[38]

Public Law 78 established an administrative framework for recruiting, contracting, and transporting bracero labor to Southwestern growers and provided guarantees that the contracts would be upheld by employers. The Department of Labor coordinated the activities of the government agencies involved in the programs. In California, primary responsibility was delegated to the Department of Employment. Public Law 78 contained many of the elements of earlier bracero programs. The Secretary of Labor was given the right to recruit Mexican workers for agricultural employment. Workers whose entry was illegal could be included if they had resided in the United States for the preceding five years. Also included were those who had previously entered under a legal contract but remained after it expired. Transportation expenses were to be paid by the federal government, but growers were to reimburse the Department of Labor for its services with an amount not to exceed $15.00 per bracero.

As in past agreements, the Secretary of Labor was required to declare that there was a labor shortage and that reasonable efforts had been made to attract domestic workers in an area before braceros could be employed. Braceros were not to be used to adversely affect the wages and working conditions of domestic workers. As before, these provisions proved to be essentially meaningless. The law was originally scheduled to expire on 3 December 1953, but it was repeatedly renewed before expiring on 31 December 1964. Until the early 1960s, extensions faced only weak opposition.

With the passage of the law, the United States was free to work out a specific bracero agreement with Mexico. This was concluded on 2 August. It was similar to previous agreements but far more detailed. Included were provisions that braceros would receive the prevailing wage, would be guaranteed employment for three-fourths of the contract period, and would be provided free transportation to and from their place of employment. It also contained basic elements of Public Law 78, the most important of which was government recruiting. Although amended in subsequent years, the 1951 agreement served as a basis for all future programs for the duration of the bracero system.

Now that the bracero system had a more permanent status, the number of braceros contracted soared. The number nearly tripled between 1950 and 1951 (67,500 to 192,000) and climbed steadily upward to a record 445,000 in 1956. Texas and California accounted for 50 to 80 percent of all the braceros contracted during any single year.

In California the new bracero agreement under Public Law 78 meant a dramatic extension of bracero employment to an expanding portion of its agricultural operations. The number of certifications issued to employers permitting them to contract braceros rose from 254 in 1952 to over 1,300 in 1955. The number of braceros hired each year in California during the mid- and late 1950s ranged from 140,000 to 185,000, making them the dominant source of field labor for fruits and vegetables.[39] In some crop areas, braceros provided virtually all the field labor. For example, in 1957 the harvest forces for San Joaquin Valley tomatoes, Imperial County lettuce, and San Diego County celery were 92, 93, and 94 percent bracero labor respectively. In 1962, bracero labor made up 82, 80, 71, and 54 percent of the seasonal labor employed in California's entire harvest of lemons, tomatoes, lettuce, and asparagus. Braceros made possible the increase in strawberry cultivation from 7,000 acres in 1951 to more than 20,000 acres by 1957. Overall, bracero labor increased as a proportion of all seasonal labor in California. In 1951, the year of the passage of Public Law 78, braceros were 15.1 percent of the seasonal work force. This proportion increased to 34.2 percent in 1957 before declining to 23.6 percent in 1962. (The last figure represents a lessened grower reliance on bracero labor due in part to increasing mechanization and growing public opposition to the bracero programs.)[40]

For domestic farm workers, the rapid growth in bracero labor meant more than increased difficulty in obtaining field work. Agricultural work became increasingly arduous: the short-handle hoe was introduced, hourly rates were substituted for piece rates, production quotas were instituted, and more time was lost moving from field to field.[41] Female and older male workers were the first to be displaced. Gradually a substantial proportion of domestic farm workers lost their jobs to braceros and could not find enough employment in the fields to survive. Especially vulnerable were members or supporters of fledgling farm labor unions, who were apparently singled out for replacement by braceros.

Large-scale displacement of domestic workers began in 1952–53 in the border counties. Domestics retreated farther north to agricultural regions in Los Angeles and Ventura counties and the San

Joaquin, Sacramento, and Napa valleys. Before the general public was aware of it, bracero-induced displacement spread throughout the state during the next seven years; by 1957, in the Peach Bowl surrounding the Sacramento Valley towns of Yuba City, Marysville, Gridley, and Live Oak, braceros, supplemented by a small force of undocumented workers, had taken many of the pruning and harvest jobs previously performed by domestic workers. There, as elsewhere, a primary labor force composed of braceros and a smaller number of undocumented workers was established. The remainder of the jobs were filled by domestic workers willing to accept the same conditions. They had no leverage to bargain for improvements. Domestic workers were rarely displaced entirely; some domestics were needed for their experience and skill, and their presence kept the labor force elastic. Smaller growers tended to use a lower proportion of braceros than did large growers and agricultural corporations. However, the overall consequences for domestic workers were demoralization, lower wages, unemployment, dislocation, a return to migrancy, and, for many, settlement in urban areas.[42]

After the initial bracero agreement under Public Law 78, the federal government moved even further toward accommodating agribusiness. The new Eisenhower administration was especially disposed during this time to follow the recommendations of corporate agriculture.[43] The most obvious illustration of this stance was the action taken by the government when Mexico balked at renewing the agreement.

The initial agreement was due to expire on 31 December 1953. During the renewal negotiations between the two governments, Mexico demanded that certain aspects of bracero contracts be strengthened to insure greater worker protection. Mexico was especially displeased about the method of determining prevailing wages. Mexican negotiators preferred a different method, possibly one in which the U.S. Department of Labor fixed the wage rate at levels to guarantee braceros a higher income. The U.S. government was not prepared to make this change; negotiations stalled; and after a fifteen-day extension, the bracero agreement expired on 15 January 1954.

The U.S. Departments of State, Labor, and Justice immediately announced that they would begin unilateral bracero recruitment on 18 January. Not only would the Mexican government have no input into the process, but braceros so contracted would be completely under the control of U.S. officials. Word spread of the U.S.'s intention, and Mexicans wishing to be contracted massed at the border. In response, Mexico posted armed guards to keep them from crossing. The result was a series of clashes from 23 January to 5 February at border crossings in Calexico and San Ysidro, California, between crowds of would-be braceros who rushed the border and Mexican guards who tried to hold them back with clubs, water hoses, and guns. Those who made it across were immediately taken by U.S. officials for contracting. The struggle was appropriately illustrated by a newspaper photograph showing an aspiring bracero being simultaneously pulled south by a Mexican border official and north by a U.S. officer.[44] Approximately 3,500 braceros were recruited in this manner in less than two weeks.[45]

The program ended on 5 February, when unilateral recruitment was declared illegal under Public Law 78. By this time immediate manpower needs had been filled. To alter Public Law 78 to allow unilateral recruitment in the future, Congress passed House Joint Resolution 355 in early March. After the phrase "pursuant to arrangements between the United States and the Republic of Mexico" was added "or after every practical effort has been made to negotiate and reach agreement on such arrangements."[46] This addition made it clear the United States could undertake unilateral recruitment in the future if Mexico rejected the terms offered by the Department of Labor essentially on behalf of Southwestern agribusiness. Faced with this show of force, the Mexican government backed down, and a new bracero agreement was quickly reached by 10 March. It left provisions of the previous agreement intact and even took away Mexico's jurisdiction in some areas.[47] With the new bracero program firmly institutionalized on terms even more favorable to growers, the desirability of employing undocumented Mexicans in the fields diminished considerably. Consequently, with grower approval and assistance, the federal government undertook a successful campaign to curtail illegal traffic across the border.

Pressure had been mounting for several years for the federal government to undertake such a campaign; in fact, Mexico had insisted that the United States commit itself to curtailing the flow before it signed the 1951 bracero agreement. In signing Public Law 78, President Truman stressed the need for stronger measures to reduce illegal immigration.[48] The situation was widely publicized in the national press during the early 1950s, partly as a result of an increase in unemployment after the end of the Korean War. The influx of undocumented workers was termed an "invasion": early in 1954, the *New York Times* featured nearly a dozen articles on the subject, one entitled "Border Invasion Declared a Peril." CBS radio aired a special documentary on 4 April on the "Wetback Problem."[49]

The most frequently mentioned solution to the problem was legislation penalizing the employers of undocumented workers, but no such legislation was passed in the early 1950s. In fact, when the flow across the border was at its peak in 1952 and 1954, senators and representatives from border states persuaded Congress to cut appropriations for the Border Patrol.[50] What appeared to be lacking was assurance that agribusiness would have an abundant supply of inexpensive and controllable labor should the volume of undocumented workers be reduced. The new bracero agreement tilted the power relationships in such a way that the number of undocumented workers in the fields could be drastically reduced without detrimental effects on agribusiness. Many growers in a remarkable reversal cooperated with the campaign against the presence of undocumented workers.

Before 1954 the primary means of dealing with undocumented Mexicans, or "wetbacks," was to legalize their presence by converting them to braceros, a process called "drying out." Worked out jointly by growers and government officials, the tactic was very successful: in 1950 there were five times more undocumented Mexicans converted to braceros than new braceros contracted.[51] The new bracero agreement made this process unnecessary.

"Operation Wetback," as it was called, commenced in June 1954 under the direction of the Commissioner of Immigration, General Joseph May Swing. It consisted of a series of deportation drives. The commissioner made considerable efforts to enlist grower support. More than 800 border patrolmen set up roadblocks in southern California and conducted raids moving south and east. Estimates placed the number of undocumented Mexicans deported during the drive at 84,000, most of these being deported from farms. Many thousands more returned to Mexico on their own in fear of arrest. The scenario was repeated in Texas, where over 60,000 people returned to Mexico to avoid arrest during the first thirty days of the sweep.[52] The extent of grower cooperation led General Swing to remark that the drive "would have been impossible without the generous cooperation extended . . . by farmers, ranchers, and growers," who "were never too busy to help in the enforcement of the laws of their nation."[53] Ernesto Galarza of the NFLU remarked that it was the change in grower attitudes toward undocumented Mexicans, rather than his union's campaign, that was responsible for the efficiency with which illegal traffic was curtailed. He concluded that by the time Operation Wet-back was launched, "the bracero system had shown its economic and political feasibility," making undocumented Mexican nationals irrelevant to grower needs.[54] Through the bracero programs and the previous "drying out" process, agribusiness had achieved a generous supply of labor on extremely favorable terms. The influx of un-documented Mexicans was dramatically reduced. Whereas 920,000 Mexicans were arrested and deported in 1954, only 222,000 were seized and deported in 1955 and the figures declined steadily—63,000 in 1956, 33,000 in 1958, and 23,000 in 1960.[55]

The problem of competition from bracero labor remained. Through-out the 1950s the NFLU's campaign against it received little support from the AFL-CIO. The union officially changed its name to the National Agricultural Workers Union (NAWU) in 1952, but its emphasis remained the same. Union officials collected evidence from domestic workers in nearly every area of the state, carefully documenting how braceros were given preferential hiring, were dis-placing domestic workers from rural communities, and were under-mining wage guarantees. By this time Galarza was virtually the only official NAWU representative in California, aided by groups of volunteers collecting testimony and affidavits. Information on the adverse effects of the bracero system and its systematic abuses was given as much publicity as possible in an attempt to generate con-troversy. According to Galarza, however, the AFL-CIO was not espe-cially interested in challenging prevailing labor relations in agricul-ture. The federation had made its peace with agribusiness, and a number of member unions were engaged in aspects of food production and distribution. In effect, the interests of field workers were ignored in order to maintain established collective bargaining relationships. From the federation's point of view, the research of the NAWU was irrelevant at best.

The AFL-CIO's antipathy to NAWU was exemplified by the estab-lishment in February 1959 of the Agricultural Workers Organizing Committee (AWOC), which rapidly undermined and replaced NAWU. (Galarza served briefly as an organizer for AWOC before becoming disaffected and leaving for the academic world.) Although AWOC's establishment was heralded by both the national press and the federation itself as a prelude to a nationwide farm worker un-ionization drive, it soon became apparent that its close ties to orga-nized labor involved serious drawbacks. The AFL-CIO was not much more serious about farm labor than the AFL had been. Franz Daniels, assistant director of organization for the AFL-CIO, candidly told an AWOC staff meeting not long after the union was established, "Don't kid yourself. Meany just got tired of going to international conventions and being needled by labor people from smaller, poorer countries, who could point out that at least they had organized farm workers, while the American labor movement hadn't. He set up AWOC to get them off his back."[56]

Norman Smith was chosen as the director of AWOC. Although he had been a United Auto Workers activist during the 1930s, Smith had had little connection with the labor movement in general during the previous eighteen years, when he was a supervisor with the Kaiser Steel Company. He had no involvement with farm labor organizing. Consequently, he had little idea of how to begin the monumental task of reaching the scattered and diverse segments of farm labor, and when successes were not forthcoming, the AFL-CIO drastically curtailed its financial support for the union.

The AWOC staff's lack of farm labor experience made their efforts especially inefficient and expensive. Key decisions were made by people unfamiliar with the life and work patterns of farm workers, and these often turned out to be paternalistic and manipulative. This problem is best illustrated by contrasting the positions of Smith and Galarza. Whereas Galarza, like Cesar Chavez later, conceived of the union as a democratic organization that would help its members develop the knowledge and skills for independent decision making, Smith frequently stated that he was unconcerned with the style of organizing as long as the job was done.[57] For all his dedication, Smith represented the kind of bread-and-butter unionism advocated by the federation. Despite its shortcomings, however, AWOC proved to be a crucial factor in the rise of farm labor militancy during the mid-1960s. AWOC locals initiated several important strikes, including the Delano grape strike in 1965. The union also inherited the role of principal opponent of the bracero system.

THE END OF THE BRACERO PROGRAMS

The failure of Congress to extend Public Law 78 beyond 1964 appears to contradict the prevailing tendency of government policies and actions to favor agribusiness. The bracero programs, perhaps the most advantageous labor supply situation ever presented to agribusiness, ended even without massive farm labor protests against its continuation. In fact, farm labor activity during the early 1960s was comparatively weak and ineffective.

Instead, the bracero system was the victim of the profound structural changes in American politics stimulated by the civil rights movement. The system's abuses and its detrimental effects on domestic agricultural workers, a large proportion of whom were Mexican Americans, attracted the attention of a number of organizations attached to or supportive of the civil rights movement. Once a connection was made between Mexican American poverty and the labor policies of the federal government, farm labor supporters advanced from criticism of the slack enforcement of bracero contracts to demands that the system be terminated. In a sense, then, massive insurgency did lead to the end of the bracero programs, but the greater part of it took place in the South rather than in the fields of California.

While the internal resources of farm workers and farm labor organizations remained small, the spread of the civil rights movement to encompass the Chicano population helped them mobilize the resources of many of the organizations and individuals supporting civil rights reforms. In addition, social changes stimulated by mass activism allowed them to mobilize a sympathetic public and stimulate opposition to Public Law 78 in Congress. The termination of the bracero system was incorporated into the goals of the civil rights movement, and a liberal-labor reform coalition attacked the privileges agribusiness had derived from public policy.

This antibracero coalition included representatives of labor, church, civil rights, civil liberties, and social action organizations, the same elements that later formed the early base of support for the Delano strike. In the early 1960s they successfully pressured a reluctant Kennedy administration into more strenuous enforcement of the terms of the bracero contracts, and later they moved the administration toward an increasingly critical appraisal of the programs. The number of organizations involved was impressive.[58] Besides the AFL-CIO and many of its member unions, these included the United Auto Workers, the International Brotherhood of Teamsters, the International Longshoremen's and Warehousemen's Union, the National Catholic Rural Life Conference, the National Catholic Welfare Council, the National Council of Churches, the Council for Christian Social Action, the Commission on Social Action of Reform Judaism, the American Friends Service Committee, the National Consumers League, Americans for Democratic Action, and the National Association for the Advancement of Colored People. One of the most active was the National Advisory Committee on Farm Labor, headed by Frank Graham, a former U.S. senator and president of the University of North Carolina, and A. Philip Randolph, vice president of the AFL-CIO. Among the committee's members were Helen Gahagan Douglas, Clark Kerr, Eleanor Roosevelt, and Norman Thomas. The committee sponsored public hearings on farm labor in February 1959, documenting, among other conditions, the decline in agricultural wages in relation to factory wages since World War II.[59]

Another group, Citizens for Farm Labor, was more explicitly opposed to Public Law 78. Organized by Henry P. Anderson, a California public health official who had investigated the impact of braceroism on farm worker housing and sanitation, its fifty-six-member advisory board included attorneys, legislators, professors, and church officials. The organization was particularly active in countering agribusiness propaganda. Others who became active in farm labor issues at this point and would remain active well into the NFWA-UFW era, were Father James L. Vizzard, S.J., director of the National Catholic Rural Life Conference, Monsignor George Higgins of the National Catholic Welfare Council, and Rev. Wayne C. Hartmire of the California Migrant Ministry of the National Council of Churches.

Stimulated by the successes of the civil rights movement and given hope by the election of John Kennedy that the nation was entering an era of social reform, many of these organizations joined those involved in farm labor organizing to mount pressure against the current bracero agreement scheduled to expire at the end of 1961. Some of their actions were loosely coordinated, but most were undertaken by individual organizations. Jointly, they pamphleted, debated agribusiness representatives, pressured individual members of Congress, documented conditions, and publicized their arguments. Their calls for reform were supported by the public indignation aroused by the CBS television documentary "Harvest of Shame," aired in November 1960.

This emphasis on mass activism as a stimulus of reforms points up the similarities between the movement against Public Law 78 and the more intensive activism of the late 1930s and the mid-1970s. It argues against the interpretation of the decline of the bracero programs as an elite-sponsored process with little mass support.[60] Elites were split on the issue. A decline in bracero utilization made the termination of Public Law 78 less traumatic for agribusiness than it would otherwise have been. The real reason for the movement's success, however, was the sympathetic national audience that farm worker protests now created.

A strike led by AWOC in the Imperial Valley lettuce fields from December 1960 to March 1961 provided strategic publicity to the anti-bracero movement. The union had several dedicated organizers, but it was hampered by a lack of support at the national level. AWOC called a strike beginning in mid-December in cooperation with the United Packinghouse Workers of America (UPWA), who were involved because packing operations previously performed in sheds had been moved into the fields. As was common practice, striking union workers were replaced by braceros at a fraction of the union wages.[61] The strike itself was well coordinated. The unions made certain that the Farm Placement Service registered strikers and they demanded that braceros be removed as required by law. The two unions also documented their claim that they had support of the overwhelming majority of the more than 3,000 domestic workers in the fields.

The braceros stayed on the job however.[62] The unions were initially hopeful that the Kennedy administration, with former CIO counsel Arthur Goldberg as the new Secretary of Labor, would be sympathetic, especially because the 1960 Democratic platform had condemned the bracero programs. But the administration ignored the unions' demand for the removal of the braceros. AFL-CIO president George Meany abruptly called off the strike and recalled Smith and other AFL-CIO organizers, and the lettuce strike was lost. One of the organizers, Clive Knowles, analyzed the strike's demise: "Later I found out that Kennedy had said to Goldberg, 'get rid of that thing'. . . . So Meany was part of that operation that Goldberg and Kennedy were putting on. In effect they were telling Meany to 'get it out of our hair, we don't have time for it.' "[63]

In June Meany announced that he was ending financial support for AWOC. Cries of betrayal rose from supporters of farm labor, and so, in January 1962, funding was restored. This resumption of support, however, was used to reassert AFL-CIO control over the union. When Meany recalled the "professional" organizers, the leadership of AWOC was assumed by volunteers, who helped create at least a half dozen autonomous unions called "area councils," which elected their own officials and made decisions and policies independent of federation control. Ties were promptly established with civil rights organizations, student groups, and liberal community organizations. AWOC began to construct a broad-based coalition and support system that went beyond established labor organizations. This offered AWOC the possibility of still greater autonomy from the AFL-CIO, so that its future would not be determined by decisions made at the federation's national level.

When financial support was restored, all this ended. The professionals returned, this time headed by C. Al Green, formerly of the building trades. The area councils were abolished, ties with outside groups cut off, and the power structure centralized more rigidly than before. AWOC changed its tactics and attempted to "organize" labor contractors as a method of organizing agricultural workers. The union obtained many "contracts," which made good publicity but meant very little.[64] AWOC was also used by the State Federation of Labor to pursue the latter's political goals, no matter how irrelevant these were to the specific interests of farm labor. Consequently, AWOC devoted the rest of 1962 to mobilizing support among farm workers for the re-election of Governor Edmund G. (Pat) Brown. Brown was at best ambivalent toward the bracero system and soon after his reinauguration went to Washington to urge the extension of Public Law 78.

Although the 1961 lettuce strike was an immediate failure, it did provide the kind of publicity about the use of braceros that fueled the campaign against Public Law 78. Some observers, in fact, marked the fallout from the 1961 strike as the beginning of the end of the system. In a less publicized confrontation, Cesar Chavez, now with Saul Alinsky's Community Service Organization, led a march of unemployed workers into the fields near Oxnard, where braceros were employed. Chavez had tried unsuccessfully for several months to persuade Farm Placement Service and Department of Labor officials to replace the braceros with domestic workers. Publicity resulting from the march led to an investigation and the resignation of the Farm Placement Bureau chief and two other officials. Another bureau official was subsequently fired for accepting bribes from Oxnard growers.[65] AWOC, meanwhile, continued its unionization campaign. From 1960 to 1962 there were 148 agricultural strikes in California, 95 percent occurring during harvest operations.[66] Wages increased, though union recognition was not granted, and the strikes served to focus attention on farm labor discontent and the impact of bracero programs on domestic agricultural labor.

Opposition to Public Law 78 was slowly building in Washington. The first indication of a shift in government policy had appeared during the late 1950s, when Eisenhower's Secretary of Labor, James Mitchell, moved to improve the enforcement of the law, especially the provisions requiring that domestic workers be offered farm employment prior to bracero importation. Mitchell later joined the liberal-labor coalition in supporting minimum-wage legislation for farm workers. He became increasingly critical of the bracero programs, and in 1960 he testified that the programs should be discontinued because of their adverse effects upon domestic workers. In that same year Representative George McGovern of South Dakota and Senator

Eugene McCarthy of Minnesota introduced legislation calling for a gradual phase out of the bracero system. They were among the first members of Congress to initiate action against Public Law 78, and both continued as leaders of the opposition until the law expired. Primarily as a result of the coalescence of antibracero senators and representatives around the McCarthy and McGovern bills, Public Law 78 was extended for only six months, rather than two years as initially proposed. This set the stage for subsequent extension fights.[67] The Kennedy administration was pursuing a less drastic course of action. Although it had refused to intervene when braceros were used to undermine the lettuce strike, the administration recommended that several alterations be made in Public Law 78 to protect domestic workers before it was extended past 31 December 1961. The law was eventually extended unamended for two years, however.

President Kennedy then attempted executive action to protect domestic workers. He directed Secretary of Labor Arthur Goldberg and his successor, Willard Wirtz, to increase bracero wages and tighten the enforcement of the contract clauses forbidding the employment of braceros in year-round jobs or to operate machinery.[68] For the first time since the program's inception, growers faced a significant barrier to their ability to dictate farm labor wages and working conditions. Several rulings by the administration gave farm labor organizers more leverage to increase the cost to growers of continued bracero use. Because Article 22 of Public Law 78 stipulated that braceros could not replace domestic workers participating in a certified strike or locked out because of a labor dispute, AWOC conducted a campaign of infiltrating crews of domestic workers, initiating strikes, and then pressuring the Department of Labor for the removal of braceros from struck fields. When it introduced this tactic, the union quickly realized, as had the NFLU before, that the regulations meant little in practice. After a 1960 strike in the tomato fields near Tracy was undermined by braceros, the union warned both the Mexican government and the new Kennedy administration that the continued use of braceros in such explosive situations threatened the health and safety of Mexican workers. In response, the Department of Labor issued two administrative rulings that gave union organizers several tactical options they had previously lacked. In the past, whenever the Department of Labor was prodded to certify a farm labor strike, braceros were removed only from the specific fields where the labor dispute was going on. In 1961 the Department of Labor ruled that in the event of a certified strike, a grower would lose all of his employed braceros, wherever they were working. It also ruled that only fifty percent of the domestic workers employed by a grower needed to go on strike in order for the department to consider certifying it, and further that in the event of a certified strike a grower's authorization to employ braceros after the strike was concluded would be suspended.[69]

Because domestic workers were seldom totally displaced in any crop area, these rulings gave AWOC an increased ability to disrupt harvest production as a protest against Public Law 78. The smaller the domestic work force, the easier it would be to initiate a certifiable strike, since fewer workers were needed to participate. As it happened, AWOC did not utilize this strategic leverage as well as it might have, because the AFL-CIO continued to be ambivalent toward a concentrated effort in farm labor organizing, but it did initiate localized strikes and petition for the removal of braceros, thus increasing in these instances the cost of bracero use. The control of the labor force was slipping out of the grasp of agribusiness, and the advantage of employing braceros declined as a result.

Opposition in Congress climaxed on 29 March 1963, when the House voted 174 to 158 against an unamended two-year extension of Public Law 78. This vote appeared to mark the end of the bracero programs. The Kennedy administration, however, bowing to direct pressure from Mexico and an appeal from Governor Brown, backed a one-year amended extension. On 20 December 1963, the law was extended for one more year, although without any of the proposed amendments. It was clear to most of those involved that Public Law 78 would not be subsequently renewed, and with surprisingly few dire predictions of economic collapse from the major growers, the last bracero agreement expired on 31 December 1964.[70] Significantly, the termination of the programs coincided with the passage of the Civil Rights Act of 1964.

The brief extensions did not indicate serious resistance. Even such long-time supporters of the law as Senator Allen Ellender argued that the 1963 extension was necessary only to provide an orderly phaseout, and during the 1964 Congressional session there was no major effort to extend the law. The most serious attempt to secure extension during 1964 came from Governor Brown. Although the California Democratic Council and the State Democratic Central Committee had opposed extension and Brown himself indicated his intention to improve farm labor wages when he assumed office in January 1959, on 13 November 1964 Brown proposed a five-year "phaseout plan" that would have extended the bracero system through 1969. Brown based his recommendation on the Giannini

Report, issued in September 1964 by the Giannini Foundation of Agricultural Economics, located at the University of California at Berkeley and endowed by the founder of the Bank of America, the late Joseph Giannini. The study, initiated at Brown's behest, concluded that termination of the bracero programs would severely affect agricultural production. Its principal author was Eric Thor, a University of California agri-economist, a long-time propagandist for agribusiness's viewpoint, and a frequent speaker at grower meetings. Both Governor Brown and the Giannini Foundation must have been embarrassed when California Director of Agriculture Charles Paul announced in June 1965 that growers had available more domestic workers than they could possibly employ and were turning large numbers away.[71]

Although the growers opposed terminating the bracero programs, few, in fact, expected to be ruined as a result. During the last five years of the system's existence, the pattern of bracero utilization had undergone several crucial changes. Essentially as a result of mechanization, the tightened enforcement of bracero contracts, and the increasing possibility that the programs would be terminated, growers had begun to rely less and less on bracero labor. The increased mechanization of the cotton harvest in particular resulted in a drastic decrease in the number of braceros. Cotton production had accounted for 60 percent of bracero employment, but by 1962 70 percent of the cotton produced nationwide was harvested mechanically, contributing to the elimination of 250,000 harvesting jobs from 1959 to 1961 alone.[72] Reflecting this trend, the number of braceros working in Texas during 1962 was only 30,000, less than 25 percent of what it had been two years before. California's total showed a somewhat less precipitous decline to 116,000 by 1962 from a high of 184,000 in 1958.[73] The number of braceros contracted nationally declined from 438,000 in 1959 to 178,000 in 1964, the last year of the programs.

As a result, a declining number of growers employed braceros. Bracero employment had already been the luxury of a relatively small number of growers; for example, during the late 1950s, 94 percent of braceros were employed by 50,000 growers in five states, while 98 percent of the nation's commercial farmers employed no braceros.[74] During the early 1960s, bracero employment became even more concentrated. The effect was to reduce the reliance of agribusiness as a whole on braceros and limit the system's advantages to fewer and fewer growers. The extension of Public Law 78 became less important to agricultural capital as a whole, and consequently, during the program's last years, the defense of the programs came mostly from the few individual growers who continued to employ large numbers of braceros, a group that was becoming increasingly isolated and burdened with a negative public image.[75] The bracero programs had enabled large growers to extend their dominance over Southwestern agriculture, but the growers were not able to hold on to them any longer.

Authorities on agricultural labor had been nearly unanimous in their belief that the bracero system had to be ended before organizing could be successful. Rev. Chris Hartmire, Jr., former director of the California Migrant Ministry, explained their reasons: "It is not possible to describe adequately the demoralizing effect this program had on domestic workers. Many strikes were crushed in advance by this demoralization; others were beaten by the use of braceros as strikebreakers or by the threatened use of braceros."[76] As if fulfilling a prophecy, the first in the series of strikes that led to the formation of the United Farm Workers and the re-emergence of widespread farm worker militancy began during the spring of 1965.

CHAPTER 9

THE FORMATION OF THE UNITED FARM WORKERS AND THE STRUGGLE FOR RECOGNITION

The farm labor struggle from the beginning of the Delano-area grape strike in September 1965 to the present can be divided analytically into three periods. Central to each were the unionization efforts of the National Farm Workers Association (NFWA) and the United Farm Workers (UFW), both directed by Cesar Chavez. The periods may be distinguished by the kinds of strategies employed by the unions and the nature of the opposition their efforts generated. As UFW officials continually emphasize, their primary concern has remained the same since the union's founding: the struggle with California growers over recognition of the UFW and the negotiation of a union contract that would significantly alter the balance of power between agribusiness and agricultural workers. The union has pursued this goal under shifts in the conditions created by the growers' various antiunion efforts and different forms of state intervention. These two variables set the context within which the struggle of the NFWA and UFW against the growers has been fought.

The lack of legislation covering agricultural labor has been a critical factor in this struggle. Until 1975 there were no legal mechanisms, on either the California or the federal level, by which agricultural workers could petition for union elections and recognition. In the absence of legal procedures, the union could undertake little beyond strikes and boycotts.

What has given the NFWA and UFW their strength and perseverance is the support and enthusiasm of a large portion of the farm worker population. In the language of our analysis, the NFWA and

UFW have been extraordinarily successful in mobilizing the internal resources of the farm worker population and sustaining that mobilization over time. Since the monetary resources of the union's constituency are generally weak, the most productive resource has been farm worker solidarity and participation. Participation has been fostered by the union's insistence on worker involvement in union activities and the local decision-making apparatus, including worker committees on ranches where it has contracts. "La Causa" embraces the spectrum of farm worker experiences. The people of the union realize that a long-term contract that upgrades agricultural work must be the primary goal, but they see the quality of agricultural employment as intimately connected with such aspects of farm workers' lives as educational attainment, the possibility of stable residence, economic security, participation in a community, a sense of achievement and self-esteem, and political involvement.

The NFWA and UFW have integrated Mexican, Chicano, and Filipino cultural and religious traditions into union philosophy and tactics. This helps explain Chavez's prominence as a charismatic figure even while the union aims toward a democratic structure and decentralization. It also partly accounts for the extraordinary identification with the union felt by many of its members, which gives the union some of its significance as a social movement.

Naturally, there are exceptions to farm worker support of the union. Agricultural workers remain a population stratified and divided by skill level, citizenship status, crop areas, residence, ethnicity, and, to a certain extent, gender. Each category derives different benefits from union participation and achievements, and at times the interests of one group conflict with those of another. Nevertheless, farm worker solidarity has been impressive, and it has been sustained for over fifteen years. The successes and failures of the NFWA and UFW have not been due to fluctuations in the resources offered by the farm worker population to the union or the ability of the union to mobilize, direct, and sustain these resources.

Rather, the struggle for unionization during the NFWA-UFW era has hinged on two factors. The first and, in a sense, primary variable is the strength of the opposition posed by growers: their degree of unity, their tactics, the cooperation of local courts and law enforcement agencies, and the other kinds of alliances developed. The power of growers has historically made it unlikely that union recognition would be won through harvest-time strikes alone. The consistent failure to "win in the fields" has triggered the product and store (that is, primary and secondary) boycott tactics initiated by the NFWA and

UFW. The second variable is the action taken by the state, and this has perhaps been the more critical one. Responses on the federal and California levels have included noninvolvement, intervention to undermine threats to the growers' control, and attempts to mediate conflict through government regulation. Intervention aimed at mediation is the most complex of these responses: it can either limit a union or help institutionalize it. Even when institutionalization of the union is a goal of state action, the form this takes conditions the organization's future. As will be shown in the case of the UFW, results can affect its ability to use tactics successful in the past, its potential to expand its organizational base to other geographical areas and agricultural products, its ability to continue as a militant grassroots movement and focal point for broader social change, and its potential to align politically with other organizations and segments of the public.

The farm worker unions thus faced different sets of challenges in the three periods following the bracero era. In each instance, the stimulus for the shift in the position of the government or the agribusiness interests was the intensity, success, and direction of agricultural labor insurgency, aided in this period by substantial support from outside the farm worker population.

THE BACKGROUND OF THE NFWA

The emergence of "La Causa" cannot be understood apart from the concurrent civil rights movement. Both the termination of the bracero system and farm worker unionization were identified with the larger goals of the movement, and its leaders admired—on both tactical and philosophical grounds—the nonviolent resistance utilized so successfully by Martin Luther King, Jr. Many of the early volunteers had previous experience in such civil rights organizations as the Congress of Racial Equality (CORE) and the Student Nonviolent Coordinating Committee (SNCC). Marshall Ganz, for example, who ran the international boycott for the UFW and served on the union's executive board, had worked as a SNCC organizer in Mississippi. The marches, demonstrations, and acts of civil disobedience that attracted public attention and support for the union were reminiscent of earlier civil rights struggles.

Before forming the NFWA in 1962, Chavez worked for ten years for the Community Service Organization (CSO) in California, a group affiliated with Saul Alinsky's Industrial Areas Foundation. The purpose of the CSO was to help the poor build a political power base in order to demand improvements in community services. Its focus was on urban areas and especially on Chicano communities, and its success was largely limited to the registration of an estimated 500,000 Chicano voters between 1948 and 1960.[1] Chavez's first contact with the CSO came in 1952, at a meeting with the CSO organizer Fred Ross in the San Jose barrio known as "Sal Si Puedes," where Chavez was living. Ross had been a director of the FSA migrant camp at Weedpatch near Arvin in the southern San Joaquin Valley from 1937 to 1942; later he would serve the NFWA and UFW as a strategic advisor and trainer of organizers. Two other people who became prominent in the UFW also worked with Chavez in the CSO: Dolores Huerta, the union's first vice president and chief contract negotiator, and Gilbert Padilla, a later vice president.

After Chavez became executive director of the CSO, he gave increasing attention to agricultural labor and specifically the injustices engendered by the bracero program. When the CSO's 1962 convention resisted his suggestion to engage in a program of full-scale farm labor organizing, Chavez resigned. At about the same time he turned down an offer by Sargent Shriver, then head of the Peace Corps, to make him a Peace Corps director for four Latin American countries.[2] Huerta and Padilla remained with the CSO for a time but soon joined Chavez in Delano, where he was organizing the NFWA.

Delano had a strategic importance as an initial operational base. It is at the center of California's table grape operations and is centrally located within the long agricultural belt stretching nearly 550 miles from Imperial Valley and Calexico near the Mexican border to Marysville and other agricultural centers in the Sacramento Valley to the North. A relatively high proportion of Delano-area farm workers are permanent residents. Unlike some other agricultural areas, Delano usually offers enough agricultural employment within commuting distance to enable many farm workers to establish homes in the area. This stable farm labor segment, mostly Mexican American, became the initial backbone of the union. Chavez's strategy was to build the union on the support of residents before attempting to organize migratory workers. Not only are more permanent workers better able to offer long-term support to a union, but they derive more immediate benefits from unionization. Hiring based on union seniority, for example, helps local workers more than migrants. Migrants are also far more vulnerable than workers having a permanent residence in the community: striking migrants have often been evicted from company-owned housing and had their meal arrangements terminated. Moreover, the annual income of migrants is lower than that of stable workers, making it particularly hazardous financially for migrants to jeopardize their harvest-time earnings.

Table grapes, the dominant crop in the Delano area, need more attention than most crops. Vines must be sprayed, trimmed,and girdled and therefore require a specialized labor force. Work on the vines occupies up to ten months of the year.[3] Thus, the proportion of stable agricultural workers in the Delano area is higher than that found in most other agricultural regions. Delano is also the winter home of a number of migratory agricultural workers who move with the grape harvest from the Coachella Valley in the south, through Arvin and Lamont in the southern San Joaquin Valley, to Delano, where the harvest continues into the fall. Many engage in off-season work on the vines, such as pruning and tying. During the early 1960s these migrants included about 1,500 Filipino men, some of whom had been imported for agricultural work during the late 1920s.[4] Many were unmarried as a result of the antimiscegenation laws that forbade them to marry white women and the general unavailability of Filipino women. Some older Filipino workers had been involved in the agricultural labor insurgency of the 1930s; agriculture was the only work they had ever known.

Chavez's organizational strategies have been extensively described elsewhere.[5] He continued the CSO style of community-based organizing rather than the more conventional farm labor union strategy of focusing on specific ranches and work-related issues. Although the unionization of farm workers was his ultimate purpose, Chavez did not initially set traditional union goals. He believed that the lack of a stable base and an ongoing organization had contributed to the weakness of past unions. He attempted to avoid similar failures by building a solid organization before embarking on strikes that would demand considerable sacrifices.[6] He first surveyed the workers he met at house meetings to find out what were their most urgent concerns. Accordingly, the NFWA's initial projects were quite modest: service centers, a burial insurance program, and a credit union.

In the spring of 1965, after the NFWA had become established, Chavez outlined his strategy of creating alliances to help build support for unionization efforts. According to Bert Corona, a long-time labor organizer and Chicano activist, Chavez asserted "that the reason the farm worker organizing drive could win in the days ahead was because they could ally themselves with a new feature in American social and political activity—the movement for civil rights, the movement of the youth and the movement of the poor—to become involved in doing something about the farm workers' needs."[7]

THE 1965 DELANO AREA GRAPE STRIKE

By 1965 the only effective AWOC local consisted of Filipino migrants. The local was headed by Larry Itliong and Ben Guines. Itliong, the southern regional director of AWOC, was the acknowledged leader among Filipino farm workers. During the thirties he was involved in several organizing efforts and strikes among agricultural workers on the West Coast; later he organized cannery workers in Alaska and southern California. He also served as vice president of a large UCAPAWA local.[8]

Even after the expiration of Public Law 78, braceros could still be used under Public Law 414 of the McCarran Act. In the spring of 1965, Secretary of Labor Willard Wirtz concluded after a visit to California that there was no need for bracero labor, but under pressure from Governor Pat Brown he declared that if enough domestic labor was not available, braceros could be recruited.[9] He set $1.40 an hour as the prevailing wage for them. That spring Coachella Valley grape growers offered domestic Filipino workers only $1.25 an hour and 10 cents a box for field packing. AWOC demanded $1.40 an hour and 25 cents a box. When the demand was refused, the union called workers out on strike. Denied access to bracero labor, the growers quickly gave in. When the grape harvest moved north to the Arvin area, the same scenario was repeated, but this time the growers held firm, and the Filipinos returned to work under the lower rate.

In the Delano area the Filipino migrants were especially vulnerable. For many, grower-owned camps had been winter homes for up to thirty years.[10] A strike might have endangered this arrangement. Nevertheless, when Delano growers offered only $1.20 an hour and 15 cents a box, many refused to leave the camps to report to work and staged what amounted to a sit-down strike.

The Delano-based NFWA was caught in a dilemma. Many of its members worked on the same ranches as the Filipinos and were sympathetic. Yet Chavez did not want to become involved in a strike at that time, estimating that the NFWA was still two or three years away from being able to sustain a major strike effort.[11] The NFWA's recent defeat in a small strike of rose workers convinced him that strikes spread the organization too thin. Moreover, the NFWA had only $87.00 in its treasury. Still, in retrospect the vote to join the strike seemed inevitable. On 16 September, Mexican Independence

Day, the NFWA membership voted overwhelmingly to join the Filipino strikers on 20 September.

The early weeks of the strike were especially memorable for the enthusiasm and hope of the Delano farm worker population. Many were shaking off the fatalism and passivity that had kept them inactive for so long during the bracero era; moving accounts can be found in several sources.[12] Support for the strike spread quickly to encompass workers in nearby towns. By October the State Farm Labor Placement Service had certified twenty labor disputes in the Delano-Earlimant-McFarland area. In addition, the NFWA was picketing at least ten other ranches.[13] Two of the ranches under strike were the DiGiorgio Fruit Corporation's 4,400-acre Sierra Vista Ranch and a 5,000-acre operation covering two counties owned by Schenley Industries. These agribusiness giants were to play a central role in the union's activities over the next three years.

The number of AWOC workers involved stayed at about 1,000, but NFWA participation grew from 500 members to over 2,000. As early as the initial strike vote, the NFWA claimed that it had authorization cards from 2,700 workers. The growers responded as they had in the past. Strikers were evicted from labor camps. If they remained, their electricity was shut off and their belongings piled onto roadways. Strikebreaking crews were recruited, some ostensibly from as far away as Texas. In testimony before the U.S. Senate Subcommittee on Migratory Labor, which met in Delano in March 1966, Dolores Huerta estimated that 2,000 Mexican aliens had been transported from the El Paso–Juarez area to break the strike.[14]

Individual growers did what they could to intimidate union pickets: they drove their pickup trucks at excessive speeds alongside picket lines, hired armed private guards, sprayed pickets with sulphur meant to be applied to roadside vines, displayed shotguns and taunted pickets to come onto their property, and beat individual pickets who came too close to their property line. As in the past, local law enforcement agencies attempted to limit the strike's effectiveness. Local courts issued injunctions limiting the number of pickets, and police and deputies detained pickets, staged mass arrests, and ignored grower harassment of those on the picket lines. At one point fifty-three people, including nineteen ministers and priests, were arrested for shouting "huelga" to workers in the fields.[15]

The NFWA soon realized that victory in the fields was unlikely, given the considerable options available to growers in the chronically oversupplied labor market and the bias of local law enforcement agencies and local courts. Few farm workers possessed the savings to sustain them through a long strike, and strike funds were not generally available. The NFWA itself was in need of money and more volunteer staff members.

Sympathizers journeyed to Delano to add their support to picket lines and help with the coordination of strike activities. Clergy were especially prominent. NFWA representatives and volunteers began to spend as much time gathering support from students, urban unions, church groups, and civil rights activists as they spent staffing picket lines. National media gave the strike considerable coverage, and the NFWA used the publicity to mobilize more direct support. This support was critical in sustaining national interest and attention long after the conclusion of the grape season. The NFWA demonstrated that it was capable of eliciting the kind of support that could increase the costs to growers of resisting unionization. In retrospect, these early efforts to mobilize and direct external support can be seen as prefiguring the far more substantial efforts undertaken by the UFW in 1967–70.

Chavez initially sought assistance as well as union volunteers from California's colleges and universities. His first appearance was on the steps of Sproul Hall at the University of California at Berkeley. The free speech movement of the previous year had politicized much of the student population, and Chavez used this development to the union's advantage. Several hours before he spoke, forty-four union members and supporters, including Chavez's wife, Helen, had been arrested while picketing. Chavez announced the arrests that day at Berkeley, Stanford, San Francisco State, and Mills College in Oakland. The students responded by donating $6,700, mostly in one-dollar bills.[16]

The union called for a grape boycott in October, about a month after the strike began. One of the first actions was to picket the docks where grapes were loaded onto ships. In San Francisco members of the International Longshoremen's and Warehousemen's Union briefly refused to load grapes. Both ILWU and Teamster members honored picket lines in other cities. By December the union had decided to concentrate its efforts on a boycott of Schenley Industries' liquor labels. The Schenley boycott introduced the strategy of taking on one grower at a time, preferably one who, like Schenley, was unusually large and had a widely recognized product label. It was helpful that Schenley was more interested in selling liquor than in promoting its grape-growing operations. Most of the corporation's nonfarm operations were unionized, and Schenley advertised heavily in labor publications. An antiunion image might be considerably damaging to sales.

In a well-publicized appearance, Walter Reuther, president of the United Auto Workers, visited Delano in December 1965. Reuther had been persuaded to visit by Paul Schrade, the UAW's western regional director and a strong supporter of the NFWA and later the UFW, whose strategy was, as he expressed it, "to put the strike on the national scene."[17] Reuther marched through the center of Delano with NFWA and AWOC pickets and later pledged $5,000 a month to support the strike, half from the AFL-CIO and half from the UAW. The national media attention the Reuther visit received helped spread support for the grape strike throughout organized labor. The visit also exacerbated the feud between Reuther and George Meany. Meany had never been enthusiastic about agricultural labor organizing, and his subsequent public statements revealed his distance from the farm worker situation. Still, AWOC was affiliated with the AFL-CIO, and Meany resented the publicity given Reuther's visit.[18] William Kircher, the federation's director of organizing, was specifically assigned by Meany to investigate the strike and assess AWOC's position. Kircher soon found that the NFWA was considerably stronger and better supported than AWOC. He subsequently began to work closely with Chavez and became the main link between the federation and the NFWA (and later the UFW) for nearly a decade.

The grape strike gained further national publicity when the U.S. Senate Subcommittee on Migratory Labor agreed to conduct hearings in California in March 1966. The chairman, Senator Harrison Williams, Jr., had introduced legislation to provide farm workers with minimum wage protection and coverage under the NLRA, a strategy initially supported by Chavez. Hearings were held in Sacramento, Visalia, and Delano, and Chavez, Huerta, and other NFWA members, as well as several large growers, testified. The most significant development of the hearings was the support expressed by Senator Robert Kennedy. Although a member of the subcommittee, Kennedy missed the first two hearings and confessed to an aide that he did not know why he was going. At the Delano hearing, however, he dominated the questioning of antiunion witnesses. In one well-publicized testimony, the Kern County sheriff, Leroy Galyen, who also had been involved in quelling the 1933 cotton strike, related the method of photographing and interrogating pickets. Pressed by Kennedy, he explained that mass arrests of pickets were conducted to eliminate the possibility of disorder. Kennedy asked on what grounds someone could be arrested without having violated a law and said, "I suggest that the sheriff read the Constitution of the United States."[19] According to Schrade, Kennedy was then in the process of re-examining his political convictions and was having long discussions with black militants and student activists. Some interpreted his support for the NFWA as somewhat opportunistic; others believed that it was sincere and deep, and that it remained so until his assassination in 1968.[20] After the hearings Kennedy was the political figure most prominently associated with the farm worker movement. He was perhaps the only national political leader the NFWA and UFW invested with their full trust and support.

While the hearings were going on, the NFWA was seeking a way of protesting an incident in which a ranch crew for Schenley sprayed pickets with insecticide and fertilizer.[21] Some members wanted to stage demonstrations at Schenley's West Coast headquarters in San Francisco. Chavez decided, however, that a march from Delano to Sacramento would serve multiple purposes. The twenty-five day, 300-mile march began on 17 March, the day after the Senate hearings concluded. The marchers were scheduled to arrive at the state capital on Easter Sunday, 10 April.

The march was inspired by the Freedom March from Selma, Alabama, two years before, but it was unique in incorporating a spirit of pilgrimage and penitence, elements in the religious background of many of the Mexican and Filipino marchers. This theme was amplified by the fact that the march took place during Lent and concluded on Easter Sunday. The march provides a striking example of the NFWA's integration of unionization efforts with the culture and history of its constituency. Patterned after the Lenten *peregrinacións* of Mexico, its theme was "Penitence, Pilgrimage, and Revolution," and its emblem was the Virgin of Guadalupe, symbolizing the struggle for social justice of the Mexican poor. Emiliano Zapata's peasant armies carried her standard during the Mexican Revolution, and the association with social revolution remains.[22]

The march gained national publicity for the boycott of Schenley products and a recently instituted boycott of DiGiorgio products. It also helped reach workers in other parts of the state. According to Chavez, the NFWA "wanted to take the strike to the workers outside the Delano area, because they weren't too enthused. They were frightened, and they really didn't know what was happening."[23] The march held nightly programs and rallies to recruit members, disseminate information on the boycott and grape strike, and elicit support. Skits by El Teatro Campesino, the NFWA's theatrical group, were especially well received. Afterwards, Chavez judged the march a powerful weapon and organizing tool.[24]

The other purpose of the march was to bring pressure on Governor Brown. Brown, who had been indifferent to the strike, was a personal friend of Robert DiGiorgio and had numerous formal and informal ties with California's agricultural corporations. Of thirteen Brown appointees to the Board of Agriculture, ten were growers, including the board's vice president, the Coachella grape grower Lionel Steinberg, and the Kern County grape grower John Kovacevich. In addition to attempting to salvage the bracero programs, Brown had pushed through the California legislature in 1959 a $2 billion water program whose primary purpose was to supply agribusiness with inexpensive water. The project would be of special benefit to the owners on the west side of the San Joaquin Valley, who included Southern Pacific (201,000 acres), Standard Oil (218,000 acres), the Kern County Land Company (450,000 acres), the Los Angeles Times Corporation (268,000 acres), and the J. G. Boswell Company (100,000 acres).[25] Policies of the Farm Placement Bureau, the Immigration Service, local law enforcement agencies, and local courts all benefited agribusiness at the expense of labor: there was no legislation to protect agricultural labor; housing, child labor, and pesticide laws were not enforced. Chavez remarked, "We know that every time we knock down one obstacle, we have five more in front of us, because the opposition has got almost everything that society has to offer in terms of structured institutions and power turned against us."[26] In fact, Chavez chose Sacramento as the marchers' destination when William Bennett, a consumer advocate and then member of the Public Utilities Commission, pointed out that California guaranteed Schenley a high price for its liquor through the California Fair Trade Act, which sets a minimum price for liquor, while agricultural workers were not guaranteed a minimum wage.[27]

William Kircher used the march as an opportunity to become better acquainted with Chavez and the NFWA. He was assessing the farm labor movement, and it was clear to him that the NFWA was the key. Accordingly, he decided during the march to phase out AWOC. Its head, Al Green, had regarded Chavez and the NFWA as a rival; he had not endorsed the march and had tried to get AWOC members to stay away. However, Filipino members of AWOC participated, and their standards shared the head of the march with the NFWA. Kircher was disturbed not only about Green's position on the march, but also about AWOC's policy of signing contracts with labor contractors and cooperating with the Teamsters in citrus industry packing houses. Shortly after the march AWOC was reduced to Larry Itliong's Delano-based operations, and Kircher began to suggest a merger of the two unions under the AFL-CIO. Chavez, however, was skeptical of the idea and afraid that a merger would undermine the NFWA's autonomy and tactical flexibility.[28]

Schenley and DiGiorgio were ideal boycott targets. Both were representative of agribusiness corporations with contractual relations with other unions. DiGiorgio was still one of the world's largest fresh fruit growers and distributors, and by 1965 it owned nearly 30,000 acres of agricultural land, including large table grape ranches near Delano, Arvin, and Borrego Springs in San Diego County. Other holdings included packing houses, cold storage plants, and a cannery. Its processing plants and warehouses, mostly associated with its subsidiaries S & W Fine Foods and TreeSweet Products, were scattered throughout the nation. Its numerous corporate interlocks included the Bank of America, which was financially tied to a large portion of California agricultural production. Robert DiGiorgio continued to be a member of the bank's board of directors, and one of the bank's vice presidents, Carl Wente, was a DiGiorgio director.[29] In its 1965 annual report, the corporation reported an income of $232 million, up from $132 million the previous year. Schenley marketed several brands of liquor and wines, while DiGiorgio had S & W and TreeSweet fruit juices: these products were the objects of the boycott.

In early 1966 the NFWA dispatched two dozen of its strikers and staff to thirteen major cities throughout the country to promote the boycotts. Boycott organizations sought help from civil rights groups, student organizations, and especially local union offices. Thousands of volunteers were recruited to pass out leaflets, picket stores, and demonstrate their support for the Delano strike. In this way a strong sense of identification and solidarity was built between the NFWA farm workers and their urban supporters.

The first breakthrough came on 6 April, while the march was in progress: Schenley Industries agreed to recognize the NFWA. It was unlikely that Schenley had been financially hurt by the boycott at this point, and it had easily harvested its grapes, but the corporation was sensitive to the publicity portraying it as a corporate giant intent on oppressing a small group of poor farm workers. Moreover, one of the heads of a bartenders' local had leaked a memo to Schenley suggesting that the Bartenders Union was considering supporting the Schenley boycott, even though that would constitute a secondary boycott, illegal under the Taft-Hartley Amendment. The contract was negotiated within three months and included a $1.75-an-hour base wage, the requirement that Schenley consult with the union before changing any work procedures or continuing operations that workers claimed were hazardous, and the replacement of the labor contractor system of worker recruitment with a union hiring hall. The last is perhaps the most significant formal change the union has instituted in the relationship between farm workers and agribusiness, and it has typically been vehemently resisted by growers.

On 7 April, the day after Schenley's recognition of the NFWA, the DiGiorgio Corporation called for secret-ballot elections on its ranches. DiGiorgio wanted a no-strike, no-boycott guarantee, which the NFWA refused to give. While the boycott against DiGiorgio's S & W Foods and TreeSweet fruit juices was stepped up, negotiations began between the NFWA and DiGiorgio representatives on election procedures. The Schenley recognition and the DiGiorgio election offer signified the first break in the growers' stance against the NFWA. DiGiorgio even suggested that agricultural labor be included under the NLRA. The DiGiorgio negotiations were the first time the NFWA dealt directly with a grower to work out procedures. Schenley apparently was resigned to NFWA recognition; DiGiorgio was not. DiGiorgio had a long history of bitter opposition to agricultural labor unionization, beginning in the 1930s and including the 1947 strike initiated by the NFLU. Chavez cited it as "one of the most unprincipled companies I've ever dealt with."[30] Most growers, he felt, would adhere to an agreement once they were pressured into it, but not the DiGiorgio Corporation. DiGiorgio was the first grower to introduce the Teamsters Union into the fields as a competitor with the NFWA.

Meanwhile the march ended as scheduled on Easter Sunday. The small group of marchers were joined by 8,000 supporters for a rally on the steps of the capitol. Included were dozens of church leaders, AFL-CIO and Teamster officials, representatives of Mexican American and civil rights organizations, and Democratic politicians and political candidates. The governor and his family, however, were not present; they chose instead to spend Easter in Palm Springs with Frank Sinatra.[31]

THE NFWA-AWOC MERGER AND THE DIGIORGIO ELECTIONS

After the march concluded, the union turned its full attention to picketing DiGiorgio ranches and promoting the boycott of DiGiorgio products. The DiGiorgio boycott was the most effective short-term boycott ever promoted by the union. While negotiating the rules and

conditions for the elections, DiGiorgio petitioned for and received a
court injunction restricting the number of pickets. In contrast to the
harassment, intimidation, and vindictiveness that had characterized
earlier Delano-area strike efforts, the early picketing of DiGiorgio
led to little direct confrontation. In fact, the court-imposed restrictions were so frustrating that the NFWA began to hold Masses and
vigils at the ranch entrance to attract the attention of workers who
remained in the fields. The corporation's antiunion efforts were not
focused on the picket line. Instead, it concentrated on lawsuits and
legal maneuvers. Size and corporate sophistication did not create a
more tolerant disposition toward the NFWA.

Negotiations continued through April and early May. Then one of
DiGiorgio's crew bosses reported to the NFWA that her foreman had
ordered her crew to sign cards authorizing their representation by
the International Brotherhood of Teamsters. She believed that her
crew preferred the NFWA and would sign its authorization cards
instead. When she was discovered passing out NFWA authorization
cards, she was promptly fired, terminating twenty-three years of
employment with DiGiorgio. In response, the NFWA walked out of
the negotiating session.[32]

The incident initiated the competition between the NFWA and the
Teamsters, and it illustrated the beginnings of close grower-
Teamster cooperation to undermine the NFWA. According to Fred
Ross, the two or three Teamster organizers assigned to the ranch had
DiGiorgio's full cooperation. In fact, organizers gave their authoriza-
tion cards to Dick Meyers, the head of DiGiorgio's agricultural divi-
sion, and Meyers in turn gave them to the supervisors.[33]

The motivation behind the entrance of the Teamsters has never
been completely understood. Several Teamster locals in San Francisco, Los Angeles, and New York were actively supporting the table
grape boycott. The union's president, Jimmy Hoffa, said in a telephone interview that the International gave support for the Modesto
local to become involved at DiGiorgio.[34] Others have maintained that
Hoffa was not enthusiastic about organizing agricultural workers;
instead, the move to organize field labor was taken by anti-Hoffa
factions, especially within the Teamsters' Western Conference.[35]
Officially the Teamster rationale was that it had extensive contracts
covering workers in canneries (including those owned by DiGiorgio),
packing sheds, and cold-storage plants, and so its actions were aimed
at protecting a jurisdictional flank. Fred Ross accepted this as the
reason.[36] At another level, the action has been associated with rivalry
within the Teamsters, a distaste for grassroots, militant unions, and
ready acceptance by growers. Whether the Teamsters made the ini-

tial decision to move into the fields or whether they were "invited" by DiGiorgio as the NFWA claimed is perhaps less important than the potential effect of replacing the NFWA. If supplanting the NFWA had not been part of their motive, they could have chosen another agricultural area in California or another product or another state to begin their efforts. Certainly subsequent Teamster interventions into organizational attempts by NFWA or the UFW involved increasingly coordinated efforts by the Teamsters and grower organizations to undermine the farm worker union's position.

In the midst of election negotiations, DiGiorgio unexpectedly announced on 20 June that elections would be held on 24 June on the Sierra Vista Ranch near Delano, the focal point of the NFWA picketing, and on the Borrego Springs Ranch in northeastern San Diego County. Elections were to be conducted according to company guidelines and supervised by an accounting firm. The NFWA was taken completely by surprise and charged DiGiorgio with negotiating in bad faith and instituting a phony election. The union received a court injunction forbidding the corporation to place the NFWA on the ballot and began immediately to urge workers to boycott the election. Nearly half of the 732 eligible workers did not vote. Of the 385 ballots cast, 284 voted for unionization; of these, 201 voted for the Teamsters. According to the NFWA, the voters included stenographers, clerks, and other nonfarm workers.[37]

The day after the election, Delores Huerta asked the Mexican American Political Association (MAPA) to bring pressure on Governor Brown for an investigation. MAPA is a political pressure group whose political recommendations can be influential in heavily Chicano precincts. Brown was in the midst of an ultimately unsuccessful re-election battle with Republican Ronald Reagan and needed MAPA support. MAPA arranged a meeting between Chavez and Brown, and the latter agreed to begin an investigation. He appointed Ronald W. Haughton, codirector of the Institute of Labor and Industrial Relations at Wayne State University, to investigate and make recommendations. Haughton's subsequent report suggested that new elections be held under the supervision of the American Arbitration Association.[38] The Teamsters and DiGiorgio had little choice but to accept, and the ground rules were negotiated for a 30 August election. Immediately after the new election agreement, DiGiorgio laid off 192 workers, many of whom, the NFWA claimed, were its supporters.

The NFWA was staking the union's future on the outcome of the DiGiorgio election. Union people did not know what tactics DiGiorgio would use to swing votes to the Teamsters, whom the corporation had

already publicly endorsed, and they were unsure of the union's
strength among the DiGiorgio workers, since many original NFWA
supporters employed by DiGiorgio had left when the strike began.
Because the boycott was the union's primary strategy, strike-related
activity had not been emphasized, and consequently there was no
reliable way to judge NFWA support. Without a victory the NFWA
might lose much of the support for the boycotts, and the possibility of
future alliances would become tenuous. Nevertheless, supporters
expected the election to demonstrate NFWA's strength among the
workers.

To insure the union's future, Chavez and other NFWA leaders
decided to merge NFWA with AWOC as an AFL-CIO affiliated
union.[39] Certainly the merger was timed to influence the election.
Those within the NFWA leadership who favored the merger argued
that the strength and protection provided by AFL-CIO affiliation
would help sway DiGiorgio workers impressed by the organizational
strength of the International Brotherhood of Teamsters, especially
since Kircher offered the NFWA a monthly organizing budget of
$10,000. Kircher provided other kinds of aid as well. When Teamster
strong-arm men physically assaulted several NFWA staff members,
he arranged through Paul Hall, the President of the Seafarers Union,
to have some vigorous Seafarer members enter the scene. After
fourteen arrived, Teamster attacks subsided.

For the NFWA leadership as a whole, the decision was not easy,
although Chavez later stated that the merger would have taken place
eventually even if the Teamster intrusion had not forced the issue.[40]
Several questions needed to be resolved about the relationship between the NFWA and the national federation, particularly the
amount of autonomy that would be permitted the union. The NFWA
leadership argued that it had to be relatively free of restrictions on its
unionization efforts because of the differences between the situations
of farm and industrial workers. The NFWA had always portrayed
itself as a democratic, participation-oriented, grassroots organization, an image that helped win support from civil rights supporters
and students. Subordination to the federation's national office would
have compromised this image and called into question the union's
avowed purposes. Moreover, the merger problems associated with the
two unions were exacerbated in this case because they were roughly
split according to ethnic composition. In fact, ethnic antagonisms
might have prevented merger altogether if it had not occurred under
the jurisdiction of a national body like the AFL-CIO.

The terms of the merger allowed Chavez the autonomy he thought
essential in strategic and tactical decision making. The union could

continue boycotts, with or without AFL-CIO endorsement, and employ volunteer organizers.[41] Even though the question had earlier split the NFWA leadership, the merger vote was nearly unanimous. The only serious opposition came from a segment of the volunteer organizers, mostly students and young people, who interpreted the merger as relinquishing control to "Big Labor." Farm workers themselves overwhelmingly voted for it.

The merger on 22 August brought into existence the United Farm Workers Organizing Committee (UFWOC). Chavez was named director and Larry Itliong, formerly of AWOC, second in command. The vice presidents were Gilbert Padilla, Dolores Huerta, and Tony Orendain of the NFWA, and AWOC's Philip Vera Cruz and Andy Imutan. One of Chavez's first acts as UFWOC director was to dissolve the agreements AWOC had signed with labor contractors. It was clear that the old NFWA grassroots style would permeate the new union. With the merger complete, UFWOC directed its attention to DiGiorgio.

The DiGiorgio elections involved workers at both the Sierra Vista Ranch near Delano and the smaller Borrego Springs Ranch in northeastern San Diego County. Fred Ross coordinated the campaign at Sierra Vista, while Chavez and Gilbert Padilla were in charge of Borrego Springs. The director of organizing for the Western Conference of Teamsters, William Grami, was in charge of Teamster efforts at both ranches. The campaign issues were surprisingly diffuse. UFWOC emphasized Robert Kennedy's investigation of the Teamsters and his subsequent charges of corruption; the Teamsters relied on grower propaganda claiming that UFWOC was a subversive organization. On the eve of the election, two major television networks predicted defeat for UFWOC. The *Los Angeles Times* reporter Harry Bernstein told Chavez that the betting in Las Vegas was three to one against his union. Even Saul Alinsky claimed that the Teamsters were too strong to be defeated.[42]

According to the election rules, every person who had worked at least two weeks at DiGiorgio since the previous September was eligible to vote. This gave eligibility to the original strikers. UFWOC strategy was to encourage the participation of these former workers, although many had left the region out of support for the NFWA strike as well as the need for employment. Hundreds of DiGiorgio strikers were bused to the election by UFWOC, some from as far away as the El Paso–Juarez area. Others traveled from the interior of Mexico. The American Arbitration Association, which supervised the election, removed the ballots to San Francisco for tabulation. Two days later, on 1 September 1966, it announced that UFWOC had won the field worker elections, with 530 votes to the Teamsters' 331. Only 12 voted for "no union." The Teamsters, as expected, won the packing sheds 97 to 45. Shortly afterwards UFWOC received a congratulatory telegram from Martin Luther King, Jr.

The next target was the huge DiGiorgio vineyard southeast of Bakersfield near Arvin, the scene of the NFLU strike twenty years earlier. Governor Brown, seeking support for his re-election campaign against Ronald Reagan, gave his personal endorsement to the UFWOC demand for an election. After a UFWOC sit-in at DiGiorgio's San Francisco headquarters, the corporation agreed to an election on 4 November. The Teamsters Union at first indicated that it would contest UFWOC but then decided against it. Of the 377 votes cast, 285 were for UFWOC.[43] The contract negotiating committee was led by Mack Lyons, a black DiGiorgio worker, who became active in the union during the strike and elections and was later elected to the union's board of directors. The negotiations continued for over three months before going to an arbitrator. Even though strikes, boycotts, and elections received most of the publicity, what was ultimately critical was the contract the union negotiated and its implementation. UFWOC was developing several basic terms, including a union hiring hall to replace the labor contractor system and strict regulation of pesticide use. Disagreements over wages were much less important than these other contract terms; changes in the method of labor recruitment and employment had the potential to alter the power relationship between agribusiness and farm workers. The hiring hall was an important provision won in the Arvin contract.

DiGiorgio at the time was planning to sell its agricultural land: the government was cutting off its supply of federally subsidized water because DiGiorgio's holdings exceeded the federal reclamation law limit of 160 acres. The union therefore wanted a successor clause so that the contract would carry over under the new ownership. The arbitrators, however, denied this, and when the corporation sold all its holdings at the end of 1968, UFWOC lost its contracts.[44]

After the contract at the Arvin Ranch was signed, in April 1967 the corporation's managers attempted to evade its terms through obstruction, noncooperation, and refusal. According to Mack Lyons, over one hundred grievances were brought by workers against the company during the first three months of the contract. Many simply could not be settled. The company also tried to undermine the hiring hall by refusing to cooperate in establishing a workers' seniority list.[45]

Meanwhile UFWOC was called upon for assistance by workers at the Perelli-Minetti Vineyards near Delano. On 9 September 1966, ten days after the first UFWOC victory in the DiGiorgio elections, wine grape workers at Perelli-Minetti struck for union recognition after a supervisor fired an entire crew. Harvest activity completely stopped for six days. UFWOC had not previously organized Perelli-Minetti; instead, it used the ranch as a place where pickets could go to work if they needed to earn money.[46] UFWOC support was strong among the company's workers. Perelli-Minetti grows its own wine grapes and produces a number of wines including Ambassador wine, Aristocrat Brandy, and Tribuno Vermouth.[47] Thus, like Schenley and DiGiorgio, it had identifiable products that could easily be made the targets of a boycott.

At first the company seemed willing to negotiate, but nine days after the strike began it announced that it had signed contracts with the Teamsters. In that time, the company had put together a strikebreaking crew who were escorted through picket lines by Teamster representatives. The Teamster incursion forced UFWOC to make a strategic decision to devote all its energies to a boycott of Perelli-Minetti wines and vermouth: its leaders reasoned that if they could not win showdowns with the Teamsters, they could expect the Teamsters to intervene continually. The table grape boycott was virtually ignored while the union sought to close off the company's retail outlets. The boycott continued for over ten months and was reported to have had a devastating financial impact on the company. Finally, in July 1967, Perelli-Minetti agreed to turn the Teamster contract over to UFWOC. At this time UFWOC and the Teamsters signed the first of what were to be several jurisdictional agreements. UFWOC agreed to recognize Teamster rights to cannery, packing house, and other nonfield workers, while the Teamsters agreed to discontinue efforts in the fields.

During 1967 and 1968 UFWOC also signed contracts with a number of other wineries that had vineyards. These included Almaden, Paul Masson, Gallo, Christian Brothers, Franzia, and Novitiate. UFWOC had won card-check elections, based on workers signing cards to authorize UFWOC to represent them, at several of these vineyards. The potential power of a UFWOC boycott made these much easier than previous victories. Yet UFWOC held only a dozen contracts covering approximately 5,000 workers, most of whom were employed in highly mechanized wine grape vineyards, and its primary purpose during this initial period was to organize the table grape workers. In the summer of 1967, UFWOC devoted its full organizational efforts to the table grape segment of agribusiness for what became a three-year struggle.

THE TABLE GRAPE BOYCOTT

In 1966 and 1967, the NFWA-UFWOC took on individual companies. Union contracts resulted from three specific product boycotts, and the unionized wine companies negotiated under the threat of further boycotts. Table grape growers, however, were beginning to coordinate their efforts to resist UFWOC. The next three years witnessed a consolidation of opposition. As a result, UFWOC had to take on an entire industry rather than a specific company.

During June and July of 1967, UFWOC conducted an organizing campaign among workers at Giumarra Vineyards, owned by the Giumarra Brothers Fruit Company. California's largest table grape grower, Giumarra owned 11,000 acres, of which 6,000 were in grapes, and employed nearly 2,500 workers at harvest time. Giumarra Vineyards had annual sales of more than $12 million, for a profit that varied between $5.5 and $7.5 million. Like many other large growers, the company received a federal subsidy—$278,000 in 1967—for leaving part of its holdings uncultivated. (Another large table grape grower, the J. G. Boswell Company, was paid a government subsidy of $3,010,000 in 1968, the largest to any one grower in the United States.)[48] When Giumarra refused to recognize UFWOC authorization cards signed by its workers and declined to meet with the union representatives, UFWOC called a meeting for a strike vote and received approval from the 1,600 to 1,800 people attending to initiate a strike on 3 August.[49]

The strike immediately reduced the Giumarra labor supply but the company then recruited a work force substantially composed of undocumented workers. Under pressure from UFWOC, the U.S. Department of Immigration removed 500 illegals from the Kern County vineyards. Giumarra, however, countered by employing "green-card" Mexican workers (i.e., workers with temporary visas) as a strikebreaking crew, contrary to government regulations forbidding the use of green-card labor in struck ranches.[50] Throughout the strike Giumarra refused to negotiate and successfully petitioned for a court injunction placing severe limits on picketing. The lack of strike benefits combined with the availability of a strikebreaking force made the strike ineffective. The failure confirmed UFWOC's conviction that struggles confined to the fields contained little hope for success. Internal resources necessary to combat such a powerful adversary were lacking.

UFWOC again turned to the consumer boycott and began to strengthen its nationwide support organizations. Farm workers, volunteers, and other union staff spread out through the country, concentrating on large cities containing the growers' primary markets. Sympathetic unions provided office space and materials, and community support groups revived to disseminate information about the boycott of Giumarra grapes.[51] Giumarra marketed its grapes under six different labels, making it difficult to identify its produce. Despite this, the boycott soon began to take effect. In response, and with the cooperation of other growers, Giumarra began after two months to ship grapes under other grower labels.[52] This tactic of questionable legality led UFWOC to re-evaluate its strategy. Since the union was essentially involved in a struggle with the entire California table grape industry (a fact reinforced by increased grower cooperation against the union), UFWOC decided in January 1968 to extend the boycott to all California table grapes. The target thus became readily identifiable, and the problem of connecting labels with particular growers was resolved.

This was the first intensive table grape boycott as well as the first rigorous test of UFWOC's strategy of mobilizing external resources to pressure growers into union recognition and contract negotiation. Since collective grower resources were considerable and were used to launch a sophisticated antiboycott campaign, support for UFWOC needed to be widespread and sustained. The elections of Ronald Reagan as governor of California and later Richard Nixon as president created two administrations sympathetic to the growers' efforts. UFWOC, on the other hand, had the advantage of a national political climate favorable to what appeared to be the modest demands of a weak union basically composed of nonwhites. UFWOC's goals could be endorsed by a wide cross-section of the population. Farm worker unionization was one of the few issues of the late 1960s about which labor leaders and union rank and file, antiwar activists, civil rights activists, students, black power advocates, most of the Chicano population, and environmental groups could agree, and UFWOC directed specific appeals to each of these constituencies. Positive response by a wide cross-section of the population helped make continued resistance to unionization expensive for the growers.

By 1969 boycott organizations had been built in forty or fifty cities, and hundreds of other communities had active boycott committees.

Particularly noteworthy were the large numbers of Chicano and student activists working with organizers from UFWOC, including 200 strikers and their families. By promoting the table grape boycott, the union developed grassroot ties with sympathetic individuals and organizations, including political leaders, church and civic organizations, and labor union locals. The AFL-CIO executive council urged its affiliates to support the boycott, and Seafarers, Longshoremen, and several Teamster locals were instrumental in keeping grapes from entering several large cities. Sympathetic grocery clerks refused to handle nonunion grapes. Protestant, Catholic, and Jewish organizations exerted moral pressure on influential figures to publicly endorse the boycott. Mayors or city councils in over three dozen cities, including New York, Cleveland, Detroit, and San Francisco, endorsed the boycott and in some cases ordered municipal agencies to cease purchasing grapes. Boycotters marched through supermarkets, confronted store managers, and blocked entrances; liberal clergy delivered sermons in support of the boycott; universities and Catholic schools suspended grape purchases and refused to deal with grocers who handled nonunion grapes. Several major grocery chains stopped carrying California table grapes because of external pressure generated in large part by secondary boycotts of their stores. The heaviest pressure was applied to the nation's two largest supermarket chains, A & P and Safeway, the latter especially notable for its multiple links to agribusiness and its antiunion policies toward farm labor.

For a time New York was nearly "shut down." The New York City government provided an initial breakthrough when in 1968 it announced that it was discontinuing its purchases of California grapes. New York itself normally provided a market for 20 percent of the California grape crop, but during the summer of 1968 grape sales dropped a remarkable 90 percent. The Transport Worker Federation urged its members in England, Sweden, and elsewhere to refuse to unload California grapes.[53] In London dock workers refused to unload 70,000 pounds during February 1969. An earlier shipment of 230,000 pounds headed for English and Swedish ports had been turned back. Boycott activities in Sweden were particularly effective. The progressive Swedish Consumer Cooperative, accounting for 30 percent of Sweden's retail grocery sales, agreed to stop purchasing California grapes. Britain and the Scandinavian countries were the largest purchasers of California grapes outside North America.[54]

During the boycott, in 1968 and 1969, UFWOC initiated strike activity in the grape fields in the Coachella Valley. The 1968 strike lasted only two weeks before being called off because of several violent incidents involving strikers. The 1969 strike likewise received little emphasis. Picketing in the fields was sustained to keep up worker support and interest and to disseminate information, but the boycott was the key to winning contracts. During these years UFWOC attempted to pressure the federal government to contain the number of illegal entrants from Mexico, who were being widely utilized in the fields and whose presence made any strike more difficult. The union also wanted stricter enforcement of regulations covering green-card workers, who were sometimes illegally employed in struck fields. Green carders constituted a large proportion of California's agricultural labor force and consequently a sizable proportion of the union's membership. Both Secretary of Labor Willard Wirtz and Attorney General Ramsey Clark ordered steps taken to cut off the flow of undocumented workers, but these had little practical effect, given the growers' desire to employ them and the contractors' willingness to smuggle them across the border for the right fee.[55]

The boycott strategy initially proved to be a difficult path. It required intensive efforts by farm workers and volunteers without prior training in organizing, and its impact was neither readily apparent nor easy to measure.[56] Impatient with the lack of immediate results from the boycott, farm workers began debating the advantages of violent tactics against the growers. Fearful of the consequences of such confrontations, Chavez called off the pickets, sent some strikers back to work to ease the union's financial strain, and, in February 1968, began the most significant of his several fasts. The theme was penitence for the union's movement toward violence. Philosophically and strategically, Chavez was committed to a Ghandian nonviolent militance.[57] A number of first-hand observers have called it the union's most important asset in winning external support for the boycotts and legislative reforms.

The fast lasted twenty-five days, and in the end Chavez became quite weak. Robert Kennedy was asked to be with Chavez when the fast ended at a Mass arranged especially for the occasion. At first Kennedy balked, concerned that his presence at such an event might be interpreted as opportunistic, but he eventually came.[58] After the Mass Kennedy was overwhelmed by farm workers who supported his candidacy for the Democratic presidential nomination. Eugene McCarthy had already entered the race for the Democratic presidential nomination against Lyndon Johnson, and there was considerable national pressure on Kennedy to run. Six days after the fast ended on

11 March, Kennedy announced his candidacy, and several days later he chose Chavez to be one of his delegates to the 1968 Democratic Convention.

Chavez prepared a statement to commemorate the end of the fast but was too weak to read it himself:

> When we are really honest with ourselves, we must admit that our lives are all that really belong to us. So it is how we use our lives that determines what kind of men we are. It is my deepest belief that only by giving our lives do we find life. I am convinced that the truest act of courage, the strongest act of manliness, is to sacrifice ourselves for others in a totally nonviolent struggle for justice. To be a man is to suffer for others. God help us to be men.[59]

UFWOC support for the Kennedy nomination epitomized the union's political autonomy from the AFL-CIO, since the federation was supporting Hubert Humphrey for the nomination. In fact, the southern California AFL-CIO regional director, Irwin Shetler, pleaded with UFWOC members not to endorse Kennedy and to back the AFL-CIO stand. After he spoke, the union voted unanimously for the Kennedy endorsement.[60]

For several weeks before the California Democratic primary, UFWOC members directed all their efforts to the campaign. They concentrated on heavily Chicano precincts in Los Angeles and several other cities, working on voter registration drives and campaigning for Kennedy. In the future the union would conduct similar campaigns for politicians it believed would represent its interests, and its influence could be crucial, as it was in this case. Observers, including reporters for the London *Sunday Times*, pointed to the UFWOC campaign as the single most decisive element in the narrow Kennedy victory.[61]

The union's support for Kennedy was no doubt due in part to the Kennedy image, his Catholicism, and the belief that his brother was a martyr. More substantially, however, Robert Kennedy had given his own unqualified support to the union and the grape boycott. According to Paul Schrade of the UAW, who knew Kennedy well and was also closely associated with UFWOC, Kennedy was always available to Chavez by phone.[62] Unlike many other political leaders, Kennedy would ask UFWOC what it wanted and what he could do to help before initiating action directly affecting agricultural labor. Dolores Huerta was walking with Ethel Kennedy just behind the senator when he was assassinated on the night of his primary victory in

California. Schrade was there as well, and was shot. Chavez had already left the victory party at the Ambassador Hotel in Los Angeles, the site of the assassination. Chavez said later that Kennedy's death represented "a tremendous setback," that "a vacuum was created when he died."[63]

UFWOC hesitated to endorse Humphrey for the presidency that November. In return for its endorsement, the union wanted Humphrey to pressure the growers to negotiate, but he would not. Only when it appeared that Nixon—who had condemned the boycott during his campaign and, with California Governor Reagan, conspicuously consumed table grapes on public occasions—could actually be defeated did UFWOC formally endorse the Democratic nominee.[64]

During this period Chavez's legislative approach was undergoing a transition crucial to the union's strategy in the years ahead. The union had always supported the inclusion of agricultural labor under the provisions of the NLRA. In the spring of 1967, Chavez and Itliong testified before a House subcommittee in favor of pending legislation to that effect.[65] This relatively simple goal continued a tradition of past attempts to bring agricultural workers under the NLRA.

The experience of strikes and boycotts, however, and a deepening understanding of the strength and complexity of the barriers to stable agricultural labor unionization convinced Chavez that inclusion within the NLRA would be counterproductive. The fault was not so much with the original NLRA as with the restrictive Taft-Hartley amendment, passed in 1947. Taft-Hartley had swung the balance of power toward the employer. It banned sympathy strikes, mass picketing, and secondary boycotts, required elected union officers to sign affidavits that they were not members of the Communist party, authorized the president to issue injunctions ordering strikers to return to work, and made unions liable for damages if their members struck in violation of union contracts. Inclusion under the amended NLRA would prohibit UFWOC from utilizing the secondary boycott and organizational strikes. An unrestricted boycott had become the union's most powerful weapon. Even if a secondary boycott was never actually undertaken, its threat could pressure supermarket chains to curtail their purchases of boycotted products. In addition, the functioning of the NLRB was not designed to accommodate agricultural work, in which harvest operations have a relatively short duration. Delays built into the cumbersome election procedure could render it meaningless, since the harvest season of peak employment might pass before elections could be held. The law also gave the grower legal maneuvers to stall strikes until the harvest season was over. Chavez was conscious that few new unions had emerged since the passage of Taft-Hartley, and he attributed this fact to the erosion of the tactical options that had helped establish CIO unions.[66]

UFWOC subsequently adopted the position to which it still adheres: any legislation covering agricultural workers must provide election machinery that is swift and geared to the specific circumstances of agricultural labor. In addition, it opposes any restriction on unionization tactics. This position was later reflected in the struggle over the provisions of the 1975 California Agricultural Labor Relations Act.

Without UFWOC support, measures to include agricultural workers under the NLRA lost momentum, although the AFL-CIO continued to support inclusion. AFL-CIO leaders were angry that Chavez had not consulted them before changing UFWOC's position and felt that the federation could not sell UFWOC's idea to Congress, since it appeared to ask for special treatment for one segment of the labor force. Growers, recognizing the tactical advantages that coverage under the NLRA would give them, came around supporting inclusion at this point, in a reversal of their former position.

Grower attempts to counter the boycott ultimately failed, despite sympathetic administrations in Sacramento and later in Washington. Governor Reagan frequently denounced the boycott as illegal and immoral and promoted California table grapes on trips throughout the nation. At the height of the boycott Reagan announced that he had "probably eaten more grapes during the past year than ever." Not only did Reagan resist all efforts to extend collective bargaining to agricultural labor, but he actively pursued progrower and antiboycott policies. He appointed growers to run California's Farm Placement Service and directed the Board of Agriculture to engage in an antiboycott campaign. The Board of Agriculture eventually waged a privately financed national publicity campaign to offset the boycott, a strategy pursued by board president Allan Grant, who also served as president of the California Farm Bureau. Reagan even went so far as to order state agencies to provide growers with welfare recipients and inmates from the state's prisons until blocked by a state Supreme Court ruling.[67] While accompanying Republican presidential nominee Richard Nixon on a campaign tour of California in September 1968, Reagan referred to picketing grape strikers as "barbarians."[68] Nixon called the boycott "illegal" and said it should be put down "with the same firmness we condemn illegal strikes, illegal lockout, or any other form of lawbreaking."[69] Nixon referred to the

NLRA as a protection for workers, without noting that agricultural workers were excluded from the law's coverage.[70]

A coalition of California agribusiness organizations hired the San Francisco–based firm of Whitaker and Baxter to generate anti-boycott publicity through a $2 million advertising and public relations campaign and promote progrower federal legislation being sponsored by Senator George Murphy of California. Whitaker and Baxter had a solid conservative reputation. In the late 1940s they were hired by the American Medical Association to defeat President Truman's national health insurance legislation and helped do so by coining the term "socialized medicine" and building a campaign around the negative connotations of the phrase. For the boycott they came up with the term "consumer rights" to counter union efforts to withold grapes from the market.

In the middle of the boycott, the Department of Defense increased its grape purchases for troops in South Vietnam. During the fiscal year 1966–67, the first year of such purchases, Defense Department table grape purchases for shipment to Vietnam amounted to 468,000 pounds. Grape purchases increased slightly—to 555,000—the next fiscal year. In fiscal year 1968–69, however, grape shipments to South Vietnam totaled 2,167,000 pounds.[71] Total table grape purchases by the department increased from 6.9 million pounds in fiscal year 1967–68 to 9.7 million pounds in fiscal year 1968–69.[72]

None of these antiboycott efforts could reverse declining grape sales. UFWOC countered Defense Department purchases and the antiboycott campaign with an increase in its own boycott activities. The union made the most of these issues. The rationale given by Defense Department officials for their increased grape purchases— such as greater "troop acceptance" of grapes—was easily pierced, and UFWOC established a connection between the boycott and the anti-war movement. UFWOC supporters in Congress, such as Senator Alan Cranston of California, harshly criticized the department's policy. More generally, the union attempted to associate its struggle with the growing anitwar movement in the same way it had earlier sought association with the civil rights movement.

Union attorneys brought a series of lawsuits against growers and their supporters, charging them with a variety of offenses: assaulting and harassing pickets, violating laws requiring safe and sanitary working conditions, undermining workers' freedom of assembly and association, violating antitrust laws, restraining trade by dividing up the grape market among themselves, maintaining artificially

high prices, and illegally using federally subsidized water.[73]
UFWOC's struggle continued to capture the imagination and sympathy of a sizable proportion of the nation's population, and the
support structure the union had built among labor unions, church
and civic organizations, civil rights organizations, Chicano groups,
and students was engaged to counter antiboycott propaganda.

Early in 1969 the union began receiving an increase in complaints
by workers that they were becoming violently ill as a result of contact
with pesticide residues on the vines. The union checked into California pesticide regulations and learned from the Department of Public
Health that the restrictions on pesticide use were too weak to prevent
adverse effects on the workers. The issue aroused major concern
among the agricultural population.[74] The pesticides used in place of
DDT-type chlorinated hydrocarbons, which in fact had not yet been
outlawed, were phosphate-based poisons that attacked the central
nervous system. At first the pesticide appeared to be simply a worker
safety problem, but public interest was engaged when tests conducted on table grapes sold at several Safeway stores—the principal
target of a recent UFWOC secondary boycott—revealed concentra-
tions far above government limits of Aldrin, a pesticide later to be
banned by the FDA as a carcinogen. The discovery of Aldrin residues
generated publicity and support for the boycott and linked injustices
in the fields with consumer interests. In response to an increasing
awareness of the dangers posed by chemical sprays, the union insisted that a strict pesticide clause be inserted into its contracts; since
then it has been especially concerned with its enforcement.[75]

U.S. Department of Agriculture statistics testify to the strength of
the boycott, although they are among the most conservative estimates of the curtailment of grape shipments—much more conservative, than, for example, estimates by many grape growers. By the
beginning of 1970, six months after the 1969 harvest peak, the
amount of unsold table grapes in cold storage was up 30 percent over
the previous year and represented over 20 percent of the total harvest. Wholesale prices were also lower than those of the previous
year. The most impressive evidence was the decline in actual grape
shipments. These fell dramatically from 1966 to 1967 and 1968. The
1967 grape harvest was unusually small and the 1968 harvest was
slightly below average, but the 1969 harvest was again normal and
roughly equivalent to the preboycott 1966 harvest. Comparing these
two years, shipments to the top forty-one grape-consuming cities,
which accounted for 75 percent of the total grape market, were down
22 percent. Figures covered May through November periods of both

years. Significantly, the decline was most substantial in the largest cities, requiring expensive diversion to secondary markets, a cost absorbed by agribusiness. For example, shipments to New York were down 34 percent; to Chicago, 41 percent; to Philadelphia, 23 percent; to Detroit, 32 percent; to Boston, 42 percent; and to Baltimore, 53 percent. Los Angeles and San Francisco were only down 16 and 19 percent respectively. Of the top ten grape-consuming cities, only Montreal showed an increase, and that was only 2 percent.[76] Coachella Valley table grape grower, Lionel Steinberg, stated that the boycott "literally closed Boston, New York, Philadelphia, Chicago, Detroit, Montreal, Toronto completely from handling table grapes."[77] Steinberg added that "it is costing us more to produce and sell our grapes than we are getting paid for them and the boycott is the major factor in this ridiculous situation. . . . We are losing maybe 20 percent of our market." Later he estimated that Coachella Valley growers lost $3 million during the 1969 harvest.[78]

Steinberg, a long-time Democrat, tried to persuade Coachella Valley grape growers to open negotiations with UFWOC in 1968 but failed to receive much support. Steinberg was one of the few political liberals among growers, but reportedly was in the past just as conservative in labor relations as his fellow growers. In January 1969 Steinberg and another Democrat, table grape grower John Kovacevich of Kern County, attempted to persuade a group of growers to meet at least privately with Chavez. A number of growers instead opened talks with the Teamsters. Steinberg, who also met with several Teamster leaders, reported that the Teamsters were ready to make an agreement with the table grape growers if it could be demonstrated that they had the necessary grower support for their attempt to represent field workers. Without giving extensive details, Steinberg recalled that Teamster officials handling these meetings wanted some assurance that Teamster contracts would become a permanent arrangement, unlike the Perelli-Minetti arrangement several years before, and requested a meeting in Governor Reagan's office to work out the agreement. For reasons that remain unclear, Reagan refused to intervene, creating disunity among the thirty grape growers who had sought out the Teamsters. Then the Teamsters themselves backed away, and as of March 1969, appeared determined not to pursue the matter.[79]

Steinberg continued his efforts to have growers meet with Chavez. Finally, after intercessions by Senator Edward Kennedy and several others, negotiations began in June 1969. Little was accomplished, and the talks broke down in July, each side blaming the other. A critical stumbling block was grower unwillingness to accept a union hiring hall to replace the labor contractor system or to guarantee workers what the union regarded as adequate pesticide protection. (These two issue have, in fact, repeatedly stalled contract negotiations.) The nonnegotiable elements of UFWOC's position in the 1969 contract talks reportedly angered Meany and led some of the union's supporters to question Chavez's judgment.[80]

Early in 1970 a committee initiated by the U.S. Conference of Catholic Bishops began a series of meetings with a number of growers as well as the UFWOC. Bishop Joseph Donnelly of Hartford, Connecticut, served as chairman, assisted by Monsignor George Higgins of Washington, D.C. Both had extensive experience in labor relations. Both sides were ready to negotiate; in fact, other growers had privately informed the bishops that if Steinberg were to reach a contract agreement, they would follow suit.

Two Coachella ranches partly owned and managed by Steinberg were the first to sign UFWOC contracts on 2 April. In an election held on two ranches owned by K. K. Larson and his brother, the union won 152 to 2. Within the next three months, UFWOC signed contracts with nearly all the Coachella Valley and southern San Joaquin Valley table grape growers. It now represented workers in 35 percent of California table grape vineyards. One of the contracts was signed with the Tenneco Corporation. Tenneco, a giant conglomerate, had recently continued its diversification from oil into other areas by moving into agriculture and was in the process of buying huge chunks of California vineyards. By 1970 it already owned more than a million agricultural acres in five states.[81] The huge Delano-area ranches, whose grapes ripen later in the season, held out.

The break in Delano occurred on 16 July, when twenty-three of the largest Delano-area growers, including Giumarra, authorized Philip Feick, Jr., of the Western Employers Council of Bakersfield, to negotiate contracts on their behalf. On 29 July all twenty-six Delano grape growers signed UFWOC contracts. Representing 50 percent of the grape harvest, these agreements brought the proportion of California's table grape industry with UFWOC contracts to 85 percent. The remaining 15 percent consisted mainly of the ten- to forty-acre holdings of small farmers in Fresno and Madera counties to the north. The union had not devoted much effort to organizing these farms. Governor Reagan announced that it was "tragic" that the grape workers who would now be covered by UFWOC contracts "had no choice in determining whether or not they want to join the union."[82]

The boycott eventually forced table grape growers to negotiate; but more than that, it made the union a political force, not only among Chicanos and farm workers but nationwide as well. Politicians found it expedient to endorse the grape boycott and make appearances with Chavez. These political alliances, which imposed few restrictions on the union, would prove to be important in the future when the Teamsters re-entered the California fields.

The early contracts with Steinberg served as a model. All contracts were for a three-year period and included a union hiring hall, formal worker grievance procedures, protective pesticide regulations, including a ban on DDT (which was outlawed by the federal government later that year) and a joint worker-grower committee to oversee pesticide use, a grower contribution of 10 cents an hour per worker to the UFWOC-sponsored Robert F. Kennedy Health Plan to support a series of UFWOC medical clinics and health programs, and a similar 2-cent-an-hour contribution to an economic development fund to help retired or disabled workers or workers who lost their jobs as a result of mechanization.[83] Wages were generally $1.75 to $1.80 an hour, plus 25 cents a box as an incentive piece rate. Annual raises were stipulated. Also guaranteed were other, mundane measures, which nevertheless were of great significance to field workers: cool drinking water, rest periods, field toilets, and prohibitions against profiteering on meal arrangements. By September, UFWOC had contracts covering 150 ranches and representing 20,000 jobs and over 10,000 members.

The contracts were assured the day before the formal signing to take place on July 29, 1970. On the eve of the new contracts, members of UFWOC's negotiating team were preparing a quiet celebration. They were interrupted by a phone call from the head of the San Francisco boycott, who informed them that Teamster officials had just signed thirty labor contracts covering field workers with Salinas-area lettuce growers.

STATE INTERVENTION AND THE RISE OF UFWOC

During the initial period of NFWA-UFWOC unionization activity, government agencies and officials supportive of agribusiness were not successful in providing a basis of unity for growers against the union, nor did they formulate a strategy of their own. Instead, the state simply continued the kinds of policies that historically had provided growers with the abundant, controllable, and inexpensive labor force they desired. However, state intervention during this period could not undermine UFWOC's effectiveness. In part this was due to the emergence of the union as a political force. While UFWOC did not force significant concessions from either the California or federal governments during this time, it did prevent the limited antiunion responses by the government or progrower politicians from being effective. Elected officials who proposed antiboycott and antistrike measures were singled out for condemnation, while those supportive of the union were endorsed and sometimes given substantial campaign help and publicity. The union generated public controversy over the lack of adequate enforcement of immigration and green-card restrictions by the Border Patrol, the Immigration Service, and the Department of Labor. Even administrations openly hostile to the union in Sacramento and Washington could not initiate effective antiunion measures at this time. While Reagan's public opposition provided ample anti-UFWOC propaganda, he was notably ineffective in mounting a legislative campaign against the union: the political forces operating in California at the time prevented any of his antiunion legislative proposals from being considered seriously.

Two conditions account for the absence of effective antiunion action on the part of the government during this period. First, UFWOC had yet to establish itself solidly through a series of labor contracts involving large numbers of field workers. Even though it had demonstrated its ability to upset normal agricultural operations, the union still had to assert its staying power. Movements of poor people, including agricultural workers, have exhibited tremendous energy and support but been short-lived. Before winning the table grape contracts, the union had little to fall back on if mass insurgency and external support ended. Union contracts were needed to translate worker support into concrete gains. These would in turn reinforce the support of its constituency and demonstrate the effectiveness of militant protest as well as give the union a more permanent position. Until gains were achieved, the union could be expected to repeat past agricultural unionization experiences: an upsurge of militancy, then a slow loss of momentum, and finally disappearance. Severe repressive action by government agencies would then be unnecessary, and perhaps counterproductive during what continued to be a reform-oriented period. In addition, widespread support for the union made repression a less attractive option. The political instability of the late 1960s and the problems of legitimacy experienced by at least the federal government placed constraints on state responses to the NFWA and UFWOC. Overt repression of a widely supported, visible, nonviolent farm worker movement with roots in both the civil rights and labor movements would be politically hazardous, especially when the support of major political figures such as Kennedy helped legitimize the union's existence and goals.

The fact that state managers were not effective in their limited antiunion responses in this period should not detract from recognizing that ultimately the foundation of the union's successes was the support of a sizable proportion of the farm worker population, especially the non-migrant, local agricultural labor force. Without this support, the boycott strategy could easily have been undermined. The extent of worker support was tested on several occasions: for example, the election at DiGiorgio, card-check elections at several other ranches, and the continuing sequence of strike activity. Demonstrations of farm worker support were critical in maintaining the legitimacy of the union in the eyes of its supporters, and it was this legitimacy that provided UFWOC with its potential to mobilize external resources.

In sum, when UFWOC table grape contracts were signed, nothing yet tried had been effective in undermining UFWOC's position. As long as the struggle was between the union and individual growers, then UFWOC's strength, including its political alliances and public support, could balance that of specific segments of agribusiness. In fact, the growers' anti-UFWOC tactics were not well coordinated. The report of the Bishops' Committee on Farm Labor in 1970 remarked, "Amazing to us was the scanty communications which the growers have with one another."[84] What anti-UFWOC elements apparently needed was a more concerted and coordinated effort against agricultural labor unionization, similar to the measures taken during the 1930s. When, however, the last of the Delano-area table grape contracts were concluded in July 1970, there was little indication of the concentrated efforts to destroy the union that would characterize the next three years.

CHAPTER 10

COORDINATED OPPOSITION

The second stage of UFWOC's struggle to gain recognition spanned the period between July 1970, immediately after the signing of the Delano area grape contracts, and the fall of 1973. It was characterized by an erosion of the formal position of the UFW. The paramount cause of this erosion was what many observers described as the collusion between the Teamsters Union and California growers, but an increase in government activity detrimental to the union was also a major factor.

This chapter will show how the context of the struggle changed. The conflict had previously been limited to the union and a segment of California growers, aided by their immediate corporate and government allies. Elements of the state, agribusiness organizations, and a major labor union, all of whom had been involved during the earlier period, stepped up their antiunion activities once UFWOC signed contracts with the grape growers. The growers became more coordinated, approaching a united stance. The anti-UFWOC tactics used earlier had not ultimately been effective. The more severe and better coordinated efforts of the second period were more successful.

Although the union would not have its status changed from that of an organizing committee to that of a chartered affiliate of the AFL-CIO until 1972, we will begin here to refer to it as the UFW (United Farm Workers of America).

THE TEAMSTER-GROWER ALLIANCE
AND THE SALINAS LETTUCE STRIKE

The Teamsters Union had collective bargaining arrangements with Salinas-area growers before 1970. Local 890 had contracts covering field truck drivers and workers in packing sheds and frozen food processing plants. In 1961 the union signed a contract covering field workers with Bud Antle, Inc. Antle signed the Teamsters' contract to thwart an organizing campaign for lettuce field workers initiated that year by AWOC and the United Packinghouse Workers. Two years later, when Antle was in financial difficulties, the Central and Southern States Pension Funds of the Teamsters loaned the company a million dollars, half of which was still outstanding in 1970. When the Antle contract was originally signed, other Salinas growers rejected a similar Teamster offer and expelled Antle from the Grower-Shipper Vegetable Association for signing a labor agreement.[1] By 1970 Salinas growers had no such reservations.

The 1970 lettuce contracts were initiated while the Teamsters were renegotiating contracts covering nonfield workers. On 23 July the Grower-Shipper Vegetable Association decided to explore the possibility of securing a Teamster contract over field workers, and the Teamsters were immediately receptive. The next day all twenty-nine growers in the association, the largest growers in the Salinas Valley, signed Teamster recognition agreements. The contracts were negotiated within the next several days. When the Teamster contracts were announced on 28 July, a number of Santa Maria and Imperial Valley growers followed suit.

Growers were clearly using the Teamsters as a weapon against the UFW. Salinas and Santa Maria lettuce workers had been asking the UFW to intervene on their behalf for the previous two years, but Chavez stalled, awaiting the outcome of the struggle with table grape growers. The UFW began more intensive organizing in lettuce fields that spring and sent letters to Salinas growers asking for recognition. Chavez had publicly announced that the lettuce fields, particularly in Salinas, would be the location of the next UFW organizing drive. Teamster incursion once again complicated the struggle.

The announcement of Teamster contracts brought immediate reaction from the workers. Widespread spontaneous work stoppages occurred in Salinas, Oxnard, and Santa Maria. A union-sponsored march on Salinas, concluding on 2 August, drew over 3,000 UFW supporters, with four columns of nearly 1,000 persons each originating in surrounding agricultural areas and converging on Salinas from different directions. Workers refused to sign Teamster authorization cards, and many who refused were fired. Despite these protests, within a week William Grami announced that the Teamsters had contracts with sixty growers and were looking for more.

The five-year contracts were recognized before the terms, including wage rates, had been agreed upon. Later, wages were set at $1.85 an hour during the harvest and $1.75 at other times. After five years rates would become $2.33 and $2.21 respectively. Hiring halls were not permitted; the hiring responsibility was left with labor contractors or the growers themselves. Workers were given no protection against pesticides beyond what already existed through legislation, nor were they protected against replacement by mechanization. In fact, workers were not even allowed to ratify the contracts, but they were required to join the Teamsters and have weekly union dues subtracted from their paychecks.

It appeared that internal politics were involved in the Teamster intervention in Salinas, and that Grami was the force behind it. Those close to the situation claimed that Grami was trying to expand his power base within the Western Conference in order to either unseat or succeed the current director, Teamster International First Vice President Einar Mohn, who was due to retire in several years. It is difficult to judge whether this reflected a personal rivalry or factionalism within the union, but the potential for expanding a power base was immense, since the Salinas and Santa Maria valleys represented over 30,000 workers between them. Grami was identified with the faction within the Teamster International that wanted to replace the union president, Frank Fitzsimmons, with Jimmy Hoffa when the latter was released from prison.[2] During the subsequent Teamster-UFW dispute, Mohn supported the Teamster position but displayed little enthusiasm for their intervention.

As in the early wine and table grape boycotts, the UFW's initial strategy was to institute boycotts against specific growers with easily identifiable products. One such grower was Inter Harvest, the nation's second largest producer of head lettuce and grower of one-fourth of all Salinas Valley lettuce, owned by United Fruit, a subsidiary of United Brands. United Fruit owned huge banana plantations in Latin America and marketed bananas under the "Chiquita" label. The company had just launched an extensive advertising campaign promoting the Chiquita label for its lettuce, celery, and artichokes. Less well advertised was the fact that eleven of the company's fifty ships were rented for use in Vietnam. If a boycott was expanded to the parent corporation, United Brands, it would include A & W root beer and Baskin-Robbins ice cream. Fresh Pict, a subsidiary of Purex, which owned 42,000 acres of land in the Southwest and Mexico, was another obvious boycott target. The union demanded that these companies rescind their Teamster contracts and recognize the UFW. To apply pressure the union announced plans for a Chiquita boycott.

The Teamsters then indicated that they wanted to re-establish their jurisdictional agreement with the UFW. Both sides began meeting on 10 August under the auspices of the U.S. Catholic Bishops' Committee on Farm Labor, headed by Monsignor George Higgins. At the initial meeting Grami declared that the Teamsters were attempting to find a method of repudiating their contracts. At the next meeting he agreed to UFW jurisdiction over field workers and said that the Teamsters would rescind their contracts on an individual basis. In response, the UFW announced a six-day moratorium before calling a Salinas area strike and later extended it to ten days.[3]

It was quite possible that reaching an agreement was the Teamsters' intention. The only result of the meetings, however, was to postpone the strike and allow the growers additional time for harvest activities. Several days later Grami announced that instead of individual contract termination, all the contracts must be rescinded or none at all. Furthermore, he would not personally sign any rescissions; that would be left to Mohn. Grami appeared to be trying to take full credit for the contracts, while shifting the blame to Mohn if they were rescinded.[4] Further meetings produced little progress. Despite increasing pressure for a strike, the UFW persuaded the workers to postpone it for several more days. The AFL-CIO and the bishops' committee also pressured the union to extend the moratorium. The UFW wanted time to tighten up a number of ranch committees and set up others to insure the strike's effectiveness. The strike was finally guaranteed on Friday, 21 August, when Herb Fleming, president of the Grower-Shipper Vegetable Association, announced that the association's members would hold the Teamsters to their contracts and had received assurances that the contracts would be honored.

The strike began the next Monday, 24 August. Estimates of the number of workers participating range from 7,000 to 10,000, with the major portion concentrated in the Salinas- and Watsonville-area lettuce and strawberry fields. Most of those on strike also walked in picket lines. Santa Maria, 200 miles to the south, also witnessed an effective strike. A majority of those who showed up for work on the first day honored the picket lines. The *Los Angeles Times* called it the "largest strike of farm workers in U.S. history."[5] Even the grower-oriented *Salinas Californian* reported that the strike had virtually shut down Salinas Valley agriculture.[6] Several days after the strike began, the State and Federal Marketing Service conservatively estimated that the volume of Salinas Valley lettuce marketed was less than half the normal amount. Produce shipments dropped from 200 to 75 railway carloads per day. The area's strawberry growers admitted that the number of strawberry crates shipped was only 14 percent of the prestrike rate.[7]

Individual growers requested and received court injunctions limiting picket activity. On 16 September Superior Court Judge Anthony
Brazil issued a permanent injunction on the assumption that the
strike was a jurisdictional dispute between the UFW and the Teamsters. These injunctions were directed against *all* picketing; past
injunctions had only limited the number of pickets. They impaired
the effectiveness of the strike by offering a pretext for arrests of
picketers. This in turn restricted the union's access to the
strikebreaking force that had replaced the original workers.

As in the DiGiorgio dispute between the UFW and the Teamsters,
burly men armed with chains and shotguns were imported by the
Teamsters to attack pickets and intimidate UFW supporters. Their
number ranged from forty to seventy. The UFW's attorney, Jerry
Cohen, was beaten unconscious and hospitalized for four days after
an assault by Teamster "guards." Shots were fired at UFW headquarters; the UFW-Watsonville office was bombed; three pickets
were shot; and bomb threats were nearly a daily occurrence. The
Seafarers Union again sent members to counter the Teamster
threats, but incidents continued for the duration of the strike. The
enormity, maliciousness, and persistence of grower-Teamster violence and their virtual impunity—especially in alliance with the
newly formed "patriotic" organizations that branded the strikers
"communist"—were reminiscent of the antiunion assaults of the
thirties.[8]

Two days before the strike began, United Fruit's vice president
announced that he had received a rescission of its Teamster contract
from Einar Mohn. An Inter Harvest manager admitted that only 108
of the firm's 1,000 workers had actually signed Teamster authorization cards, and a card check tabulated by Monsignor Higgins revealed that the vast majority of Inter Harvest field workers wanted
UFW representation. Negotiations were held, and an agreement was
reached on 31 August, just after a Chiquita boycott was announced.
Chavez called the contract one of the best initial contracts in the
union's history. The base wage jumped from the prestrike level of
$1.75 an hour to $2.10; other gains included the union hiring hall,
some pesticide controls and a prohibition of DDT, inclusion of crew
bosses under the contract (a demand that Inter Harvest had especially resisted during negotiations), and the normal grower contribution to the union's health and welfare fund.[9] Teamster guards, with
the apparent cooperation of some Inter Harvest truck drivers under
Teamster contract, shut down Inter Harvest shipments for over a
week in protest.

After completion of the Inter Harvest agreement, the UFW initiated a boycott of Purex. Several days later the Purex Corporation's president, William Tincher, was ready to recognize the UFW and had received a Teamster rescission. Later, contracts were was also signed with D'Arrigo, Pick 'N Pak (a strawberry subsidiary of Dole), Brown and Hill Tomato Packers, and the large Delfino artichoke grower. The combined contracts covered approximately 15 percent of the head lettuce grown in California and Arizona.

By mid-September the Salinas Valley harvest was coming to an end. Court injunctions and Teamster intimidation, combined with a lack of strike funds and the usual availability of strikebreakers, had cut into the effectiveness of the strike. However, the regular work force had amply demonstrated its support for the UFW. The strike, possibly the largest to that point in California's agricultural history, and certainly the largest since the 1930s, was extremely well coordinated.[10] Fred Ross, who was present for the duration of the strike, said that he had never seen such complete cooperation from the farm workers as in Salinas.[11] But as before, the strike could not by itself force grower concessions: the growers had too many alternatives, their allies were too powerful, and farm worker resources were too limited. After strike activity had severely curtailed harvest operations for several weeks, strikers began to return to work out of financial necessity, and within a month crop shipments were at two-thirds of the normal volume. The UFW decided again to initiate a product-wide boycott, this time of head or iceberg lettuce. The immediate stimulus was the 16 September ban on picketing in the Salinas area. Bud Antle, Inc., the nation's largest producer of head lettuce, was singled out for special consideration. Like many of the larger agribusiness corporations, Bud Antle had financial ties with corporations involved in collateral operations. The most significant of these was the Dow Chemical Corporation, whose products were being boycotted by antiwar organizations because Dow produced much of the napalm dropped during the Vietnam War. Dow also produced agricultural pesticides and fertilizers and was supplying Antle with lettuce wrapping, pesticides, and produce boxes. In addition, Antle was leasing over 3,000 acres of agricultural land from a Dow subsidiary, the Dow Chemical Financial Corporation, in exchange for a minority interest in Antle, Inc. Antle had previously sold Dow 17,000 acres.[12]

Because of Antle's long-standing Teamster contract, on 6 October Judge Gordon Campbell ordered the UFW to cease the boycott of Bud Antle products. The UFW ignored the injunction, and after Chavez declared that the boycott was still being promoted during a court deposition in late November, the judge sentenced Chavez to jail for contempt of court.[13] Chavez entered the Salinas jail on 4 December, and farm workers set up twenty-four-hour vigils outside. The jailing received extensive coverage in the national media. Ethel Kennedy, the widow of Robert Kennedy, and Coretta King, widow of Martin Luther King, Jr., visited Chavez in jail. On 24 December the California Supreme Court ordered Chavez released pending a hearing on the UFW's appeal of Judge Campbell's ruling. Over a year later, on 15 April 1971, the court overturned the injunction against the Antle boycott.

Other injunctions forbidding UFW picketing were consolidated and also appealed by the union. On 29 December 1972 the California Supreme Court voted 6 to 1 to overturn the injunctions and ruled that the UFW picketing was legal.[14] The injunctions had been issued under the California Jurisdictional Strike Act, which protects neutral employers from competing unions, but which does not apply when employers interfere with the designation of the union. The Supreme Court decision lent further credibility to the UFW claim that grower-Teamster agreements were "sweetheart contracts." The court stated that the growers had invited the Teamsters into the situation primarily to avoid dealing with the UFW. The decision read in part:

> from a practical point of view an employer's grant of exclusive bargaining status to a non-representative union must be considered the ultimate form of favoritism, completely substituting the employer's choice of unions of his employees' desires. . . .
>
> In sum, we conclude that an employer who grants exclusive bargaining status to a union which he knows does not have the support of his employees may not thereafter call upon the state to enjoin concerted activities by a competing union.
>
> There is no suggestion in the record that the Growers, before taking such a step, attempted to ascertain whether their respective field workers desired to be represented by the Teamsters, or, indeed, that the question of their field workers' preference was even raised as a relevant consideration. . . .
>
> Although there is some dispute as to the precise number or percentages of field workers favoring either the Teamsters or the UFWOC, it appears clear that by mid-August at least a substantial number, and probably the majority of the applicable field workers desired to be represented by the UFWOC rather than the Teamsters.[15]

In March 1971 the UFW and the Teamsters signed another jurisdictional agreement. Einar Mohn indicated that the Teamsters wanted to relinquish their lettuce contracts. Teamster contracts were to remain in effect, but they would be unenforced until growers and the UFW agreed to a contract. While negotiations continued, the UFW suspended the lettuce boycott.

After five months the negotiations broke off, and the lettuce boycott resumed. The UFW claimed that the growers were not serious about reaching an agreement, but the union itself was under pressure from the AFL-CIO to arrive at a compromise. To expose the growers' strategy, Chavez, certain that the union would not have to sign a bad contract, agreed to all their demands, but the growers still would not agree to a contract.[16] Even after the negotiations ceased, Teamster contracts remained unenforced.[17] By prolonging what appeared to be insincere negotiations, lettuce growers obtained six months of relief from boycott pressures, and the 1971 harvest was completed without serious disruptions.

STATE OBSTRUCTION TO UNIONIZATION

The next several years witnessed a decisive shift in the context of the struggle. In the past, progrower intervention by government agencies and officials may have given growers added support and resources, but it had not altered its basic direction and emphasis. However, after the failure to resolve the UFW-Teamster dispute over the Salinas and Santa Maria valley lettuce contracts, attempts were made to legislate severe restrictions upon the UFW's activity. Up until this time the UFW had not encountered the kind of concentrated and coordinated efforts to weaken it by utilizing political and legislative channels that would increasingly characterize the next phase of the struggle.

Old forms of government assistance to growers were again employed. For example, late in 1970 the union received information that the Defense Department had drastically increased its purchases of lettuce grown by Bud Antle, Inc. Antle, which produces 11 percent of the nation's head lettuce, accounted for 9.9 percent of the department's lettuce purchases in 1969 and 8.3 percent in 1970. In the first quarter of 1971, its share skyrocketed to 29.1 percent. Moreover, Antle lettuce was brought at prices substantially higher than the market price. At the same time, department purchases of UFW-contracted lettuce dramatically declined. The Defense Department, as it had done several years before during the table grape boycott, was helping offset the possible effects of the lettuce boycott by providing an expanded market to a boycotted product. In response, on 6 January 1971 the UFW filed suit against Secretary of Defense Melvin Laird and Bud Antle, Inc., in U.S. District Court.[18]

The bulk of government actions against the UFW, however, took the form of legislation. Legislation to outlaw many of the union's tactical options was introduced in a number of key agricultural states in 1971. The American Farm Bureau coordinated these measures, while the Nixon administration spearheaded the attack by introducing similar legislation in Congress. The various pieces of legislation contained similar proposals. All included provisions for secret-ballot elections for agricultural workers, but all outlawed the secondary boycott. Elections would have been easy for growers to circumvent, since "cooling-off" periods that would effectively encompass a harvest period were often stipulated. Some bills even outlawed harvest-time strikes altogether. Many made it difficult for seasonal workers to vote and also limited the issues that could be resolved by collective bargaining; some, for example, would have excluded the union hiring hall and pesticide controls.

The Nixon administration revealed its proposals in 1971. Officials in the departments of Agriculture and Labor launched a campaign to promote the legislative package, claiming that it was similar to the NLRA. The proposed election machinery would make it difficult, if not impossible, for seasonal workers to vote. Workers were to give ten days' notice before striking, and growers could invoke a thirty day cooling-off period. This insured that harvest strikes would be difficult to undertake legally. The secondary boycott was outlawed. The proposed agricultural labor relations board that was to enforce this legislation would be controlled by the Department of Agriculture.[19]

The new attacks put the union on the defensive and drained its resources. The UFW had to open a number of campaigns to counter the legislative proposals, and this curtailed its focus on the lettuce boycott. Chavez claimed that the legislative fights "slowed us down terribly."[20] One of the reasons the earlier table grape boycott was so effective was that the union had concentrated all its energy on it. Such singular attention could not be given to the lettuce boycott. The union had to devote significant energy to campaigns in Oregon, Washington, Arizona, New York, Florida, and California.

One of the first legislative struggles took place in Oregon, where the legislature passed a bill banning both secondary and primary boycotts, harvest-time strikes, and collective bargaining over pesticide control. Mass demonstrations in the state capital of Salem and threats of a possible boycott of Oregon lumber pressured the Republican governor, Tom McCall, to veto the bill.[21]

The struggle in Florida centered on another segment of migratory agricultural workers, mostly black, who are hauled up and down the Atlantic coast by labor contractors. This work force is supplemented by imported labor from the Caribbean. The UFW won contracts in the spring of 1972 at several Florida citrus orchards owned by large corporations diversified into agriculture, including the Minute Maid division of Coca Cola. Shortly afterward an antiunion bill was introduced in the Florida legislature: several of its supporters publicly described it as anti-UFW legislation.[22] The union campaigned against the provision outlawing agricultural union hiring halls and attempted to expose the abuses of the labor contractor system in Florida agriculture. In so doing the union unveiled a system that was far more exploitative than the one in California. Several cases were discovered of workers being held by labor contractors on threat of death as virtual slaves. After media attention to these scandals and UFW objections, the proposed legislation died in committee on 7 April 1972.[23]

In Arizona, in May 1972, Republican governor Jack Williams signed a Farm Bureau–sponsored bill into law within forty-five minutes of its passage (a record) to avoid union pressure for a veto. Agricultural strikes could not be called unless workers certified the strike by secret ballot supervised and certified by a seven-person state board appointed by the governor. The law also offered growers a number of possible procedural delays to circumvent the certification of harvest-time strikes. In addition, growers faced with such strikes could be granted a ten-day restraining order. Union hiring halls in agriculture were outlawed, as were negotiations over mechanization. Secondary boycotts were outlawed, and primary boycotts were restricted to those naming the specific producer of the boycotted commodity. This would make a general product boycott illegal.[24]

The UFW chose to stage its major battle against such legislation in Arizona. Chavez assigned Jim Drake, Leroy Chatfield, and Marshall Ganz to launch a recall campaign against the governor to provide a warning to progrower politicians in other states. The campaign was extraordinarily successful in activating farm workers and others in this normally conservative state. Local AFL-CIO officials credited the campaign with opening up Arizona politics. Several other successful recall campaigns were initiated there, and the UFW's registration of nearly 100,000 voters was credited with the election of several Chicano and Navajo candidates for state and local offices over the next several years.[25] The union secured 168,000 signatures, of which 108,000 were eventually declared valid. Arizona election officials delayed in checking the signatures, however, and by the time ensuing appeals forced their certification, it was too close to the 1974 gubernatorial election to schedule a recall election.

A progrower farm labor bill passed the California Assembly Labor

Committee in June 1971. Before it came to a vote before the Ways and Means Committee, the union sponsored a rally of 2,000 farm workers on the steps of the state capitol. UFW officials pressured legislators to defeat the bill, and shortly afterward Assemblyman Willie Brown, chairman of the Ways and Means Committee, announced that the bill was dead.

The Farm Bureau then wrote a similar piece of legislation and placed it before the voters as a ballot initiative, Proposition 22, on the 1972 general election ballot. It was one of the most restrictive anti-UFW bills proposed anywhere in the country. It outlawed secondary boycotts and placed such severe restrictions on primary boycotts that they would be virtually impossible to initiate. It required ten-day strike notice and provided for a sixty-day cooling-off period. The provisions for free elections virtually insured that they could not be held during the peak harvest season by stipulating that they could only take place when the number of temporary employees did not exceed the number of permanent ones. Unions were prohibited from negotiating over work rules, and growers, even under union contracts, were allowed to hire nonunion workers.[26] The UFW perceived the fight against Proposition 22 as a life-and-death struggle and ignored the lettuce boycott in order to concentrate on defeating the initiative. The issue was far graver than any specific conflict with a segment of the growers. If the initiative passed, the union's future would be in jeopardy.

The UFW campaign picked up momentum and valuable media exposure when it pressured California Secretary of State Jerry Brown to file suit to remove the proposition from the ballot. The union presented Brown with affidavits from many of those who had signed initiative petitions reporting the proposal had been misrepresented to them. Handwriting experts verified that entire pages of petitions had been signed by the same person and that thousands of the signatures were forged. Brown charged that those behind Proposition 22 had engaged in what "may represent the gravest case of election fraud in recent history to get it before the voters in November."[27] Although Brown's suit was dismissed, it placed the grower-financed campaign on the defensive. Despite the expenditure of nearly $500,000 by its proponents, the proposition was defeated by a margin of 58 to 42 percent. In the end, the UFW succeeded in preventing the passage of restrictive legislation in all but three states: Arizona, Idaho, and Kansas.

In March 1972 Peter Nash, a conservative Republican recently named by Nixon as chief counsel for the NLRB, filed suit in federal court to prohibit the UFW from utilizing the secondary boycott. The suit claimed that the UFW was now covered under the terms of the NLRA because in the union's current strike and boycott campaign against nine small Napa Valley wineries, several of the strikes involved workers employed in commercial sheds, an operation covered by the NLRA. Nash contended that this placed all aspects of the union's activities under the board's jurisdiction. By this time three of the board's five members were Nixon appointees, including the chairman, Edward Miller, who had compiled a strong antilabor record. Previously, the board had always recognized that the UFW was not covered by the NLRA. If Nash's ruling was sustained, the union would be deprived of the secondary boycott without gaining any of the NLRA's benefits.[28]

The UFW responded quickly. Contending that the ruling was politically motivated, it called vaguely for a boycott of the Republican party. This took the form of massive letter-writing campaigns, the picketing of Republican headquarters in 150 cities, and threats of demonstrations at the upcoming 1972 Republican National Convention, then scheduled for San Diego. The fact that it was a national election year undoubtedly stimulated involvement in supportive efforts. Over one million letters were reportedly sent to the party's national chairman, Senator Robert Dole. Numerous Democrats publicly pledged their support, including Senators Edward Kennedy and George McGovern. The United Auto Workers promised to mobilize the resources of its locals to provide support. Two months after the campaign began, Nash agreed to drop the charges, and the UFW in turn discontinued the boycott of the wineries and promised not to attempt to organize nonagricultural workers.

That summer the Democratic party drafted a platform that included support for the lettuce boycott. The UFW had been an early and active supporter of Senator McGovern, while the Teamsters endorsed President Nixon, and the national AFL-CIO withheld its endorsement. The nationally televised convention gave considerable media attention to the lettuce boycott. After it concluded, the president of Inter Harvest claimed that lettuce shipments from Salinas fell 20 percent, costing growers an estimate $200,000 a day in lost sales.[29]

The period from 1970 through 1972 was dominated by a increasingly coordinated assault on the UFW. The forms taken by anti-UFW actions in this period were significant. Rather than overtly repressive, in many cases they seemed at first glance to be compatible with farm worker interests. The Teamsters were an established union with considerable resources; they might, in theory, be better able to represent the interests of the workers than the UFW. All the anti-UFW legislative proposals contained provisions granting agricultural workers the right to secret ballot elections for union designation. By obscuring the real nature of these developments, growers and sympathetic legislators and government officials hoped to maintain their own credibility while making it virtually impossible for the UFW to continue to exist; it was to appear that the union itself was at fault for its loss of membership and failure to become established. Even though Teamster-grower collusion prevented the UFW from obtaining contracts from the majority of lettuce growers, the legislative onslaught against the UFW was a pronounced failure, especially given the money and energy devoted to attacking the union. This inability to drive a wedge between the UFW and its supporters and prohibit most of the union's activity led to an even more direct attack on the UFW, one that made no effort to mask its purposes.

After the re-election of President Nixon and the defeat of Proposition 22 in November, a rapid series of events set the stage for a UFW strike in the Coachella Valley in April 1973. It occurred after the Teamsters signed contracts with the grape growers immediately upon the expiration of the UFW contracts. This represented perhaps the most severe assault on the union in its history.

NIXON, THE TEAMSTERS, AND THE GROWERS

The UFW had expected that the renewal of its 1970 table grape contracts, due to expire during the spring and summer of 1973, would generate grower opposition, and it did. The growers objected primarily to the UFW hiring hall, claiming that it had been inefficient and was disliked by many of the workers. While there was some substance to grower claims—due in part to the union's lack of administrative experience—the UFW pointed out that the growers themselves had engaged in deliberate manipulation to undermine the hiring hall's effectiveness and were placing the blame on the union in hopes of generating worker discontent. According to the union, Lionel Steinberg, a grower who was generally cooperative with the hiring hall system, experienced few difficulties.[30] The issue of the union hiring hall versus the labor contractor proved to be a cruical factor in the Teamster intervention in the California grape fields in 1973.[31]

Another factor in the Teamster intervention was the involvement of the Nixon administration. The Teamsters International had developed extraordinarily close ties to the administration. Nixon appointed Fitzsimmons to the Wage and Price Board in 1971, and the Teamster president remained a loyal member after AFL-CIO officials had quit the board and publicly denounced its policies. The Teamster front office enthusiastically supported Nixon's re-election in 1972, and it was reported that Fitzsimmons' attacks on Senator McGovern were written in the White House. It was also believed that White House counsel Charles Colson had devised the terms of Nixon's pardon of ex-Teamster president Jimmy Hoffa for Fitzsimmons' benefit. Hoffa was serving a thirteen-year sentence for pension fund fraud and jury tampering, and was pardonned with the requirement that he could not discuss union matters or run for a union office until 1980. This effectively removed Hoffa as an immediate threat to Fitzsimmons, who most observers felt would lose in a union race against Hoffa.

According to a *New York Times* story, Teamster officials admitted that their close association with the administration was of little benefit to union members; the White House gave little support to Teamster legislative proposals and other goals. The chief beneficiary appeared to be Fitzsimmons, and not only through Nixon's prevention of a Hoffa challenge to the union presidency. The Justice Department dropped the prosecution of a fraud case against Fitzsimmon's son, Richard, and denied an FBI request to seek court approval for additional wiretaps to investigate an alleged plan for organized crime to use Teamster pension funds to set up bogus health and dental care plans.[32] The Teamster president supported Nixon virtually until his resignation. Just two months before Nixon left office, the union was revealed as the largest outside financial contributor to the National Citizens' Committee for Fairness to the Presidency, whose primary concern was to block Nixon's impeachment.[33]

The initial manifestation of the coalition between the Teamsters Union, the American Farm Bureau, the California growers, and the Nixon administration occurred on 12 December 1972, when Fitzsimmons addressed the American Farm Bureau Convention in Los Angeles. It was an unprecedented appearance for a labor leader. In his speech Fitzsimmons proposed an "alliance" between his union and the conservative grower organization. There is little question that this served as a signal to agribusiness in general and California growers in particular. Although Fitizsimmons chastized growers for having "nineteenth century attitudes" toward farm labor, he saved his strongest criticisms for Chavez and the UFW, calling the union "a revolutionary movement that is perpetrating a fraud on the American public."[34] The next day the convention voted to recommend that agricultural labor be brought under the NLRA, an action that the Farm Bureau had always staunchly opposed in the past. After his address, Fitzsimmons discussed farm labor organizing with officials of the Teamster Western Conference, including Mohn and Grami. The meetings produced the Teamsters' Agricultural Workers Organizing Committee, with Grami as its director.

The invitation for Fitzsimmons to address the Farm Bureau had been arranged by the Nixon administration. Officially, this was accomplished by Undersecretary of Labor Charles Sibelman, but many observers believed that Colson was its instigator, since Colson was one of Nixon's chief liaisons with the Teamsters and organized labor in general. On 2 December Colson met with Nixon and Fitzsimmons, and a few days later he resigned as White House chief counsel to join a Washington, D.C., law firm. That same day Fitzsimmons announced that the Teamsters Union was transferring all its legal business to that firm, and Colson received a $100,000-a-year retainer from the union. George Meany's executive assistant, Thomas Donahue, said that he was convinced that the Teamsters re-entered the fields primarily to destroy the UFW, and that the decision was made at the highest levels within the Nixon administration and the union. From his knowledge of Colson's function within the administration and his activity afterward, Donahue concluded that Colson was the primary architect of the alliance.[35]

Further evidence of the administration's anti-UFW activity was contained in two memoranda written by Colson to the NLRB and the Justice and Labor departments. In essence they stated that these agencies should not intervene in the Teamster-UFW struggle unless their actions would be harmful to the UFW. The first memo, written during May 1971, said in part, "Only if you can find some way to work against the Chavez union should you take any action." Less than a year later, the NLRB attempted to outlaw the UFW's use of the secondary boycott. In the second memo written in 1972, Colson wrote, "We will be criticized if this thing gets out of hand and there is violence, but we must stick to our position. The Teamsters Union is now organizing in the area and will probably sign up most of the grape growers this coming spring, and they will need our support against the UFW."[36] This was written well in advance of Fitzsimmons' Farm Bureau speech.

On 29 December 1972 the California Supreme Court issued the ruling previously described: the lettuce and vegetable growers who signed with the Teamsters in 1970 had done so without consulting the workers in an attempt to avoid a UFW organizing drive. Three weeks later, on 16 January 1973, William Grami announced that the Teamsters had renegotiated their contracts with these growers and were considering organizing "disgruntled" workers currently under UFW contracts. The new contracts were signed while the 1971 jurisdictional agreement with the UFW was still in effect and while their original contracts remained unenforced. Reported to cover 30,000 workers, they offered considerably better wages than previously but contained low pension and unemployment benefits. More importantly, the hiring hall, pesticide controls, inclusion of foremen under the contract, and protection against the adverse effects of mechanization were still missing. Les Hubbard, a spokesman for the growers' negotiating committee, commented, "We demanded no more evidence of Teamster support from the workers than we did on the original contract."[37]

Meanwhile, on 9 January, William Spaulding, an attorney who represented several Coachella Valley growers negotiating with the UFW over contract renewal, characterized the union's negotiators as vindictive, "highly emotional and irresponsible," and unconcerned about the well-being of the growers.[38] Later events suggested that the growers were not negotiating seriously but rather were stalling until the expiration of the UFW contracts permitted them to sign with the Teamsters. During the talks the growers demanded that the UFW give up the hiring hall and pesticide control clause, perhaps the union's two least negotiable positions.[39] Chavez himself felt that the UFW might have renewed its contracts if it had been willing to give up these two features, but that was impossible.[40]

In a deposition taken in 1974 as evidence in a suit against the Teamsters International and the Western Conference by several rank and file Teamsters, David Smith, an attorney for the Coachella Valley growers, testified that on 24 January 1973 approximately twenty-five growers or their representatives held an unpublicized meeting with Teamster officials at the El Morocco Motel in Indio. The head Teamster representative present was Ralph Cotner, who was working directly under Grami. Although Cotner, Grami, and Mohn made no mention of the meeting in their depositions on the suit, Smith's recollections were detailed. At the start of the meeting, Cotner announced the Teamsters' intention to organize agricultural workers and answered numerous grower questions. It was not a formal negotiating session, but the growers present were particularly interested in whether the Teamster agreements provided for a union hiring hall. Cotner assured them that they did not.[41] It is possible that the meeting was a more of a formal strategy session than Smith's cautious answers indicated. For its part, the UFW claimed that the growers and Teamsters worked out the details of their contracts during the meeting, although it offered no evidence to substantiate this.

The depositions of Grami and Mohn inadvertently revealed more evidence to support the charge that the growers and Teamsters had entered into an alliance for the purpose of destroying the UFW.[42] According to the two Teamster officials, petitions presented to the growers included the names of packing and shed workers asking for Teamster recognition. However, there was no record of any serious Teamster efforts to sign contracts covering workers in packing sheds, as Smith's deposition verified: the Teamsters had contracts covering field workers, but not the shed workers whom they had traditionally represented. A year after they signed the Coachella contracts, the Teamsters were covering no packing sheds affiliated with these growers.

On 19 March the Teamsters announced that they had signed two-year contracts with the National Farm Contractors Association covering the workers employed by its members. About half of the 800 farm labor contractors in California were members.[43] Earlier, on 14 February, a confidential letter mailed to farm labor contractors from the association's president, Guinn Sinclair, reported that the agreement with the Teamsters was near and added, "it will be a death blow to the hiring hall and Chavez's ambition to become Commissar of California."[44]

On 5 April the table grape growers walked out of negotiating sessions with the UFW, and on 15 April all but two Coachella Valley grape growers signed four-year contracts with the Teamsters. Cotner claimed that he petitioned for recognition after obtaining signatures from 4,100 agricultural workers in the valley. These were never verified; they were simply given to the growers. The UFW claimed fraud, and a reporter for the *Riverside Press Enterprise* said that the local farm labor service had informed him that only 1,200 to 1,500 people were working in agriculture in the valley at the time the petitions were supposedly circulated.[45] On 10 April a committee of church leaders, congressmen, and labor leaders headed by Monseigneur Higgins polled farm workers in thirty-one fields and reported that 795 were for the UFW, 80 for the Teamsters, and 78 for no union.[46]

The UFW renegotiated its contract with Steinberg around this time before it was due to expire. It contained adjustments in hiring hall procedures to allow grower input. Teamster and UFW contracts were roughly equivalent in terms of wages but differed vastly in control over hiring and working conditions. As before, Teamster contracts did not include a hiring hall, ranch committees, pesticide controls, or adequate grievance procedures.

On 13 April, two days before the UFW contracts expired, over 1,000 workers overwhelmingly voted to strike any grape grower signing a Teamster contract. On 16 April approximately 2,000 workers began the strike, which effectively stopped the grape-thinning process. During the Coachella strike, eighteen separate court injunctions limiting picketing were issued. An injunction covering a Tenneco-owned field actually outlawed all picketing. By the end of the first week, more than 300 had been arrested. Later the injunctions were rewritten to allow unlimited picketing sixty feet away from a struck field.

Strikebreaking crews were imported, many coming from the Mexican border areas. The Teamsters immediately secured "guards," most of them paid $50.00 a day plus $17.50 for expenses, according to Grami's testimony. He believed that most were unemployed Teamsters from other locals but admitted that they were not necessarily Teamster members. He also denied employing "Hell's Angels–types."[47] UFW members claimed that the Teamster guards, who numbered about 350, carried grape stakes, clubs, baseball bats, metal pipes, metal chains, and knives. Many were massive men weighing up to 300 pounds.

The picket lines were an extraordinary sight. On the far side of the road were UFW pickets, marching, singing, and chanting. On the side adjacent to the struck field were Teamster guards, taunting UFW pickets. In between was a line of Riverside County deputy sheriffs, keeping the two groups separated. Behind the Teamsters were the people in the fields, who under the circumstances could do little but remain there. The UFW credited the sheriff's department with a semblance of impartiality in its enforcement of the law, something the union claimed was absent later in the season in the San Joaquin Valley. One UFW organizer commented that the concentrated presence of the sheriff's department prevented many serious assaults by the Teamster guards.[48] Some guards in fact spent almost as much time verbally harassing the sheriffs as they did the UFW pickets.

The police were unable to prevent all violence, however. Beginning in June, Teamster guards began openly to assault UFW pickets. Although both UFW members and Teamsters were arrested in a number of confrontations, the sheriff's deputies testified that the battles had been initiated by the Teamsters. One Teamster revealed that the violence was in response to an order given by Ralph Cotner, who was officially in charge of Teamster organizing in Coachella.[49] In one of the most publicized attacks, Father John Banks sustained three broken bones in his face when he was smashed without warning by a Teamster guard while having breakfast in a restaurant with a reporter for the *Wall Street Journal*. Scores of people were injured in a series of violent skirmishes. Fifty-six were hurt when Teamster guards charged UFW pickets at an asparagus field. Two guards were charged with attempted murder after they stabbed a farm worker six times with an ice pick; a farm worker's family barely escaped death when their small trailer was set on fire while they slept; even factfinders sent into the Coachella Valley by Fitzsimmons were attacked and beaten by guards under Cotner's command.

On 28 June an estimated forty guards armed with lead pipes, chains, brass knuckles, and grape stakes charged 200 pickets around the John Kovacevich ranch near Arvin in the southern San Joaquin Valley, where the grape harvest was beginning. Four of the injured pickets required hospitalization. One sixty-year-old man was severely beaten and sustained a skull fracture and cracked ribs. Twenty-five Teamsters were arrested, but the Kern County district attorney, Al Leddy, dropped charges on all but one, who was later acquitted. The national media attention given to this and previous assaults forced the Teamsters to withdraw their guards on 5 July. By that time the harvest, and with it the strike, had moved into the San Joaquin Valley. As it turned out, the guards were not needed to disrupt strike efforts there.

Throughout the strike the AFL-CIO offered its strongest support of the UFW to date. On 18 April Meany, who had been noticeably noncommittal in his public statements, condemned the actions of the Teamsters in signing the contracts and added, "They are clearly union busting in a concerted campaign to wipe out the United Farm Workers. This is the most despicable strikebreaking, union-busting activity I have ever seen in my lifetime in the trade union movement."[50] Several days later the AFL-CIO executive board announced that it was raising $1.6 million for the UFW strike fund by means of a membership levy. Thus, the Coachella strike became the first well-financed, well-planned farm worker rebellion in California history. Up to $75.00 a week per person was given out in strike benefits. For this reason the strike was a successful show of force, although the contracts were lost. Because of the readily available supply of surplus labor, the strike was only partly effective in halting production. Although the UFW never officially acknowledged this, some of its members claimed that a disproportionately high number of regular workers who did not strike were young Filipinos, who reportedly harbored resentment over what they perceived as Mexican American domination of the union. On the other hand, a significant number of recruited strikebreakers left the fields to join the strike. Many of the remaining strikebreakers were undocumented workers inexperienced at grape harvesting. Work proceeded slowly; grapes were often poorly packed; and wholesale prices dropped while grower costs increased. According to the Federal Market News Service, as of 27 June grape shipments were only 44 percent of what they had been the previous year. Prices were below the break-even price, except for the grapes harvested under UFW contract.[51]

During the early part of the strike, Jane Yett Kiely, a student of the Graduate Theological Union in Berkeley who had been placed with Safeway Stores, Inc. as an intern, issued a report on the UFW-Teamster dispute. Because Safeway was the target of a UFW secondary boycott as a result of its proagribusiness policies and its handling of large quantities of non-UFW head lettuce, two Safeway vice presidents arranged for Ms. Kiely to undertake an independent investigation of the situation and make recommendations. As part of the project, she interviewed Einar Mohn on 5 February 1973. In response to a question about the role of farm workers within the Teamsters Union, Mohn replied:

> We have to have them in the union for a while. It will be a couple of years before they can start having membership meetings, before we can use the farm workers' ideas in the union. . . . I'm not sure how effective a union can be when it is composed of Mexican-Americans and Mexican nationals with temporary visas. Maybe as agriculture becomes more sophisticated, more mechanized, with fewer transients, fewer green carders, and as jobs become more attractive to whites, then we can build a union that can have structure and that can negotiate from strength and have membership participation.[52]

Asked whether the Teamster contracts contained any protection against the hardships caused by mechanization of the harvest, Mohn responded:

> No, that isn't a problem to solve in this way [by contract provisions]. Shortage of jobs is the problem. If there weren't such a shortage of jobs, Mexican-Americans could get jobs. I don't know what will happen to the Mexican-Americans. After all, you can't expect whites to step aside and let Mexican-Americans and Negroes have the (machine) jobs they have had for years.[53]

Ms. Kiely's recommendation to Safeway Stores was "that Safeway boycott the lettuce of growers with Teamster contracts and other growers who have dealt unfairly with the workers' desires for a union."[54] Safeway did not accept her advice.

During this period several UFW-organized strikes in Arizona resulted in substantial wage gains for some of the workers. These strikes were illegal under the proagribusiness legislation passed the previous year, but the law was never enforced.[55]

When the California strike spread north into the San Joaquin Valley, however, UFW pickets were met with considerable resistance by the sheriff's departments of Kern, Tulare, and Fresno counties. As in Coachella, San Joaquin growers signed Teamster contracts as soon as UFW contracts expired. One of these was Gallo Wine, which had had a UFW contract for six years before it expired on 15 April. Earlier Teamster organizers had been chased out of the fields by Gallo workers when they attempted to meet with them. Then Gallo began to fire workers who were especially supportive of the UFW and demanded that the UFW give up the hiring hall and the union's right to determine union seniority before it would renew its contract. When Gallo signed a four-year Teamster contract on 10 July, the strike began. According to Fred Ross, 125 of Gallo's permanent workers walked out, leaving the fields to specially recruited strikebreaking crews. Eighty of the Gallo strikers went to work on the UFW boycott.[56] Seventy striking families were forcibly evicted by sheriff's deputies from Gallo-owned labor camps. Some had worked for the winery for fourteen years.[57] Shortly afterward the UFW announced a boycott of Gallo wines.

Throughout the valley, restrictive injunctions were issued by the local courts, resulting in mass arrests as before. While police in the Coachella Valley had rarely initiated acts of violence themselves, police in the San Joaquin Valley were extremely aggresive in attempting to enforce injunctions against picketing and mass demonstrations. Their actions recalled the vigilante tactics used to smash unionization efforts in the valley during the 1930s. The police charged picketers with clubs and mace, often beating or macing them whether they were resisting arrest or not. Some UFW pickets testified that on occasion Teamster officials or management personnel would put on deputy badges and join in the beatings or even make arrests.[58] That summer the UFW counted forty-four people who had been beaten by the police. The police also made arrests at strikers' homes at two or three in the morning. Police helicopters flew over the pickets, showering them with small rocks and dirt clods stirred up by the blades. A number of AFL-CIO officials on the scene testified to the viciousness of police attacks; several were themselves beaten and arrested by the police.[59] "They don't arrest us for trespassing," Chavez charged. "They beat the hell out of us, both men and women." Nearly 3,600 UFW members and supporters were arrested over the summer, including over 70 priests, nuns, and ministers and the seventy-six-year-old Dorothy Day of the Catholic Worker organization.

Throughout the summer Meany and Fitzsimmons held meetings to resolve the dispute. On 1 August Meany announced that the basis for an agreement had been reached. Fitzsimmons ordered an immediate halt to Teamster organizing, while Mohn and Chavez worked out the final terms of the new jurisdictional agreement, which again was designed to allow the UFW full jurisdiction over field workers. While negotiations were in progress on 10 August, all twenty-nine Delano area table grape growers whose UFW contracts had expired recently, signed Teamster contracts. This prompted Chavez to walk out of the meeting, charging the Teamsters with once again negotiating in bad faith. Later both Fitzsimmons and Mohn publicly repudiated the contracts, claiming that orders to cease organizing were still in effect.

Negotiations between the Teamsters and the AFL-CIO began again in Washington in late September, and a new agreement was announced on 27 September. Among those participating in the negotiations were Fitzsimmons, Mohn, Meany, Chavez, and AFL-CIO vice president Paul Hall. Under the terms of the agreement, the Teamsters were to rescind all the table and wine grape contracts they had signed the previous spring and summer and were to cease organizing agricultural workers altogether. They would retain the previous lettuce and other row crop contracts until their expiration in July 1975, at which time they would not be renewed. Meany and Fitzsimmons were designated as the final arbitrators of the agreement. For their part, the UFW would cease the lettuce boycott, would not challenge Teamster jurisdiction over workers involved in the processing, warehousing, and transporting of produce, would support a direct extension of the NLRA to cover agricultural labor, and would comply with the rules and policies of the AFL-CIO in future boycotts.[60] Generally this was believed to mean that the UFW would now have to seek the approval of the AFL-CIO's executive council before launching a boycott. Meany further announced that all parties understood that the agreement was fully complete and not subject to further negotiation.[61]

The next day Fitzsimmons announced a delay. According to UFW sources, Fitzsimmons had consented to sign the agreement and indi-

cated that it should be brought to him right away for that purpose.
When AFL-CIO and UFW officials arrived at Fitzsimmons' office,
Charles Colson was there, and Fitzsimmons said that he wanted the
Teamsters' lawyers to examine the language of the agreement. After
a series of delays, Fitzsimmons announced on 15 November that the
Teamsters would honor the contracts they had signed, including
those in the Delano area. On the sixteenth Meany issued a statement
condemning the Teamsters for reneging on the agreement. He promised full AFL-CIO support to the UFW and added, "It appears the
Teamsters have decided that their interests lie in maintaining the
alliance they have created with these employers, rather than maintaining their integrity as trade unionists."[62]

Several reasons for the union's reversal have been suggested by
those close to the situation, who assume that the Teamsters were
sincere in approving the initial agreements. Meany himself was
reputed to believe that agribusiness representatives had put pressure on Fitzsimmons. The Teamsters had been worried about possible
grower reaction if they were to renounce their contracts and had
wanted the AFL-CIO to indemnify them for any financial loss from
grower lawsuits.[63] Other sources in the AFL-CIO and UFW maintain
that Colson, acting as a Teamster attorney, personally advised Fitzsimmons not to sign the agreement. Colson's presence at what should
have been the official signing gives credibility to this argument.
Meany and the AFL-CIO at that time were calling for Nixon's impeachment, and Nixon would not have wanted Fitzsimmons, his
strongest supporter in labor circles, to enter into any agreement with
the federation.[64]

In the meantime the strike had come to a tragic conclusion. While
the police continued to break up picket lines and stage mass arrests,
the growers began to hire private armed guards, and strikebreakers
began to arm themselves. Incidents of shooting directed at UFW
members and supporters, mostly on the picket line, began around 1
August and increased in frequency. One picket was shot in the
shoulder and another in the hip. A third sustained flesh wounds in
the head. A number of shots were fired at a picket line containing
Chavez's son, Fernando. Police made no attempt to disarm the
strikebreakers, and no arrests were made.

Shortly after midnight on 14 August, across from the union's office
in Arvin, one of the few Arab members of the UFW, Nagi Daifullah, a
farm worker from Yemen and a UFW picket captain, was killed in a
scuffle with a Kern County deputy. The deputy had directed a small
group of mostly UFW members gathered outside a bar to disperse or
face arrest. After a bottle was thrown, Daifullah began to run. The

deputy chased him and knocked him to the pavement, rendering him unconscious, and then dragged him back to the bar, leaving a trail of blood. Daifullah never regained consciousness and died the next evening from a skull fracture. Eyewitnesses claimed that the deputy had hit him over the head with a flashlight, but the deputy insisted that he only hit his shoulder and that the fatal injury was sustained in the fall. The death was ruled accidental.

The UFW immediately organized a funeral procession and utilized the event to pull Arab strikebreakers out of the fields. Daifullah himself was one of 1,200 workers from Yemen imported to the valley during the earlier grape strike, and most of his countrymen had lived in labor camps in relative obscurity. Their main contact with the outside was channeled through Arabic-speaking labor contractors. Ethnic differences compounded by severe isolation made them prime candidates for strikebreakers.

Two days later, on a silent picket line near Giumarra's vineyard mourning Daifullah's death, sixty-year-old Juan de la Cruz, one of the original 1965 strikers, was fatally shot by someone driving past in a pickup truck. A twenty-year-old male alternately identified as a farm worker and a labor contractor was charged with the shooting. Three years later he was acquitted by a jury that accepted his claim that he had fired in self-defense in response to a hail of rocks from pickets.[65]

Immediately Chavez ordered all picket lines removed. After the funerals, which were attended by 5,000 people, hundreds of strikers and supporters were dispatched throughout the United States to begin the second boycott of table grapes and a secondary boycott of Safeway Stores. The two deaths were the primary motive for the abrupt shift in emphasis, but there were others. Since early in the strike, pressure had been mounting for a renewal of the table grape boycott, since this vehicle had been effective before. Moreover, the UFW was simply out of money. It had spent $3 million on the strike, including all of the $1.6 million from the AFL-CIO. Nearly all went toward paying strike benefits.[66]

The year was a disaster for the UFW in terms of contract and membership figures. At its height the year before, the union held more than 150 contracts covering 50,000 workers and had around 30,000 year-round members. By the end of the fall harvest, it was reduced to less than a dozen contracts covering 6,500 workers, and the union could claim no more than 12,000 members.[67] But Chavez maintained that the strike was successful even though the contracts were lost because it hurt the growers financially. Those in the regular labor force who did not join the strike—disproportionately Filipino,

Anglo, and Arab workers, supplemented by specially recruited un-documented Mexican nationals—brought in the harvest, but UFW sources indicated that the work force was only half the normal size in many fields. The volume of grapes in cold storage climbed dramati-cally, indicating a restriction of their normal markets, and the union maintained that growers secretly destroyed huge quantities of grapes at night. When the leaves came off the vines in the fall, grapes were revealed still on the vines.

Perhaps more significantly, Chavez claimed that the strike helped solidify the workers' support for the union. Beatings and jailings had been an educational experience that deepened understanding and commitment. According to Chavez, "Unlike the lettuce workers, the fresh grape workers in the Union weren't radical before the strike." The jailings served to "expose the workers to an entirely different view of their Union, looking from the inside out through the bars. And they voted to go to jail every time."[68]

Nevertheless, the union's inability to hold on to the table grape contracts once again demonstrated the structural powerlessness of agricultural labor and the weakness of farm workers' internal re-sources. For the time being, the growers prevailed, although only with the assistance of powerful allies, and UFW supporters began to wonder whether the union had a future. The 1973 grape strike illustrated the divisions within the farm worker population. The union's constituency was segmented according to ethnicity and citizenship status. Growers and Teamster organizers did what they could to exacerabate these splits, but the UFW itself had antagonized segments of the farm labor force through its determination of worker seniority and membership in "good standing." Perhaps this was in-evitable because the changes the union sought to achieve were pro-found, but animosity toward the union made a significant number of regular farm workers unwilling to participate in strikes or offer any other forms of support to the union.

The UFW was once again faced with the necessity of mobilizing its external resources. The brutality used against grape strikers and their supporters on the picket lines proved to be an asset. Grower and Teamster arguments were effectively delegitimized by media cover-age of unprovoked attacks and assaults by Teamster guards and sheriff's deputies. In a period of declining social consciousness and increasing conservatism, such brutality may have been necessary to activate and sustain support for still another international product boycott. The UFW had not chosen its circumstances, but it attempted to exploit them to its own best advantage.

CHAPTER 11

STATE MEDIATION BY LEGISLATION

The latest period of agricultural unionization efforts has been characterized by state attempts to mediate grower-labor conflict through the legislative process. The California Agricultural Labor Relations Act (ALRA) of 1975, sponsored by Governor Jerry Brown, is the prime example of such mediation. This legislation appeared only after ten years of virtually continuous turmoil through farm worker strikes and consumer boycotts. The production and distribution ends of agricultural goods were both unstable. Coordinated efforts by growers and several governmental agencies, officials, and legislative bodies had tried and failed to undermine the latest agricultural unionization movement. Every indication pointed to a future of unresolved conflicts, continued farm labor insurgency, and heightened political pressure from the UFW and its supporters. Under these circumstances, legislation regulating agricultural capital-labor disputes seemed an attractive and feasible policy objective to many government officials. In this respect the history of the current unionization movement parallels that of the 1930s, when continued agricultural labor unrest generated massive coordinated repressive efforts and, following their failure to halt continued agricultural labor protests, elements of the state attempted to mediate the struggle by providing certain guarantees to labor.

Reform was not automatically conceded however; it was won by labor. In the ten years following the Delano grape strike, the UFW had become effective in mobilizing its resources and channeling its strength in the directions that offered the greatest rewards. The conflict that began as a strike against a group of table grape growers had escalated to embrace powerful corporate agriculture organizations and finally reached the level of the state. The strong support of several California legislators, the ability to apply effective pressure on others, and the political advantage demonstrated to several politicians, including Jerry Brown, of being associated with or supportive of farm worker goals—all these resources were critical to the UFW in securing the passage of the ALRA.

THE RETURN TO THE BOYCOTT

The renewed table grape boycott began with considerable momentum. Numerous church organizations, including the National Conference of Bishops and the World Council of Churches, endorsed it. On a trip to Europe in the fall of 1974, Chavez obtained promises to coordinate a European boycott from British, Norwegian, and Swedish unions and was received by Pope Paul VI. During the winter of 1973–74, the use of the secondary boycott against supermarket chains began to effect results. Several chains sought court injunctions against pickets. But there were indications of a far more serious threat to the union. Late in the fall of 1973, the California Farm Bureau and the Mexican government proposed a renewal of the bracero program. This proposal was later discussed by Secretary of State Henry Kissinger and Mexican president Luis Echevarria during a meeting in Mexico City. A year later, on 21 October 1974, President Gerald Ford again discussed a renewed bracero agreement with Echeverria, and both countries planned to set up a commission to study the question of Mexican nationals working in the United States.[1] Any renewal of the bracero program could have disastrous consequences for the extension or even the survival of farm labor unionization.

In September 1973 the UFW held its first constitutional convention in Fresno. Its status had been changed from an organizing committee to an independent union affiliated with the AFL-CIO during the previous year. The constitution to be ratified at the convention formalized the structure of the union, which was built upon ranch committees. It gave membership status to volunteers who worked for the union for at least six months and stipulated that labor contractors could not be given union membership. Chavez was unanimously elected the union's president, with Dolores Huerta as first vice president and two Filipinos, Philip Vera Cruz and Pete Velasco as second and third vice presidents. Vera Cruz had been president of the NFLU in 1950. Gilbert Padilla was elected secretary-treasurer.

All would serve on the union's executive board along with Marshall Ganz, Mack Lyons, Eliseo Medina, and Richard Chavez.

Speakers at the convention included Senator Edward Kennedy, Seafarers Union president Paul Hall, representing Meany, and United Auto Workers president Leonard Woodcock. At a later press conference, Kennedy expressed the view that the NLRA would not provide suitable coverage for farm worker unionization and said that he was receptive to UFW recommendations on labor legislation. Woodcock pledged to continue his union's $10,000-a-week contribution to the UFW.[2]

Despite the support given to the renewed boycott by the UAW, the Longshoremen, and several AFL-CIO affiliated unions, the AFL-CIO, which had endorsed the 1968 table grape boycott but none of the others, hesitated to endorse it. The money provided by the federation was exclusively for strike benefits, not boycott operations. Although the federation publicly supported the union's efforts, many sources within the UFW indicated that there had always been tensions between the two. Meany was reportedly unhappy with the entire series of UFW boycotts. The problem was not the idea of a boycott in itself: some AFL-CIO affiliates carry on boycotts that are endorsed and publicized by the federation: the contemporaneous Farah products boycott was an example. Meany's (and the federation's) distance stemmed rather from the nature of the UFW as a militant, grassroots movement with a radical tenor. The union had ties with antiwar organizations, left activists, and other community organizations outside the labor movement. The UFW opposed the Vietnam War virtually from its founding and spoke out against the repression of domestic radical organizations, the increasing power of American-based multinational corporations, and U.S. military intervention. The 1973 convention adopted a resolution that urged the United States to withhold diplomatic recognition of the Chilean military junta, and convention delegates stood in memory of the assassinated Chilean president, Salvadore Allende.[3]

The federation was also generally resistant to labor issues that went beyond wages and benefits. Meany was especially hostile to the idea of worker participation in management or control over work.[4] Control over hiring and working conditions received primary emphasis in UFW campaigns. It has been reported that Meany was particularly concerned about the union hiring hall and discussed it with Chavez on at least one occasion.

The UFW's autonomy within the AFL-CIO created additional friction. According to Jim Drake, who had been with the union since

1962 and had particularly close contact with Chavez, UFW autonomy "drives Meany up the wall."[5] The union's unconventional operations made it suspect; it did not conform to the federation's image of a "responsible" labor union. The union's advertising on college campuses for volunteer community organizers to work for the boycott was incomprehensible to unions accustomed to employing highly paid professional organizers. In fact, the UFW's use of volunteer workers recruited from campuses and nonwhite urban areas as well as from the farm worker population has always been distrusted by the federation. (The practice generated controversy within the union as well, but it worked quite well as long as the volunteers were committed to following the union's policies, were willing to work extraordinarily long hours, and did not attempt in their work to impose their own ideological purposes at variance with the union's.)[6] Chavez was deeply committed to this form of recruitment and declared that he would resign if it was discontinued, at least under the union's current circumstances. The union offices were most often situated in older buildings, and the union fleet of cars consisted mostly of superannuated compact models. The unconventionality of operations during this period was perhaps epitomized by the union's practice of paying its staff, including Chavez, $5.00 a week plus providing room and board.

For most of its history, the union remained independent of AFL-CIO policies and protocol. The federation was rarely consulted before the union undertook new strategies and boycotts. Meany was sometimes pressured to keep the UFW in line by affiliated unions that regarded the secondary boycotts as contrary to their interests, but there was little the federation could do except cut off support, and reduction of support for the UFW generated criticism and hurt the federation's image.

The UFW also made political endorsements independent of the AFL-CIO. In fact, it paid little attention to what the AFL-CIO did in these matters and based its support rather on how effectively the candidate could help the union or whether he or she emphasized more general issues compatible with the union's own perspective. In 1968 the UFW supported Robert Kennedy while the federation endorsed Hubert Humphrey; in 1972 it endorsed George McGovern while the federation remained uncommitted. The union actively supported Tom Hayden for the California Democratic nomination for U.S. senator in 1976, while most of organized labor endorsed the incumbent, John Tunney. Some years before, Chavez endorsed Black Panther party member Bobby Seale for mayor of Oakland.

The UFW's identity as a social movement of largely nonwhite agricultural workers within a broader movement of poor people gave the AFL-CIO "nothing but headaches," according to Jim Drake. Up until 1973 the union had virtually no direct contact with Meany. William Kircher served as a buffer between the union and Meany for eight years, until he was moved to an executive position in the Culinary Workers Union in 1973. Without Kircher to explain and interpret the union's behavior to the federation, direct contact between the two began to heighten the tension between the UFW and the AFL-CIO front office.

Moreover, the federation's understanding of the agricultural labor situation was inadequate. After an AFL-CIO executive council meeting in February 1974, Meany told reporters that events of the previous summer indicated that the UFW had lost the support of the workers: "After all it was Chavez's own people who went to work behind the picket lines in Coachella, and that didn't indicate much support from the workers for Chavez."[7] Later he added: "But the thing that I'm disappointed about Cesar is that he never got to the point that he could develop a real viable union in the sense of what we think of as a viable union."[8] Meany indicated that he believed the $1.6 million given to the union the previous spring to be utilized as strike benefits had been wasted, since it had not resulted in immediate contracts.

The federation did not abandon the UFW, because it needed the union. According to a *Washington Post* story confirmed by UFW staff members, the AFL-CIO used the union to bolster its own image. The federation could always point to its support for the UFW to answer criticisms that it had lost interest in organizing and represented an aristocracy of labor. Meany himself needed to regain some of the legitimacy he had lost through his tacit support of Nixon and the war in Vietnam. The UFW could play the role of the conscience of the labor movement to the advantage of the federation. As the *Post* put it, "Standing by Cesar Chavez, Mr. Meany keeps company with a militant folk hero. In contrast, Mr. Fitzsimmons . . . looked like a moral bum."[9] Similarly, the *Los Angeles Times* labor writer Harry Bernstein wrote that 1972 represented Meany's most insecure period in recent years largely because of his neutrality in the presidential election, which "disgusted" many other union leaders. A number of union leaders privately characterized Meany as "a reactionary advocate of the status quo."[10] Support for Chavez and the UFW improved Meany's stature while permitting him to maintain essentially the same policies and beliefs as before. Others within the UFW and the federation believed that the AFL-CIO was using the union as a weapon in its ongoing struggle with the Teamsters. Since the Teamsters Union had been expelled from the federation for corruption in 1957, it had periodically raided AFL-CIO affiliated unions. Continued support for the UFW represented a stand against the Teamsters.

The UFW in turn needed the federation's support and endorsement of the boycott in order to isolate the Teamsters. With a united labor front in support of the UFW, the Teamsters' argument that they had legitimate interests in organizing agricultural labor would appear weak and self-serving. To get the endorsement, the UFW was willing to give up one of its most strategic and useful weapons.

Pressure on the AFL-CIO to persuade the UFW to discontinue the secondary boycott of supermarket chains was especially strong from the Butchers and Retail Clerks unions; in Ohio, the Retail Clerks union ran full-page newspaper advertisements against the UFW supermarket boycott because members feared the loss of their jobs. There was also pressure from the UAW, even though the boycott had no direct effect upon its members. On 8 April 1974 Meany announced that the AFL-CIO was endorsing the boycott of head lettuce and table grapes. In return the UFW agreed to give up the boycott of retail outlets where other AFL-CIO affiliates had members working, and this effectively ended the secondary boycott of supermarket chains, most notably Safeway and A&P. The federation did not endorse the boycott of Gallo and Franzia wines, since the AFL-CIO affiliated Glass Bottle Blowers Association and Distillery Workers Union had contracts with these firms.

Some members of the UFW executive board resisted this concession, but Chavez convinced them that the union had a greater need for the endorsement of the AFL-CIO.[11] Several union members claimed that the secondary boycott was losing its effectiveness anyway, and that the injunctions and lawsuits it generated tied up the union's resources. Most felt, however, that the loss of the secondary boycott was a damaging blow, severely limiting the options available to the union. Fred Ross termed it "a stab in the back" by the AFL-CIO.[12] It took away the primary incentive for supermarket chains to stop handling the boycotted product. Even though the agreement could be reversed if the union decided it needed the secondary boycott more than the federation's endorsement, it set a precedent. It represented the largest concession yet to the AFL-CIO and moved the union in the direction of increasing conformity with the more conventional labor union model. It is significant that the UFW was essentially forced into the compromise by the nature of the opposition it faced.

With the AFL-CIO's endorsement, relations between the two organizations improved substantially. The federation issued repeated public statements denouncing the Teamsters and calling for support for the grape and lettuce boycotts, and member unions offered unprecedented aid. During the summer of 1974, the boycott staff cultivated the support of other unions to the fullest possible extent. Chavez began spending more time developing ties with other unions, and they responded with support, publicity, and donations. Chavez addressed the UAW national convention in Los Angeles in June, where he reportedly drew the greatest applause of the convention. In mid-June he travelled to Los Angeles again and over three days met with representatives or attended meetings of the County Federation of Labor, the Laborers' Union, the Longshoremen's Union, the Retail Clerks, the Electrical Workers, the Hotel, Restaurant and Bartenders Union, the Laundry Workers, the California Federation of Teachers, the Public Employee Department of the county federation, the Communication Workers of America, the Los Angeles–Orange Counties Organizing Committee, and the Rubber Workers.[13] In July the Los Angeles County Federation of Labor, AFL-CIO, paid to display 140 signs endorsing the lettuce and grape boycotts on city buses.

In response to the AFL-CIO endorsement, Fitzsimmons sent letters to AFL-CIO affiliated unions throughout the country threatening to cease cooperation with unions supporting the boycott. This was interpreted as meaning that the unions could not expect the Teamsters to respect their picket lines or cooperate in any way at the local level.[14] The threat posed a problem for unions having especially close relationships with the Teamsters.[15]

Throughout 1974 the union received reports of declining grape sales. Gallo wine was similarly affected. The year after the boycott began, figures showed Gallo sales nationwide to be down as much as 20 percent. Lettuce sales were reportedly not so strongly affected. The lack of the secondary boycott was clearly hampering the union's efforts. It became increasingly difficult for the union to pressure supermarket chains to take grapes off the market. The Food Council, which represents most of the supermarket chains, took a strong stand to keep grapes on the market in Los Angeles, where the union was concentrating its boycott efforts. Formerly cooperative markets and chains informed boycott organizers that they could not go against the council.

In January 1974 M. E. "Andy" Anderson was appointed by Fitzsimmons to replace Einar Mohn as director of the Teamsters' Western Conference. William Grami's failure to be appointed was attributed to the repercussions of Teamster violence in the fields during the previous year.

In 1974 the Teamsters Union made its first attempt to represent itself as a union committed to servicing farm labor contracts. On June 5 Fitzsimmons announced the chartering of the union's first farm worker local. Local 1973, as it was called, was named after the year that the Teamsters' efforts to organize agricultural labor, to quote Fitzsimmons, "reached a turning point."[16] The headquarters were in Monterey, with offices in seven California agricultural centers. The local was structured to make it appear competitive to the UFW in offering service to the workers. It was directed by David Castro, the recent head of a Teamster cannery workers' local in Hayward. It employed a number of Chicano organizers, and some of its eighty-five staff members were to aid farm workers seeking social services. But the local held no membership meetings, elected no officers, and sent no delegates to any convention or caucus. From the outset it was placed in trusteeship by the Western Conference and was under the control of Mohn and Grami. Its mode of operation and the lack of farm worker participation reflected the remarks Mohn had made to Jane Yett Kiely for her report to Safeway during the year before.

Only six months after its inception, the local was all but dismantled. The headquarters were moved south to Delano and were used only to service contracts in that immediate area. Other contracts were assigned to existing Teamster locals in agribusiness centers. In November, just before the move to Delano, Ralph Cotner, who had replaced Grami as director of organizing, fired thirty staff members, including many of the Chicano organizers and social service staff. Subsequently Cotner was given a lesser assignment in Arizona; Grami appeared to be out of agricultural labor at last.

UFW strike activities during the spring and summer of 1974 were limited. As in the late 1960s, picket lines were maintained mostly for the purpose of disseminating information to workers in the field and conveying the union's presence. Union members in agricultural areas claimed that many of the permanent table grape workers had left growers who signed with the Teamsters, and the present harvest crews were less skilled, making the harvest less efficient. Both union and newspaper reports testified to the dramatic growth in the proportion of illegals in the fields, many of them working under Teamster contracts.

A considerable number of small, spontaneous strikes throughout the summer were aided by the UFW. A successful strike among 150 strawberry pickers in Watsonville near Salinas resulted in 20 percent wage gains and a UFW contract. Encouraged by this success, strawberry pickers near Oxnard in Ventura County staged a spontaneous walkout. Nearly 2,000 workers participated, making the strike well over 50 percent effective. Growers answered with court injunctions, and the Ventura County sheriff's department made mass arrests to enforce them. They were joined by units of the Los Angeles County and Ventura County tactical squads, who engaged in the kind of intimidation that was utilized the previous summer in the San Joaquin Valley. As earlier, the police used low-flying helicopters to disperse pickets. Strikers did not succeed in winning a contract. The critical element during this phase of the UFW's history, however, was not in the fields or in the supermarkets, but rather in the legislative arena.

LEGISLATIVE STRATEGY

The latest Teamster incursion caused several shifts in the UFW's tactical emphasis. Chavez later said that he had decided that the union should promote legislative solutions just before its convention in September 1973.[17] As noted above, the union developed closer relationships with the AFL-CIO and affiliated unions in part to insure their support for subsequent legislative efforts.

Events during 1974 made the legislative strategy more attractive. Democrats were in the majority in both houses of the California state legislature, and the 1974 elections added to their predominance. Before 1974 a proposal sympathetic to the UFW would have faced the near certainty of a veto by Governor Reagan. The election of Jerry Brown as governor in November 1974 removed that obstacle.

The development of the California Agricultural Labor Relations Act was an attempt by the state to mediate a long-term struggle between dominant and insurgent groups by curbing the power of the insurgents while at the same time trying to insure their existence. The act gave the UFW a legislative foundation that it could use to become permanently established, but it also circumscribed its future options. That these restrictions appeared at the time to be relatively limited, especially when compared to past grower-supported legislation, was an indicator of the kind of political power and support the union had built. In order to secure this resolution, however, the Brown administration undermined a consistently pro-UFW bill that had a good chance of passage during the 1974–75 legislative session.

The passage of the California ALRA was widely interpreted as a victory for the UFW, and this interpretation was advantageous for Brown. In reality, it was more of a compromise, and its long-term effects remain unclear.

When Ronald Reagan announced that he would not seek reelection, the Democratic party appeared to be in a solid position to capture the governorship in 1974. Interviews with UFW staff members did not reveal any predominant union preference in the Democratic gubernatorial primary held on 4 June.[18] The UFW limited its activity in the Democratic primaries to help for congressional candidates pledged to support its legislative proposals. Boycott organizers too were especially concerned with reaching politically influential people who could make up a support group for UFW-endorsed legislation.[19] Former UFW national legislative director Art Torres was elected to the California Assembly from the 56th District of Los Angeles.

Two days after Jerry Brown's victory in the Democratic primary, he met with Chavez in Los Angeles, just before the latter's address to the UAW convention. Brown wanted the UFW's endorsement, but Chavez insisted that the decision had to be made by the union's executive board.[20] Later it was discovered by union staff that Brown was seeking a united labor endorsement that would include the Teamsters. Although Chavez declined to be part of such an arrangement, the UFW endorsed Brown on its own and campaigned for his election.

In 1974 the UFW was putting together its own legislative package, drawn up by Chavez and UFW attorney Jerry Cohen with the help of the head of the California AFL-CIO, Jack Henning, and cosponsored by two Democratic assemblymen, Richard Alatorre of East Los Angeles and Richard Burton of San Francisco. The proposed legislation would create a three-member "Agricultural Workers Commission," to be appointed by the governor. The commission would comprise one representative each from agricultural employers, agricultural workers, and the public. It would supervise secret-ballot elections for union recognition and would have full access to labor camps and the records of unions and growers. Before an election was held, the commission would require authorization cards for a specific union signed by at least 50 percent of the workers employed at a particular time, provided that number was at least 50 percent of the harvest-time peak. Another union could be placed on the ballot if it received authorization cards signed by an additional 10 percent of the employed workers. The option of voting for no union would be provided. The election would be held within seven days of the presentation of a valid petition. Action on challenges would be delayed until after the election, thus preventing procedural delays from circumventing the possibility of elections during peak harvest periods. Strikers could vote if they had not accepted permanent employment elsewhere, while strikebreakers hired after the commencement of a strike could not vote. (This clause was designed to keep growers from recruiting special crews for the purpose of voting against a particular union.) In order to be designated the sole bargaining agent, a union would have to win at least 50 percent of the votes. If there were three or more choices on the ballot and none received more than 50 percent, a runoff election would be held.

The legislation was aimed at promoting industrial rather than craft unionization. It specified a number of unfair labor practices, by both unions and employers, that could invalidate an election. The commission could certify a union if it determined that a majority of the workers were engaged in a recognition strike. This gave unions alternative ways of achieving recognition. Under some circumstances, the union could challenge existing contracts. Most importantly, the legislation placed no restrictions on secondary or primary boycotts, strikes, or issues open to negotiation between a union and an employer. The bill was supported by the California State AFL-CIO; its primary opponents were the Teamsters and growers.[21] The Teamsters wanted a law that broke up ranches into several craft bargaining units.

The bill was introduced in the California legislature in 1974 and was narrowly approved (41–31) by the Assembly on 19 August. Two days later, however, the Senate voted 19–16 against suspending the rules to allow the measure to be heard at the last regularly scheduled meeting of the Industrial Relations Committee for the 1973–74 session.[22] Although the UFW condemned the vote, the legislation had at least been given a trial run to ascertain the support for the measure. Had it been allowed to proceed further, sources in the UFW acknowledged, the Industrial Relations Committee might have added Teamster-sponsored amendments that would have made it unacceptable, and there was also the likelihood of a Reagan veto. The union was quite pleased with the support for the proposed legislation. Alatorre said that he would introduce it again the following year, when prospects for its passage would be even more favorable.

While the bill was in the legislature, the UFW sought Jerry Brown's endorsement of it. Leroy Chatfield, formerly on the staff of the UFW and head of the boycott in Los Angeles, had become one of Brown's campaign advisors. The union's attorney, Jerry Cohen, tried to contact Brown for an endorsement through Chatfield, but Brown hesitated. The UFW, used to recalcitrant politicians, decided to apply direct pressure. It placed twenty pickets at Brown's campaign office in San Francisco, and they pledged to stay until they secured an endorsement. This they shortly received.[23] Later, during his campaign, Brown consistently emphasized his support for the UFW and declared that one of his first priorities would be to seek passage of legislation aimed at providing secret-ballot union elections for agricultural workers. Most observers believed that this meant the Burton-Alatorre bill, since Brown had already endorsed the measure.

The UFW's power to mobilize quickly for its legislative agenda was demonstrated in July 1974, when Democratic Assemblyman Howard Berman introduced an agricultural labor bill with a progrower Republican assemblyman, Robert Wood, from the Salinas Valley. The measure was placed in direct competition with the Burton-Alatorre bill. Berman had just been appointed Democratic majority leader by Assembly Speaker Leo McCarthy, who had never particularly favored UFW-sponsored legislation. His bill contained several provisions unacceptable to the UFW. It stipulated craft rather than industrial union organization, outlawed the use of a secondary boycott to gain recognition, and set up pre- instead of post-election grievance hearings. Although Berman indicated that he was open to amendments to the measure, the union wanted no competition for the Burton-Alatorre bill and asked Berman to withdraw his sponsorship. When he refused, the union's hundred-member Los Angeles boycott staff spent a Sunday leafleting Berman's 57th District, which encompassed an affluent and relatively liberal section of West Los Angeles. The leaflets denounced Berman, asked voters to write or call him, and gave his local and Sacramento office telephone numbers. His district responded, and on Monday Berman contacted the UFW Los Angeles office to ask the union to call off its campaign. He also heard from a number of prominent local Democratic party leaders who had been mobilized by the boycott staff. He at first promised he would withdraw his advocacy and then reversed himself, but the bill was never seriously considered.

After Brown's election and inauguration, the UFW staged a march on Gallo wine headquarters in Modesto as a show of force. On 1 March, addressing 15,000 supporters during a rally at the conclusion of the march, Chavez pointed toward Sacramento and said that if Brown reneged on his promise to sign a bill guaranteeing secret elections, "we may have to march on Sacramento as we did when his daddy was in office." Chavez was specifically referring to the recently reintroduced Alatorre measure.[24] Reports reached the union that Brown had not liked the remark but had begun working on such legislation. Shortly afterward the union had an all-day meeting with Brown and his staff to let them know what had to be covered. When the meeting concluded, Chavez was confident that Brown would come up with an acceptable bill.[25]

The fact that Brown was now engaged in writing an agricultural labor relations bill in itself indicated a change in expected strategy. Most observers believed that Brown would sanction the Alatorre proposal. Ron Taylor, a long-time reporter on California agricultural labor, wrote early in 1975 that the Alatorre bill was given a "good chance" of passing during the current legislative session and that Brown was expected to sign it into law.[26] The union expected Brown's own proposal to be modeled after the Alatorre measure, if it was not its near duplicate.

On 10 April Brown announced his proposal. It was more similar to the Berman bill of the previous year than the Alatorre measure; in fact, Berman was sponsoring the bill in the State Assembly while Democrat John Dunlop of Napa introduced it in the State Senate. The legislation actually was written under the direction of Secretary of Agriculture, Rose Bird, and based in part on the provisions of the NLRA. The UFW immediately denounced the bill as deceptive and vowed to fight against several of its provisions. The proposed legislation was similar to Alatorre's in that it set up a five-person Agricultural Labor Relations Board to supervise secret-ballot union elections. The method of securing an election and the 50 percent figure needed to certify a union as sole bargaining agent were also similar. Elections would be held quickly, during peak harvest time, after valid petitions had been received by the board. No restrictions were placed on primary boycotts, harvest-season strikes, or the issues that could be covered by contract negotiations.

The UFW objected to the provision that limited the union's right to engage in a secondary boycott. A secondary boycott could be undertaken only after a union had won an election; it could be used only to pressure reluctant growers into negotiating a contract. As in the Berman bill, the secondary boycott could not be utilized to gain union recognition as a bargaining agent. The UFW claimed that the bill was worded in such a way that it might in practice nullify the use of secondary boycotts altogether. The proposal outlawed the use of recognition strikes as an alternative to the election procedure. Jerry Cohen further claimed that the legislation would divide laborers into separate craft unions rather than organize them on a ranch basis in the agricultural equivalent of industrial organization. The union wanted a specific clause outlawing existing agricultural contracts in order to nullify current Teamster agreements.[27] It promised to fight the bill and reasserted its preference for the Alatorre proposal.

Alatorre accused Brown of ignoring his pledge to uphold the Alatorre bill and charged that Brown's ambition for higher political office was behind his actions. Other Chicano legislators called the proposal racist. The Teamsters withheld any immediate reaction but later opposed the bill. Their main concern was the ability to maintain the contracts they already had, and the language of the proposal was ambiguous on the status of existing contracts after the law took effect. The Teamsters claimed that the law would invalidate their contracts even before a petition for an election was submitted. (Chavez, who wanted the bill to do just that, agreed that it was unclear on the issue.) Grower reaction was rather mild. Les Hubbard, the spokesman for the Western Growers Council, commented that "for many growers, the bill from Brown was a pleasant surprise."[28]

Brown immediately began to lobby interested parties for support for his bill. He concentrated on supermarket industry executives and church organizations generally sympathetic to the UFW. By 1 May he had met with the Western Conference of Catholic Bishops, Protestant church leaders, prominent black ministers, the Southern California Council of Churches, and the Southern California Board of Rabbis, in addition to officials of unions and food industries.[29] His tactic was to cut into the bases of support for both the growers and the UFW, so that both sides would be pressured to accept his compromise proposal.

Although six bills dealing with agricultural labor relations were introduced into the state legislature, only three were seriously considered—Brown's, Alatorre's, and a proposal sponsored by Republican Assemblyman Kenneth Maddy of Firebaugh and Democratic Senator George Zenovich of Fresno and backed by growers and the Teamsters Union. When a showdown appeared imminent in the Assembly Labor Relations Committee, Brown began to meet with UFW and grower representatives to initiate changes in his bill. After a series of such meetings, Brown announced on 5 May an amended version of his proposal. Observers believed that most of the changes were in favor of the UFW. Although the restrictions on the secondary boycott remained, ranch instead of craft unionization was clearly specified, and a new provision was added to prohibit either a grower or a union from selecting employees for the sole purpose of voting in an election. The Teamsters took no part in the negotiations and continued their opposition to the proposal.[30]

The UFW formally endorsed the bill on 8 May, following endorsements by grower representatives and key legislators, including Alatorre and Zenovich.[31] Reflecting the coalition that had finally pieced it together, it was now the Alatorre-Zenovich-Dunlop-Berman Agriculture Labor Relations Act. Later the Teamsters Union dropped its opposition when the proposal was further amended to state specifically that existing contracts would not be invalidated when the law went into effect.[32] Chavez won an addition stating that existing contracts could not be used for delaying elections. The Building Trades Union and the Packinghouse Workers agreed to drop their opposition when a similar amendment was inserted exempting their members from the law's coverage. After it was clear that the compromise version would pass, an anonymous grower expressed regret about the earlier Teamster contracts: "We might never have had any union if we hadn't cooperated with the Teamsters to keep Chavez out."[33]

At Chavez's urging Brown called a special legislative session to vote on the bill so that it would go into effect in late summer rather than 1 January, as originally scheduled. On 26 May the Senate passed the bill 31–7, and three days later the Assembly approved it 64–10. Brown signed it into law a week later. It was to go into effect 28 August, in time for the fall grape harvest.

On 26 July Brown announced the appointment of the Agricultural Labor Relations Board's five members. Heading the board was Catholic Bishop Roger Mahoney of Fresno. Also appointed were former UFW staff member Leroy Chatfield, who had served on Brown's campaign staff before becoming the governor's director of administration; Richard Johnson, a grower attorney who headed the Agricultural Council of California; Joseph Ortega, a Chicano attorney for the Los Angeles Model Cities Program; and Joseph Grodin, a law professor at the Hastings School of Law in San Francisco and a former attorney for the Teamsters as well as a number of construction workers' unions.[34] The board came under attack by the growers and Teamsters for its alleged pro-UFW bias, although Mahoney stated that he had never personally endorsed UFW boycotts.

At the UFW convention, which was held in August, a resolution was adopted censuring Senator John Tunney for favoring legislation to include agricultural workers under the NLRA and his failure to support the UFW's boycotts.[35]

ELECTIONS AND OPPOSITION

The time between the passage of the ALRA and its effective date witnessed several controversial developments. Since most growers realized that few elections would result in a rejection of union representation, many of them began directly to help Teamster organizers reach the work force while preventing their UFW counterparts from doing the same.

The UFW needed to reach the workers to explain its position and lobby for their votes. The union's supporters who relied on union reports rather than an understanding of labor relations in agriculture would have been surprised to learn that worker support was actually problematic. The farm workers were a heterogeneous population, split by differences in race and ethnicity, stability of residence, occupational classification, interests in agricultural labor as a career, citizenship status, involvement in previous struggles, and ideological orientation. The UFW was more representative of some segments of the labor force than others. Although its past strikes had been well supported and many other spontaneous walkouts had sought help from the union, the strongest UFW members and supporters were those with relatively stable residence. For migrants, the hiring hall instituted by the UFW was sometimes inconvenient and even detrimental. Local workers employed in a specific area all year would have an edge in seniority over migrants and could be guaranteed a stable employment pattern, whereas migrants would not have this advantage.

Least in favor of the UFW were the undocumented workers whose employment options might be drastically limited by the operation of a union hiring hall based on seniority. Although the union did not attempt to sort out people according to their citizenship status except for strikebreaking crews, illegals who are not regular workers would have a low job priority under a hiring hall simply because they probably would have little seniority. For the previous several years, reports indicated a growing number of illegals engaged as agricultural workers. Federal officials estimated that during the 1975 summer harvest, up to one-third of the harvest crews were composed of illegals.[36] The UFW charged that the presence of illegals was especially strong in areas where there had been previous labor controversy, such as the table grape regions.

Besides the problems associated with appealing to this diverse population, the original UFW strikers, who were the union's strongest supporters, had discontinued working on their ranches because of the strikes. The law allowed strikers to vote, but the determination of who was eligible was difficult, as were the problems associated with trying to contact those eligible but no longer employed and insuring their participation in the elections. The UFW needed to win the approval of a significant proportion of those employed at technically struck ranches, many of whom were part of the original strikebreaking crews.

Coupled with these problems was the fact that on many ranches the Teamsters were the incumbents. The UFW had fewer than 20 contracts covering approximately 10,000 of California's 220,000 agricultural workers during peak season, while the Teamsters claimed over 400 contracts covering approximately 50,000.

The fact that the benefits stipulated in Teamster contracts reportedly did not always reach the workers and that in some instances contracts had gone unenforced for years deprived the Teamsters of the full advantages of their incumbency. Recognizing that they needed a strong bargaining position to keep the workers' votes, they renegotiated their contracts with 135 growers, most involved in lettuce. On 17 July 1975 the Teamsters announced that the new contract terms would increase wage and fringe benefits 25 percent. The minimum wage was raised from $2.50 to $2.95 an hour. Piece rates also increased between 4 and 6 percent.[37] At the same time, Teamster organizers began to use a more militant tone in order to refute the UFW's charges of sweetheart contracts.[38]

The UFW had the advantage of its reputation as a militant organization with strong cultural attachments to Chicano and Filipino agricultural workers, and it was credited with being the primary force behind the gains of farm labor over the past ten years. Statistics from the California Departments of Labor and Agriculture showed that farm wages increased 120 percent between 1964 and 1974, compared with a 59 percent rise for industrial workers. This brought the average hourly wage of farm workers to 62 percent of the industrial wage, compared with 45 percent a decade before.[39] Long periods of unemployment still kept most below the poverty level, but many workers testified that UFW presence in an area by itself caused wages to rise, since growers wanted to prevent a strike.[40]

But the UFW still had to struggle against the traditional passivity of the agricultural work force. Although the union had done much in its ten-year history to activate the work force, intimidation still was prevalent, especially in the form of dismissals because of support for the UFW. It needed to contact field workers in order to solicit their support. The most efficient way was to meet on the ranches, since many of the migrants lived there and had little contact with the outside community, but the union was denied access to ranches by most of the growers. Throughout the summer there were reports of UFW organizers being thwarted in their attempts to reach workers. Many were arrested and some assaulted. At the same time, many of the same growers allowed Teamster organizers free access to workers even during work hours.[41] UFW protests notwithstanding, there was nothing illegal in this differential treatment, at least until the ALRA went into effect. It added to the atmosphere of tension, fear, and intimidation, which intensified as the date of potential elections drew nearer. Growers were clearly using all the tactics at their disposal to sway the elections against the UFW.

In a controversial decision the ALRB granted union organizers access to growers' property despite grower contentions that this ruling violated their rights. Organizers were allowed on ranches one hour before and after the work day and up to one hour during the lunch and rest periods. Unions were limited to two organizers per thirty workers. As the initial election petitions were being filed, a temporary restraining order against the access rule was issued by the U.S. District Court in Fresno on 3 September.[42] The order was sought by the South Central Farmers Committee, the group of table grape growers concentrated around Delano who had been the target of the 1965 Delano grape strike. Many previously cooperative growers immediately barred UFW organizers from their property.[43] On September 18 the California Supreme Court ordered the access rule enforced pending a court review. On 4 March 1976 the same court upheld the access rule. However, the UFW had been denied access during much of the critical first three weeks of the elections, which were concentrated in the Salinas and Delano areas. The access controversy indicated the resistance the growers would mount against the implementation of the ALRA.

During the first month of elections, the UFW won 86, with a total of 13,410 votes (52 percent). The Teamsters won 73, with 8,037 votes (31 percent), while the "no union" option won 19, with 4,175 votes (17 percent). After the second month, the UFW had won 114 contests and the Teamsters 86. Thirty-six of the UFW victories were on ranches covered by current Teamster contracts.[44] The UFW maintained its right to negotiate a contract with Inter Harvest by beating the Teamsters by 1,167 votes to 28. Nearly 80 percent of eligible Inter Harvest workers voted. The Teamsters won a substantial victory at Bud Antle, Inc., in Salinas. Neither union dominated the elections in the Delano-area grape vineyards or the Salinas-area lettuce and vegetable fields. This meant that the Teamsters lost their jurisdiction over a number of ranches where they had previous contracts. However, the Teamsters were generally stronger on ranches where they already had a contract, while the UFW won most of the elections on ranches that had not previously been under union contract.

Whether the election results could be treated as an accurate indicator of union preference was questionable. Many growers vigorously and legally tried to persuade the workers in their employ to vote for the Teamsters. There were also reports of numerous violations of the law: alleged grower and Teamster intimidation of the work force through threats of dismissal or the firing of UFW supporters; hiring of crews recruited principally to vote for either the Teamsters or no union; and continued denial of access to UFW organizers even after the restraining order was lifted. The UFW filed more than 100 complaints of irregularities with accompanying worker affidavits during the first few weeks of the elections. Chavez charged that the board was not properly enforcing the law and claimed that "20 to 30 percent of the workers are not voting because of fear, intimidation and threats."[45] In fact, two members of the board estimated that the grower interference had lowered the UFW's share of the vote by 15 to 20 percent.[46]

Faced with a degenerating situation, the board leveled unfair labor practice charges against several growers and tightened the enforcement of the law. The growers were charged with having illegally discharged workers for their support of the UFW and having further "interfered with, restrained and coerced" UFW supporters.[47] It also charged a supervisor of a major table grape grower, the M. B. Zaninovich Company, with threatening to kill workers if they supported UFW.[48] The Joseph Gallo Company, headed by the younger brother of Ernest and Julio Gallo of Gallo Wines, was charged with numerous unfair labor practices, including the removal of UFW supporters from the company's housing camp and hiring workers on the basis of union preference.[49] The imposition of harsher penalties for violations and the appointment of a special enforcement team to oversee elections and related activities appeared to diminish the frequency of grower abuses. On 16 October a report by a group of AFL-CIO leaders headed by Paul Hall found "widespread intimidation of workers by growers and Teamsters, inadequate investigation of those charges by the ALRB and incomplete law enforcement." Several of the group acknowledged, however, that enforcement had recently improved.[50]

Increased enforcement appeared to influence the election results in the UFW's favor. Between 7 October and 29 October, the UFW increased its share of the total election victories from 52 to 57 percent, while the Teamsters gained slightly from 31 to 38 percent and the "no union" option declined sharply from 14 to 5 percent.[51] The *Los Angeles Times* reported that almost all Teamster victories were on ranches where the growers had sided with the Teamsters; this was legal, but it gave the Teamsters an advantage.[52] When elections were held in December and January in the Imperial Valley near the Mexican border, the UFW won eleven out of the twelve contests. By this time, the UFW said, the enforcement of the ALRA had dramatically reduced the intimidation of the agricultural workers.[53]

A Louis Harris poll released in October 1975 reported continued nationwide support for the UFW-initiated boycotts. Of those surveyed, 12 percent responded that they were boycotting table grapes; 11 percent were boycotting head lettuce; and 8 percent were boycotting Gallo Wines. These figures indicated that the boycotts may have been the most effective union boycotts of any product in U.S. history. The UFW itself was supported by 45 percent of the respondents, compared with 7 percent support for the Teamsters and 14 percent support for the growers; 35 percent were undecided. Support for the UFW was strongest among college-educated and professional people.[54]

Once the increased enforcement of the law had resulted in a greater proportion of UFW victories, opposition to the law itself was increasingly voiced by both growers and Teamsters. The board, deluged with elections to supervise, ran out of operating funds and went into debt. The California legislature was scheduled to consider in January 1976 additional appropriations to keep the board functioning until the beginning of the new fiscal year in July. Since it was considered an emergency measure, the appropriation needed a two-thirds majority to pass. Individual growers, the California Farm Bureau, and Teamster officials all demanded alterations in the law before the board received additional funds: drastic modification or elimination of the access rule, an extension of the time between the filing of an election petition and the actual election from seven to twenty-one days, the definition of labor contractors as employers, and a reduction of the financial liabilities of growers found guilty of violations. Some of these changes would bring the law more into line with present NLRA guidelines. The board ceased operations on 6 February 1976, when advocates of the emergency appropriation could not generate the two-thirds majority needed for passage. The Senate voted 20 to 15 to sustain the appropriation, 7 votes short of the necessary number. Opposition to the appropriation was composed largely of Republicans and rural Democrats. Grower-backed legislation to amend the law failed badly, as did several compromise plans.

Because it had ceased operations, the board could not certify one of the final elections, a critical UFW victory over the Teamsters (462 to 311) at the five lettuce-producing Bruce Church Farms located in

Fresno, Salinas, Lost Hills, Santa Maria, and Imperial County. In the absence of certification, the Teamsters kept their jurisdiction over the ranches.

Governor Brown took a firm stand against the amendment of the law. As a candidate for the Democratic nomination for president, Brown used a three-state AFL-CIO conference in San Francisco as a forum to denounce legislative opposition to the appropriation as "an unholy alliance with those whose only interest is in profits, anti-union activities, and 'right to work' laws."[55] Several attempts to resolve the appropriation dispute failed, and the board did not receive operating funds until the beginning of the new fiscal year. Meanwhile, board members Leroy Chatfield, Joseph Grodin, and Joseph Ortega had resigned, along with the board's general counsel, Walter Kintz. Chatfield left to become a special assistant in Brown's presidential campaign.

In response to what Chavez referred to as the "political football" future of the law, the UFW organized a massive petition drive to place an agriculture labor relations initiative on the November 1976 ballot. If passed, the law could be changed only by a ballot referendum, thus preventing the legislature from holding up implementation. Besides being an attempt to insure the continuous operation of the board, the proposition strategy was also an effort by the UFW to preserve its current level of independence. Approved as a ballot initiative, the law would be more difficult to amend in the future. It would form a barrier to future restrictions against the UFW that would be especially welcome when the political forces that secured the passage of the ALRA lost momentum and the union was once again placed on the defensive. The initiative would also make the UFW less susceptible to pressure from supporters, especially the AFL-CIO and Democratic politicians, to accept the curtailment of its independence in order to reach compromises in the future.

The UFW obtained nearly twice the 312,000 signatures required to qualify its initiative for the ballot. The initiative, Proposition 14, was essentially the same as the ALRA, including the limitations placed on secondary boycotts. However, the controversial access rule was now written into the law, changing its status from that of a procedural regulation and rendering it more secure against future alteration. Initial polls indicated public approval of Proposition 14. It was endorsed by Brown, Democratic presidential candidate Jimmy Carter, many of the former ALRB officials, and most California Democratic party leaders, including Senator John Tunney. The growers, however, mounted an efficient, well-financed advertising campaign asserting that the access rule was a violation of the right of private property and relating it to increasing government intervention into the private lives of citizens. In the first post-Watergate national election, the campaign had widespread appeal, and the proposition was badly defeated by a 60 to 40 percent margin.

During the summer of 1976, the UFW continued its practice of involvement in political campaigns. It endorsed Jerry Brown for the Democratic presidential nomination and gave him credit for not yielding to agribusiness pressure to amend the ALRA. The union worked for Brown in the California primary and lent help in other states where he was campaigning. Later Chavez delivered Brown's nominating speech at the Democratic National Convention. The UFW also mounted a successful voter registration drive in conjunction with its efforts to pass Proposition 14, using funds provided by the Democratic National Committee and channeled through the California Democratic committee. This drive registered over 200,000 voters and primarily benefited such Democratic candidates as Jimmy Carter and incumbent Senator John Tunney, although neither was successful in California.

The UFW also endorsed opposition candidates and organizations. It actively worked for the senate candidacy of Tom Hayden against John Tunney in the California Democratic primary. Dolores Huerta addressed a rally sponsored by the People's Bicentennial Commission in Washington, D.C., in July 1976, and later, in February 1977, Chavez participated in a Santa Barbara conference designed to help build a broad base of support for Hayden's Campaign for Economic Democracy.

In June 1976 the UFW, the Teamsters, and grower representatives began secret deliberations aimed at working out another jurisdictional agreement between the two unions. Brown was credited with having arranged the meetings.[56] An agreement was reached in January 1977, and the formal signing by Chavez, Fitzsimmons, and Anderson took place on 10 March, after technical details had been worked out. The agreement gave the UFW jurisdiction over workers covered by the ALRA, while the Teamsters would limit themselves to organizing workers covered by the NLRA. The Teamsters indicated that they were ceasing their agricultural labor organizing activities and would not seek to renew their current contracts when they expired, except for the one with Bud Antle. The agreement would cover thirteen western states and run five years, although the actual terms of the last three years remained to be worked out.

Like previous jurisdictional agreements, this one made the UFW the primary labor organizer for California farm workers. Chavez indicated that the union would concentrate on building a more stable base in California before moving into other states. He promised to increase the union's efforts to secure representation for agricultural workers under the ALRA.

CHAPTER 12

STATE MEDIATION AND RESISTANCE

Even after the UFW-Teamster agreement of March 1977 allowed the UFW jurisdiction over organizing field workers, the UFW was still far from signing contracts with all the growers on whose ranches the union had won elections. The struggle to win against the Teamsters in elections supervised by the ALRB had occupied most of the period between 1975 and early 1977. During this period the board failed to rule expeditiously on nearly a thousand unfair labor practice charges filed against California growers for violations of the ALRA during the election process. The delays in legal response forced workers to wait up to two years for their elected bargaining agent to be certified.[1]

The UFW won thirty-three of the forty-eight nondairy farm elections supervised by the ALRB between 1 December 1976 and the end of the fiscal year on 30 June 1977. Of the 9163 farm workers voting in the forty-eight elections, 5,593 voted in favor of the UFW, 1,904 for no union representation, and 460 for other unions; 1,206 votes were challenged. The ALRB certified twelve of the thirty-three elections as won by the UFW and thus made it possible for contract negotiations to begin with the twelve ranches.[2] The union had about seventy contracts with California growers early in 1977. It had 250 in 1973 at the height of its success, but the 1977 figure was a decided improvement over the low of twelve contracts to which the union was reduced when the growers first chose to sign with the Teamsters.[3]

The end of Teamster competition removed only one of many obstacles. The UFW charged that Coachella Growers, Inc., the largest citrus grower in the Coachella Valley, began a campaign of harassment against UFW supporters immediately after the election victory. The company ceased to provide a bus to bring the workers residing in Coachella to the citrus groves in Blythe, a hundred miles away. The labor camp began to offer housing only to male workers and charged the occupants double rent. The company dropped the price paid for picking lemons from $14.00 a bin to $12.00 and provided work only three days a week. The UFW claimed that the company was trying to force workers to quit and thereby lose both their jobs and their seniority. Over a series of contract negotiating sessions the year after the UFW had been certified, the company refused to modify its stance on key items. It refused to use the hiring hall for regular hiring of fewer than a hundred people, disallowed the first step of the grievance procedure if the company did not agree with the union that there was a grievance, refused access to company property for union business, and rejected union medical and pension plans.

The UFW also brought charges of unfair labor practices against Hemet Wholesale, a nursery in the San Jacinto Valley, which sold potted plants to commercial nurseries. It was the first time the ALRB was asked to rule on such charges against an employer who had begun contract negotiations with a union. The UFW accused the nursery, a major farm employer, of stalling contract negotiations for eighteen months following the union's victory in an election at the firm in September 1975 and firing six workers after they became involved in union organizing activities. The ALRB eventually ruled that the nursery was guilty of unfair labor practices in the case and ordered that the workers be reinstated with back pay.[4]

In the aftermath of an election conducted by the ALRB among Tenneco employees in Indio and Thermal, the UFW brought charges of union busting against the company. The election produced 177 votes for the UFW and 120 votes for no union, but the results were not final because 100 additional votes had been challenged. The UFW charged Tenneco with paying antiunion workers to talk other workers into voting against the UFW, trying to stop UFW organizers from talking to employees in a Tenneco farm labor camp, threatening workers with loss of jobs or lower pay during a worker meeting the day after the election, and refusing twice to give employee lists to the ALRB staff in Coachella.[5]

The ALRB issued a series of unfair labor practice charges against the E & J Gallo Winery over the union representation campaign before the 1975 election, in which the Teamsters Union was the apparent winner. The ALRB cited thirty-four alleged instances of surveillance by Gallo personnel, including the photographing of workers meeting or attempting to meet with UFW organizers. The complaint claimed favoritism for the Teamsters in terms of access to the fields, the use of Gallo-owned vehicles, and distribution and promotion of literature. The ALRB also charged that Gallo fired two farm workers because of their work for and membership in the UFW.[6] After lengthy hearings, David C. Nevins, administrative law judge for the ALRB, ruled that the election at Gallo should be set aside because the company had created a "police state atmosphere." He accepted most of the UFW allegations against Gallo as true and found that the company had openly sided with the Teamsters to defeat the UFW, allowed the Teamster organizers to campaign without interference, kept UFW supporters under constant surveillance by security guards in uniform, photographed, "restrained and coerced" them, and fired two employees who showed open support for the UFW.[7]

Six Delano area table grape growers of the South Central Farmers Committee delayed signing a contract with the UFW for over two years after the union won secret-ballot elections in 1975, and the union accused them of failing to negotiate in good faith. The companies were M. Caratan, Inc., Nick Bozanich, Jr., Jake J. Cesare & Sons, Jack Radovich, Sam Barbic, and Tex-Cal Land Management, Inc. They were represented in negotiations by the law firm retained by the South Central Farmers Committee, which also represented Giumarra, Tenneco, and Coachella Growers. The firm actively worked against the ALRA and by November 1977 had reached only one collective bargaining agreement for its clients whose workers had voted to be represented by the UFW. The union protested that contract meetings were not long enough or frequent enough to make real progress and that constant struggle over minor issues delayed agreements: the delays were all the more unwarranted since the companies were dealing with their second UFW contracts and were already familiar with most of the contract language.

At Giumarra Vineyards of Bakersfield, the largest table grape operation in the United States, the ALRB conducted an election in September 1977. Of 1,900 workers eligible to cast ballots, 900 voted for "no union," 673 voted for the UFW, and 172 ballots were challenged. In February 1978 the ALRB issued forty-four charges of unfair labor practices against Giumarra, ranging from threats of firing and other reprisals against workers who favored the UFW to refusal to rehire them. The ALRB complaint called for ten remedies, including rehiring discharged employees with back pay, public apology, and a declaration to its employees that it would not engage in such conduct in the future.[8]

Throughout 1977 the ALRB was a crucial element in the UFW's strategy for securing contracts on ranches where elections had been won during the previous two years. Documenting unfair labor practices and seeking administrative review began to replace the boycott as the most effective way to secure contracts. On 31 January 1978, Chavez officially suspended the boycott of nonunion table grapes and lettuce. The spokesman for the UFW, Marc Grossman, said that the boycott was no longer needed because of the effectiveness of the ALRA; future boycotts would be aimed at labels of individual growers who refused to negotiate a contract once their workers voted for UFW representation.[9] Sources within the union still viewed the boycott as an important weapon for gaining a contract or improving one, but it was no longer the only option—or even the first choice of options.[10] By the time the boycott was ended, the UFW had won over 250 elections; the ALRB had certified over 180 victories; the union had signed over 80 contracts covering about 25,000 workers; and negotiations were in progress with another 100 growers.

From a base of organized workers representing a quarter of the union's strength at the height of its success in the early seventies, the UFW launched a major public campaign on behalf of farm workers in 1978. Chavez told a committee of the regents of the University of California in February that Governor Brown should appoint a blue-ribbon committee to determine how many California farm workers had been displaced from their jobs as a result of machines developed by researchers at the University of California. He told them that university research should benefit everyone: the workers who might be displaced as well as the employers who have already profited from breakthroughs in agricultural technology. He noted that in 1977 the university had opposed a UFW-sponsored bill that would have required the university to make "social impact" statements about its agricultural research. Tom Hayden, a later speaker, supported Chavez, stating that research in the university is aligned with the interests of agribusiness and therefore that the university is incapable of objectivity in gauging the impact of such research. He announced that his campaign for Economic Democracy would join the UFW to press for legislation requiring impact statements and levying a tax on agricultural machines, with the proceeds to be used for programs to retrain displaced farm workers for other occupations.[11]

In May 1978 the UFW reached a contract agreement with seven

Delano-area table grape growers. It was the first contract since 1970 and covered nearly 20 percent of the estimated 8,000 grape field workers in the Delano area. The agreements raised wages from $3.25 to $3.50 an hour and included pensions and other benefits. The new contracts eliminated the hiring hall and allowed direct grower hiring through their own central hiring system. It represented a major exception to the union's steadfast defense of the hiring hall in the face of growers' intensive objections. Chavez declared that the UFW would not automatically waive its hiring hall demand for other growers but would be willing to "discuss a similar change if workers get the right things in return."[12] Observers regarded the suspension of the hiring hall system as a mark of the UFW's weakness among table grape workers in the Delano area, once the heart of the farm worker movement.[13] Nevertheless, the union won a contract from growers who resisted signing one for over two and a half years after the UFW won elections on their ranches.

Beginning in late 1977 and 1978, the UFW extended support to farm labor strikes outside California for the first time since 1974. Over the previous three years the union had ceased organizing in Texas and Arizona to concentrate on the struggle in California. In Texas workers formed the independent Texas Farm Workers union (TFW), led by Antonio Orendain. In April 1978 the UFW leader in Texas, Jose Saldana, called for a union election for the workers of the Griffin and Brand Produce Company of McAllen, who were involved in a four-week-old onion strike; the election, he said, could avoid future confrontations. UFW supporters were able to gather authorization cards from 450 Griffin and Brand workers. There was no mechanism in Texas law to force a union election, despite the signed authorization cards, unless Griffin and Brand sought an injunction against further union organizing; in that event, a judge could order a union election at his discretion. Even without legal guarantees, the call for an election still had certain weight as a moral force, since the company had always claimed in the past that workers on Griffin and Brand farms did not want a union.[14]

In Arizona organizing was undertaken by the Maricopa County Organizing Project (MCOP), a nonprofit organization formed to improve farm worker wages and working conditions. Although MCOP was not a union, it conducted a strike of over 2,500 farm workers for better piece-rate wages during the onion harvest of November 1977 near Pheonix in Maricopa County. Chavez visited the picket lines in the vegetable fields on 21 November, promised immediate financial and legal assistance from the UFW, and offered UFW help in negotiating a contract for the onion workers if they and MCOP requested.[15]

In the summer of 1978, the UFW answered an appeal for assistance from melon workers in Yuma, Arizona. On Tuesday, 13 June Cesar Chavez and Helen Chavez joined about forty workers on the picket line at the G & S Produce Company melon fields, although Judge Bill Helm had issued an order prohibiting all picketing. Shortly after the Chavezes' arrival, a half-dozen Yuma County sheriff's deputies appeared. Judge Helm's injunction was read, and it was announced that the pickets would be arrested if they refused to leave. Chavez asked the workers to move away from the area while he and Helen remained to be arrested. Brought before Judge Helm, they declined both bail and a release on their own recognizance because they felt that accepting either would legitimize an order that violated First Amendment rights to freedom of speech. They were imprisoned. The next day they went before the same judge. Threats had been received in the jail overnight, and the county attorney argued that the Chavezes should be released from the Yuma facility. The UFW attorney argued that they should stay. Judge Helm denied the UFW's motion to suspend or modify his injunction, saying that the workers were satisfied with what the growers offered them and that UFW picketing would raise "the fear of intimidation." He ordered the Chavezes released from jail and instructed them to return for trial Friday. Upon leaving the jail, they were greeted by 600 farm workers waiving UFW banners. On Friday they were given six-month suspended sentences for contempt.[16]

By the fall of 1978 the UFW was looking toward organizing in New Mexico as well as in Florida, Washington, Arizona, and Texas, where it was already active. Thirty-five contracts were signed in 1978 to bring the UFW total to over 125 contracts and 30,000 members. Besides support for the Yuma melon strike, the UFW focused its energy on Florida, where it renegotiated the citrus contract with Coca Cola's Minute Maid division in Florida and offered aid to 2,000 tomato workers in Homestead. It also expanded its service center and membership drive in the Rio Grande Valley of Texas and participated in work stoppages in the onion harvest there and a legislative campaign to extend unemployment compensation to farm workers. The major test of the union, however, was to come in December and January, when it had to renegotiate contracts covering 20,000 workers for sixty-six growers in the vegetable industry from the Salinas Valley to Arizona.

THE IMPERIAL VALLEY
VEGETABLE CONTRACT DISPUTE

As contracts with vegetable growers expired at the beginning of the new year, lettuce workers started a walkout at California Coastal Farms in El Centro and Salinas on Friday, 19 January 1979. By noon Monday, sanctioned strikes had spread from Cal Coastal to Sun Harvest, Vessey & Co., and Saikhon Farms. The strikes involved 1,750 workers statewide. Imperial County Superior Court Judge Donald Work granted grower requests for a temporary restraining order against the walkout at Saikhon and Vessey. The UFW disobeyed the order and extended the strike to Joseph Maggio and LuEtte Farms in El Centro. Growers attempted without success to recruit strikebreakers in Mexico and then prepared to make citizen's arrests at UFW picketlines. Ron Hull, vice president of the Imperial Valley Growers Association, said, "The plan is to begin citizen's arrest of some of the strikers. The sheriff will not arrest them, but has said he will take them into custody if growers make the citizen's arrest."[17]

Negotiations going on in San Diego between the UFW and twenty-eight California and Arizona lettuce growers reached a stalemate after two months. Growers refused to consider any pay increase above the 7 percent raise they offered, arguing that the 7 percent limit was in keeping with President Carter's Wage and Price Stability Council guidelines. The union demanded a one-year contract with hourly wage increases to $5.25 from the existing level of $3.70. Farm workers were decades behind industrial workers in wages and benefits. The UFW noted that a 7 percent raise would simply maintain the gap between farm labor income and that of other workers. Unprocessed foods were not covered by the price guidelines, and the price of a box of lettuce had risen 110 percent in 1978. Moreover, the majority of vegetable industry workers were earning less than $4.00 an hour, the rate below which the president's wage guidelines were not supposed to apply.

The growers hired a Los Angeles public relations firm, the "Dolphin Group," to manage media coverage during the strike. The company, headed by William Roberts, had coordinated press converage for various grower causes and conservative political campaigns, including Ronald Reagan's. The firm shortly began to use southern California media to call for volunteers to harvest the struck fields.

A "Committee for Fair Negotiations," organized by Roberts to influence public opinion, initiated a volunteer lettuce-picking drive during the second week of the walkout. Growers sent high school students and company supervisors to harvest lettuce as the market price per carton of lettuce rose, partly in response to the strike. Firms not being struck began to make bonanza profits.

On Thursday, 25 January, growers made citizen's arrests of sixty-four strikers at Vessey and Saikhon Farms. By noon Friday the UFW had extended the strike to seven companies. In an interview in Los Angeles with a *Salinas Californian* reporter, Doug Foster, Chavez raised the possibility of a nationwide boycott of lettuce if growers attempted to bring in strikebreakers.[18] On Monday afternoon a grower-recruited team attempted to leave a struck field with several thousand cartons of harvested lettuce. The grower crews were pelted with rocks, lettuce was scattered, a windshield was smashed, and two company vehicles were set on fire. Two UFW strikers were arrested, but they were freed from police custody by the other pickets. During the melee two sheriff's deputies suffered minor injuries, and a UFW striker sustained hip injuries when a car from the grower caravan charged into the strikers' line. Marc Grossman, the UFW spokesman, charged that growers were waging a "deliberate campaign of intimidation and violence." He reported that Vessey security guards had beaten a UFW striker, who received a depressed skull fracture and required intensive care in El Centro Community Hospital.[19] When police discovered firebombs near the office of Saikhon Farms, arguments broke out between growers and the union about which side was actually the source of the earlier fires.

The following day ALRB agents gained an injunction against two lettuce growers and the UFW to limit the number of UFW pickets, prohibit physical assaults on either side, and force growers to disarm company security guards. The growers reported that 300 volunteers appeared to pick lettuce in struck fields on "Volunteer Harvest Day" on 31 January. In the fields bands of security guards carried clubs, mace, and firearms; a pack of attack dogs was also in readiness.

By the end of the month, the strike affected 3,000 workers statewide, and 16,000 individuals including family members and strikers. More than half of the farm labor force in the Imperial Valley was affected. On 2 February Chavez addressed a rally of 3,000 in Calexico, calling the lettuce strike a "dream realized, a dream that at one time we thought impossible." He spoke of going to California cities to seek moral and financial support and again raised the possibility of a nationwide lettuce boycott and an extension of the strike to additional growers in the Imperial Valley.[20] Two days later a grower employee was arrested for waving a shotgun at 300 pickets near the Joseph Maggio fields, and nine UFW pickets were arrested for rock throwing. California Attorney General George Deukmejian sent growers and the UFW a telegram on Monday, 5 February, reporting Justice Department observers' feeling that "the potential for violence is increasing" and calling on leaders to "take all steps necessary to prevent violence from erupting." Tension increased as more strikebreakers moved into the Imperial Valley. Except for the two enjoined not to use firearms, growers were reported to have increased their use of armed security guards. The Lyon's International Strike Force of Los Angeles was supplying guards at a charge of $38,000 per week, according to a grower expert.[21] Later in the week Ku Klux Klan posters appeared around El Centro, and workers found crosses in the fields of some struck ranches. On Friday the Imperial County sheriff reported that gunshots had been fired into the air at a labor camp site where pickets were marching; pellet gun blasts hit a farm labor bus without breaking the glass; and an arson-caused fire burned several thousand cartons stored by Maggio. The following day the UFW launched a walkout at the Bruce Church Company, one of the top three producers in the vegetable industry, and the Admiral Packing Company, bringing the total number of struck companies to ten and involving 4,300 workers.

On Saturday afternoon about eighteen UFW strikers left their picket lines at a ranch owned by Mario Saikhon, where a strikebreaking crew of seventy was working. The six men in front had moved 180 yards inside the lettuce field when shots were fired by two men and a third blocked their retreat with cross fire. Five of the men reached a fence and high grass after the shooting began. The sixth, twenty-seven-year-old Rufino Contreras of Mexicali, was hit with a .38 caliber bullet below the right eye. His brother, Luis Contreras, also a striker, was eight feet away when Rufino was shot. Gunfire continued for fifteen minutes and prevented Luis and the other pickets from coming near Rufino. An ambulance arrived an hour after the shooting and took Contreras to El Centro Community Hospital, where he was pronounced dead twenty minutes later. He left a wife and two children. Rufino Contreras, his brother, Luis, and his father, Lorenzo, had moved to Mexicali from a village in Oaxaca. The family together gave Saikhon twenty years of labor. Rufino was a seasonal worker on melon and lettuce harvests, which gave him work seven months a year and earned him about $8,000, working six days a week.[22] Three Saikhon employees were booked on murder charges and released on bail which ranged from seven to eight thousand dollars.

That night Chavez urged strikers to channel their anger into mourning for the worker killed: "The greatest tribute we can pay to Rufino Contreras is winning the strike." At a mass attended by 2,000 in Calexico that Sunday, Chavez declared a moratorium on all picketing until the funeral for the young striker and invited the assembled people, who were wearing black armbands and carrying mourning banners, to join him in a fast. He called for two outside investigations and proposed a general work stoppage by all the 7,000 UFW workers in the Imperial Valley. In a public statement he said, "We do not hold all growers responsible, but we do hold accountable those greedy employers who would trade blood for money." The official growers' response: "Cesar Chavez must be held accountable because . . . the tactics of orchestrated terrorism and rioting are his."[23]

Governor Jerry Brown joined the 5,000 mourners who attended the funeral and marched in the procession through Calexico to the grave site on 14 February. In the eulogy Chavez said, "When they spoke out against the injustice they endured, the company answered them with bullets. The company sent hired guns to quiet Rufino Contreras. Wherever farm workers organize, they stand up for their rights and strike for justice, Rufino Contreras is with them." Brown sat next to Chavez at the funeral and later declined grower requests that he intervene in contract negotiations.[24] A week later, the three Saikhon employees were arraigned for the murder of Contreras. Leonardo Alfreda Barriga, a foreman from Calexico, Anthony Andreas San Diego, a temporary foreman from Nipomo, and Froylan Perez Mendoza, from Mexicali, were released on $50,000 bail posted by their employer.

THE SALINAS VALLEY VEGETABLE STRIKE

As harvest activity increased in the Salinas Valley to the north, the ALRB investigated UFW complaints that a California Coastal Farms foreman had brandished a weapon at pickets and company complaints of strike damage and injury to workers, company vehicles, and equipment. Monterey County Superior Court Judge Richard Silver barred the company and union from possessing firearms and other weapons and limited the number of UFW pickets to a maximum of 150 per field. He subsequently ruled, in an unprecedented decision, that UFW strikers had the right of regulated access to struck fields to talk with nonstrikers. This gave the union a way to challenge the 1,000 strikebreakers Sun Harvest claimed to have recruited, as well as those at California Coastal and Bruce Church.

On 27 February Chavez announced an international boycott of Chiquita bananas aimed at pressuring Sun Harvest, a subsidiary of United Brands, to reach a new contract. Chiquita bananas were responsible for more than 20 percent of the gross sales of United Brands. Chavez said the boycott was an attempt to persuade Sun Harvest to engage in good faith negotiations and a response to its use of strikebreakers and intimidation.[25] The company was expected to experience economic losses on two fronts because of the combined strike and boycott. Its prime competitor in the lettuce industry was Bud Antle, which had a Teamster contract and was profiting vigorously as the strike caused shortages in the lettuce supply and the price rose to $12.00 per carton. Bud Antle was moreover a subsidiary of Castle and Cooke, which markets Dole bananas, the major competitor of Chiquita in American markets.

To strengthen its position in the vegetable strike, the UFW made plans to revive and expand the national boycott against all lettuce except that produced by Bud Antle, which was under a Teamster contract.

On Wednesday the next week, caravans of striking Salinas field workers set out before dawn for the fields of companies having UFW contracts. The strikers called for a one-day total shutdown for a mass march and rally led by Chavez. It was the third major UFW march in Salinas in the union's history. That afternoon Chavez told the more than 4,000 strikers and supporters assembled that Salinas would be the focal point of the strike when the peak lettuce harvest began in April. That evening he told a fund-raising rally in Sacramento that neither Governor Brown's personal influence nor third-party mediation would affect the strike as long as growers held to a 7 percent wage rate limit. (Rural legislators had been calling for the Federal Mediation Service to be brought in, and growers were pressing Brown to influence Chavez to end the stalemate in the negotiations.) Chavez denied that negotiations had reached an impasse. He argued that the process of bargaining had not even begun, since the growers refused to negotiate in good faith. The 7 percent proposal was a take-it-or-leave-it offer, and the UFW had filed an unfair labor practice charge with the ALRB about it. If the board determined that the growers were not acting in good faith, they would have to "make whole" striking workers for wages lost during the negotiating period.[26]

As the lettuce harvest approached its peak in Salinas, the growers and union traded accusations. Growers were preoccupied with gaining the safe use of strikebreakers, while the UFW was concerned about the behavior of armed security guards. Growers accused union pickets of rock throwing, window smashing, trespassing on private property, and loud verbal abuse of "replacement workers." The UFW was apprehensive because sheriff's deputies were finding that private security guards hired by the growers were carrying loaded weapons in violation of a court order limiting the use of firearms. The UFW charged that local law enforcement showed partiality to growers. The Salinas UFW director, Bill Granfield, declared that deputies were making arrests for rock throwing and "minor offences on peaceful picket lines" well after the crimes were supposed to have occurred; there was in addition a general pattern of foot-dragging in processing arrested strikers. Arrested pickets were placed on hold for the Border Patrol after booking, and those taken into custody were often treated roughly.[27]

In Washington on 17 April during a media tour of major U.S. cities, Chavez charged President Carter with failing to enforce laws against the importation of alien workers: the freedom of growers to transport, house, feed, hire, and pay illegal immigrants as strikebreakers was a threat to the existence of the UFW. He asserted that the use of illegal aliens as strikebreakers was intensifying the potential for the kind of violence that had occurred in the Imperial Valley.[28]

Democratic Senator Harrison Williams of New Jersey, chairman of the Senate Committee on Labor and Human Resources, prepared for hearings in Salinas later in the week on the working and living conditions of migratory workers. Growers complained that the hearings would simply provide Chavez with a public relations forum. Eight growers and grower associations were invited to testify and were offered up to two hours each to present any information they chose. Only two accepted. On 26 April, the first day of the hearings, growers held a press conference to charge that the hearings were inflammatory because they were being held in Salinas in the middle of a strike and unnecessary and irrelevant because the strike was a local problem and not a matter for Senate discussion.

Senator Williams opened the hearings with criticism of local growers for their "irresponsible and unfortunate" refusal to testify.[29] The hearings offered an opportunity to engage in constructive dialogue, he added, but the growers apparently preferred a monologue through the medium of costly full-page ads in the New York and Washington news media.

Chavez was the first witness to give testimony. He focused on injustices committed against farm workers, including violence against strikers. One central concern was the dismissal earlier that week of the murder charges against the three Imperial Valley ranch foremen charged with shooting Rufino Contreras. Chavez called on three Imperial Valley workers for testimony concerning the attack, and Jerry Cohen asked Senator Williams to pursue an investigation of the murder by the Justice Department's Civil Rights Division. Chavez denounced law enforcement agencies for taking the side of the growers. He charged the Border Patrol with harassing strikers on the picket line but refusing to raid struck fields and giving growers unlimited access to illegal alien strikebreakers. He said that the Immigration and Naturalization Service was refusing to take action on the specific information supplied by the UFW on the presence of illegal aliens in strikebreaking crews in Salinas. He declared that the only neutral agency involved was the ALRB, and it was consequently being attacked by the growers.

In the afternoon Sun Harvest attorney Joseph Herman testified that his company supported placing farm workers under the NLRA instead of enacting a national law based on the California ALRA. He criticized the ALRA for being hostile to business interests, especially in allowing the state to find growers guilty of not bargaining in good faith and levying heavy economic penalities under its "make whole" remedy. He also objected to the ALRA's authorization of secondary boycotts, such as the current one against Chiquita bananas. The NLRA did not contain these provisions present in the California law. He charged that the ALRB encouraged farm workers to organize, rather than simply allowing them to, and he concluded by accusing the UFW of massive violence and terrorism in the 1979 vegetable strike.

Monsignor George Higgins, secretary of research for the National Catholic Conference and head of a blue-ribbon investigative panel, testified that violence occurred in the Imperial Valley because of the presence of armed private security guards. The committee called in by Chavez to investigate the killing of Contreras had concluded that one of the major factors leading to violence was the use of dogs and armed guards in the fields.

Gerald Brown, chairman of the ALRB, defended the agency in testimony on Friday, emphasizing that the board had brought democratic procedures to the work site in almost 800 secret-ballot elections involving more than 70,000 farm workers in the three and a half years of its existence. He described criticism of the agency as misdirected, since responsibility for the new contract rested with the negotiating parties, the union and the growers. While the agency could penalize either side for refusing to bargain in good faith, it could not force them to agree.

That afternoon Senator Williams declared that he was still convinced that farm workers needed national protection under a law similar to the California act that would take into account the special circumstances of agriculture. He also said that he would ask the Civil Rights Division of the Justice Department to review the circumstances of the Contreras shooting.

In the wake of the hearings and criticism by the UFW, the Immigration and Naturalization Service increased its staff in Central California and established a command post in Salinas. It assigned seven additional officers to the staff of five permanent Border Patrol agents in the valley. Raids in the first seven days of May led to the arrest of more than 500 illegal aliens, most of them working as strikebreakers. Raids tripled the number of arrests of undocumented aliens normally made during the lettuce harvest in Salinas. UFW Secretary-Treasurer Gilbert Padilla met with Lionel Castillo, the commissioner of the Immigration and Naturalization Service, to insist that the agency file criminal charges against growers for harboring and transporting illegal aliens and to complain that the raids were not including the labor camps.

UFW pressure for more Border Patrol raids brought criticism from the director of MCOP in Arizona. Lupe Sanchez, the director of the organization that represented undocumented workers in Arizona, sent an open letter to Chavez: "We must urge you to stop all actions that would create a greater division among workers (undocumented and documented)."[30] UFW spokesman Marc Grossman said the UFW was like any labor union in not wanting to watch idly while its strikes were being broken, and strike coordinator Marshall Ganz accused MCOP of being "a bunch of students and do-gooders" whose jobs were not being threatened.[31] Both said that the UFW had had some success in organizing and representing undocumented workers, but that progress could occur only under a law guaranteeing the right of farm workers to organize and bargain collectively.

In the first week of May, UFW strikers found thirty-five high school students working in a thinning and hoeing crew on property leased from Sun Harvest. Pickets saw a bus from King City High School dropping off students next to the Sun Harvest field and a foreman coming out to drive them to the work site. School officials acknowledged that students were recruited under the Work Experience Program. Officials posted announcements about field jobs in school bulletins with all the other employment listings, although students were informed that a strike was in progress. A Work Experience instructor signed them up, filled out the required work permits, and turned over the list to the recruiter's son, who was a student at the school. The superintendent of the high school insisted that the park across from the struck field was a "normal stop" for the school bus and that school personnel had fulfilled their duties by informing student workers of the strike and encouraging them to talk to their parents. An official of the County Office of Education said that the state education code discouraged what King City High School officials had done, since it required employment to be in the best interest of the students, and this work was placing them in a hazardous situation. The UFW filed an unfair labor practices complaint with the ALRB, charging King City High School officials with recruiting students as strikebreakers and transporting them to the job site.[32]

As continued attempts at negotiation proved indecisive, the UFW called a walkout of more than 1,000 farm workers at nonstruck companies. The show of solidarity was aimed at pressuring twenty-eight growers into a favorable contract settlement. The entire Salinas membership left their jobs to reinforce picket lines and cut into vegetable production. Union members joined roving caravans of 150 to 200 persons and moved from farm to farm, attempting to disrupt production. Militants chased nonunion field workers from the job site at struck companies. Confrontations erupted between the strikers and strikebreakers or private security guards. One strikebreaker stabbed a UFW picket with a lettuce knife at a Sun Harvest field. Another strikebreaker was hospitalized for observation after being beaten when strikers rushed a field where he was working. Scores of strikers and nonunion workers were injured in scattered incidents. Sheriffs arrested 122 people over a hundred-mile radius as a result of field confrontations. Governor Jerry Brown sent telegrams to Cesar Chavez and Mike Storm, the president of the Grower-Shipper Vegetable Association, saying, "For the well-being of California, I urge you to promptly return to the bargaining table and negotiate in good faith until an equitable contract is reached."[33]

Two days later contract talks abruptly stopped. Jerry Cohen charged that growers were acting as if they were trying to break the union. Grower representatives said that the outstanding differences with the union were beyond economics. Mike Storm asserted that such "management rights" as elimination of the union hiring hall and an easing of restrictions on dismissals were more important than wages.[34] When talks resumed amid rumors of a new Teamster Local 890 contract with Bud Antle, growers appeared to be divided on how to proceed. Sun Harvest's largest competitor in lettuce production was said to be on the verge of offering a large jump in hourly wages for general field work, up to a minimum of $5.00 by September. Sun Harvest's vice president, Roland Kemp, responded quickly to the news of the Antle contract. Kemp, a former high-ranking employee of

Castle and Cooke and a veteran of nine strikes by banana workers at the company's plantations in Honduras and Costa Rica, said that his company " 'would be happy to settle for the Antle contract,' because minimal restrictions on 'management control' would be worth the additional pay."[35]

Recognizing that contract agreements were still far away after seven months on strike, Chavez and a group of a hundred striking farm workers launched a major new campaign on 31 July. The UFW organized a twelve-day march from San Francisco to Salinas to publicize the vegetable strike, win urban support, and mobilize farm workers. At the beginning of the march, Chavez addressed a rally attended by over 1,000 people in San Francisco's Union Square. He declared that the union would begin in earnest to pursue the consumer boycotts announced three months before. The focus would be on United Brands as the owner of Sun Harvest. The UFW was asking consumers to boycott both Chiquita bananas and the products of other United Brands subsidiaries, A & W root beer and John Morrell meats.

The day the UFW began its campaign in San Francisco, the president of Sun Harvest, Carl Sam Maggio, sent a telegram to the union headquarters in Keene indicating that the company was willing to enter binding arbitration with the possibility of signing a separate contract with the UFW, independent of the rest of the vegetable industry. He offered to enter intense negotiations for twenty days and asked the UFW, if no agreement was reached, to accept the choice of an impartial arbitrator between the company's and the union's final offers. He denied that the march and the UFW's threat of a general strike in the vegetable industry were responsible for the offer.[36] The UFW subsequently rejected the proposal as being the same as one it had rejected three months earlier.

The 140-mile march and boycott represented an escalation of UFW strike activity. During previous struggles to win contracts, marches were called to marshall support. During the Delano grape strike of 1965, the UFW marched on Sacramento. In 1970 the union marched into Salinas to begin the lettuce strike that led to contracts with the vegetable industry. In 1975 another statewide march was called on Modesto during the struggle with Gallo. The renewal of the boycott in the union's longest and largest strike demonstrated the union's recognition that farm workers might again have to depend on urban volunteer organizers to win contracts.

While the march was in progress, the Teamsters reached a tentative agreement for 2,400 workers under contract with Bud Antle. The company offered to pay $5.00 an hour and, it was reported, agreed to keep hourly wages 25 cents above the wages its competitors paid under UFW contracts. For months the UFW's demands for a $5.25 minimum had been denounced as exorbitant and inflationary. Vice President Kemp said that Sun Harvest "would accept the economics in the Bud Antle contract if the 'language' provisions outlining strict management control of hiring and firing could be adopted as well."[37]

As the march of 600 supporters neared Salinas, Chavez began an all-water fast. He had fasted before in protest, to pressure growers or win a strike or cause farm workers to continue a strike. The new fast was not for nonviolence but for "patience and love." The following day a hundred workers from Meyer Tomato and the Gonzales Packing Company, large tomato growers with expired UFW contracts, walked off their jobs to join the "March for Justice." A contingent of farm workers marching to Salinas from the south grew steadily as non-striking laborers engaged in work stoppages along the route. The UFW hoped that such expressions of solidarity would convince growers that the union had the support and resources to conduct a general strike in the Salinas Valley.

As Chavez arrived in Salinas, heading a protest march 5,000 strong, he appeared unsteady and weary from twelve days of marching and six days of the fast. Governor Brown joined the march beside Chavez as the demonstration passed through east Salinas neighborhoods and he addressed the rally the UFW called the largest gathering of farm workers in the history of California. In his speech to the crowd, estimated at over 12,000, Brown said, "I call on the growers to settle now. Don't make the mistake that these farm workers don't have the power to launch strikes, boycotts, and everything else that is necessary to win."[38]

The following day, at the end of the UFW's biannual convention, Chavez announced a favorable contract settlement with Meyer Tomato. Two of the contract provisions had never been gained in a previous farm labor agreement: cost of living protection against inflation and a full-time UFW representative to be paid by the company. Other provisions included an increase in the base wage for transplanters to $5.00 an hour and a guarantee that no seniority worker would be displaced because of mechanization.

A week later a second contract was successfully negotiated with another tomato grower, the Gonzales Packing Company. The Gonzales settlement agreed to the provisions of the Meyer contract except for the one concerning mechanization. Both sides instead agreed that mechanization would not be introduced that year. Negotiations about future mechanization would begin, and if no agreement was reached, the UFW retained the right to strike. The union continued its separate talks with two lettuce firms, West Coast Farms and Sun Harvest. Other lettuce companies responded to the report of the Meyer and Gonzales breakthroughs by declaring that tomato companies had little in common with the lettuce industry.

On Sunday, 26 August, the UFW won its first agreement in the lettuce strike. The new contract with West Coast Farms included a minimum hourly wage of $5.00 for general field labor, an increase in the piece rate from 58 cents to 75 cents a carton, UFW retention of the right to strike if mechanization displaced 20 percent of the workers in any job classification, and a union representative paid by the company. The chief UFW negotiator, Jerry Cohen, observed that it would be difficult for the lettuce companies to depreciate the importance of the new settlement as they had with the tomato contracts. Because of a 1977 arbitration agreement with the UFW, West Coast Farms did not renegotiate the noneconomic portions of the old contract: rules covering hiring and firing, grievance procedures, and determination of union membership in good standing. According to Andrew Church, negotiator for the industry group, "Under the agreement, they [West Coast Farms] did not have an opportunity to negotiate about language. And this whole strike has centered on the issues of quality control and control of the ranch. . . . We are not going to be flocking to sign the same old contract that gives control of the ranch to the workers."[39]

Following the settlement with West Coast Farms, several nonunion firms rushed to match or surpass the new wage increases. Hundreds of nonunion field workers stopped work to demand equivalent wage improvements. At Frudden Farms, a tomato company, 200 workers struck and filed a petition with the ALRB for a representational election. Companies responding with immediate wage increases may have been attempting to forestall UFW organizing drives.

The major breakthrough of the strike came on 31 August when the UFW won an agreement with Sun Harvest for a new three-year contract covering about 1,200 workers. The contract called for an immediate hourly minimum wage of $5.00 an hour and a piece rate of 75 cents a carton, with cost of living adjustments. Sun Harvest agreed to pay two full-time union representatives to act as liaisons between the company and the union, and the contract provided for binding arbitration to resolve any dispute over mechanization. The UFW officially ended the boycott of United Brands products; all the union's resources would be focused on an international boycott of iceberg lettuce, especially the Red Coach lettuce produced by Bruce Church.[40]

More than 1,300 workers walked off their jobs at the operations of eight major growers on Wednesday, 5 September, to demand agreements patterned after the Sun Harvest contract. The firms affected by the walkouts had not been struck previously, although strike authorization votes had been taken in the spring. Workers demanded immediate separate negotiations: that is, negotiations independent of the industry group of sixteen growers whose negotiations with the UFW had been stalled since July.

The Mann Packing Company, the largest broccoli packer in the United States, reached a contract with the UFW on Monday, 10 September, in separate negotiations. The new agreement followed the Sun Harvest pattern but added a higher piece rate for broccoli workers. The industry group was still further divided that week when four more firms removed themselves from umbrella negotiations. Andrew Church withdrew from his position as chief negotiator just as a settlement seemed imminent, saying that he decided to withdraw when it became clear that there were irreconcilable differences among the growers participating in the industry group.[41]

By the middle of the week the UFW had won a total of eleven contracts. The new agreements meant that the majority of agribusiness firms that had begun negotiating with the UFW a year before had settled their differences and entered into three-year contracts. The Sun Harvest settlement again provided a model, with the hiring hall retained and binding arbitration of disputes over mechanization. Five Salinas Valley companies, including Bruce Church, and five Imperial Valley firms still resisted the contract terms established at Sun Harvest and remained without agreements.

CAMPAIGN IN THE VEGETABLE INDUSTRY

As the lettuce season drew to a close in the Salinas Valley, the focus of the strike shifted back to the Imperial Valley. Tensions increased at picket lines as strikebreakers began to harvest winter lettuce. On Friday, 2 November, scores of farm workers were injured in the worst incidence of violence in over four months. UFW National Executive Board member Jessica Govea said that the injuries occurred when a car carrying five union members was forced off the road by a vehicle belonging to a company supervisor, and the strikers were attacked with tire irons. She reported that a sheriff's deputy witnessed the beatings and, only when carloads of other strikers began to stop at the scene, did the deputy take out a shotgun and intervene in the clash.[42] UFW striker Juan Ortiz del Campo and four other strikers were arrested by Imperial County Sheriff's deputies and charged with attempted murder, assault with a deadly weapon, and terrorism. No charges were filed against strikebreakers or company employees. Del Campo was held on $25,000 bond, and the four others were held on bonds that ranged from $5,000 to $12,000. After spending over seven hours in jail, del Campo began vomiting, and UFW officials insisted he be allowed to go to the hospital. He was admitted to El Centro Community Hospital and was discovered to be suffering from a depressed skull facture. On Saturday he underwent surgery to remove two pieces of bone that had been shattered in the fight. He was placed in intensive care and listed in stable condition with major head injuries.[43]

The ALRB investigated the outbreak of violence and issued a formal complaint on Tuesday, 20 November, charging that foremen employed by Growers Exchange started the attack which led to the injuries. In the first ever ALRB charge against a law enforcement agency, the board charged the Imperial County Sheriff's Department with unfair labor practices by enforcing the law in "a prejudicial manner." Board attorney Maurice Jourdane said deputies demonstrated bias by "just investigating the strikers and not doing anything about the strikebreakers."[44] The complaint also charged deputies with refusing any medical attention to del Campo and holding him in jail for eight hours despite the serious injuries he sustained. The same week the ALRB began to hold training sessions with the deputies to talk about the farm labor law and its application.

Meanwhile Sun Harvest workers voted in elections on 13 December at eight locations in California and Arizona for the first company-wide ranch committee. Thirty-one candidates actively campaigned within the union for five positions. For the first time in the UFW's history, the president and vice president of the newly elected ranch committee would be paid by the company to work full-time on union business. The 1979 contracts with Sun Harvest and other growers created these positions for union representatives.

Contract negotiations proceeded with both sides recognizing that wages were no longer a significant obstacle. Imperial growers were now paying the prevailing wage set earlier in the year by Salinas growers. Nonunion companies were often willing to pay a premium in the hope of avoiding a union organizing drive. On 15 December Admiral Packing reached a settlement with the UFW. Six days later Growers Exchange, one of the big five producers in the lettuce industry, settled differences with the union. The agreement provided a

$5.00 hourly minimum and 75 cents a carton lettuce piece rate. Three Salinas Valley companies remained without contracts: Bruce Church, California Coastal, and O.P. Murphy. Eight growers in the Imperial Valley failed to reach a settlement since the beginning of the economic conflict with the UFW nearly a year earlier. These were Colace Brothers, Gourmet Harvesting and Packing, Luette Farms, Carl Joseph Maggio, Joe Maggio, Martori Brothers Distributors, Vessey & Co., and Mario Saikhon.

On 15 January 1980 San Diego Municipal Judge T. Bruce Iredale held a preliminary hearing on the charges against the five UFW strikers arrested on 2 November. He threw out the charges of conspiracy to commit terrorism and declared the statute had not been drafted for use in strike situations. The judge also dismissed all charges against four of the five union members because Imperial County law enforcement made a shoddy preparation of the case and illegally coached strikebreakers who were to be called as witnesses. In a telephone interview with reporter Doug Foster, Judge Iredale said, "I think what they tried to do was the dirtiest thing I had ever heard of." He stated deputies showed the prospective witnesses booking photographs of the defendants just three days before the preliminary hearing, contrary to accepted practice and a court order requiring a live lineup. He declared, "It's something I'm not proud of, and it made me realize why they had brought in an outside judge." He went on to say "if this [improper police action] had happened in San Diego, heads would fall."[45] Of the five UFW members originally arrested, only del Campo would now be tried.

In the spring of 1980 UFW organizing spread to workers outside the vegetable industry, whose wages were lagging behind the terms won in the strikes in the Imperial and Salinas Valleys. On Friday, 11 July, ratification was confirmed for a new three-year contract between the UFW and the Vintner Employers Association. It covered approximately fifteen hundred workers employed by Almaden, Paul Masson, Minstral, and Las Colinas Vineyards. The agreement provided wage increases from $3.80 to a new hourly minimum of $5.10, with hourly and cost-of-living increases during the remaining two years of the contract. More importantly the settlement included what could become a model mechanization clause for grapes and other crops. The contract stipulated that growers who were now engaged in nearly 100 percent hand harvesting would be mechanized by no more than 30 percent by 1983, and must guarantee that seniority workers would suffer no income loss by the shift to greater machine harvesting. The agreement further stated that seniority farm workers would have first claim on the jobs of operating grape harvester machines when they were introduced.[46]

On 21 July farm workers began a strike that spread to more than two thousand workers in garlic and six other crops in the San Benito and Santa Clara Counties. The strike lasted nineteen days until growers offered to raise the hourly minimum from $3 to $4 with $2.50 a basket piece rate in order to get workers back on the job pending elections and certification of a bargaining agent. Growers without union contracts raised wages to the new level to forestall organizing drives on their ranches. The union planned to continue its drive to win elections that would eventually yield a master contract for the region.[47]

When the harvest of winter iceberg lettuce began again in the Imperial Valley in January 1981, the UFW quietly shifted to an alternative strategy. Although the strike was still technically in effect as it entered its third year, the union ceased picketing struck ranches and instead allowed its members to return to work. It concentrated its efforts on winning a great number of complaints it filed against growers before the ALRB. The board still had 800 charges in its active file remaining to be resolved. One of the complaints of bad faith bargaining could require growers to be subject to the make-whole remedy by which they would be required to pay UFW members back pay for the entire time they were on strike.

The boycott against Bruce Church's "Red Coach" brand lettuce continued throughout the year, but the company did not settle its differences with the UFW despite its economic losses. Union officials reported that the boycott succeeded in closing off markets in major metropolitan areas like Chicago, New York, and Boston, and was further promoted by sending mobile teams to cities like Atlanta and Montgomery. Nevertheless, the company appeared determined to cause the UFW to force a contract through the remaining legal avenues.[48]

The UFW lost a vote to represent workers of E. & J. Gallo Vineyards in a ballot count from one of the first elections conducted under the ALRA five years earlier. The final results gave the Teamsters 237 votes to 234 for the UFW. Later in the year the board threw out the Gallo election because it was tainted by many instances of employer violation of the law. If the UFW wants to represent Gallo workers in the future, it will most likely have to begin a new organizing drive, perhaps a strike and even a boycott, all of which would be difficult since Gallo has had years "to build the kind of work force it wants," according to Chris Hartmire, now UFW executive assistant.[49]

By February 1982, the UFW had won 162 contracts. Negotiations were underway with another eighty-nine companies, involving approximately 25,000 workers. Half of these concerned renegotiated contracts; the rest were new settlements. Much of the year before had been spent in negotiations following from favorable ALRB decisions affecting workers whose elections had taken place up to six years earlier. In the fall of 1982 the UFW faces the challenge of gaining renewals of the three-year contracts with the vegetable industry, due to expire at this time.[50] It remains to be seen how these renegotiations will be affected by the ability of other growers originally struck in 1979 to continue to resist contract settlements with the union.

PROSPECTS AND DILEMMAS

A substantial challenge to the UFW has become the repeated attempts to amend the ALRA. Agribusiness-supported legislation to this effect has been repeatedly introduced into the California legislature by Republicans and conservative Democrats. The agribusiness strategy seems to be to keep pushing such amendments until political forces in California allow its passage. Governor Brown has so far vetoed three grower-backed alterations which have passed the legislature. These were intended to erode the UFW's ability to determine what constitutes good standing within the union's membership. The latest attempt would repeal the ALRA and replace it with an "Agricultural Labor-Management Relations Act," conforming to NLRA provisions including Taft-Hartley. Such a law would permit a governor to request a court injunction prohibiting a farm worker strike if "public health and safety" are jeopardized. Both the right of access of union organizers to farm workers living on company property and ALRA provisions requiring prompt certification elections and designating industrial (as opposed to craft) bargaining units would be eliminated.[51] The union's use of secondary boycotts would be curtailed, and decertification of a union would be easier. Other spot bills have been prepared which would erode individual provisions of the law: a union's right to determine good standing among its members, the make-whole remedy, determination of union seniority, decertification procedures, definition of bargaining units, and election procedures.

With the decline of the UFW's ability to mount a crisis in agriculture, due in part to its own successes, the union has taken a more conventional approach to protecting the ALRA and building its political power: campaign contributions and loans to supportive political figures. The recent increase in these expenditures is remarkable.

According to a report filed with the California secretary of state, the UFW donated $287,000 to political candidates during 1980 compared to only $53,000 in 1978. In fact, the 1980 UFW total was greater than the 1978 figures for the Western Growers Association ($221,000) and the California Farm Bureau ($211,000).[52] Of course, this is still well below the total for combined political contributions for all agribusiness organizations and individual growers.

Most of the UFW's contributions during the 1980 elections went to California legislative candidates who supported Howard Berman, the union's choice for Assembly speaker. Berman, considered a strong UFW supporter, challenged Assembly speaker Leo McCarthy in 1979, and the switch of votes by two Chicano Assembly members from Los Angeles closely identified with the UFW, Richard Alatorre and Art Torres, kept McCarthy from a narrow victory. However, in a showdown for Assembly speaker between Berman and Willie Brown, Jr., on 1 December 1980, both Alatorre and Torres switched their votes to Brown after Brown reassured them that he had no intention of attempting to change the ALRA. The actions of Alatorre and Torres reportedly infuriated Chavez, especially since Republican Assembly leader Carol Hallett, whose husband is a pesticide dealer, swung conservative Republicans, including lesiglators from agricultural areas, behind Brown. Alatorre and Torres backed Brown after determining that Berman could not win and after Brown told them he had not struck a political bargain with pro-grower legislators.[53] Although this has been interpreted as a defeat for Chavez, former speaker McCarthy was never very supportive of the UFW, and Brown will likely be more favorable toward the union. Also, Brown may be in a better position to support the interests of urban Chicanos than Berman.[54]

Despite its gains under the ALRA, the UFW has not been able to expand rapidly. Although it has a potential membership of 200,000 in California alone, the union currently has only 30,000 members. Agribusiness has yet to accept the unionization of its field workers, and individual growers do whatever they can to inhibit the process. As a result, the number of unfair labor practice charges lodged by the UFW has doubled since 1978. Growers use more sophisticated strategies, such as employing labor consultants whose purpose is to aid growers in obstructing unionization. Also, some growers appear to have put their resources behind a few attempts by workers to decertify the UFW, and attorneys for one such group of workers are also lawyers for the Western Growers Association.[55] Such attempts may be preceded by growers filling crews with antiunion workers.

Growers may also find advantages in provoking farm worker strikes if they think that these will be viewed by the larger public with much less sympathy for the workers than in the past. Negative reactions to strikes could promote an agribusiness strategy of seeking voter approval through a statewide initiative of altering or replacing the ALRA. A properly orchestrated strike may also be profitable for the growers. For example, in a study of the 1979 Imperial Valley lettuce strike, a group of agricultural economists from the University of California at Berkeley wrote that the limited strike-induced lettuce harvest reduction of 50 percent pushed lettuce prices up 400 percent. The resultant earnings for growers was $76 million, compared to an estimated $35 million if no strike had occurred. Growers who were not struck informally shared their windfall profits with struck growers, and this was later expanded through the creation of a strike insurance policy written by a Bermuda company, Quail Street Casualty, Ltd. Growers throughout California and Arizona now participate in the strike insurance program.[56] Growers are also utilizing shortcomings in the ALRA and its implementation to tie up the union in costly legal battles that sometimes take years to resolve. For example, the ALRB spends over 30 months on the average to resolve union complaints of unfair labor practices, and the UFW has charged that the board is reluctant to speed up the process as well as use its power to seek court injunctions against growers who are in violation of the law.[57]

Similar to the original NLRA, the ALRA is proving indecisive for one critical aspect of unionization: contract resolution through genuine collective bargaining. Many industrialists during the 1930's resisted unionization at this stage. They were required under the NLRA to bargain in good faith, but the lack of good faith on the part of employers was difficult to prove.[58] Delays built into cumbersome procedures often postponed eventual unionization for years after a union had been certified as sole bargaining agent. The NLRA does not compel unions and management to reach a contractual agreement; it merely stipulates sincere negotiations by both sides. The ALRA similarly has not prevented the growers from avoiding contract negotiations. Although an accurate figure is difficult to calculate, perhaps as many as 30 percent of all UFW election victories have not yet resulted in contracts. Seven of the twenty-eight Imperial Valley growers involved in negotiations with the UFW remain unsigned, as do Salinas-based Bruce Chruch and California Coastal Farms.[59]

Federal government expansion into labor-management relations during World War II pressured recalcitrant industrialists to settle with unions in order to prevent labor disputes, and the remaining barriers to mass production unionism were eliminated. Such intervention is not likely for farm workers. Instead, pressure on growers for contract negotiations can be mounted through strikes, boycotts, and charges of bad faith bargaining. This last option may prove to be decisive. The seven Imperial Valley growers who have not yet signed UFW contracts have all been found guilty by the ALRB of bad faith bargaining and have appealed the board's rulings to the courts. Andrew Church, who has been representing California Coastal Farms estimates that if these rulings are upheld by the courts, the institution of a make-whole remedy may cost as much as $3 million to $5 million a firm.[60] If such rulings hold, the risks growers undertake in delaying unionization illegally become considerable.

Although legal procedures may eventually prove favorable to the UFW, they do result in considerable delays before election victories can result in actual gains. Continually fighting such battles may be intensely frustrating, and the process hardly inspires the spirit of solidarity among farm workers. Impatience with the slow pace of progress may have contributed to a recent airing of dissatisfaction within the UFW. Internal dissent and cleavages are nothing new to the union, but they have not taken on as much prominence. At the UFW's fifth constitutional convention in Fresno in September 1981, approximately fifty delegates walked out when they were accused of being traitors for nominating a slate of three candidates for the union's board of directors in opposition to three incumbents supported by Chavez. Dissatisfaction apparently revolved around delays in payment from the union's pension and medical fund, a lack of personnel to assist arbitration and negotiation, and a perceived trend toward union acceptance of low wage settlements.[61]

More serious are the number of high-level union personnel who have left the UFW during the past several years. These include, among others, Jerry Cohen, chief counsel and director of the legal office for seventeen years, Marshall Ganz, the union's chief organizer for nearly fifteen years, Gilbert Padilla, one of the union's founders and its secretary-treasurer, Jessica Govea, director of the union's health service program, and Marc Grossman, spokesman for Chavez and long-time UFW leader. Ganz, Padilla, and Govea were also UFW executive board members. Some of the staff departures stemmed from an atmosphere of suspicion within the union of disloyalty among its officials. In fact, vague, unsubstantiated charges were subsequently made by some still in the UFW that several former union officials were now working against the union. Chavez himself charged at the union's convention that "malignant forces" inside and outside the UFW are "jointly struggling to destroy our union" including "persons who once worked within our organization."[62] The UFW has had a persistent problem in handling internal dissent among its officials, organizers, and other staff, and this inability has often precipitated dismissal of staff, charges of authoritarianism leveled against Chavez, and a preoccupation with the presence of leftists and others having "their own agenda" within the union. The latest split, however, appears to be the most serious yet, and now that the union is more firmly established, internal problems take on a greater significance in influencing its future.

A far more formidable threat is that posed by the possibility of a renewed bracero agreement. President Reagan included an experimental Mexican "guest worker" program in his administration's proposals for changes in immigration policy announced 30 July 1981. The program would allow the admission of 50,000 Mexicans a year during a two-year experiment.[63] The administration cloaked its plan with the rationale that it was an attempt to regain control of the U.S.-Mexican border in order to reduce the number of undocumented workers in the United States. It needs to be remembered, however, that illegal immigration from Mexico reached unprecedented heights during the middle of the 1942–64 bracero programs.

The institution of a "guest worker" program at this time would most likely forestall unionization and legislative reform by supplying Southwestern agribusiness with an abundance of low wage labor. Given the priorities and orientation of the Reagan administration as well as vehement opposition to the United Farm Workers' strikes and consumer boycotts by Reagan while governor of California, a guest worker program supervised by the present administration would almost certainly be designed and implemented in ways that would attempt to reduce labor costs to growers and return control of every aspect of farm labor employment to employers.

One potential complication for the union was averted when the Teamsters announced on 25 February 1982 that Western Conference leaders voted unanimously to extend the five-year-old jurisdictional agreement with the UFW.[64] An imminent challenge will be the renewal of the three-year contracts with many of the Salinas and Imperial Valley lettuce and vegetable growers when they expire during 1982. It is as yet unclear whether another strike will need to be undertaken.

Although the passage of the ALRA has not proven to be the smooth resolution to agricultural capital-labor conflicts that some observers expected and also has not been without negative consequences for the UFW, the law does set an important precedent. It is likely that mediation efforts will continue under the aegis of state regulation. The ALRA may prove especially significant if it is taken as a model for future legislation in other states or at the federal level, since it offers an alternative to the inclusion of agricultural workers under the NLRA. However, a repeal of Taft-Hartley (something for which labor has not been able to muster enough legislative or executive support) might make inclusion under the NLRA more acceptable to the UFW, especially if the California law is subsequently altered to the advantage of agribusiness. The outcome of future struggles is very much still to be determined.

CHAPTER 13

CONTROL STRUGGLES AND STATE MEDIATION

A review of farm labor unionism supplies a key to our understanding of working-class history. Analysts of American labor conflicts have focused on the militancy of industrial, urban workers as a source of data for theories of labor unionism and state mediation of class conflicts. The effect has been to view the labor movement in terms of white workers and to treat minority laborers as peripheral to worker initiatives. By focusing exclusively on the mobilization of the urban white segment, they have neglected significant long-term patterns of militancy in the agricultural working class. We have sought to redress this bias by arguing that farm workers showed a persistent tendency to mobilize around nonwage or "control" issues, even though they have been among the lowest-paid groups in the United States.

We have also demonstrated that state intervention has been critical to defining capital-labor relations in agriculture. In examining the shifting functions of the state with respect to farm labor insurgency, two patterns can be distinguished. The dominant one is the use of a variety of formal and informal mechanisms that operate in the direct interests of large growers. During several crises in agricultural production stemming from farm labor insurgency, however, a second pattern has emerged as elements of the state seek to mediate the struggle between agricultural labor and capital by offering significant guarantees to labor. Analyzing the differences between the two modes of state response is necessary for understanding not only the present period but also the potential of agricultural labor to pursue further social change. Both control issues and state mediation will be further considered in this chapter.

Control Issues and Agricultural Labor

The traditional paradigm of labor relations in America tends to see wage issues as the dominant expression of worker protest. The Wisconsin school, as represented by Commons and Perlman, emphasizes working-class pragmatism and economism.[1] This tradition generally treats trade unions as pursuing "bread-and-butter" issues and trimming their aspirations to an evolutionary accommodation to the structure of American capitalism. Workers are viewed as primarily job and wage conscious. Kerr, Dunlop, and others define the organizing principle of worker protest as concern with the job and job conditions within an essentially reformist ideology. They predict a long-run decline in strikes by workers as capitalism advances.[2] Accordingly, the traditional approach to labor relations tends to play down the significance of strike activity and regard contract negotiations at the bargaining table as more representative of class conflict. Wage issues are the primary area of contention.

In contrast to the traditional paradigm, other authorities and interpreters of labor militancy, many of them Marxists, focus on control issues as they are defined by workers in advanced sectors of production. Serge Mallet, for example, describes control issues for French workers in sectors having a high organic composition of capital.[3] Andre Gorz discusses skilled European workers with stable and fully institutionalized labor unions.[4] Stanley Aronowitz is likewise most concerned with skilled and educated workers in the United States, viewing seasonal agricultural workers as mainly casual labor "not employed in the expansion of capital" and a displaced segment of the population who owe their marginality to mechanization.[5]

Other analysts have not been so exclusively concerned with studying the most advanced sectors of the working class. Historians who examine American labor movements within a framework of class struggle have been concerned with identifying the mobilizing objectives of unskilled as well as skilled labor, nonunionized as well as unionized workers; David Montgomery and Jeremy Brecher have contributed to this research. They reassert the relevance of strikes and identify patterns of demands that moved beyond economism toward control issues.[6] However, researchers have yet to agree on a distinctive set of criteria to identify a control struggle as opposed to an economistic one. Control issues vary according to the relations of production as shaped by sector, firm, geographical location, characteristics of workers, and shifts in the standard of living. Gorz and Mallet acknowledge this problem, but they simply offer examples of control and economistic objectives rather than a detailed analysis of the nature of the differences between them.

There have been several recent attempts by Marxian theorists to analyze tendencies within worker protests that lead to control struggles. Examining the strike activity of French workers in the 1960s and 1970s, Mallet treats two trends as indicators of such struggles: action challenging the ends of production, and action critical of employer arbitrariness and capitalist norms for the exploitation of labor.[7] According to Mallet, a challenge to exploitation is accessible at times to unskilled workers, whereas questioning the goals of production is possible only for the most educated workers in advanced industries. For both groups of workers, control struggles are expressed by qualitative questions rather than quantitative (wage) issues. Mallet has proposed that workers in modern sectors of production can aspire to take managerial control over policy and the general orientation of the enterprise. In contrast, workers in traditional sectors have a more defensive struggle—against harsh work rhythms, for example, and for job security, improvements in work schedules, and control of wage setting—that does not lead to control of management.[8]

Gorz outlines some of the political dimensions of control issues.[9] His provocative thesis is that a basic lack of liberty is intrinsic to the modern work situation. The suppression of civil liberties on the job presents a permanent menace to public liberties. If a labor union wants to exercise countervailing power, it must move beyond wage demands toward a challenge to the basis of exploitation. In general, such control questions as Gorz proposes are aimed toward adapting the production process to worker needs, narrowing the area of management's arbitrary power, and gaining workers autonomous power in company decision making. Like other analysts, however, Gorz is mainly concerned with the problems and prospects of trade unions in the industrial sector and at a stable state of membership and institutionalization. His framework does not cover the situation of farm workers.

In *Workers' Control in America*, David Montgomery argues that militant organizing around control issues among American workers reached far beyond the sphere of influence of the IWW, to which historians have tended to confine their observations on control struggles. Montgomery proposes that the customary image of IWW protest as far outside the mainstream of American labor development is misleading. He identifies tactics of mass involvement, direct challenges to managerial authority, and contempt for established AFL voluntarism in the U.S. trade union movement-not merely episodes, but outstanding characteristics of American labor struggles that can be observed continuously during the era he studies. Montgomery distinguishes two currents of working-class struggle in industrial sector unionism. One source of militancy emerged from skilled workers' opposition to detailed supervision by managerial officials and erosion of the power of craft workers by production engineering. Craft workers opposed the influence of scientific management, which undermined their superior knowledge of their work and degraded their functions to a continuum of specialized machine tending. The division of the crafts cheapened worker skills and power within the labor process. Their struggle over control issues emanated from the employers' subordination of the crafts to the accumulation of capital. Then there were conflicts involving the unskilled. The militancy of laborers and operatives was prompted primarily by wage questions.[10]

The two currents can both be regarded as part of the same general pattern of working-class struggle. Both involve a willingness to use direct action tactics, and, as Montgomery seems to imply, both control issues and wage issues have served to mobilize, unify, and educate the working class.[11] He does not expect the unskilled labor force to engage in qualitative control strikes, but in the wage strikes of unskilled laborers and operatives, Montgomery sees evidence that contradicts the prevailing belief in the docility of immigrants. He proposes that there is ample data supporting a contrary characterization: when economic conditions permitted, unskilled workers took action from a sense of gross injustice and united to pursue a common goal within their ethnic communities.[12]

The mobilization of agricultural workers has not been examined in light of the contrast between economism and control. One reason for the omission is, of course, the fact that most interpretations of labor struggles have been based on data for white, urban, skilled and industrial workers. In view of the arguments presented earlier in this chapter, we might expect labor struggles among agricultural workers to center on wages since they have traditionally been unskilled and among the lowest wage groups in the working class. Instead, we have found that nonwage, qualitative issues have a prominence at least equal to that of wages in many farm worker strikes. Throughout this century, agricultural workers in California from a variety of ethnic and racial backgrounds have lived at or near subsistence levels and repeatedly struggled over control as well as wage issues.

Montgomery regards as control struggles strikes for union recognition, the dismissal of unpopular foremen or the retention of popular ones, the enforcement of work rules, the regulation of layoffs or dismissals, and the eight-hour day and also expressions of sympathy or solidarity with other groups of workers.[13] Mallet's definition encompasses struggles for control over employment and hiring, work conditions (especially health and safety), classification, and work organization and hours.[14] The issues from farm worker strikes that most closely parallel Montgomery's and Mallet's definitions are strikes to abolish the labor contractor system and protests concerned with job safety, the timing of work and the amount of production, tools and equipment, hiring and seniority, meals and sanitary conditions in the labor camps, and the bonus system. In the UFW era, control issues have included attempts to gain union recognition and eliminate labor contractors, institute a hiring hall and seniority system, end child labor, establish ranch committees, control pesticide use, and regulate the mechanization of agricultural work. Farm worker demands are control issues because they oppose the arbitrary power of the employer and the prevailing norms of exploitation in agriculture. Although the strike issues of farm workers stop short of managerial control, they still represent attempts to gain a necessary qualitative improvement in the balance of power with the growers, and have not been compromised for wages.

Our study of farm labor protest supports Montgomery's thesis by showing that like the industrial struggles, the agricultural sector showed ample evidence of continuous activity emphasizing direct action and control. Moreover, strikes by rural laborers in California give evidence that *unskilled* workers too organize around control issues: both wage and nonwage control issues proved capable of mobilizing agricultural labor. Furthermore, this pattern was visible in California from the outset: in agricultural organizing by ethnic clubs and unions, IWW activity, CAWIU and UCAPAWA strikes, union opposition to the bracero programs, and, most notably, current UFW efforts.[15]

Why has control been important to these unskilled workers who have neither craft to defend nor power from superior work knowledge compared to the employer? Their interest is explained in part by Harry Braverman in *Labor and Monopoly Capital*. Control over the labor process has always been central from the point of view of employers. For the sake of expanding profits, capitalists had to remove control over the labor process from the workers and retain it themselves. The transition from control by the worker to control by

the capitalist was experienced by the worker as a progressive aliena-
tion from the process of production. For capitalists it was the problem
of "management."[16] The same method of reordering the labor process
to centralize control in the hands of employers was applied to a wide
variety of occupations. First, the labor process was dissociated from
workers' skills so that it became independent of tradition, craft, and
worker knowledge. Then all possible conceptual work was removed
from the point of production. Finally, employers used their monopoly
over knowledge of work to control each aspect of the labor process and
the manner of execution.[17]

The result was a transformation of working people into factors of
production and instruments of capital.[18] As both Montgomery and
Braverman state, this was a condition repugnant to its victims, no
matter what their level of skill or pay. It violated the human conditions of work, not because laborers were destroyed as human beings,
but because they were utilized in inhuman ways. At the same time,
each new generation of workers had to be habituated to the capitalist
mode of production because they were plunged into working "from
the outside," from the reserve. Workers were acclimatized through
the destruction of any other way of living (a result of the evolution of
capitalism), powerful economic forces, and corporate employment
and bargaining policies.[19]

The centralization of control in agriculture has produced an extreme case of the attempt to de-skill productive activity, as well as a
chaotic pattern of employment and way of life for farm workers and
their families. Growers have successfully used their control over the
labor force to insist upon a plentiful supply of labor at low wages,
manipulate immigration policy, repress unionization attempts with
the help of the state, secure contract labor from Mexico, and promote
a labor contractor system that promised to leave intact the pattern of
employer control and exploitation of the work force. Farm workers
have responded with control demands that have become more
sharply defined in each succeeding period of mass insurgency. The
early California ethnic clubs sought to gain some order in the hiring
process to the point of enforcing closed shop conditions whenever
possible. IWW militancy focused on the effects of exploitative conditions on the everyday lives of farm workers. A succession of unionization efforts in the 1930s generated demands for the abolition of the
labor contractor system and wide-ranging issues related to the
day-to-day experience of making a living as a farm worker: protests
over housing, sanitary conditions, discrimination, the length of the
work day, medical services, transportation, and work implements.

More than any previous unionization effort, the UFW has been able to move beyond wage demands in favor of objectives oriented toward control over the labor process. It has insisted on the hiring hall in an attempt to gain control over hiring and in order to include seniority rights and exclude child labor, remove the arbitrary control over the work force embodied in the labor contractor system, and insure a correspondence between the number of workers needed for a job and the number supplied. All of these functions of the hiring hall are aimed at narrowing the sphere of management's arbitrary power and adapting the system of production to the needs of workers in a way not possible before UFW-led farm worker insurgency. Pesticide control clauses in UFW contracts have attempted to modify the technique of production and challenge employers' prerogatives where the health and safety of field laborers and consumers were concerned. Both pesticide limitations and the hiring hall have been crucial issues of contention between growers and the UFW.

Most UFW officials are convinced that if the organization is to follow up on the enforcement of its contracts, the most effective way is to delegate authority to the ranch committees; large numbers of individualized contracts, with all their regional variations, have been difficult to administer from a central union headquarters. Differences in crops, size of ranch operations, requirements for packing, stages of mechanization, types of pesticide usage, and even composition of the labor supply all reinforce a need for effective ranch committees.

The union's insistence on its own program of demands was one reason the contract renegotiation for table grapes broke down in 1973; growers favored the Teamsters Union, which promised no hiring hall or pesticide restrictions. The UFW refused to compromise its opposition to agribusiness practices, even when threatened with extinction by grower opposition. When the union has pursued its own program on control issues, it has placed farm workers in an offensive rather than defensive position; it raised consciousness and increased workers' competence and knowledge of the agribusiness system. Mass involvement has been a critical difference between the UFW and the Teamsters. The UFW has aimed to create autonomously functioning, locally elected ranch committees with the authority to enforce contracts, negotiate over the implementation of contract provisions, and settle grievances. In contrast, the Teamsters Union was without functioning locals for farm workers, not to speak of ranch-level organizations, and it left to the labor contractor system the task of determining employment circumstances.

TRANSITIONAL REFORMS AND FARM LABOR UNIONISM

When farm workers succeeded in organizing, was there any reason to look to their unionization struggles for anything more than an attempt to improve their standard of living against particularly severe and long-standing domination by growers? Whether one considers the farm worker movement an extension of bread-and-butter unionism seems to rest on whether one considers the hiring hall and pesticide control a minimum trade unionist program. As is evident from the Teamsters' policy for field laborers, both the hiring hall and pesticide control could be excluded from a business union's program. In agriculture, as in some areas of industry, a union with a gradual policy of wage gains and a modicum of fringe benefits still represents a short-run improvement for workers compared to no union at all. If denied an organized means of expressing discontent, workers might regard union bargaining for simple wage improvements as a passable trade union program, given the lack of alternatives. The growers' opposition to UFW demands showed the extent to which hiring and pesticide use were regarded as the prerogative of the employer. Growers would cede to lower management and even labor contractors the power associated with the hiring hall, but they vehemently resisted granting it to the union because this power challenged management's ultimate authority. Growers have been willing to make concessions on wage demands, the real bread-and-butter issues, but not on control, because the cost of wage increases may be passed on to the consumer, whereas control concessions have a different kind of "cost."

As organizing objectives, the hiring hall and pesticide issues have been attainable only by mass worker involvement and support. They have stimulated political awareness around such concerns as child labor, the premature aging and disability of farm workers, political participation and permanent community residence, consumer protection, and control over the labor process. The struggle for pesticide restrictions, the hiring hall, and the elimination of the labor contractor have not aimed to abolish profits or give political control to the working class. Where successfully implemented, however, they have provided a meaningful link between the union's daily actions and the goals of reducing exploitation, guaranteeing stable employment, elevating the standard of living, and eroding the domination of grower profit over the human needs of workers.

The object of struggle has not been ownership but, rather, the way labor processes have been organized and carried out. The California growers' hundred-year history of antipathy toward farm worker organizations would seem arbitrary if one did not recognize what has been at stake: the method of supervision and control over the work force. In fact, previous analyses without the benefit of a Marxian interpretation saw the struggle between growers and field laborers as a problem of race relations or a result of the scale and technological sophistication of agricultural operations. Both explanations neglected the fact that similar types of exploitation and resistance appeared during the rise of agrarian capitalism in England, among a racially homogeneous population and at a much lower level of technical development and size of farming operations.[20]

THE RELEVANCE OF CONTROL ISSUES

We have argued that control issues have been important in every major period of mass militancy among farm workers in this century, particularly during the Depression of the 1930s and the UFW era. In certain disputes, control issues were the most important reasons for a strike's occurrence, but they were not the mobilizing factor in every dispute: many strikes took place simply over wages. The prominence of control issues in farm worker struggles is related to prevailing social patterns within agricultural production. The lack of control over the labor process has led to low wages and unstable job prospects. Economic insecurity has driven farm workers into migrancy to maintain a livelihood. Forced to follow the crops, they have had little chance to gain stable residency so that their children can have an uninterrupted education and their families a chance for continuity in health care and participation in community life. Exploitation in work has been directly linked with oppression in other areas of life. Poverty has interacted with every facet of farm worker experience to promote their disenfranchisement. The control issues for which farm workers have struggled have been essential, if only to humanize their daily existence. The connection between personal life and the labor process could scarcely be more complete than it is for agricultural wage labor: the organization of work clearly has determined almost all aspects of their everyday lives.

The pattern of agricultural employment has also made it unlikely that the situation of farm workers could be improved without a combined strategy involving control and wages. The typical means by which the labor process in California agriculture has been organized, the labor contractor system, is characterized by the clear subordination of the workers to the contractor and the primary identification of the contractor with the grower. The pattern of abuses connected with the system has reinforced farm workers' powerlessness and made it necessary in most cases for farm workers to seek the abolition of the labor contractor system and the institution of an alternative. The most frequent alternative has been union recognition. In a few special cases involving the ethnic clubs, the crew leader or contractor was "organized" to serve as a spokesperson in bargaining for the interests of the workers. But for most of farm labor history, growers have successfully maintained the norm of worker subordination characteristic of the labor contractor system. Until workers gained control over hiring, there could be no guarantees of seniority, no end to child labor, and no stability for the work force.

Control has also been crucial because historical experience has shown that wage gains alone are temporary and must be won again and again on the successive jobs of harvest workers. The potential to mechanize the harvest and increase energy-intensive methods of farming imposes a limit on the economic goals that can be achieved. Thus, the structure of the farm workers' situation restricts the usefulness of economism as a solution to their problems.

The UFW is now in a position to realize lasting changes in the control of the labor process: a union able to abolish the labor contractor system has the potential to change not only hiring, but even the form of supervision and control over the work force. But even if growers ultimately accept the UFW as a legitimate bargaining agent for farm labor, there are important barriers to the UFW's ideas on control. A primary source of difficulty is the maintenance of union security through practices associated with hiring and membership status. Observers have long noted that the hiring hall primarily benefits local, resident labor: people who can, for example, be reached by a telephone chain. Workers who are discontented with delays at the hiring hall are tempted to go directly to a grower for employment. The result is dissension and the ironic situation in which the union must have workers employed directly by the grower taken off the payroll. When the union succeeds in winning the right to be the sole determinant of what constitutes "membership in good standing" as a condition of hiring, it finds itself criticized not only by growers anxious to weaken identification with the union, but also by elements within its own memberhsip who are unconvinced by its militant rationale and resent pressure to take an active part in picketing, mass demonstrations, and strike meetings. For its part, union leadership has tended to be uncompromising in its demands for loyalty, commitment, and personal sacrifice. What the UFW asks of its members in the name of solidarity contrasts dramatically with the requirements of conventional unions, which are satisfied when the rank and file pay dues regularly and vote occasionally. While UFW demands can be understood in the context of its fight to survive against strenuous agribusiness opposition, it is nevertheless true that the union calls for a level of activism many regard as extraordinary. Furthermore, union officials are predominantly Chicano and male, whereas union membership is more diverse—involving many women and groups with other ethnic and citizenship status—and the general farm labor force is more varied still. Internally, differences of interests exist and arise continually. Whether they are addressed consciously or not, they are an enduring source of potential weakness to the maintenance of identification and solidarity.

It is also questionable whether the union can put decentralized power into practice. Observers report conflicting opinions within UFW leadership on how much the union can and should rely upon ranch committees without specific instructions from headquarters in La Paz. At the same time, growers remain reluctant (at best) to take their ranch committees seriously enough to work with them toward resolving issues of contract enforcement and grievances at the local level, let alone hammering out provisions of new contracts. Ranch committees, where they are operable, sometimes work in a climate of ambiguous authority in the shadow of Chavez's determination to attend to the most minor details of union operations himself whenever he chooses. It remains to be seen whether the union can create something more than the highly visible but largely ineffective local committees found in other unions. For it must be added that problems associated with union security and decentralization are not unique to the UFW, or to the agricultural sector itself, for that matter. Individual examples of largely successful attempts to resolve similar problems exist elsewhere in the American labor movement. Moreover, the UFW has been confronted with these difficulties virtually from its inception. Its tentative resolutions have often had results that were at least acceptable, and it has won quite a number of ALRA elections in the process.

POWER AND ORGANIZATIONS

The experiences of labor insurgents in agriculture can inform our understanding of how poor people in general manage to evoke concessions from elites and force changes in institutions. Our findings both support and qualify the important and provocative thesis offered by Frances Fox Piven and Richard Cloward in their book *Poor People's*

Movements: Why They Succeed, How They Fail.[21] The authors drew illustrations for their argument from the unemployed workers' movement during the Depression, the industrial workers' movement in the same period, the civil rights movement, and the welfare rights movement of the 1960s.

Piven and Cloward found that protest movements by the poor are conditioned by the fact that a very limited range of options for protest are available and normal institutional patterns do not provide an opportunity for the poor to advance their own interests. As a result, their primary power is to disrupt normal operations through mass defiance, whether the target is welfare offices, government agencies, places of employment, or public facilities. Protests are more likely to have an impact when protesters have a crucial function in an institution or when powerful groups have a pronounced interest in its smooth functioning.

In responding to unrest, placation is usually the most attractive option available to political elites. Mass insurgency tends to occur during extraordinary periods, often involving electoral crises. Ignoring insurgency or responding solely through repression may increase electoral dissatisfaction and the delegitimation of elites. Thus, political leaders usually offer immediate concessions, especially when the private sector is also demanding that they "do something." Economic elites may, however, initially oppose concessions, particularly if these appear to represent a break with the usual pattern of government accommodation to their interests. During periods of electoral instability, the alliance between private and public power may be temporarily weakened. In such situations, the defiant poor may achieve gains.

Concessions usually include attempts to channel the energy and anger of the protesters into more legitimate and less disruptive forms of political behavior. Leaders may be provided with government positions and brought into contact with institutional power. Electoral avenues not previously available may open up. Administrative grievance procedures to route protest into bureaucratic organizations may be designed. Channeling political behavior may function to dissipate protest and remove the threat of disruption, even though it may also yield tangible gains.

At the same time, some government measures are intended not to conciliate protesters but rather to undermine whatever sympathy the insurgent group has won from a wider public. New programs, policies, or legislation may make it appear that demands are being met, thus answering the moral claims of protesters but in fact yielding little in practical results. For example, many of the antipoverty and model cities programs of the 1960s served to placate liberal sympathizers without having much of an impact on poverty.

Conciliation and manipulation in turn help change the political climate that initially gave rise to disruptions. When protest subsides, concessions may be withdrawn. Since the poor no longer pose a threat of disruption, they no longer exert leverage on political leaders. Thus, there is no further need for conciliation. Some concessions, however, are not withdrawn. Instead, they become institutionalized. Some reforms, even though vehemently opposed by powerful groups, may later prove to be compatible with the interests of these groups. For example, industrialists resisted unionization, but once unions were established, they found them a convenient mechanism for regulating and disciplining the labor force. Southern economic elites similarly resisted granting blacks the franchise, but once the civil rights movement forced this and related concessions, Southern elites discovered that their interest in maintaining castelike race relations in the South had drastically diminished with the mechanization of agriculture and increased industrial growth there.

Thus, if protests, especially by the poor, win reforms, they win what historical circumstances have already made ready to be conceded. Reforms, however, are not easily granted; rather, they are forced by people taking the only options available to them within the limits imposed by historical circumstances.

The predominant error made by activists engaged in helping the poor is their failure to recognize the structural and institutional constraints placed on poor people's movements. Activists instead attempt what is not possible: to build effective, formal, permanent mass-membership organizations to sustain the political power of the poor after periods of mass defiance subside. Even though elites may solicit input from such organizations, they are responding to insurgency, not to the supposed strength of the organization itself. When insurgency subsides, most organizations also disappear. Those able to survive abandon their militancy and instead become dependent on elites rather than on a mass base.

By concentrating on organization-building during periods of insurrection, organizers unwittingly contribute to the blunting of protest. Instead of attempting to escalate the momentum of mass defiance, activists collect dues, enroll protesters in organizations, and draft constitutions. Because they are not in institutional positions to pursue their own interests under "normal" circumstances, the poor need to use periods of collective mobilization to win what they can while it is possible. Endeavoring to achieve what is not possible, leaders and organizers fail to exploit these opportunities fully.

Piven and Cloward's findings are relevant to the circumstances of agricultural labor in California. Agricultural production has always been central to the economy of California; thus, the cooperation of farm workers has been essential. The possibility of withholding cooperation through strikes, slow-downs, intentionally deficient work, and boycotts gives agricultural workers impressive leverage to force concessions. However, this potential has been infrequently realized despite numerous instances of protest because large growers have been able to manipulate the labor supply through coordinating the actions of various agribusiness organizations and government agencies to their own advantage. The alliance between political and economic elites has been a particularly fruitful one for the growers.

Mass disruption of agricultural production has been a prerequisite for government mediation and temporary or permanent concessions to labor. Citizens' groups, political leaders, church organizations, and the farm workers themselves repeatedly called on the government to institute agricultural labor reforms. But it was only when agricultural labor utilized its potential for mass defiance that either growers or government responded.

Japanese workers effectively used the harvest-time strikes and slowdowns mobilized by local Japanese labor associations to make them the highest-paid source of field labor by 1907 and to provide them with enough income to purchase or lease agricultural lands for themselves. The strikes and labor boycotts mounted by the IWW, an organization minimally concerned with formal membership roles and dues collections, stimulated legislation improving some of the worst conditions of migratory workers just before World War I. Most CAWIU-led strikes during 1933, including a number of general or crop-wide walkouts, achieved grower concessions despite mass arrests, violent attacks on pickets, and the deportation of many Mexican strikers. Later, during the 1930s, UCAPAWA, which consciously attempted to build itself up as a stable, mass-based, formal membership organization, was most successful when coordinating spontaneous strikes. The gains the UFW has achieved have been based on mass defiance through strikes and consumer boycotts.

If unionization of the agricultural labor force does become permanent, it is entirely possible that after violently resisting farm labor organization for nearly a century, growers will accommodate themselves to the change and attempt to turn it to their advantage. Unionization does provide a mechanism to rationalize the agricultural labor force through providing job security, seniority, higher wages, and adequate health care and protection. Union hiring halls may in the long run be more efficient and stable recruitment and job placement mechanisms than labor contractors, whose supply of workers is chronically uncertain. The UFW has recently begun reminding growers that labor contracts give a union the right to use disciplinary procedures to forestall or end wildcat strikes and slowdowns. A more stable, permanent labor force in agriculture may be more compatible with the long-term interests of agribusiness, especially as it becomes increasingly mechanized, than an array of continually shifting sources of labor composed of workers of various ethnicities and citizenship status supplemented at times by children, students, housewives, unemployed persons discharged from the relief rolls, and "patriotic" citizens' organizations.

Before the UFW, however, all concessions granted by either growers or government were temporary. After labor acquiescence was restored, gains were erased by further manipulation of the labor market, persecution of leaders, and repression of organizations. What differentiates the present period of organizing is precisely the persistance of the UFW as an organization and its ability to use insurgency to win agricultural labor legislation in California similar in effect to the gains the NLRA represented to industrial workers.

The success of the UFW certainly qualifies Piven and Cloward's thesis. Perhaps the termination of the bracero program by itself would have stimulated farm labor insurgency and grower concessions. However, it is clear that the UFW sustained and channeled that insurgency while building itself as an organization. Part of the reason some concessions become permanent is perhaps that their beneficiaries are capable of fighting against their destruction. Lacking the basis for mass defiance, organizations are the most feasible means available to defend gains on a continuing basis.[22]

Viewed in this way, reforms that are not withdrawn after insurgency subsides take on a dialectical character. Rather than simply being prefigured by institutional arrangements, reforms may simultaneously attempt to manipulate or co-opt *and* offer structural changes in class relations. Concessions to farm workers ceded during times of crisis and later institutionalized may well fit into the needs of capital accumulation by those in control of agricultural production, but these changes may also shift the balance of power in the direction of labor and encroach on the prerogatives of capital. The altered social relations of production in agriculture can then provide the basis for future demands and organizational action. This leads us back to a consideration of state mediation.

THEORIES OF THE STATE AND FARM LABOR HISTORY

State efforts aimed at mediating the conflict between agricultural labor and capital have been undertaken only after prolonged periods of farm labor unrest in which external sources of support were cultivated and mobilized to offset the weak institutional position of farm workers. These sources helped sustain extended periods of insurgency and offered some degree of protection from political reprisals. Movements toward mediation during the late 1930s and the UFW era were preceded by nearly a decade of intense labor unrest, widespread farm worker strikes, and continuous unionization efforts. In the latest effort, the consumer boycott was effectively used as well. These activities disrupted a significant proportion of agricultural production. During UFW-led insurgency, both production and marketing functions proved unstable. Moreover, the labor organizations had built a political power base on support from other organizations and political leaders. This factor appears to be crucial. Outside support was used to push government agencies and elected officials toward a favorable resolution of labor's demands.

After prolonged struggles that could be neither endured nor eliminated, segments of the state moved toward an accommodation based on the recognition of at least the more moderate aspirations and goals of labor organizations and the promotion of their institutionalization. In other words, the state attempted to achieve temporary equilibrium through guaranteeing some of the economic interests of agricultural labor and undermining the short-term economic interests of agricultural capital. Currently the California ALRA provides a mechanism for the institutionalization of agricultural unions. Although its long-term effects remain unclear, the pattern of implementation thus far demonstrates that it can be used effectively by the UFW to unionize the farm labor force and win for labor increased control over work. State mediation has the potential not only to establish the UFW but also to permit it to continue pursuing control issues.

Our model of the state incorporates two contradictory themes. First, many state activities and expenditures create and sustain conditions necessary for profitable capital accumulation in the monopoly sector. Among these activities are the protection of dominant classes and the reproduction of class relationships. During periods of protest by members of subordinate groups, as noted above, the state seeks either to constrain insurgents through law enforcement bodies and the courts or channel and mediate conflict in a direction that minimizes its significance in challenging the dominance of capital. Reforms will be undertaken in ways that depoliticize and circumscribe conflict.

However, the ability of the state to act effectively in the interests of the dominant classes is limited by the strength of class struggle and the desire of state officials to mediate crises successfully. The functions of the state are not determined only by structural relationships within capitalism; state structures are also objects of class struggle. Democratic processes provide mechanisms of influence that can sometimes be effectively used by groups demanding major reforms. As a result, the internal structure of the state as well as policy choices emanating from it are "simultaneously a *product*, an *object* and a *determinant* of class conflict."[23]

When state structures and policies are successfully shaped by the capitalist class or devoid of working-class input, interventions are bound by the imperatives imposed by capital accumulation. Interventions under either condition politically neutralize the working class by channeling its demands into outcomes that have little effect on prevailing class relations. The state's institutional bias toward prevailing relationships is left intact. When working-class pressures are strong, however, state intervention may be contradictory. State actions will ordinarily mediate conflict in ways that attempt to alleviate what is perceived as the immediate source of discontent. Reforms may not be able to prevent future insurgency, simply because they do not alter the underlying causes of conflict. Contradictions then become manifest in different forms. In fact, to the extent that the state is politically unable to neutralize the segments of the working class making demands, state intervention may create a situation in which subsequent demands are more directly concerned with restructuring basic class relationships. This possibility depends on the results of mediation attempts and how these shape future class struggles. In other words, class struggles translated into the political arena shape the historical development of reforms and state agencies designed to facilitate mediation.

Before we apply this model to an analysis of the ALRA, several qualifications should be made. As the preceding chapters demonstrate, state mediation for the most part has been absent during agricultural capital-labor conflicts. Instead, powerful government agencies either directly represented certain specific capitalist interests or were disproportionately staffed by individuals with ties to such interests. Mediation efforts by the California government began only after the election of governors (Culbert Olson in 1938 and Jerry Brown in 1974) who were more independent from specific grower interests than their predecessors had been.

Moreover, state mediation refers to the dominant state response. While segments of the state attempt to enforce concessions, other government agencies and officials resist altering their old patterns. This is readily apparent under the ALRA: board officials have repeatedly intervened to stop local officials from arresting UFW organizers and member for practices authorized by the law. The persistence of antilabor activities on the local level suggests the ease with which law enforcement, the courts, and local officials could revert back to past practices if the ALRA was seriously weakened or repealed.

STATE MEDIATION IN THE CURRENT PERIOD

We will now attempt to integrate insights of the theories of the capitalist state into an analysis of the recent mediation efforts by the California government. We have already explained how prolonged insurgency by labor that is also translated into political power forces the state into mediation and attempts at reform. The state then attempts to depoliticize the struggles of the working class by placing restrictions upon the insurgent groups, and this may be accomplished by integrating these groups within state structures. As a result, the kinds of reforms most likely to be attempted may be advantageous to labor, but at the same time they may limit its power to mobilize insurgency and force further structural changes in the future. Mediation may channel the struggle into narrower economic issues. Potential reforms that attempt structural changes, leave labor unrestricted, and enhance the possibility of future demands will most likely not engender government support.

All these processes are fraught with conflict, tension, and contradictions. The outcome of a reform effort is not predetermined, but rather is a result of pressures upon and within the state emanating from the strengths of conflicting classes and groups. State managers as a group have no preconceived notion of how to resolve such conflicts. Still, they must contend with the pressures created by their relationship to the capital accumulation process to resolve conflict and insurgency in certain directions. State mediation usually results in attempts to neutralize the insurgent segment. The specific result of mediation reflects the strength and characteristics of the competing parties.

One aspect of this conflict has not been given proper emphasis: government concessions must be implemented, and implementation provides new battlegrounds for the conflict within a more limited domain. Although particular segments of capital or their representatives often participate in working out compromise arrangements, implementation of the agreement is not insured. Intense conflicts may occur after state mediation because of attempts by corporations to circumvent, ignore, or resist government regulations.

The attempt by the California and federal governments in the late thirties to provide support for agricultural unionization did not create a situation in which unionization progressed far enough for state-induced restraints to be carried out. The present mediation attempt by the California government, however, does include limited restrictions on the activities of agricultural unions. The ALRA can best be interpreted as an attempt at mediating the struggle between large-scale agricultural interests and labor, a struggle that has marked most of California's history and that was exceptionally strong during the ten years before the enactment of the law. As noted, mediation has attempted to circumscribe the conflict. The legislation modified the UFW's position by placing limitations on the options it could utilize to gain union recognition, primarily through restrictions on the use of secondary boycotts and recognition strikes. The acceptance of these conditions by the UFW was made easier by the fact that the union had previously suspended all secondary boycott activity in order to secure AFL-CIO endorsement of its primary boycott of head lettuce and table grapes. Once accepted, the legislation limited the focus of the struggle. With the secondary boycott in effect, the union had been engaged in a struggle not only with a specific segment of growers, but with much of the food industry, including supermarket chains. It focused attention on the entire food-for-profit system with its mutually sustaining elements. The conflict now involved only the growers and the union. Although the UFW threw its full weight behind the compromise once it was reached, the Brown bill undermined the union's effort to utilize the state legislative apparatus as a vehicle for the pursuit of its own interests. In competition with Brown's initial proposal, the UFW-backed legislation quickly lost momentum. The union's political strength, however, protected it from having to make further concessions: additional restrictions would have probably aroused UFW opposition to the entire proposal and eroded Brown's credibility as well as the possibility of the bill's passage.

The process of securing grower compliance now became primary. Once the secondary boycott was eliminated, the growers lost the basis of the support they had had from other segments of the food industry. Through the governor's office and the ALRB, the California government confronted the more parochial interests of growers and their legislative allies, who were attempting to modify the law to their own advantage and against its intended purpose. Grower pressure to modify the law intensified after it became clear that it was helping to establish the UFW as a permanent force in California agriculture. The resistence of the Brown administration to grower pressure indicates that for the present, at least, the law represents a continuing effort to accommodate capital-labor conflict under the aegis of state regulation, rather than an attempt to undermine the UFW.

The California government has been able to mediate the struggle between agricultural capital and labor by serving as an integrative mechanism. Mediation was accomplished despite the short term interests of agribusiness in a passive, inexpensive, and controllable labor force. It should be noted again that there is no one factor that compels the state to attempt mediation. It is more accurate to say that the state can be pushed toward mediation by strong, prolonged, and potentially effective efforts to achieve social change by an organized subordinate group that does not dissolve in the face of repressive tactics or whose repression is politically hazardous.

Although we have emphasized state mediation, interventions, and policies in describing the dominant government response to particular situations, we do not mean to imply that the internal structure of the state is unitary. The specific composition of state authority determines the kinds of response initiated by government. In other words, since the state mediates between demands made upon it and its responses to those demands, the specific composition of the state at any given time encourages some policy options and discourages others. Class struggles are not only the impetus behind attempts at state mediation but also help determine the internal composition of the state, which in turn is instrumental in determining the specific form mediation will take. Thus, it is clear that particular government officials and agencies influence mediation efforts. Governor Brown's legislative resolution of UFW unionization efforts, the California legislature's passage of the ALRA, and the ALRB's pattern of enforcement of the law are all outcomes of underlying political forces and struggles. This understanding justifies a focus on individuals, like Brown, who help shape the contours of mediation. A group struggling for change must be able to exert political power, both to help determine the internal composition of the state and to promote policies congruent with its interests.

The fact that the UFW is in a position to exert such power is related to the important place of agricultural production in California's economy. At the same time, the importance of agricultural production is a powerful incentive for state managers—such as Brown and key legislators—to seek a resolution that minimizes the possibility of future disruptions and preserves a healthy investment climate. It is thus quite understandable that even state officials with a history of support for farm worker demands have an interest in restricting the options available to the UFW: the restrictions reflect the proven power of the union to precipitate a crisis in sectors of agricultural production and distribution.

The power the UFW has been able to exert on a political level stems from its widespread backing by the farm worker population, boycott supporters, and others who endorsed the union's goals. The union has been singularly successful in winning electoral support for candidates who agree to represent its political interests: Robert Kennedy's victory in the 1968 California Democratic presidential primary is the best-known example. The union's impact has been felt even in races where its candidate has not been victorious. Its support for Tom Hayden in the 1976 Democratic primary helped create dissatisfaction with the incumbent, John Tunney, that contributed to his defeat by the Republican candidate, S. I. Hayakawa, in the November general election. Also, the union's support of Howard Berman for California Assembly Speaker in 1979 prevented the re-election of Leo McCarthy to that post, even though Berman subsequently lost the speakership election to Willie Brown, Jr. In this way the UFW has exercised a limited veto power over some Democratic party candidates.

Similarly, the relationship between Jerry Brown and the UFW has been one of mutual dependence. The UFW has needed someone like Brown to represent its basic interests on the political level, and Brown has been constrained not only by agribusiness interests but also by his need for political support and legitimacy. The logical resolution for Brown has been to pursue agricultural labor policies that are at a minimum acceptable both to the UFW and to agribusiness; for the UFW the relationship between the union and the governor has been a vacillation between support of and criticism for Brown's policies.

The UFW has remained relatively free from constraints imposed by more powerful organizations, such as the AFL-CIO and the Democratic party. It has accepted such compromises as the curtailment of the secondary boycott in 1974 in order to win AFL-CIO endorsement for its primary boycotts, but it has also pursued policies and endorsed candidates different from those favored by the AFL-CIO and other labor organizations as well as the majority of Democratic leaders. The extent of the UFW's autonomy, however, rests on a precarious balance. Perhaps one of the reasons the union has supported the Campaign for Economic Democracy initiated by Tom Hayden's senatorial campaign is that this coalition, if it ever develops, has the potential of offering the UFW political support and thus reducing the need for future compromises with the AFL-CIO or Democratic party regulars.

To summarize: The success of the state in mediating conflicts and acting as an integrative mechanism is problematic. It is not true that the state grants only minimal and co-optable reforms. The reforms undertaken and their implementation depend on specific circumstances, such as the nature of the underlying forces and the internal composition of the state. As Andre Gorz has argued, it seems possible as well as desirable to pursue structural, or transitional, reforms that have the potential to force a realignment of power between dominated and dominant classes.[24] These reforms then become the basis for further actions aimed at overcoming the contradictions imposed by a capitalist mode of production. To be effective, such reforms should be constituted in ways that keep subordinate classes and their organizations relatively independent from restrictive government legislation. Thus, reformers may avoid seeing their gains rendered less effective either through implementation and enforcement procedures or through future debilitating restrictions.

PROSPECTS FOR THE FUTURE

Several implications follow from the foregoing analysis. It seems increasingly likely that the UFW will dominate future efforts to organize agricultural labor in California. As the history of agricultural labor unionization in California has demonstrated, growers and their allies possess too many resources and options for a farm labor union by itself to force permanent concessions. An agricultural labor movement must drive a wedge between the state and corporate agriculture, making it increasingly costly to continue past patterns of government accommodation to the growers. In this sense, the UFW needs the state, or rather a segment of it. Two factors will largely determine the long-range effects of state mediation: the institution-alization of a conflict and the effects of institutionalization on the UFW as a militant, democratically-organized union.

The theories of the capitalist state that we have found useful suggest that the institutionalization of the conflict between agri-cultural capital and labor will carry with it attempts to limit the options available to the UFW and narrow its focus to more conven-tional demands. We have already noted the restrictive aspects of the ALRA. In addition, the mechanisms of farm labor elections and labor contract negotiations have proven to be cumbersome and time-consuming, and tend to monopolize the UFW's attention. The time needed to secure labor contracts encourages the union to confine its activities to California. Other agricultural unions patterned after the UFW have arisen in Ohio, Arizona, and Texas. Although in some cases their organizers are former UFW officials, the UFW has not yet established formal linkages.

Perhaps more significantly, the UFW must defend itself against future restrictions and changes in the law detrimental to its in-terests. A change of administrations in California could bring about new legal obstacles. With the decline of produce boycotts and the emergence of an election mechanism, the network of support groups the union relied upon in the past has been eroded. Whether it can be recreated if needed in the future is problematic.

David Montgomery's analysis of the effects of the NLRA of 1935 raises issues relevant to the future of the present farm worker move-ment. Activity by the federal government in support of unionization during the Depression was simultaneously liberating and co-optative for workers. Labor struggles and government response lifted the burden of absolute managerial control from the work force. In addi-tion to securing wage gains, union contracts won workers power on the job. Management was obliged to deal with workers' elected repre-sentatives, and the workers were accorded some degree of protection against company favoritism and arbitrary dismissals. But institu-tionalization also created processes through which the rank and file could be disciplined and brought under tighter control and labor organizing constrained from threatening the prevailing market and profit mechanisms. Additionally, industrial unions were subjected to more rigid legal and political controls. Management, once it accepted the existence of unions, encouraged the development of union struc-tures and policies most adaptable to corporate goals. And the process of seeking advantageous rulings from government agencies strengthened the importance of union officials relative to union members.[25]

Thus, institutionalization may move the UFW into a more defensive position. Piven and Cloward's study of poor people's movements argues that when the leaders of such movements turn away from encouraging disruption and toward building organizations, the power of the movements declines.[26] The UFW does not appear at present to conform to this pattern; it has been the UFW as an organization that has mobilized, directed, and sustained insurgency, creating a crisis in agricultural production through strikes and consumer boycotts. In 1979 the UFW successfully concluded its largest strike since 1973; some observers, including several growers, believe it was the UFW's largest and most effective strike to date. Nevertheless, the possibility remains that the union may turn more exclusively toward organization building at the expense of its ability to mobilize insurgency once its institutional position has become more firmly established. Indeed, there are compelling reasons why the UFW should pursue more defensive strategies. Agribusiness has not completely accepted the existence of either the union or the ALRA, and the organized growers have attempted to use the resources at their disposal, including their political allies in the California legislature, to undermine the law's effectiveness through alterations of strategic provisions or limitations on the law's jurisdiction. Ironically, the UFW now finds itself in the position of defending a state structure while agribusiness fights for change.

It is not difficult to imagine a situation in which the UFW's power to win elections would be seriously undermined and the union effectively prevented from expanding. Although UFW-led strikes and boycotts continue, there is no longer a crisis in agribusiness operations. The political climate that produced the ALRA has now changed, and the California governor elected in 1982 will almost certainly be less sympathetic to the UFW than Governor Brown is. Agribusiness may begin to prevail in its attempts to alter the ALRA, and an amended law may restrict rather than facilitate agricultural unionization. A "guest worker" program has been proposed; if undertaken by the Reagan administration, its effects will most likely be similar to those of the 1942–64 bracero programs: worker demoralization, the displacement of domestic workers, a decline in living and working standards, and the defeat of unionization efforts.

In addition, the question remains whether the UFW can consolidate enough power to implement fully the gains it appears to be in the process of winning. In particular, it is unclear whether the UFW can succeed in permanently eliminating the labor contractor system and build the power of ranch-level committees. Can it influence the trend toward agricultural mechanization so that labor displacement and dislocation are minimized and the present farm workers are offered the opportunity for better positions within agricultural production?

Whereas some analysts, including Piven and Cloward, argue that the erosion of the ability of movements like the UFW to pursue extensive changes stems from the interest of their leadership in building an organization or in the process of institutionalization itself, we propose that a critical variable is the success of the state in restricting the possible activities and demands of such an organization, limiting its political impact, and channeling its efforts into areas more compatible with the long-term interests of capital. Such confinement is neither inherent in the process of institutionalization nor a necessary outcome of state mediation. Rather, it depends on the power of opposing sides translated to the political level.

The UFW seems to recognize this situation. Its future as an organization capable of generating structural reforms may be influenced more by its ability to stay free of constraining state regulation than by any struggle with a particular segment of agribusiness. It is this aspect of agricultural labor relations within California and elsewhere in the United States that may be the most significant during the next decade.

NOTES

INTRODUCTION

1. For example, Ronald B. Taylor, *Chavez and the Farm Workers* (Boston: Beacon, 1975); Jacques E. Levy, *Cesar Chavez: Autobiography of La Causa* (New York: W.W. Norton, 1975); Sam Kushner, *Long Road to Delano* (New York: International Publishers, 1975); and Dick Meister and Anne Loftis, *A Long Time Coming: The Struggle to Unionize America's Farm Workers* (New York: Macmillan, 1977).

2. See David Brody, *Workers in Industrial America* (New York: Oxford, 1980); David Montgomery, *Workers' Control in America* (New York: Cambridge University Press, 1979).

3. C. Wright Mills, *The Power Elite* (New York: Oxford, 1956), pp. 3–29. We are indebted to Dick Flacks for this interpretation.

CHAPTER 1

1. For example, between 1930 and 1954 the size of the average farm in California increased 37 percent; between 1954 and 1969, over 100 percent. The number of small farms in California has declined from 135,676 in 1930 to 80,848 in 1964. See Robert C. Fellmeth, *Politics of Land* (New York: Grossman, 1973), p. 79.

2. Ibid., pp. 78–79; Mark Day, *Forty Acres: Cesar Chavez and the Farm Workers* (New York: Praeger, 1971), p. 37.

3. Stephen H. Sosnick, *Hired Hands: Seasonal Farm Workers in the United States* (Santa Barbara: McNally and Loftin, West, 1978), p. 18.

4. Ibid., p. 19.

5. California Employment Development Department, Sacramento, Cal., *California Rural Manpower Report*, annual issues 1966–1975, as cited by Sosnick, *Hired Hands*, p. 7.

6. For example, Department of Agriculture statistics from the early 1970s listed the average annual income of year-round farm workers in the United States as $4,358. Migrant seasonal farm workers had an average income of $3,350 a year. While the average income of agricultural labor in California has been slightly higher than the national average, by 1975 the California average hourly wage for agricultural labor was slightly less than half the

average hourly wage of the state's manufacturing workers. According to the U.S. Census, in 1969 agricultural workers had the lowest median income for male workers in all but three California counties. See Sue Eileen Hayes, *Industrial Response to Agricultural Labor Relations Act* (Austin, Tex.: Center for the Study of Human Resources, University of Texas, 1979), pp. 13, 96–99.

7. Andre Gorz, *Strategy for Labor: A Radical Proposal* (Boston: Beacon Press, 1964), pp. 35–41; David Montgomery, *Workers' Control in America* (New York: Cambridge University Press, 1979), pp. 1–7, 98–99.

8. Gorz, *Strategy*; Montgomery, *Worker's Control*, pp. 91–112; Serge Mallet, *Essays on the New Working Class* (St. Louis: Telos, 1975).

9. Mayer N. Zald and John D. McCarthy, eds., *The Dynamics of Social Movements* (Cambridge, Mass.: Winthrop, 1979), pp. 1–5; Anthony Oberschall, *Social Conflict and Social Movements* (Englewood Cliffs, N.J.: Prentice-Hall, 1973); Charles Tilly, *From Mobilization to Revolution* (Reading, Mass.: Addison-Wesley, 1978).

10. Peter Bachrach and Morton Baratz, *Power and Poverty, Theory and Practice* (New York: Oxford University Press, 1970), p. 54.

11. Theo J. Majka, "Poor People's Movements and Farm Labor Insurgency," *Contemporary Crises* 4 (July 1980): 283–308.

12. Oberschall, *Social Conflict*, p. 140.

13. James O'Connor, *The Fiscal Crisis of the State* (New York: St. Martin's Press, 1974), pp. 5–6. For a related approach to the accumulation-legitimation dichotomy, see Claus Offe, "The Theory of the Capitalist State and the Problem of Policy Formation" and "Introduction to Legitimacy Versus Efficiency," both in *Stress and Contradiction in Modern Capitalism*, ed. Leon N. Lindberg, Robert Alford, Colin Crouch, and Claus Offe (Lexington, Mass.: D. C. Heath, 1975), and Claus Offe, "Political Authority and Class Structure," in *Critical Sociology*, ed. Paul Connerton (London: Penguin Books, 1976).

14. See Nicos Poulantzas, *Political Power and Social Classes* (London: New Left Books, 1973); *Classes in Contemporary Capitalism* (London: New Left Books, 1975); "The Problem of the Capitalist State," *New Left Review* 58 (November–December 1969), 67–78; and his interview with Henri Weber, "The State and the Transition to Socialism," *Socialist Review*, no. 38 (March–April 1978), 9–36.

15. Poulantzas, *Political Power*, pp. 44–47.

16. Ibid., pp. 187–94.

17. See Alan Wolfe, "New Directions in the Marxist Theory of Politics," *Politics and Society* 4 (1974): 140–43; David A. Gold, Clarence Y. H. Lo, and Erik Olin Wright, "Recent Developments in Marxist Theories of the Capitalist State," *Monthly Review* 27, no. 5 (1975): 38; Gosta Esping-Andersen, Rodger Friedland, and Erik Olin Wright, "Modes of Class Struggle and the Capitalist State," *Kapitalistate*, no. 4–5 (1976): 189–90; and Michael Reich and Richard Edwards, "Political Parties and Class Conflict in the United States," *Socialist Review*, no. 39 (May–June 1978): 38–42.

18. Theda Skocpol, "State and Revolution: Old Regimes and Revolutionary Crises," *Theory and Society* (January–March 1979): 7–15; Boris Frankel, "On the State of the State: Marxist Theories of the State after Leninism," *Theory and Society* 7 (January–March 1979): 204–11; and Fred Block, "The Ruling Class Does Not Rule: Notes on the Marxist Theory of the State," *Socialist Revolution*, no. 33 (May–June 1977), 6–28.

CHAPTER 2

1. George F. Seward, *Chinese Immigration in Its Social and Economic Aspects* (New York: Charles Scribner's Sons, 1881), pp. 14–29.

2. Ibid., pp. 30–36.

3. Mary Roberts Coolidge, *Chinese Immigration* (New York: Henry Holt, 1909), pp. 339–40.

4. Seward, *Chinese Immigration*, pp. 37–50.

5. Ira B. Cross, *A History of the Labor Movement in California* (Berkeley: University of California Press, 1935), p. 74.

6. Ibid., pp. 78–79.

7. Alexander Saxton, *The Indispensable Enemy: Labor and the Anti-Chinese Movement in California* (Berkeley: University of California Press, 1971), pp. 69–70.

8. Cross, *History of the Labor Movement*, p. 80.

9. Lucile Eaves, *A History of California Labor Legislation* (Berkeley: University Press, 1910), pp. 126–27.

10. Saxton, *The Indispensable Enemy*, pp. 94–101.

11. Ibid., p. 103.

12. Cross, *History of the Labor Movement*, pp. 84–85.

13. Coolidge, *Chinese Immigration*, p. 261.

14. Cross, *History of the Labor Movement*, pp. 81–86.

15. Eaves, *California Labor Legislation*, p. 148.

16. Saxton, *The Indispensable Enemy*, pp. 105–6.

17. Cross, *History of the Labor Movement*, p. 89.

18. Eaves, *California Labor Legislation*, p. 150.

19. Saxton, *The Indispensable Enemy*, p. 114.

20. Cross, *History of the Labor Movement*, pp. 89–92.

21. Saxton, *The Indispensable Enemy*, p. 119.

22. Ibid., pp. 116–26.

23. Ibid., pp. 123–27.

24. Hubert Howe Bancroft, *History of California*, vol. 7 (San Francisco: History Company, 1890), pp. 404–6.

25. Saxton, *The Indispensable Enemy*, pp. 129–30.

26. Coolidge, *Chinese Immigration*, p. 119.

27. Saxton, *The Indispensable Enemy*, p. 128.

28. Cross, *History of the Labor Movement*, pp. 117–19.

29. Saxton, *The Indispensable Enemy*, p. 139.

30. Ibid., p. 172.

31. Ibid., pp. 167–72.

32. Ibid., p. 215.

33. Ibid., pp. 216–17.

34. Carey McWilliams, *Factories in the Field* (Boston: Little, Brown, 1939; reprint ed., Santa Barbara: Peregrine, 1971), pp. 59–65.

35. Saxton, *The Indispensable Enemy*, p. 4.

36. Coolidge, *Chinese Immigration*, p. 382.

37. Saxton, *The Indispensable Enemy*, p. 3.

38. Ibid., p. 210.

39. Herbert Hill, "Anti-Oriental Agitation and the Rise of Working Class Racism," *Society*, January–February 1973, p. 46.

40. Saxton, *The Indispensable Enemy*, p. 211.

41. Cross, *History of the Labor Movement*, p. 171.

42. Eaves, *California Labor Legislation*, p. 193–94.

43. Saxton, *The Indispensable Enemy*, p. 230.

44. Eaves, *California Labor Legislation*, p. 196.

CHAPTER 3

1. H. A. Millis, *The Japanese Problem in the United States* (New York: Macmillan, 1915), p. 3.

2. Ibid., p. 103.

3. Ibid., p. 105.

4. Carey McWilliams, *Factories in the Field* (Boston: Little, Brown, 1939; reprint ed., Santa Barbara: Peregrine, 1971), pp. 111–12.

5. Ibid., p. 106.

6. Carey McWilliams, *California: The Great Exception* (New York: Current Books, 1949), p. 153.

7. Paul S. Taylor, *Mexican Labor in the United States*, vol. 1 (Berkeley: University of California Press, 1928), pp. 6–10.

8. Millis, *Japanese Problem*, pp. 110–12.

9. McWilliams, *Factories in the Field*, p. 107.

10. Ibid., p. 83.

11. Stuart Marshall Jamieson, *Labor Unionism in American Agriculture*, U.S. Department of Labor, Bureau of Labor Statistics, Bulletin no. 836 (Washington, D.C.: Government Printing Office, 1945), p. 56.

12. Herbert Hill, "Anti-Oriental Agitation and the Rise of Working Class Racism," *Society*, January–February 1973, p. 53.

13. Yamato Ichihashi, *Japanese in the United States* (Stanford, Cal.: Stanford University Press, 1932), p. 172.

14. Jamieson, *Labor Unionism*, pp. 53–54.

15. U.S. Commission of Immigration, *Reports*, vol. 24, "Immigrants in Industries: Agriculture" (Washington, D.C.: Government Printing Office, 1911), p. 27.

16. Jamieson, *Labor Unionism*, p. 53.

17. Ira B. Cross, *A History of the Labor Movement in California* (Berkeley: University of California Press, 1935), pp. 263–64.

18. Nels Anderson, *Men on the Move* (Chicago: University of Chicago Press, 1940), pp. 295–96.

19. McWilliams, *Factories in the Field*, p. 111.

20. Ichihashi, *Japanese*, pp. 188–89.

21. Ibid., p. 184.

22. Millis, *Japanese Problem*, pp. 134–35.

23. Ibid., p. 134.

24. Roger Daniels, *The Politics of Prejudice: The Anti-Japanese Movement in California and the Struggle for Japanese Exclusion*, University of California Publications in History, vol. 71 (Berkeley: University of California Press, 1962), p. 10.

25. Ichihashi, *Japanese*, p. 190.

26. Jeffery M. Paige, *Agrarian Revolution* (New York: Free Press, 1975), p. 16.

27. Carey McWilliams, *Prejudice, Japanese-Americans: Symbol of Racial Intolerance* (Boston: Little, Brown, 1944), pp. 16–19.

28. Daniels, *Politics of Prejudice*, pp. 34–37.

29. Ibid., pp. 31–43; McWilliams, *Prejudice*, pp. 25–31.

30. Millis, *Japanese Problem*, pp. 16–18.

31. Millis, *Japanese Problem*, p. 201.

32. Eldon R. Penrose, *California Nativism: Organized Opposition to the Japanese, 1890–1913* (San Francisco: R and E Research Associates, 1973), pp. 84–85.

33. Ibid., pp. 76–78.

34. Daniels, *Politics of Prejudice*, p. 87.

35. Millis, *Japanese Problem*, pp. 205–6.

36. Ichihashi, *Japanese*, pp. 269–70.

37. Ibid., p. 193.

38. Daniels, *Politics of Prejudice*, p. 88.

39. McWilliams, *Prejudice*, p. 64.

40. McWilliams, *Factories in the Field*, p. 116.

41. E. G. Mears, *Resident Orientals on the American Pacific Coast* (Chicago: University of Chicago Press, 1928), pp. 253–54; McWilliams, *Prejudice*, p. 65.

42. Ichihashi, *Japanese*, p. 193.

43. Carey McWilliams, *Brothers under the Skin* (Boston: Little, Brown, 1951), pp. 111–16.

CHAPTER 4

1. Paul F. Brissenden, *The IWW: A Study of American Syndicalism* (New York: Russell and Russell, 1920; reprint ed. 1957), pp. 208–9.

2. Stuart Marshall Jamieson, *Labor Unionism in American Agriculture*, U.S. Department of Labor, Bureau of Labor Statistics, Bulletin no. 836 (Washington, D.C.: Government Printing Office, 1945), pp. 59–63; Philip S. Foner, *History of the Labor Movement in the United States* (New York: International Publishers, 1965), pp. 261–67; Cletus E. Daniel, "In Defense of the Wheatland Wobblies: A Critical Analysis of the IWW in California," *Labor History* 19 (1978): 485–509; Melvyn Dubofsky, *We Shall Be All: A History of the Industrial Workers of the World* (Chicago: Quadrangle, 1969), pp. 294–300.

3. Jamieson, *Labor Unionism*, p. 62; Dubofsky, *We Shall Be All*, p. 297.

4. Carey McWilliams, *Factories in the Field* (Boston: Little, Brown, 1939; reprint ed., Santa Barbara: Peregrine, 1971), p. 162.

5. Foner, *History of the Labor Movement*, p. 261.

6. Daniel, "Wheatland Wobblies," p. 494.

7. Jamieson, *Labor Unionism*, pp. 62–63.

8. Daniel, "Wheatland Wobblies," p. 496.

9. Ibid., pp. 498–500.

10. Foner, *History of the Labor Movement*, p. 276; Daniel, "Wheatland Wobblies," p. 503.

11. Foner, *History of the Labor Movement*, pp. 276–77.

12. Sam Kushner, *Long Road to Delano* (New York: International Publishers, 1975), pp. 50–51.

13. Daniel, "Wheatland Wobblies," p. 497.

14. Foner, *History of the Labor Movement*, p. 280.

15. Carleton H. Parker, *The Casual Laborer and Other Essays* (New York: Harcourt, Brace, and Howe, 1920), pp. 114–15.

16. Selig Perlman and Philip Taft, *Labor Movements*, vol. 4 of *History of Labor in the United States, 1896–1932*, ed. John R. Commons (New York: Macmillan, 1935), p. 386.

17. William Preston, *Aliens and Dissenters: Federal Suppression of Radicals, 1903–1933* (Cambridge, Mass.: Harvard University Press, 1963), pp. 40–41.

18. Parker, *Casual Laborer*, p. 190.

19. Foner, *History of the Labor Movement*, p. 277–78.

20. Perlman and Taft, *Labor Movements*, p. 420.

21. Brissenden, *The IWW*, p. 282.

22. James Weinstein, *The Corporate Ideal in the Liberal State: 1900–1918* (Boston: Beacon Press, 1968), p. 238.

23. Jamieson, *Labor Unionism*, p. 65; Kushner, *Long Road*, p. 52.

24. Perlman and Taft, *Labor Movements*, p. 432; Brissenden, *The IWW*, pp. x–xi.

25. McWilliams, *Factories in the Field*, p. 172.

26. Daniel, "Wheatland Wobblies," p. 506.

27. Jamieson, *Labor Unionism*, p. 64; Daniel, "Wheatland Wobblies," pp. 507–8.

28. Jamieson, *Labor Unionism*, pp. 57–58.

29. Mark Reisler, *By the Sweat of Their Brow: Mexican Immigrant Labor in the United States, 1900–1940* (Westport, Conn.: Greenwood Press, 1976), p. 24.

30. Ernesto Galarza, *Merchants of Labor: The Mexican Bracero Story* (Charlotte/Santa Barbara: McNally and Loftin, 1964), p. 29; Reisler, *By the Sweat of Their Brow*, p. 27.

31. Reisler, *By the Sweat of Their Brow*, pp. 30–32.

32. Ibid., pp. 32–33.

33. Stuart Ward, "The Mexican in California," vol. 21, no. 1 of *The Commonwealth*, part 2, no. 12 (San Francisco: Transactions of the Commonwealth Club of California, 23 March 1926), p. 5.

34. McWilliams, *Factories in the Field*, p. 125.

35. Nels Anderson, *Men on the Move* (Chicago: University of Chicago Press, 1940), p. 296.

36. Reisler, *By the Sweat of Their Brow*, p. 207.

37. Ibid., p. 173.

38. Ibid., p. 203.

39. McWilliams, *Factories in the Field*, p. 127.

40. "The Mexican," Ward, pp. 6–7.

41. William H. Kirkbride, "An Argument for Mexican Immigration," vol. 21, no. 1 of *The Commonwealth*, part 2, no. 12 (San Francisco: Transactions of the Commonwealth Club of California, 23 March 1926), p. 14.

42. Abraham Hoffman, *Unwanted Mexican Americans in the Great Depression* (Tucson: University of Arizona Press, 1974), p. 28.

43. Bruno Lasker, *Filipino Immigration to the United States* (Chicago: University of Chicago Press, 1931), p. 21.

44. Ibid., p. 23.

45. Ibid., pp. 48–51.

46. Jamieson, *Labor Unionism*, p. 74.

47. U.S. Congress, Senate Committee on Education and Labor, Subcommittee to Investigate Violations of the Rights of Free Speech and Assembly and Interference with the Right of Labor to Organize and Bargain Collectively, Pursuant to S. Rev. 226, 74th Cong., 1940, *Hearings*, part 47, p. 17217; part 54, p. 19780 (hereinafter referred to as La Follette Committee).

48. Ibid., part 54, p. 19861; McWilliams, *Factories in the Field*, pp. 190–93; Jamieson, *Labor Unionism*, pp. 70–72.

49. Reisler, *By the Sweat of Their Brow*, p. 78.

50. Paul Taylor and Tom Vasey, "Contemporary Background of California Farm Labor," *Rural Sociology* 1 (1936): 403–4.

51. La Follette Committee, part 47, p. 17227.

52. Reisler, *By the Sweat of Their Brow*, p. 80.

53. Jamieson, *Labor Unionism*, p. 76.

54. Kushner, *Long Road*, p. 61.

55. Ibid., p. 63.

56. McWilliams, *Factories in the Field*, pp. 132–33.

57. Ibid., p. 199.

58. Reisler, *By the Sweat of Their Brow*, p. 80.

59. Ibid., p. 215.

60. Hoffman, *Unwanted Mexican Americans*, pp. 39–41.

61. Reisler, *By the Sweat of Their Brow*, pp. 217–18.

62. Hoffman, *Unwanted Mexican Americans*, pp. 39–41.

63. Ibid., p. 82.

64. Ibid., p. 100.

65. Ibid., p. 106.

66. Emory S. Bogardus, *The Mexican in the United States* (Los Angeles: University of Southern California Press, 1934; reprint ed., New York, Arno Press and the New York Times, 1970), pp. 90–91.

67. Hoffman, *Unwanted Mexican Americans*, p. 106.

68. Lasker, *Filipino Immigration*, p. 34.

69. Carey McWilliams, "Exit the Filipino," *Nation*, 4 September 1935, p. 265.

CHAPTER 5

1. Mark Reisler, *By the Sweat of Their Brow: Mexican Immigrant Labor in the United States, 1900–1940* (Westport, Conn.: Greenwood Press, 1976), p. 233.

2. Stuart Marshall Jamieson, *Labor Unionism in American Agriculture*, U.S. Department of Labor, Bureau of Labor Statistics, Bulletin no. 836 (Washington, D.C.: Government Printing Office, 1945), p. 85.

3. Ibid., pp. 85–113; Dorothy Ray Healey, Phonotape 49A, Bancroft Library, University of California, Berkeley, Cal.

4. Orrick Johns, *Time of Our Lives: The Story of My Father and Myself* (New York: Octagon Books, 1937), pp. 329–33.

5. Norman Mini, "That California Dictatorship," *Nation*, 20 February 1935, p. 224.

6. Jamieson, *Labor Unionism*, p. 98.

7. Carey McWilliams, *Factories in the Field* (Boston: Little Brown, 1939; reprint ed., Santa Barbara: Peregrine, 1971), pp. 196–97.

8. Jamieson, *Labor Unionism*, p. 100.

9. Ibid., p. 104.

10. Ibid., p. 427.

11. Healey, Phonotape 49A.

12. Ibid.

13. Ibid.

14. Mini, "California Dictatorship," p. 226.

15. *Rural Worker*, National Committee to Aid Agricultural Workers, Washington, D.C., vol. 1, no. 15, November 1936, p. 2.

16. Dick Meister and Anne Loftis, *A Long Time Coming: The Struggle to Unionize America's Farm Workers* (New York: Macmillan, 1977), p. 37.

17. Ibid., pp. 37–38; Paul W. Taylor, interview, Berkeley, Cal., August 1975.

18. Jamieson, *Labor Unionism*, p. 109.

19. Reisler, *The Sweat of Their Brow*, pp. 242–43.

20. Jamieson, *Labor Unionism*, p. 106.

21. Caroline Decker Gladstein, Phonotape 49A, Bancroft Library, University of California, Berkeley, Cal.

22. Meister and Loftis, *Long Time Coming*, p. 37.

23. McWilliams, *Factories in the Field*, p. 224.

24. Jamieson, *Labor Unionism*, p. 112.

25. Lew Levenson, "California Casualty List," *Nation*, 29 August 1934, pp. 243–45.

26. U.S. Congress, Senate Committee on Education and Labor, Subcommittee to Investigate Violations of the Right of Free Speech and Assembly and Interference with the Right of Labor to Organize and Bargain Collectively, Pursuant to S. Rev. 226, 74th Cong., 1940, *Hearings*, part 69, pp. 25317–31 (hereafter referred to as La Follette Committee).

27. Nels Anderson, *Men on the Move* (Chicago: University of Chicago Press, 1940), p. 297.

28. La Follette Committee, *Hearings*, part 55, pp. 20075–91; 20235–48.

29. Clarke A. Chambers, *California Farm Organizations* (Berkeley: University of California Press, 1952), p. 39.

30. La Follette Committee, *Hearings*, part 55, p. 20242.

31. Ibid., part 55, p. 20248.

32. McWilliams, *Factories in the Field*, p. 232.

33. La Follette Committee, *Hearings*, part 49, p.17917.

34. La Follette Committee, *Reports*, 78th Cong., 2d session, part VIII, pp. 1152–53.

35. Carey McWilliams, *Ill Fares the Land: Migrants and Migratory Labor in the United States* (New York: Barnes and Noble, 1942; reprint ed., 1967), pp. 25–27.

36. Ibid., p. 27.

37. John Steinbeck, "Dubious Battle in California," *Nation*, 12 September 1936, pp. 302–3.

38. Sam Kushner, *Long Road to Delano* (New York: International Publishers, 1975), p. 85.

39. Frank J. Taylor, "The Right to Harvest," *Country Gentleman*, October 1937, p. 72.

40. McWilliams, *Factories in the Field*, p. 242.

41. Ibid., p. 242.

42. Jamieson, *Labor Unionism*, p. 120.

43. Ibid., pp. 124–25; McWilliams, *Factories in the Field*, pp. 244–45.

44. Jamieson, *Labor Unionism*, pp. 125–27; McWilliams, *Factories in the Field*, pp. 249–52.

45. *New Republic*, 30 September 1936, p. 210.

46. Jamieson, *Labor Unionism*, p. 140.

47. Ibid., p. 146.

48. *New Republic*, 28 July 1937, p. 327.

49. Ibid., p. 328.

50. Robert F. Wagner, Introduction to *The Wagner Act: After Ten Years*, ed. Louis G. Silverberg (Washington, D.C.: Bureau of National Affairs, 1945), p. 3.

51. David Brody, *Workers in Industrial America: Essays on the 20th Century Struggle* (New York: Oxford, 1980), pp. 100–112, 120–35.

CHAPTER 6

1. U.S. Congress, House Select Committee to Investigate the Interstate Migration of Destitute Citizens, Pursuant to H. Res. 63, 491, 629, 76th Cong., and H. Res. 16, 77th Cong., 1941, *Report on Interstate Migration*, part 4, p. 364 (hereafter referred to as Tolan Committee).

2. Gove Hambidge, "Farmers in a Changing World—A Summary," in *Yearbook of Agriculture, 1940*, U.S. Department of Agriculture (Washington, D.C.: Government Printing Office, 1940), p. 71.

3. Tolan Committee, p. 294.

4. Chester C. David, "The Development of Agricultural Policy Since the End of the World War," in *Yearbook of Agriculture, 1940*, pp. 313–14; and Charles H. Hession and Hyman Sardy, *Ascent to Affluence: A History of American Economic Development* (Boston: Allyn and Bacon, 1969), pp. 631–32.

5. Tolan Committee, p. 427.

6. John H. Kolb and Edmund deS. Brunner, *A Study of Rural Society* (Boston: Houghton Mifflin, 1952), p. 89.

7. Ibid., pp. 88–89.

8. Tolan Committee, pp. 300–302.

9. Ibid., p. 304.

10. Ibid., p. 337.

11. Ibid., pp. 403–4.

12. Studs Terkel, *Hard Times: An Oral History of the Great Depression* (New York: Pantheon, 1970), p. 53.

13. Tolan Committee, p. 313.

14. Ibid., p. 323.

15. Ibid., p. 368.

16. Ibid., p. 383.

17. *Migratory Labor in American Agriculture: Report of the President's Commission on Migratory Labor* (Washington, D.C.: Government Printing Office, 1951), p. 91.

18. Tolan Committee, pp. 446–47.

19. Ibid., p. 451.

20. Ibid., pp. 451–53.

21. Ibid., pp. 453–55.

22. U.S. Congress, Senate Committee on Education and Labor, Subcommittee to Investigate Violations of the Right of Free Speech and Assembly and Interference with the Right of Labor to Organize and Bargain Collectively, Pursuant to S. Res. 226, 74th Cong., 1940, *Hearings*, part 47, p. 17463 (hereafter referred to as La Follette Committee).

23. Dixon Wecter, *The Age of the Great Depression, 1929–1941* (New York: Macmillan, 1948), p. 149; and Tolan Committee, p. 464.

24. Tolan Committee, p. 464.

25. Ibid., pp. 429–31.

26. La Follette Committee, p. 17389.

27. Ibid., p. 17421.

28. Ibid.; Stuart Marshall Jamieson, *Labor Unionism in American Agriculture*, U.S. Department of Labor, Bureau of Labor Statistics, Bulletin, no. 836 (Washington, D.C.: Government Printing Office, 1945), p. 80.

29. La Follette Committee, p. 17218.

30. Ibid., pp. 17240–41.

31. Ibid., p. 17423.

32. Walter J. Stein, *California and the Dust Bowl Migration*, Contributions in American History, no. 21 (Westport, Conn.: Greenwood Press, 1973), pp. 3–16.

33. Ibid., p. ix.

34. Ibid., p. 46.

35. See John Steinbeck, *Their Blood Is Strong* (San Francisco: Simon J. Lubin Society, 1938).

36. Carey McWilliams, *Factories in the Field* (Boston: Little, Brown, 1939; reprint ed., Santa Barbara: Peregrine, 1971), p. 305.

37. Stein, *Dust Bowl Migration*, pp. 227–28.

38. La Follette Committee, *Hearings*, part 53, pp. 19467–68.

39. John Steinbeck, *Their Blood Is Strong*, p. 3.

40. Stein, *Dust Bowl Migration*, pp. 37–38.

41. La Follette Committee, *Reports*, no. 1150, pp. 384–85.

42. Carey McWilliams, *Ill Fares the Land: Migrants and Migratory Labor in the United States* (New York: Barnes and Noble, 1942; reprint ed., New York: Arno, 1976), p. 47.

43. Harry Schwartz, *Seasonal Farm Labor in the United States*, Columbia University Studies in the History of American Agriculture, No. 11 (New York: Columbia University Press, 1945), p. 26.

44. McWilliams, *Ill Fares the Land*, p. 344; Stein, *Dust Bowl Migration*, pp. 140–44.

45. Clarke A. Chambers, *California Farm Organizations* (Berkeley: University of California Press, 1952), pp. 83–84, 90.

46. Stein, *Dust Bowl Migration*, pp. 149–55.

47. McWilliams, *Factories in the Field*, p. 297.

48. Stein, *Dust Bowl Migration*, pp. 171–75.

49. Ibid., p. 167.

50. McWilliams, *Factories in the Field*, pp. 303–4.
51. Ibid., p. 303.
52. Stein, *Dust Bowl Migration*, p. 249.
53. McWilliams, *Factories in the Field*, p. 298.
54. Stein, *Dust Bowl Migration*, p. 181.

CHAPTER 7

1. Robert E. Burke, *Olson's New Deal for California* (Berkeley: University of California Press, 1953), p. 3.
2. Carey McWilliams, *The Education of Carey McWilliams* (New York: Simon and Schuster, 1979), p. 68.
3. Burke, *Olson's New Deal*, p. 4.
4. Ibid.
5. McWilliams, *Education*, p. 70.
6. Burke, *Olson's New Deal*, pp. 21–22.
7. Ibid., pp. 18–19.
8. Stein, *Dust Bowl Migration*, p. 116.
9. Clarke A. Chambers, *California Farm Organizations* (Berkeley: University of California Press, 1952), p. 84.
10. Walter J. Stein, *California and the Dust Bowl Migration*, Contributions in American History, no. 21 (Westport, Conn.: Greenwood Press, 1971), p. 82.
11. Carey McWilliams, *Factories in the Field* (Boston: Little, Brown, 1939; reprint ed., Santa Barbara: Peregrine, 1971), pp. 289–90.
12. McWilliams, *Factories in the Field*, p. 294.
13. Burke, *Olson's New Deal*, p. 79.
14. Ibid., p. 87.
15. Stein, *Dust Bowl Migration*, p. 257.
16. Chambers, *California Farm Organizations*, p. 92.
17. Carey McWilliams, *Ill Fares the Land: Migrants and Migratory Labor in the United States* (New York: Barnes and Noble, 1942; reprint ed., 1967), p. 13.
18. Stein, *Dust Bowl Migration*, p. 117; McWilliams, *Education*, p. 77.
19. Carey McWilliams, "What's Being Done about the Joads?" *New Republic*, 20 September 1939, p. 179.
20. Ibid., p. 178.
21. McWilliams, *Ill Fares the Land*, p. 41.
22. Stein, *Dust Bowl Migration*, p. 126.
23. Burke, *Olson's New Deal*, pp. 129–31.
24. Alden Stevens, "100,000 Political Footballs," *Nation*, 19 July 1941, pp. 52–53.
25. Burke, *Olson's New Deal*, pp. 141–43.
26. Stein, *Dust Bowl Migration*, pp. 194–95.
27. Ibid., p. 192.

28. Ibid., p. 196.

29. "Help for the Joads," *Nation*, 21 December 1940, p. 622.

30. Ibid.

31. McWilliams, *Education*, p. 78.

32. Gerald S. Auerbach, *Labor and Liberty: The La Follette Committee and the New Deal* (New York: Bobbs-Merrill, 1966), pp. 180–81.

33. McWilliams, *Education*, pp. 78–79.

34. U.S. Congress, Senate Committee on Education and Labor, Subcommittee to Investigate Violations of Free Speech and Assembly and Interference with the Right of Labor to Organize and Bargain Collectively, Pursuant to S. Res. 226, 74th Cong., 1940, *Hearings*, parts 47–75 (hereafter referred to as La Follette Committee).

35. Auerbach, *Labor and Liberty*, p. 191.

36. Carey McWilliams, "The Joads on Strike," *Nation* 4 November 1939, p. 489.

37. Chambers, *California Farm Organizations*, p. 51.

38. McWilliams, *Education*, p. 78.

39. Stein, *Dust Bowl Migration*, p. 244.

40. Ibid., pp. 244–45.

41. Sam Kushner, *Long Road to Delano* (New York: International Publishers, 1975), p. 92.

42. Stein, *Dust Bowl Migration*, p. 245.

43. Ibid., p. 252.

44. Stuart Marshall Jamieson, *Labor Unionism in American Agriculture*, U.S. Department of Labor, Bureau of Labor Statistics, Bulletin no. 836 (Washington, D.C.: Government Printing Office, 1945), p. 165.

45. Porter L. Chaffee, ed., "The Contract Labor System in California Agriculture," Federal Writers' Project, Oakland, Cal., 1938, Bancroft Library, University of California, Berkeley, Cal.; Jamieson, *Labor Unionism*, pp. 171–79.

46. Jamieson, *Labor Unionism*, pp. 171–72.

47. La Follette Committee, *Hearings*, part 51, p. 18623.

48. McWilliams, "The Joads on Strike," p. 489.

49. La Follette Committee, *Hearings*, part 51, pp. 18633–54.

50. Ibid., p. 18664.

51. Ibid., p. 18922.

52. Ibid., part 62, p. 22066.

53. Jamieson, *Labor Unionism*, p. 186.

54. Harry Schwartz, "Recent Developments among Farm Labor Unions," *Journal of Farm Economics* 23 (1941): 837.

55. Jamieson, *Labor Unionism*, pp. 179–85.

56. Stein, *Dust Bowl Migration*, pp. 266–68.

57. La Follette Committee, *Reports*, 78th Cong., 2d sess., no. 398, pp. 1526–27.

58. Stein, *Dust Bowl Migration*, p. 268.

59. Ibid., pp. 269–71.

60. Ernesto Galarza, *Farm Workers and Agri-Business in California, 1947–1960* (Notre Dame, Ind.: University of Notre Dame Press, 1977), pp. 102, 107–8.

61. McWilliams, *Factories in the Field*, p. 306.

62. David Brody, *Workers in Industrial America* (New York: Oxford University Press, 1980), pp. 100–12; David Montgomery, *Workers' Control in America* (New York: Cambridge University Press, 1979), pp. 163–66.

63. Brody, *Workers in Industrial America*, pp. 112–16.

CHAPTER 8

1. J. F. Otereo, "Immigration Policy: Drifting toward Disaster," *AFL-CIO American Federationist* 88 (February 1981):4.

2. Ernesto Galarza, *Merchants of Labor: The Mexican Bracero Story* (Charlotte/Santa Barbara: McNally and Loftin, 1964), p. 47.

3. Otey M. Scruggs, "Evolution of the Mexican Farm Labor Agreement of 1942," *Agricultural History* 34 (1960):140–41.

4. Richard B. Craig, *The Bracero Program: Interest Groups and Foreign Policy* (Austin: University of Texas Press, 1971), p. 39.

5. Scruggs, "Mexican Farm Labor Agreement," p. 148.

6. Craig, *Bracero Program*, p. 45.

7. Galarza, *Merchants*, pp. 121–259; Nelson Copp, *Wetbacks and Braceros: Mexican Migrant Laborers and American Immigration Policy, 1930–1960* (San Francisco: R and E Research Associates, 1971), pp. 34–89; Truman E. Moore, *The Slaves We Rent* (New York: Random House, 1965), pp. 87–99; Ernesto Galarza, *Farm Workers and Agri-Business in California, 1947–1960* (Notre Dame, Ind.: University of Notre Dame Press, 1977), parts 2 and 3.

8. President's Commission on Migratory Labor, *Migratory Labor in American Agriculture* (Washington, D.C.: Government Printing Office, 1951), pp. 56–59.

9. Derived from U.S. Department of Agriculture and U.S. Department of Labor data as cited in J. Craig Jenkins, "The Demand for Immigrant Workers: Labor Scarcity or Social Control," *International Migration Review* 12 (1978):529. Utilizing the same data, Jenkins found that braceros had a strong negative effect on farm wages (r = −.56), whereas the effect of undocumented workers was weaker (r = −.27). More significantly, correlating the annual number of collective actions undertaken by farm labor unions as indexed by the *New York Times* with the number of braceros contracted, Jenkins found that the presence of braceros significantly dampened union activity (r = −.56). The effect of undocumented workers on union activity was also negative but very slight (r = −.04). Although undocumented workers were often employed as strikebreakers, their presence apparently was not enough to prevent strikes, a point obvious to witnesses of the strike activity initiated by the NFWA and UFW during later years.

10. Galarza, *Merchants*, pp. 121–82, 224; Ellis W. Hawley, "The Politics of

the Mexican Labor Issue, 1950–1965," *Agricultural History* 40 (1966):162–63).

11. Carey McWilliams, *North from Mexico* (New York: J. B. Lippincott, 1949; reprint ed., New York: Greenwood Press, 1968), p. 266.

12. Galarza, *Merchants*, p. 51.

13. McWilliams, *North from Mexico*, p. 266.

14. Varden Fuller, *Labor Relations in Agriculture* (Berkeley: Institute of Industrial Relations, University of California, 1955), p. 11.

15. Galarza, *Merchants*, p. 51.

16. Craig, *Bracero Program*, p. 54.

17. Ibid., p. 63.

18. Galarza, *Merchants*, pp. 52–53.

19. Ibid., p. 54.

20. Ibid., p. 59; Jenkins, "Demand for Immigrant Workers," p. 519.

21. Galarza, *Farm Workers*, p. 37.

22. Ernesto Galarza, *Spiders in the House and Workers in the Fields* (Notre Dame, Ind.: University of Notre Dame Press, 1970), pp. 13–15.

23. Ibid., pp. 16–17.

24. Galarza, *Farm Workers*, pp. 100–101, 108.

25. Galarza, *Merchants*, p. 216.

26. *Farm Labor Organizing, 1905–1967: A Brief History* (New York: National Advisory Committee on Farm Labor, 1967), p. 37.

27. Ibid., pp. 38–39.

28. Joan London and Henry Anderson, *So Shall Ye Reap* (New York: Thomas Y. Crowell, 1970), p. 44.

29. Galarza, *Spiders*, pp. 77–78.

30. Ibid., p. 30.

31. Galarza, *Merchants*, p. 123.

32. Ronald B. Taylor, *Chavez and the Farm Workers* (Boston: Beacon Press, 1975), p. 71; Galarza, *Spiders*, pp. 40–48.

33. Galarza, *Spiders*, p. 48.

34. Ibid., p. 295.

35. Ibid., pp. 227–28.

36. Ibid., pp. 256–58.

37. Galarza, *Merchants*, pp. 183–84.

38. Hawley, "Politics of the Mexican Labor Issue," p. 160.

39. Galarza, *Merchants*, pp. 79–80.

40. Max J. Pfeffer, "The Labor Process and Corporate Agriculture: Mexican Workers in California," *Insurgent Sociologist* 10 (Fall 1980):32; Galarza, *Farm Workers*, pp. 32–35.

41. Galarza, *Farm Workers*, p. 149.

42. Ibid., pp. 226–30.

43. Craig, *Bracero Program*, p. 105.

44. Ibid., p. 113.

45. Galarza, *Merchants*, p. 66.

46. Craig, *Bracero Program*, pp. 113–18.

47. Ibid., p. 122.

48. Hawley, "Politics of the Mexican Labor Issue," p. 160.

49. Jorge A. Bustamente, "Undocumented Immigration from Mexico: Research Report," *International Migration Review* 11 (1977):149–50.

50. Galarza, *Merchants*, p. 61.

51. Ibid., p. 63.

52. Copp, *Wetbacks and Braceros*, p. 40.

53. Galarza, *Merchants*, p. 70.

54. Ibid., p. 70.

55. Jenkins, "Demand for Immigrant Workers," p. 529.

56. Quoted in London and Anderson, *So Shall Ye Reap*, p. 46.

57. Ibid., p. 135.

58. Craig, *Bracero Program*, pp. 142–43, 161–62, 175–76, 197.

59. National Advisory Committee on Farm Labor *Report on Farm Labor*; Public Hearings, Washington, D.C., 5–6 February, 1959 (New York, 1959), p. 25.

60. For an example of such an interpretation, see J. Craig Jenkins and Charles Perrow, "Insurgency of the Powerless: Farm Worker Movements (1946–1972)," *American Sociological Review* 42 (1977):249–68.

61. Sam Kushner, *Long Road to Delano* (New York: International Publishers, 1975), pp. 109–10.

62. Moore, *Slaves We Rent*, pp. 156–57.

63. Quoted in Kushner, *Long Road*, p. 113.

64. London and Anderson, *So Shall Ye Reap*, pp. 56–60.

65. Kushner, *Long Road*, p. 117.

66. Pfeffer, "Labor Process," p. 36.

67. Craig, *Bracero Program*, pp. 155–62.

68. Hawley, "Politics of the Mexican Labor Issue," pp. 173–74.

69. Pfeffer, "Labor Process," p. 38.

70. Craig, *Bracero Program*, pp. 182–97.

71. William Turner, "No Dice for Braceros," *Ramparts*, September 1965, pp. 18–20, 26.

72. "Machines Will Replace Domestics as Well as Braceros," *Congressional Record* 109, part 10 (29 July 1963), pp. 13590–91.

73. Craig, *Bracero Program*, p. 182.

74. Hawley, "Politics of the Mexican Labor Issue," p. 157.

75. Robert L. Bach, "Mexican Immigration and U.S. Immigration Reforms in the 1960s," *Kapitalistate*, no. 7 (1978):68–71; Hawley, "Politics of the Mexican Labor Issue," p. 176.

76. Quoted in Kushner, *Long Road*, p. 115.

CHAPTER 9

1. Interview with Fred Ross, Los Angeles, May 1974.

2. Sam Kushner, *Long Road to Delano* (New York: International Publishers, 1975), p. 151.

3. John Gregory Dunne, *Delano* (New York: Farrar, Straus, and Giroux, 1967; rev. ed., 1971), p. 14.

4. Ronald B. Taylor, *Chavez and the Farm Workers* (Boston: Beacon Press, 1975), p. 110.

5. For example, see Cesar Chavez, "The Organizer's Tale," *Ramparts*, July 1966, pp. 43–50.

6. Ross interview, May 1974.

7. Quoted in Kushner, *Long Road*, p. 122.

8. Ibid., p. 83.

9. Jacques E. Levy, *Cesar Chavez: Autobiography of La Causa* (New York: W. W. Norton, 1975), p. 182.

10. Taylor, *Chavez*, p. 124.

11. Ross interview; Levy, *Cesar Chavez*, p. 183.

12. See Eugene Nelson, *Huelga!: The First Hundred Days of the Great Delano Grape Strike* (Delano, Cal.: Farm Worker Press, 1966); Peter Matthiessen, *Sal Si Puedes* (New York: Delta, 1969), pp. 111–48; Taylor, *Chavez*, pp. 125–9, 145–56; Levy, *Cesar Chavez*, pp. 181–93.

13. Taylor, *Chavez*, p. 146.

14. Ibid., p. 148.

15. James P. Degnan, "Monopoly in the Vineyards: The Grapes of Wrath Strike," *Nation*, 7 February 1966, p. 152.

16. Levy, *Cesar Chavez*, pp. 192–93.

17. Kushner, *Long Road*, p. 153.

18. Taylor, *Chavez*, p. 158.

19. Ibid., pp. 165–67.

20. Kushner, *Long Road*, p. 163.

21. Dunne, *Delano*, p. 131.

22. Luis Valdez, "The Tale of the Raza," *Ramparts*, July 1966, pp. 40–43.

23. Quoted in Levy, *Cesar Chavez*, p. 207.

24. Ibid., p. 210.

25. William Turner, "Bracero Politics: A Special Report," *Ramparts*, September 1965, pp. 14–32.

26. Quoted in Levy, *Cesar Chavez*, p. 195.

27. Ibid., pp. 206–7.

28. Taylor, *Chavez*, pp. 170–73.

29. Turner, "Bracero Politics."

30. Levy, *Cesar Chavez*, pp. 235–36.

31. Dunne, *Delano*, p. 134.

32. Taylor, *Chavez*, pp. 187–88.

33. Interview with Fred Ross, Los Angeles, June 1974.

34. Taylor, *Chavez*, pp. 188–89.

35. Interview with Vivian Drake, Los Angeles, June 1974.

36. Ross interview, June 1974.

37. Levy, *Cesar Chavez*, p. 231.

38. Ibid., p. 233.

39. Ross interview, June 1974.

40. Levy, *Cesar Chavez*, p. 239.

41. Joan London and Henry Anderson, *So Shall Ye Reap* (New York: Thomas Y. Crowell, 1970), p. 157.

42. Levy, *Cesar Chavez*, pp. 243–44.

43. Taylor, *Chavez*, p. 203.

44. Levy, *Cesar Chavez*, pp. 255–56.

45. Ibid., pp. 253–56.

46. Taylor, *Chavez*, p. 203.

47. Nicolas C. Mills, "Workers on the Farms," *New Republic*, 23 September 1967, p. 9.

48. Robert Sherrill, "Reaping the Subsidies," *Nation*, 24 November 1969, pp. 561–66; and *El Malcriado*, UFW bimonthly, Keene, Cal., 15 June 1968.

49. Levy, *Cesar Chavez*, p. 264.

50. Doug Adair, "Cesar Chavez's Biggest Battle," *Nation*, 11 December 1967, pp. 627–28.

51. Ross interview, June 1974.

52. Ibid.

53. London and Anderson, *So Shall Ye Reap*, p. 160; Kushner, *Long Road*, pp. 178–79; Taylor, *Chavez*, pp. 229–36; and Ronald B. Taylor, "The Boycott and the NLRA," *Nation*, 12 May 1969, pp. 591–93.

54. *El Malcriado*, 15 February 1969.

55. Taylor, *Chavez*, pp. 218–19.

56. Ross interview, June 1974.

57. Levy, *Cesar Chavez*, pp. 269–71.

58. Ibid., p. 285.

59. Matthiessen, *Sal Si Puedes*, pp. 195–96.

60. Kushner, *Lond Road*, pp. 166–67.

61. Ibid., pp. 167–68.

62. Ibid., p. 164.

63. Levy, *Cesar Chavez*, p. 290.

64. Matthiessen, *Sal Si Puedes*, pp. 315–16.

65. *El Malcriado*, 24 May 1967.

66. Interview with Jim Drake, Los Angeles, July 1974.

67. London and Anderson, *So Shall Ye Reap*, p. 161.

68. Matthiessen, *Sal Si Puedes*, p. 312.

69. Ibid.

70. Taylor, *Chavez*, p. 236.

71. *El Malcriado*, 1 February 1969.

72. Levy, *Cesar Chavez*, p. 302.

73. Ibid., p. 303.

74. Ruth Harmer, "Poisons, Profits and Politics," *Nation*, 25 August 1969, pp. 134–37.

75. Ronald Taylor, "Nerve Gas in the Orchards," *Nation*, 22 June 1970, pp. 751–53.

76. *El Malcriado*, 1 January 1970.

77. Levy, *Cesar Chavez*, p. 296.

78. Dick Meister and Anne Loftis, *A Long Time Coming: The Struggle to Unionize America's Farm Workers* (New York: Macmillan, 1977), pp. 161–62.

79. Levy, *Cesar Chavez*, pp. 298–99.

80. Ibid., pp. 301–2.

81. Ibid., pp. 308–9.

82. Ibid., p. 329.

83. *El Malcriado*, 1 July 1970.

84. Mark Day, *Forty Acres: Cesar Chavez and the Farm Workers* (New York: Praeger, 1971), p. 145.

CHAPTER 10

1. Dick Meister and Anne Loftis, *A Long Time Coming: The Struggle to Unionize America's Farm Workers* (New York: Macmillan, 1977), p. 170; Sam Kushner, *Long Road to Delano* (New York: International Publishers, 1975), pp. 197–98.

2. Jacques E. Levy, *Cesar Chavez: Autobiography of La Causa* (New York: W. W. Norton, 1975), p. 355; Meister and Loftis, *Long Time Coming*, p. 212.

3. Levy, *Cesar Chavez*, pp. 337–43.

4. Ibid., p. 355.

5. *Los Angeles Times*, 26 August 1970.

6. *Salinas Californian*, 24 August 1970.

7. *El Malcriado*, 15 September 1970; Meister and Loftis, *Long Time Coming*, p. 168.

8. For an especially comprehensive discussion of the contract negotiations and the earlier discussion with the Teamsters and the intimidation by Teamster guards, see Levy, *Cesar Chavez*, pp. 337–424. Levy illustrates the day-to-day decisions and negotiations top UFW officials are faced with and the tactics growers, Teamsters, and the UFW utilize. His book also captures the UFW's style of operation and helps explain how it adds to the growers' mistrust of the union.

9. Ibid., pp. 308–9; *El Malcriado*, 1 October 1970.

10. Interview with Venustiano Olguin, La Paz, Cal. April 1974.

11. Interview with Fred Ross, Los Angeles, June 1974.

12. *El Malcriado*, 1 February 1971; Meister and Loftis *Long Time Coming*, p. 171.

13. Levy, *Cesar Chavez*, pp. 425–30.

14. *Los Angeles Times*, 30 December 1972.

15. *R. T. Englund* v. *Cesar Chavez*, California Supreme Court, Sup., 105 *California Reporter* (December 1972), pp. 525–39.

16. Levy, *Cesar Chavez*, pp. 437–38.

17. Ronald B. Taylor, *Chavez and the Farm Worker* (Boston: Beacon Press, 1975), p. 290.

18. Robert C. Fellmeth, *Politics of Land* (New York: Grossman, 1973), p. 53; *El Malcriado*, 15 January 1971.

19. Taylor, *Chavez*, pp. 277–78.
20. Quoted in Levy, *Cesar Chavez*, p. 449.
21. Ibid., pp. 449–52.
22. *El Malcriado*, 28 April 1972.
23. Levy, *Cesar Chavez*, pp. 453–62.
24. *New York Times*, 11 June 1972.
25. Levy, *Cesar Chavez*, pp. 463–68.
26. *Los Angeles Times*, 21 September 1972; Meister and Loftis, *Long Time Coming*, pp. 181–82.
27. Ibid.
28. *Los Angeles Times*, 10 March 1972 and 11 March 1972; *New York Times*, 25 March 1972.
29. John Banks, "Coachella Valley: Struggle for Self Determination," *Christianity and Crisis*, 9 July 1973, p. 136.
30. Interview with Vivian Drake, Los Angeles, June 1974; Meister and Loftis, *Long Time Coming*, pp. 173–74.
31. Peter Barnes, "Cesar Chavez and the Teamsters," *New Republic*, 19 May 1973, pp. 14–15.
32. *New York Times*, 17 March 1974; Meister and Loftis, *Long Time Coming*, pp. 184–85.
33. *Los Angeles Times*, 21 June 1974.
34. *Los Angeles Times*, 13 December 1972; Meister and Loftis, *Long Time Coming*, p. 184.
35. Interview with Thomas Donahue, Delano, Cal., July 1974.
36. Levy, *Cesar Chavez*, p. 473.
37. *San Francisco Chronicle*, 17 January 1973.
38. *Los Angeles Times*, 11 January 1973.
39. Levy, *Cesar Chavez*, p. 477.
40. Ross interview, June 1974.
41. Deposition of David E. Smith, 2 May 1974, *Mauricio Terrazas, et al.* v. *Frank Fitzsimmons, et al.*, United States District Court, Central District of California, No. 74-1426-RJK.
42. Deposition of William Grami, 26 February 1974, and Deposition of Einar Mohn, 26 February 1974, *Mauricio Terrazas, et al.* v. *Frank Fitzsimmons, et al.*
43. *Los Angeles Times*, 20 March 1973.
44. *El Malcriado*, 23 March 1973.
45. Taylor, *Chavez*, p. 293.
46. Levy, *Cesar Chavez*, p. 478.
47. Deposition of William Grami, 26 February 1974, *Maurico Terrazas, et al.*, v. *Frank Fitzsimmons, et al.*
48. Vivian Drake interview.
49. Taylor, *Chavez*, pp. 302–3.
50. Ibid., p. 297.
51. *El Malcriado*, 13 July 1973; Meister and Loftis, *Long Time Coming*, p. 187.

52. Jane Yett Kiely, "Report to Safeway on the Lettuce Labor Dispute," San Francisco, mimeo, 1973, p. 20.

53. Ibid.

54. Ibid., p. 21.

55. Interview with Jim Drake, Santa Barbara, Cal., April 1974.

56. Ross interview, June 1974.

57. Levy, *Cesar Chavez*, p. 495.

58. Barbara Baer and Glenna Matthews, "The Women of the Boycott," *Nation*, 23 February 1974, pp. 232–7.

59. Levy, *Cesar Chavez*, pp. 495–504.

60. *AFL-CIO News*, 24 November 1973.

61. Ibid.

62. *San Francisco Chronicle*, 11 November 1973.

63. *El Malcriado*, 29 March 1974; Meister and Loftis, *Long Time Coming*, p. 195.

64. Kushner, *Long Road*, p. 219; Meister and Loftis, *Long Time Coming*, p. 196.

65. *Los Angeles Times*, 17 August 1973; Meister and Loftis, *Long Time Coming*, pp. 190–91; Kushner, *Long Road*, pp. 209–10.

66. Levy, *Cesar Chavez*, p. 511.

67. Meister and Loftis, *Long Time Coming*, p. 190.

68. Quoted in Levy, *Cesar Chavez*, p. 512.

CHAPTER 11

1. *Los Angeles Times*, 22 October 1974.

2. *Fresno Bee*, 23 September 1973.

3. Sam Kushner, *Long Road to Delano* (New York: International Publishers, 1975), p. 215.

4. *Los Angeles Times*, 1 September 1974.

5. Interview with Jim Drake, Los Angeles, June 1974.

6. This analysis is based on the authors' observations while working for the UFW as well as numerous interviews conducted with long-time UFW staff members. One of the objectives of the interviews was to ascertain the kind of relationship between the UFW and the AFL-CIO. The above conclusions are similar to those of others who have written about the UFW from direct observation.

7. *Los Angeles Times*, 23 February 1974.

8. Ronald B. Taylor, *Chavez and the Farm Workers* (Boston: Beacon Press, 1975), p. 317.

9. *Washington Post*, 11 October 1973.

10. *Los Angeles Times*, 1 September 1974.

11. Field notes, Los Angeles, June 1974.

12. Interview with Fred Ross, Los Angeles, May 1974.

13. *Los Angeles Citizen*, 14 June 1974.

14. *Los Angeles Times*, 18 April 1974.
15. Interview with Vivian Drake, Los Angeles, July 1974.
16. *Los Angeles Times*, 6 June 1974.
17. Jacques E. Levy, *Cesar Chavez: Autobiography of La Causa* (New York: W. W. Norton, 1975), p. 528.
18. Field notes, Los Angeles, June 1974.
19. Interview with Fred Ross, Los Angeles, June 1974.
20. *Los Angeles Times*, 23 June 1974.
21. *Los Angeles Times*, 6 March 1974 and 22 August 1974.
22. *Los Angeles Times*, 22 August 1974.
23. Taylor, *Chavez*, p. 329.
24. *Los Angeles Times*, 2 March 1975.
25. Levy, *Cesar Chavez*, p. 528.
26. Ronald B. Taylor, "Something Is in the Wind," *Nation*, 22 February 1975, pp. 206–9.
27. *Los Angeles Times*, 12 April 1975: *San Diego Union*, 11 April 1975.
28. *Los Angeles Times*, 12 April 1975.
29. *Los Angeles Times*, 29 April 1975.
30. *Los Angeles Times*, 6 May 1975.
31. *Los Angeles Times*, 8 May 1975.
32. *Los Angeles Times*, 20 May 1975.
33. *Los Angeles Times*, 30 May 1975.
34. *Los Angeles Times*, 27 July 1975.
35. *Los Angeles Times*, 16 August 1975.
36. *San Francisco Chronicle*, 24 August 1975.
37. *Los Angeles Times*, 18 July 1975.
38. *Los Angeles Times*, 17 August 1975.
39. Ibid.
40. Field notes, Los Angeles, July 1974.
41. *Los Angeles Times*, 5 August 1975.
42. *Los Angeles Times*, 4 September 1975.
43. *Los Angeles Times*, 5 September 1975.
44. *Los Angeles Times*, 8 October 1975; Vernon M. Briggs, Jr., Walter Fogel, and Fred H. Schmidt, *The Chicano Worker* (Austin: University of Texas Press, 1977), p. 70.
45. *Los Angeles Times*, 11 September 1975.
46. *Los Angeles Times*, 30 September 1975.
47. *Los Angeles Times*, 20 September 1975.
48. *Los Angeles Times*, 26 September 1975.
49. *Los Angeles Times*, 27 September 1975.
50. *Los Angeles Times*, 17 October 1975.
51. *Los Angeles Times*, 30 October 1975.
52. *Los Angeles Times*, 26 December 1975.
53. Ibid.
54. *Los Angeles Times*, 30 October 1975.
55. *Los Angeles Times*, 7 April 1976.
56. *Los Angeles Times*, 11 June 1976.

CHAPTER 12

1. The most complete sources of public information on major events and activities involving UFW after it won major elections under the ALRA are found in the *Salinas Californian, Riverside Press-Enterprise, Fresno Bee, Los Angeles Times*, and *Imperial Valley Press*.

2. *Fresno Bee*, 8 July 1977.

3. *Imperial Valley Press*, 25 April 1977.

4. *Riverside Press-Enterprise*, 28 July 1977.

5. *Riverside Press-Enterprise*, 29 April 1977.

6. *Fresno Bee*, 4 May 1977.

7. *Los Angeles Times*, 9 December 1978.

8. *Los Angeles Times*, 2 February 1978.

9. *Los Angeles Times*, 1 February 1978.

10. Interviews with Rev. Wayne C. Hartmire, Los Angeles, Cal., September 1979, and Jerome Cohen, Salinas, Cal., September 1979.

11. *Los Angeles Times*, 17 February 1978.

12. *Los Angeles Times*, 9 July 1978.

13. Interviews with Rev. Wayne C. Hartmire, Los Angeles, Cal., September 1979; Jerome Cohen, Salinas, Cal., September 1979; and Doug Foster, Salinas, Cal., 1979.

14. *The Monitor*, 11 April 1978.

15. *Guardian*, 7 December 1977.

16. *Los Angeles Times*, 25 June 1978.

17. *Salinas Californian*, 25 January 1979.

18. *Salinas Californian*, 29 January 1979.

19. *Salinas Californian*, 30 January 1979.

20. *Los Angeles Times*, 2 February 1979.

21. *Salinas Californian*, 5 February 1979.

22. *Los Angeles Times*, 15 February 1979.

23. *Los Angeles Times*, 12 February 1979.

24. *Salinas Californian*, 14 February 1979.

25. *Salinas Californian*, 27 February 1979.

26. *Salinas Californian*, 8 March 1979.

27. *Salinas Californian*, 12 April 1979.

28. *Salinas Californian*, 18 April 1979.

29. *Salinas Californian*, 26 April 1979.

30. *Salinas Californian*, 1 May 1979.

31. Ibid.

32. *Salinas Californian*, 11 May 1979.

33. *Salinas Californian*, 12 June 1979.

34. *Salinas Californian*, 14 June 1979.

35. *Salinas Californian*, 16 July 1979.

36. *Salinas Californian*, 31 July 1979.

37. *Salinas Californian*, 4 August 1979.

38. *Salinas Californian*, 13 August 1979.

39. *Salinas Californian*, 27 August 1979.

40. *Salinas Californian*, 1 September 1979.

41. *Salinas Californian*, 13 September 1979.

42. *Salinas Californian*, 3 November 1979.

43. *Salinas Californian*, 5 November 1979.

44. *Salinas Californian*, 22 November 1979.

45. *Salinas Californian*, 17 January 1980.

46. *Salinas Californian*, 7 and 12 July 1980.

47. *Salinas Californian*, 9 August 1980.

48. Chris Hartmire, telephone interview, 1 February 1982.

49. Ibid.

50. Ibid.

51. *California AFL-CIO News*, 20 February 1981.

52. *Salinas Californian*, 1 November 1980.

53. *Los Angeles Times*, 4 December 1980; *Sacramento Bee*, 5 December 1980.

54. *Sacramento Bee*, 5 December 1980.

55. *Los Angeles Times*, 25 October 1981.

56. *Los Angeles Times*, 15 January 1982.

57. *Los Angeles Times*, 25 October 1981.

58. David Brody, *Workers in Industrial America* (New York: Oxford University Press, 1980), pp. 107–12.

59. *Salinas Californian*, 24 January 1981; *Los Angeles Times*, 15 January 1982.

60. Ibid.

61. *Los Angeles Times*, 6 and 7 September 1981; *New York Times*, 12 December 1981.

62. Ibid.; *Los Angeles Times*, 25 October and 13 November 1981.

63. *New York Times*, 31 July 1981.

64. *Los Angeles Times*, 4 and 26 February 1982.

CHAPTER 13

1. Selig Perlman and Philip Taft, *Labor Movements*, vol. 4 of *History of Labor in the United States, 1896–1932*, ed. John R. Commons (New York: Macmillan, 1935).

2. Clark Kerr, John T. Dunlop, Frederick H. Harbison, and Charles A. Myers, *Industrialism and Industrial Man* (Cambridge, Mass.: Harvard University Press, 1960), pp. 208–16.

3. Serge Mallet, *Essays on the New Working Class* (St. Louis: Telos, 1975), pp. 68, 105.

4. Andre Gorz, *Strategy for Labor: A Radical Proposal* (Boston: Beacon, 1964), p. 9; "Workers' Control Is More Than Just That," in *Workers' Control*, ed. by Gerry Hunnius, G. David Garson and John Case (New York: Vintage, 1973), p. 328.

5. Stanley Aronowitz, *False Promises: The Shaping of American Working Class Consciousness* (New York: McGraw-Hill, 1973), p. 11.

6. David Montgomery, "The 'New Unionism' and the Transformation of Workers' Consciousness in America, 1909–22," *Journal of Social History* 7 (1974): 509–29, and *Workers' Control in America* (New York: Cambridge University Press, 1979); and Jeremy Brecher, *Strike* (San Francisco: Straight Arrows, 1972), p. 316.

7. Mallet, *New Working Class*, p. 92.

8. Ibid., pp. 105–6.

9. Gorz, *Strategy*, pp. 35–41.

10. Montgomery, *Workers' Control*, especially chap. 4 and 5.

11. Montgomery, "New Unionism," pp. 519–20.

12. Ibid., p. 514.

13. Ibid., p. 515.

14. Mallet, *New Working Class*, pp. 87, 102–4.

15. Linda C. Majka, "Labor Militancy among Farm Workers and the Strategy of Protest: 1900–1979," *Social Problems* 28 (1981): 536–44.

16. Harry Braverman, *Labor and Monopoly Capital: The Degradation of Work in the Twentieth Century* (New York: Monthly Review, 1974), pp. 53–59; Mongomery, *Workers' Control*, pp. 1–44.

17. Braverman, *Labor*, pp. 113–19.

18. Braverman, *Labor*, pp. 113–19; David Brody, *Workers in Industrial America* (New York: Oxford, 1980), pp. 9–14; Montgomery, *Workers' Control*, pp. 101–3.

19. Braverman, *Labor*, pp. 139–51.

20. Linda C. Majka, "Farm Workers, Labor Unionism, and Agrarian Capitalism" (Ph.D. diss., University of California, Santa Barbara, 1978), pp. 30–74; William Hasbach, *A History of the English Agricultural Labourer*, trans. Ruth Kenyon, with a preface by Sidney Webb (London: P. S. King, 1908; reprint ed. New York: A. M. Kelley, 1966); Joseph Arch, *Joseph Arch: The Story of His Life, Told by Himself*, 2d ed. (London: Hutchinson, 1898); Arthur Clayden, *The Revolt of the Field* (London: Hodder and Stoughton, 1874).

21. Frances Fox Piven and Richard Cloward, *Poor People's Movements: Why They Succeed, How They Fail* (New York: Pantheon, 1977).

22. For a more detailed critique of Piven and Cloward, as well as an evaluation of their critics, see Theo Majka, "Poor People's Movements and Farm Labor Insurgency," *Contemporary Crises* (1980): 283–308.

23. Gosta Esping-Anderson, Rodger Friedland, and Eric Olin Wright, "Modes of Class Struggle and the Capitalist State," *Kapitalistate* 4-5 (Summer 1976), p. 191, emphasis in original.

24. Gorz, *Strategy*, pp. 35–41.

25. Montgomery, *Workers' Control*, pp. 163–66.

26. Piven and Cloward, *Poor People's Movements*, pp. ix–xiii.

BIBLIOGRAPHY

Adair, Doug. "Cesar Chavez's Biggest Battle." *Nation*, 11 December 1967, pp. 627–27.

Anderson, Nels. *Men on the Move*. Chicago: University of Chicago Press, 1940.

Arch, Joseph, *Joseph Arch: The Story of His Life, Told by Himself*. 2d ed. London: Hutchinson, 1898.

Aronowitz, Stanley. *False Promises: The Shaping of American Working Class Consciousness*. New York: McGraw-Hill, 1973.

Auerbach, Gerald S. *Labor and Liberty: The La Follette Committee and the New Deal*. New York: Bobbs-Merrill, 1966.

Bach, Robert L. "Mexican Immigration and U.S. Immigration Reforms in the 1960s." *Kapitalistate* 7(1978):63–80.

Bachrach, Peter, and Morton Baratz. *Power and Poverty, Theory and Practice*. New York: Oxford University Press, 1970.

Baer, Barbara, and Glenna Matthews. "The Women of the Boycott." *Nation*, 23 February 1974, pp. 232–37.

Bancroft, Hubert Howe. *History of California*. Vol. 7. San Francisco: History Company, 1890.

Banks, John. "Coachella Valley: Struggle for Self Determination." *Christianity and Crisis*, 9 July 1973, pp. 132–37.

Barnes, Peter. "Cesar Chavez and the Teamsters." *New Republic*, 19 May 1973, pp. 14–15.

Block, Fred. "The Ruling Class Does Not Rule: Notes on the Marxist Theory of the State." *Social Revolution*, no. 33 (May–June 1977):6–28.

Bogardus, Emory S. *The Mexican in the United States*. Los Angeles: University of Southern California Press, 1934; reprint ed., New York: Arno Press and the New York Times, 1970.

Braverman, Harry. *Labor and Monopoly Capital: the Degradation of Work in the Twentieth Century*. New York: Monthly Review, 1974.

Brecher, Jeremy. *Strike*. San Francisco: Straight Arrow, 1972.

Briggs, Vernon M., Jr., Walter Fogel, and Fred H. Schmidt. *The Chicano Worker*. Austin: University of Texas Press, 1977.

Brissenden, Paul F. *The IWW: A Study of American Syndicalism*. New York: Russell and Russell, 1920; reprint ed. 1957.

Brody, David. *Workers in Industrial America*. New York: Oxford, 1980.

Burke, Robert E. *Olson's New Deal for California*. Berkeley: University of California Press, 1953.

Bustamante, Jorge A. "Undocumented Immigration from Mexico: Research Report." *International Migration Review*" (1977):149–77.

California Employment Development Department, Sacramento, Cal. *California Rural Manpower Report*. 1966–1975.

Chaffee, Porter L., ed. "The Contract Labor System in California Agriculture." Federal Writers Project, Oakland, Cal., 1938. Bancroft Library, University of California, Berkeley, Cal.

Chambers, Clarke A. *California Farm Organizations*. Berkeley: University of California Press, 1952.

Chavez, Cesar. "The Organizer's Tale." *Ramparts*, July 1966, pp. 43–50.

Clayden, Arthur. *The Revolt of the Field*. London: Hodder and Stonghton, 1874.

Coolidge, Mary Roberts. *Chinese Immigration*. New York: Henry Hold, 1909.

Copp, Nelson. *Wetbacks and Braceros: Mexican Migrant Laborers and American Immigration Policy, 1930–1960*. San Francisco: R and E Research Associates, 1971.

Craig, Richard B. *The Bracero Program: Interest Groups and Foreign Policy*. Austin: University of Texas Press, 1971.

Cross, Ira B. *A History of the Labor Movement in California*. Berkeley: University of California Press, 1935.

Daniel, Cletus E. "In Defense of the Wheatland Wobblies: A Critical Analysis of the IWW in California." *Labor History* 19(1978).

Daniels, Roger. *The Politics of Prejudice: The Anti-Japanese Movement in California and the Struggle for Japanese Exclusion*. University of California Publications in History, vol. 71. Berkeley: University of California Press, 1962.

Davis, Chester C. "The Development of Agricultural Policy since the End of the World War." In *Yearbook of Agriculture, 1940*. U.S. Department of Agriculture. Washington, D.C.: Government Printing Office, 1940.

Day, Mark. *Forty Acres: Cesar Chavez and the Farm Workers*. New York: Praeger, 1971.

Degnan, James P. "Monopoly in the Vineyards: The Grapes of Wrath Strike." *Nation*, 7 February 1966, pp. 151–54.

Dubofsky, Melvyn. *We Shall Be All: A History of the Industrial Workers of the World*. Chicago: Quadrangle, 1969.

Dunne, John Gregory. *Delano*. New York: Farrar, Straus, and Giroux, 1967; rev. ed., 1971.

Eaves, Lucile. A History of California Labor Legislation. Berkeley: University Press, 1910.

Englund, R. T. v. Cesar Chavez, California Supreme Court, Sup., 105 *California Reporter*. December 1972, pp. 521–39.

Esping-Anderson, Gosta, Rodger Friedland, and Erik Olin Wright. "Modes of Class Struggle and the Capitalist State." *Kapitalistate* 4–5 (1976):186–220.

Farm Labor Organizing, 1905–1967: A Brief History. New York: National Advisory Committee on Farm Labor, 1967.

Fellmeth, Robert C. *Politics of Land.* New York: Grossman, 1973.

Foner, Philip S. *History of the Labor Movement in the United States.* New York: International Publishers, 1965.

Frankel, Boris. "On the State of the State: Marxist Theories of the State after Leninism." *Theory and Society* 7 (1979):199–242.

Fuller, Varden. *Labor Relations in Agriculture.* Berkeley: Institute of Industrial Relations, University of California, 1955.

Galarza, Ernesto, *Farm Workers and Agri-Business in California, 1947–1960.* Notre Dame, Ind.: Univesity of Notre Dame Press, 1977.

———. *Merchants of Labor: The Mexican Bracero Story.* Charlotte/Santa Barbara: McNally and Loftin, 1964.

———. *Spiders in the House and Workers in the Fields.* Notre Dame, Ind.: University of Notre Dame Press, 1970.

Gold, David A., Clarence Y. H. Lo, and Erik Olin Wright. "Recent Developments in Marxist Theories of the Capitalist State." *Monthly Review* 27, no. 5. (1975): 29–43.

Gorz, Andre. *Strategy for Labor: A Radical Proposal.* Boston: Beacon Press, 1964.

———. "Workers' Control Is More Than Just That." In *Workers' Control,* edited by Gerry Hunnius, G. David Garson, and John Case. New York: Vintage, 1973, pp. 325–43.

Grami, William, Deposition, 26 February 1974. *Mauricio Terrazas, et al. v. Frank Fitzsimmons, et al.* United States District Court. Central District of California. No. 74-1426-RJK.

Hambidge. Gove. "Farmers in a Changing World—A Summary." In *Yearbook of Agriculture, 1940.* U.S. Department of Agriculture. Washington, D.C.: Government Printing Office, 1940.

Harmer, Ruth. "Poisons, Profits and Politics." *Nation,* 25 August 1969, pp. 134–37.

Hasbach, William. *A History of the English Agricultural Labourer.* Translated by Ruth Kenyon, with a preface by Sidney Webb. London: D. S. King, 1908; reprint ed. New York: A. M. Kelley, 1966.

Hawley, Ellis W. "The Politics of the Mexican Labor Issue, 1950–1965." *Agricultural History* 40 (1966): 157–76.

Hayes, Sue Ellen. *Industrial Response to Agricultural Labor Relations Act.* Austin, Tex.: Center for the Study of Human Resources, University of Texas, 1979.

"Help for the Joads." *Nation,* 21 December 1940, p. 622.

Hession, Charles H., and Hyman Sardy. *Ascent to Affluence: A History of American Economic Development.* Boston: Allyn and Bacon, 1969.

Hill, Herbert. "Anti-Oriental Agitation and the Rise of Working Class Racism." *Society* (January–February 1973): 43–54.

Hoffman, Abraham. *Unwanted Mexican Americans in the Great Depression.* Tucson: University of Arizona Press, 1974.

Ichihashi, Yamato. *Japanese in the United States.* Stanford, Cal.: Stanford University Press, 1932.

Jamieson, Stuart Marshall. *Labor Unionism in American Agriculture.* U.S. Department of Labor, Bureau of Labor Statistics, Bulletin no. 836. Washington, D.C.: Government Printing Office, 1945.

Jenkins, J. Craig. "The Demand for Immigrant Workers: Labor Scarcity or Social Control." *International Migration Review* 12 (1978): 514–35.

Jenkins, J. Craig, and Charles Perrow. "Insurgency of the Powerless: Farm Worker Movements (1947–1972)." *American Sociological Review* 42 (1977): 249–68.

Johns, Orrick. *Time of Our Lives: The Story of My Father and Myself.* New York: Octagon Books, 1937.

Kerr, Clark, John T. Dunlop, Frederick H. Harbison, and Charles A. Myers. *Industrialism and Industrial Man.* Cambridge, Mass.: Harvard University Press, 1960.

Kiely, Jane Yett. "Report to Safeway on the Lettuce Labor Dispute." San Francisco: mimeo, 1973.

Kirkbride, William H. "An Argument for Mexican Immigration." Vol 21, no. 1 of *The Commonwealth*, part 2, no. 12. San Francisco: Transactions of the Commonwealth Club of California, 23 March 1926.

Kolb, John H. and Edmund deS. Brunner. *A Study of Rural Society.* Boston: Houghton Mifflin, 1952.

Kushner, Sam. *Long Road to Delano.* New York: International Publishers, 1975.

Lasker, Bruno. *Filipino Immigration to the United States.* Chicago: University of Chicago Press, 1931.

Levenson, Lew. "California Casualty List." *Nation,* 29 August 1934, pp. 243–45

Levy, Jacques E. *Cesar Chavez: Autobiography of La Causa.* New York: W. W. Norton, 1975.

London, Joan, and Henry Anderson. *So Shall Ye Reap.* New York: Thomas Y. Crowell, 1970.

"Machines Will Replace Domestics as Well as Braceros." *Congressional Record* 109, part 10. 29 July 1963, pp. 13590–91.

McWilliams, Carey. *Brothers under the Skin.* Boston: Little, Brown, 1951.

———. *California: The Great Exception.* New York: Current Books, 1949.

———. *The Education of Carey McWilliams.* New York: Simon and Schuster, 1979.

———. "Exit the Filipino." *Nation,* 4 September 1935, p. 265.

———. *Factories in the Field.* Boston: Little, Brown, 1939; reprint ed., Santa Barbara: Peregine, 1971.

———. *Ill Fares the Land: Migrants and Migratory Labor in the United States.* New York: Barnes and Noble, 1942; reprint ed., New York: Arno, 1976.

———. "The Joads on Strike." *Nation,* 4 November 1939, p. 489.

———. *North from Mexico.* New York: J. B. Lippincott, 1949; reprint ed., New York: Greenwood Press, 1968.

———. *Prejudice, Japanese-Americans: Symbol of Racial Intolerence.* Boston: Little, Brown, 1944.

———. "What's Being Done about the Joads?" *New Republic*, 20 September 1939, pp. 178–80.

Majka, Linda C. "Farm Workers, Labor Unionism, and Agrarian Capitalism." Ph.D. dissertation, University of California, Santa Barbara, 1978.

———. "Labor Militancy among Farm Workers and the Strategy of Protest: 1900–1979." *Social Problems* 28 (1981): 533–47.

Majka, Theo J. "Poor People's Movements and Farm Labor Insurgency." *Contemporary Crises* (1980): 283–308.

El Malcriado. UFW publication, bimonthly. Keene, Cal.

Mallet, Serge. *Essays on the New Working Class.* St. Louis: Telos, 1975.

Matthiessen, Peter. *Sal Si Puedes.* New York: Delta, 1969.

Mears, E. G. *Resident Orientals on the American Pacific Coast.* Chicago: University of Chicago Press, 1928.

Meister, Dick, and Anne Loftis. *A Long Time Coming: The Struggle to Unionize America's Farm Workers.* New York: Macmillan, 1977.

Migratory Labor in American Agriculture: Report of the President's Commission on Migratory Labor. Washington, D.C.: Government Printing Office, 1951.

Millis, H. A. *The Japanese Problem in the United States.* New York: Macmillan, 1915.

Mills, C. Wright. *The Power Elite.* New York: Oxford, 1956.

Mills, Nicolaus C. "Workers on the Farms." *New Republic*, 23 September 1967, pp. 157–59.

Mini, Norman. "That California Dictatorship." *Nation*, 20 February 1935, pp. 224–25.

Mohn, Einar. Deposition. 26 February 1974. *Mauricio Terrazas, et al. v. Frank Fitzsimmons, et al.* United States District Court. Central District of California. No. 74-1426-RJK.

Montgomery, David. "The 'New Unionism' and the Transformation of Workers' Consciousness in America 1909–22." *Journal of Social History* 7 (1974): 511–30.

———. *Workers' Control in America.* New York: Cambridge University Press, 1979.

Moore, Truman E. *The Slaves We Rent.* New York: Random House, 1965.

National Advisory Committee on Farm Labor. *Report on Farm Labor.* Public Hearings. Washington, D.C. February 5–6, 1959. New York, 1959.

Nelson, Eugene. *Huelga!: The First Hundred Days of the Great Delano Grape Strike.* Delano, Cal.: Farm Worker Press, 1966.

Oberschall, Anthony. *Social Conflict and Social Movements.* Englewood Cliffs, N.J.: Prentice-Hall, 1973.

O'Connor, James. *The Fiscal Crisis of the State.* New York: St. Martin's Press, 1974.

Offe, Claus. "Introduction to Legitimacy Versus Efficiency." In *Stress and Contradiction in Modern Capitalism*, edited by Leon N. Lindberg, Robert Alford, Colin Crouch, and Claus Offe. Lexington, Mass.: D.C. Heath, 1975.

————. "Political Authority and Class Structure." In *Critical Sociology*, edited by Paul Connerton. London: Penguin Books, 1976.

————. "The Theory of the Capitalist State and the Problem of Policy Formation." In *Stress and Contradiction to Modern Capitalism*, edited by Leon N. Lindberg, Robert Alford, Colin Crouch, and Claus Offe. Lexington, Mass.: D. C. Heath, 1975.

Otereo, J.F. "Immigration Policy: Drifting toward Disaster." *AFL-CIO American Federationist* 88 (February 1981).

Paige, Jeffery. *Agrarian Revolution*. New York: Free Press, 1975.

Parker, Carleton H. *The Casual Laborer and Other Essays*. New York: Harcourt, Brace, and Howe, 1920.

Penrose, Eldon R. *California Nativism: Organized Opposition to the Japanese, 1890–1913*. San Francisco: R and E Research Associates, 1973.

Perlman, Selig, and Philip Taft. *Labor Movements*. Vol. 4 of *History of Labor in the United States, 1896–1932*, edited by John R. Commons. New York: Macmillan, 1935.

Pfeffer, Max J. "The Labor Process and Corporate Agriculture: Mexican Workers in California." *Insurgent Sociologist* 10 (Fall 1980).

Piven, Frances Fox, and Richard Cloward. *Poor People's Movements: Why They Succeed, How They Fail*. New York: Pantheon, 1977.

Poulantzas, Nicos. *Classes in Contemporary Capitalism*. London: New Left Books, 1975.

————. *Political Power and Social Classes*. London: New Left Books, 1973.

————. "The Problem of the Capitalist State." *New Left Review* 58 (November–December 1969): 67-78.

————. Interviewed by Henri Weber. "The State and the Transition of Socialism." *Socialist Review*, no. 38 (March–April 1978): 9–36.

President's Commission on Migratory Labor. *Migratory Labor in American Agriculture*. Washington, D.C.: Government Printing Office, 1951.

Preston, William. *Aliens and Dissenters: Federal Suppression of Radicals, 1903–1933*. Cambridge, Mass.: Harvard University Press, 1963.

Reich, Michael, and Richard Edwards. "Political Parties and Class Conflict in the United States." *Socialist Review*, no. 39 (May–June 1978): 37–57.

Reisler, Mark. *By the Sweat of Their Brow: Mexican Immigrant Labor in the United States, 1900–1940*. Westport, Conn.: Greenwood Press, 1976.

Rural Worker. National Committee to Aid Agricultural Workers, Washington, D.C. Vol. 1, no. 15. November 1936.

Saxton, Alexander. *The Indispensable Enemy: Labor and the Anti-Chinese Movement in California*. Berkeley: University of California Press, 1971.

Schwartz, Harry. "Recent Developments among Farm Labor Unions." *Journal of Farm Economics* 23 (1941): 833–42.

————. *Seasonal Farm Labor in the United States*. Columbia University Studies in the History of American Agriculture, no. 11. New York: Columbia University Press, 1945.

Scruggs, Otey M. "Evolution of the Mexican Farm Labor Agreement of 1942." *Agricultural History* 34 (1960): 140–49.

Seward, George F. *Chinese Immigration in Its Social and Economic Aspects.* New York: Charles Scribner's Sons, 1881.

Sherrill, Robert. "Reaping the Subsidies." Nation, 24 November 1969, pp. 561–66.

Skocpol, Theda. "State and Revolution: Old Regimes and Revolutionary Crises." *Theory and Society* 7 (January–March 1979): 7–95.

Smith, David E. Deposition. 2 May 1974. *Mauricio Terrazas, et al. v. Frank Fitzsimmons, et al.* United States District Court. Central District of California. No. 74-1426-RJK.

Sosnick, Stephen H. *Hired Hands: Seasonal Farm Workers in the United States.* Santa Barbara: McNally and Loftin, West, 1978.

Stein, Walter J. *California and the Dust Bowl Migration.* Contributions in American History, no. 21. Westport, Conn.: Greenwood Press, 1971.

Steinbeck, John. "Dubious Battle in California." *Nation*, 12 September 1936, pp. 302–4.

————. *Their Blood Is Strong.* San Francisco: Simon J. Lubin Society, 1938.

Stevens, Alden. "100,000 Political Footballs." *Nation*, 19 July 1941, pp. 52–54.

Taylor, Frank J. "The Right to Harvest." *Country Gentleman*, October 1937.

Taylor, Paul S. *Mexican Labor in the United States.* Vol. 1 Berkeley: University of California Press, 1928.

Taylor, Paul S., and Tom Vasey. "Contemporary Background of California Farm Labor." *Rural Sociology* 1 (1936).

Taylor, Ronald B. "The Boycott and the NLRA." *Nation*, 12 May 1969, pp. 591–93.

————. *Chavez and the Farm Workers.* Boston: Beacon Press, 1975.

————. "Nerve Gas in the Orchards." *Nation*, 22 June 1970, pp. 751–52.

————. "Something Is in the Wind." *Nation*, 22 February 1975, pp. 206–9.

Terkel, Studs. *Hard Times: An Oral History of the Great Depression.* New York: Pantheon, 1970.

Tilly, Charles. *From Mobilization to Revolution.* Reading, Mass.: Addison-Wesley, 1978.

Turner, William. "Bracero Politics: A Special Report." *Ramparts*, September 1965, pp. 14–32.

————. "No Dice for Braceros." *Ramparts*, September 1965, pp. 14–26.

U.S. Commission of Immigration. *Reports.* vol. 24. "Immigrants in Industries: Agriculture." Washington, D.C.: Government Printing Office, 1911.

U.S. Congress, House Select Committee to Investigate the Interstate Migration of Destitute Citizens, Pursuant to H. Res. 63, 491, 629, 76th Cong., and H. Res. 16, 77th Cong. 1941, *Report on Interstate Migration*, part 4.

U.S. Congress, Senate Committee on Education and Labor, Subcommittee to Investigate Violations of the Rights of Free Speech and Assembly and Interference with the Right of Labor to Organize and Bargain Collectively, Pursuant to S. Rev. 226, 74th Cong., 1940. *Hearings*, part 47, Part 54.

Valdez, Luis. "The Tale of the Raza." *Ramparts*, July 1966, pp. 40–43.

Wagner, Robert F. Introduction to *The Wagner Act: After Ten Years*, edited by Louis G. Silverberg. Washington, D.C.: Bureau of National Affairs, 1945.

Ward, Stuart R. "The Mexican in California." vol 21, no. 1 of *The Commonwealth*, part 2, no. 12. San Francisco: Transactions of the Commonwealth Club of California, 23 March 1926.

Wecter, Dixon. *The Age of the Great Depression, 1929–1942*. New York: Macmillan, 1948.

Weinstein, James. *The Corporate Ideal in the Liberal State: 1900–1918*. Boston: Beacon Press, 1968.

Wolfe, Alan. "New Directions in the Marxist Theory of Politics." *Politics and Society* 4 (1974): 131–60.

Zald, Mayer N., and John D. McCarthy, eds. *The Dynamics of Social Movements*. Cambridge, Mass. Winthrop, 1979.

INDEX

AFL. *See* American Federation of Labor

Agricultural Adjustment Act or "Triple A," 102, 104, 129

Agricultural Adjustment Program, 103

Agricultural Labor Relations Board (ALRB), 237, 239, 242

Agricultural Labor Subcommittee of California Chamber of Commerce, 88

Agricultural Workers Industrial League (AWIL), 69

Agricultural Workers Organization, 60

Agricultural Workers Organizing Committee (AWOC), 157, 158, 201; AFL-CIO control over, 161; and Delano grape strike, 172–76; merger with NFWA, 179, 182

Alatorre, Richard, 234–37, 239, 271

Alatorre-Zenovich-Dunlop-Berman Agricultural Labor Relations Act. *See* California Agricultural Labor Relations Act

Alien Lands Act of 1913, 47–48, 76

Alien Lands Act of 1920, 49

Alinsky, Saul, 162, 183; Industrial Areas Foundation, 169

Almaden Winery, 185, 268

ALRA. *See* California Agricultural Labor Relations Act

American Farm Bureau, 213–14

American Federation of Labor (AFL), 9, 10, 35, 44, 60, 279; anti-Asian policy, 40; bias against non-whites, 75, 94; and CAWIU, 82; control over nonfield workers, 127; exclusion of Filipinos, 72; and FALA, 130; and Mexican labor, 63; and NAWU, 157; nonsupport of rural unions, 52, 69; part of anti-bracero coalition, 159; and small farm unions, 92–94; strikes by affiliates, 80, 92; and Wheatland Defense Fund, 54

American Legionaires, 45, 69, 88, 91

American Sugar Refining Co. *See* Sugar Trust

American-Hawaiian Steamship Co., 89

Anderson Clayton Company, 78

Anderson, Dewey, 118–20

Anderson, Henry P., 160

Anderson, M. E., 231

Aronowitz, Stanley, 277

Arthur, Chester A., 30

Associated Farmers, 85–87, 107, 109, 132, 147; anti-Semitism, 90; collusion with growers, 115–20; funds for, 89; involvement in repression, 88, 92, 93, 128, 134; and La Follette Committee, 125, 126, 129; membership of, 88–90; opposition to unions, 87, 90

Atcheson, Topeka, and Santa Fe Railroad, 89

AWIL. *See* Agricultural Workers Industrial League

AWOC. *See* Agricultural Workers Organizing Committee